Principles of Political Ecology

Principles of Political Ecology

Adrian Atkinson

Belhaven Press
London

First published in Great Britain in 1991 by
Belhaven Press (a division of Pinter Publishers),
25 Floral Street, London WC2E 9DS

British Library Cataloguing in Publication Data
A CIP catalogue record for this book is available from the British Library

ISBN 1 85293 178 7 (hb)
    1 85293 183 3 (pb)

Typeset by Communitype Communications Ltd.
Printed and bound by Biddles Ltd.

Contents

Preface and Acknowledgements

This book is one of the outputs of a rather long drawn-out enterprise. The first conscious stimulus was the 1973 oil crisis. At the time I was engaged in studying the process of suburbanisation on the East Coast of the United States within the framework of a Master's degree course in urban and regional planning. Clearly, I realised, the oil shortage and price rise and the inconveniences to life which these caused were not in themselves any immediate harbinger of the apocalypse and would soon sort themselves out. But this occurrence both reoriented my research and set in motion a train of thinking, and eventually a way of life, that has led *inter alia* to the writing of this book.

Already, starting at the end of the 1960s, I had spent the best part of three years travelling to and around Asia, following out my curiosity to experience the rich variety and beauty of landscapes and cultures which that part of the world displays. I had gone into this with a thorough education in European culture and was proud of Europe's achievements; in encountering other cultures it took time for me to learn to appreciate the subtleties and come to some understanding of the different foundations upon which other cultural manifestations are built and hence the different meanings attaching to the structure of everyday life. In time a feeling of regret grew up in me in seeing how insistently European culture, in the form of the universalistic 'modernisation' project, was erasing these cultural differences and creating a uniform, even monotonous, single culture — often flagrantly inappropriate to these other circumstances. Perhaps I was simply being romantic and should be thankful that at least I was able to experience this cultural richness where it will no longer be available to subsequent generations. However, the thought processes that opened up following the 1973 oil crisis were altogether less reconcilable to resignation: I became increasingly convinced that in its present form the modernisation project is akin to the project of the Pied Piper, leading the world on a hiding to nothing. The destruction of particular cultures I was witnessing is merely the prelude to the destruction of the basis for any culture.

Over the second half of the 1970s I was employed in planning consultancy both in the UK and in various other countries and it became ever clearer that the concerns about growing environmental destruction resulting from the modernisation process that had emerged in the early 1970s were being totally disregarded in the actuality of the kinds of development projects and programmes which I was being employed to plan. At the end of the 1970s I therefore sought funding to investigate more closely the reasons why the political process was so resistant to environmentalist concerns; this resulted in my obtaining two years of Social Science Research Council funding, as it then was, to carry out doctoral research in the planning studied programme at the London School of Economics (LSE).

Coming from a background in musical and visual culture and via architecture into planning, I was a complete neophyte to philosophical and discursive modes of analysis and communication and it took two years to work my way out of technocratic approaches to the problematic in question and into some sort of understanding of the shape which this work would have to take. For tutorage in 'academic discipline' I had the support of the LSE. But with regard to content and orientation, I looked to the ecology movement. With no previous knowledge of the existence of the movement, I started by holding, and recording, long, semi-structured interviews with over 30 activists in the movement and from these I obtained both an initial reading list and an orientation and intuition with regard to where the real answers to the ecological problematic might lie. These I continued to pursue through the libraries and at the same time through participation in the activities and debates of the growing ecology movement. Over the 1980s I was fortunate to be able to continue all this work on the proceeds of very part-time university teaching and freelance consultancy work in planning — increasingly on environmental and energy issues — in the UK and overseas.

The doctorate proved to be a robust framework upon which to structure the theoretical side of the project. An early part of the work, conducted in the form of an 'antithesis', comprised an investigation of the claims of, on the one hand, resource and environmental economics, and on the other, government managerialism to solve the environmental problematic. These were found to fall fundamentally short of the depth of change required based as they are in the first instance on a naïve faith in science and simplistic assumptions about human nature and in the political sphere upon short term realpolitik.

The thesis process was in no way an end in itself and the dissertation was completed in 1987, using only part of the accumulated material. To a certain extent this material could be fed into the debates of the movement itself samizdat-style as Roneoed discussion papers or through the array of journals servicing the needs of the movement. The depth of theory which the movement was capable of sustaining was — and at the time of writing remains — limited and hence in important respects incoherent and blind to some very important issues and problem areas relating to the needs of the movement. On the other hand, with the exception of a few isolated academics developing their own projects and seminars, the theoretical side of the ecological project failed to materialise; there was simply insufficient critical mass to generate a generalised debate with a steady stream of relevant books and/or any academic journal within the pages of which such a debate might be coherently conducted. Although I am critical of the meagre literature that did appear in the course of my research, I should say that I was grateful for whatever did appear and on the whole there was communication and support amongst the few academics pursuing these lines of thought and research.

Some of the reasons for the problem of a lack of any substantial research in this area are spelled out in the initial chapters of this book. However, the point is not to winge but rather to make a coherent enough contribution across a wide enough spectrum of intellectual discourse to precipitate a more generalised debate and in particular to impress upon a whole range of disciplines, that have paid virtually no attention to the relevance of the environmental problematic to their subject matter, (though I am sure many of the academics in question are very concerned about the destruction of the Brazilian rainforests and probably are also at the forefront of local recycling efforts!) the importance of the issues to these disciplines.

Of course the effort that went into this book might well come to nothing. So far previous efforts to develop theory relevant to the ecological problematic have been almost entirely ignored even within the disciplines out of which they have been produced and this attitude to ecological theory may continue. On the other hand the response could be very hostile. Certainly I have had some feedback upon the mode of discourse and content of aspects of the argument laid out in the following pages that is extremely dismissive. I should say that I am not at all sure that I am the right individual to be attempting to put these arguments together at all: as already noted, I did not come to this work in any way possessing the intellectual background to most of the disciplinary areas over which I have trespassed, and in some cases passed summary judgement, in this text. So I cannot in, as it were humanistic, principle justify taking offence to being spat in the eye by academics who have committed their lives to given lines of enquiry within hallowed frames of reference and who feel that I have entirely misconstrued the nature and importance of their work. I would only feel hurt if this amounted to no more than an excuse to continue to ignore the implications of the ecological problematic on their work — not to mention their lifestyle.

Indeed, a further problem could well lie in the general line of argument presented in this book being accepted, but severed from the question of praxis. So it is necessary to stress that if the elements of theory contained herein do prove to be broadly acceptable, if this acceptance is not accompanied by the adoption of relevant praxis, then the purpose of the argument will have failed as surely as — and perhaps more problematically than — if they are ignored or loudly rejected. The ecological problematic is, in the end, a question of our way of life including out attitudes, aspirations and outlook, not merely a matter of the way we think, write and talk about matters.

It must be clear from the above that choosing whose help and support to acknowledge here as contributing to this book is very problematic because its sources are so diverse and diffuse. Michael Hebbert, as my supervisor at the LSE, who waited so patiently for me to collect my thoughts, together with the other academic staff, students and outside lecturers set the research on course in the structural sense. I must also acknowledge on this score my teaching colleagues at the now sadly demised Planning School of the Architectural Association and also at the Development Planning Unit of University College London. Although I would not want to give offence, I would wish to acknowledge the importance in particular of the lectures of Mike McKenna which provided me with a trajectory into philosophy — from Descartes and Hume to Hegel and Marx — which has been axiomatic in the whole construction of theory set out in this book. I say this might give offence not merely because I may have misconstrued what Mike had to say but because the last time we met, in a reunion of the AA Planning School staff, Mike dominated the proceedings with a total refutation of the existence of the ecological problematic based upon what was clearly a structured quest for data and arguments to substantiate his case!

My debt to activists in the Green movement runs into hundreds of names. In the first instance I must thank all those I interviewed in 1980, many over several hours and some more than once, who provided me with the orientation that has sustained my turning upside down the conventional approaches to knowledge in order, I hope, to adequately address the concerns which they expressed in those early days of the research. They are: Michael Allaby, Vic Anderson, Frankie Ashton, Peter Berry, Godfrey Boyle, Tom Burke, Czech Conroy, John Davoll, Digby Dodd, Paul Ekins, Dave Elliott, Tony Emerson, Edward Goldsmith, Robin Grove-White, Peter Harper, Julian Lessey, Julia Leyden, Clive Lord, Gerrard Morgan-Grenville, Robin Oakley-Hill, Jonathan Porritt, Sid Rawl, Graham Searle, Martin Stott, Len Taitz, David Taylor, Peter Taylor, Gordon Thompson, John Todd, Jonathan Tyler, Tony Webb, Leslie and Tony Whittacker and Sally Willington. For support in terms of the orientation of the thought processes, rather than any specific contribution to the more esoteric and complex argument, my debt extends to the many participants at meetings, conferences and workshops that are a regular feature of participation in the development of the Green movement, where 'personalities' are less important than the unity of purpose, the 'superorganic' spirit of the movement as it develops through all its participants and extends out across the consciousness of society at large. This I sense as the main contributor to the content of this book.

Finally I wish to thank Iain Stevenson and Belhaven Press for having nursed and processed the book into being in such an apparently effortlessly efficient manner.

The *natural sciences* have been prolifically active and have gathered together an ever growing mass of material. But philosophy has remained just as alien to them as they have remained alien to philosophy. Their momentary union was only a *fantastic illusion*. The will was there but not the means... But natural science has intervened in and transformed human life all the more *practically* through industry and has prepared the conditions for human emancipation, however much its immediate effect was to complete the process of dehumanization. *Industry* is the *real* historical relationship of nature, and hence of natural science, to man. If it is then conceived as the *esoteric* revelation of man's *essential powers*, the *human* essence of nature or the *natural* essence of man can also be understood. Hence natural science will lose its abstractly material, or rather idealist, orientation and become the basis of a *human* science, just as it has already become though in an *estranged* form — the basis of actual human life. The idea of *one* basis for life and another for *science* is from the outset a lie... The whole of history is a preparation, a development for '*man*' to become the object of *sensuous* consciousness and for the needs of 'man as man' to become [sensuous] needs. History is itself a *real* part of *natural history* and of nature's becoming man. Natural science will in time subsume the science of man just as the science of man will subsume natural science: there will be *one* science.

Karl Marx (1975: 355): 'Economic and Philosophical Manuscripts'

1 Introduction

The accumulation of ideas and analyses that is to be found on the following pages has been impelled by a sense of crisis. In truth crisis is a relative phenomenon. Life for the average citizen today may possess a sense of movement, even of excitement, without yet precipitating any sense of crisis. Life for many, particularly for an older generation that knew far less wealth and freedom of movement in their youth and who lived through the crisis of total war, involves an overwhelming sense of well-being. Many of the younger generation who have found their way into stable life patterns, new homes, young families and secure employment, have no sense beyond certain colourful images passing across their television screens from time to time that humanity might be in any way at a watershed in its existence. Even if there is a sense of crisis, it is not something that affects many people immediately or, in so far as they might be aware of it and in some way concerned, that they feel they can do much about.

Amongst those who do perceive our age as one of crisis, there are two almost completely different sets of notions as to what is involved. On the one hand, most immediately, we are confronted with the collapse of the ideas and structures which defined the contours of social and political life throughout much of the 20th century. This has been referred to as, *inter alia*, the advent of post-industrial society, the demise of Fordism, the rise of postmodernism, the collapse of social democracy, socialism and communism and the rise of the New Right. Some kind of break has occurred at the level of economic structures and beyond that, cultural values and outlook. The overt symptoms are: rapid changes in the structures of employment and, with this, attitudes to work; the continued acceleration of the flow of ever more exotic consumer goods, coupled with the growth of a significant underclass, living on run-down housing estates or in cardboard cities, without access to the means to satisfy even basic needs; a retreat of the belief in, and the actuality of, the omnipotence of the state as provider of basic welfare; and, most dramatically, the abandonment of 'communism' as the ruling political ideology and structure in the Soviet Union and Eastern Europe. For many these changes have precipitated personal crises that turned to new opportunities or resignation, but the general reaction has not been one of the kind of tension associated with crisis but rather of a quiet falling away of value structures into a life process that seems effortlessly to carry all along with it. In so far as this has generated a sense of crisis, this has been one of intellectual concern with the wisdom of the changes in train and an anxiety with regard to the ultimate social, political and cultural settlement that might evolve out of the current rapid metamorphosis.

On the other hand, and seemingly at a greater distance from our everyday lives, there has been a growing concern that the way in which our society is making use of the biosphere is not sustainable even in the medium term. Rapidly growing population and per-capita consumption of resources, mismanagement of these resources and generation of pollution which further spoils resource potential and directly affects the health of increasing numbers of people: these are the major components of a complex of problems that has led environmentalists to the conclusion that the world cultural system is heading for self-destruction on an apocalyptic scale. Initially this sense of crisis, too, has been an overwhelmingly intellectual concern amongst a very small proportion of the population at large: there was very little to prove that this contention might be valid. Increasingly, however, symptoms of the kinds of problems which the environmentalists have been pointing to have materialised and, with these, the sense of concern of the environmentalists has spread as a kind of nagging worry in the background of the general consciousness.

Although the initiation of the environmental movement coincided with the first awareness of the advent of post-industrialism (Touraine (1974)) and the demise of social democracy (MacIntyre (1968), Lipietz (1986)) in the late 1960s, these two sets of concerns, the two forms of perception of the existence of a modern crisis, failed to inform one another; they have, as it were, passed one another by in the night, accumulating their evidence and analyses as if the other did not exist. It is the intention of this book — and of political ecology generally — to address the whole range of concerns that inform the sense of crisis coming both from the collapse of social democracy and Fordism, on the one hand, and the growth of environmental problems on the other. Political ecology is about building a radically new social, political and cultural world out of the ruins of the old, one which will obviate the environmental catastrophe ahead and establish an economic and social system which incorporates a sustainable relationship between society and nature.

The onset of the Industrial Revolution in England in the early 19th century was disruptive and bewildering in a similar manner to the current 'postmodern' era (Polanyi (1940); Smelser (1960); Thompson (1968)). The configuration of social forces and ideological predispositions was fundamentally different from that which currently prevails but the same urge manifested itself to devise principles upon which to structure the passage out of the perceived crisis. The 'principles of political economy' (Steuart (1770); Ricardo (1817); Malthus (1836); Atkinson (1840); Mill (1848)) that became the guiding ethic and creed of the bourgeois masters of the age have survived and spread across the globe to dominate thinking about meaning and normative structure in the modern world, in the form of the 'world economic system'. Indeed, these principles did not merely survive: today their guardians openly contend that they have now triumphed over the Marxist 'critique of political economy' which, for 150 years, has shed powerful light on the injustice and unreason that flowed from the principles of political economy.

The fundamental principle of political economy is that individual and sectional interests not only do compete for the possession of resources but that this competition is healthy and should be encouraged. The critique of political economy, initiated by the Owenite socialists (Bray (1839); Hodgskin (1825, 1827); Thompson (1824)) and extended by Karl Marx[1] focused on the inherent injustice of political economy and ultimately on the irrationality which the antagonisms, an inevitable corollary to systemic competition, bring to the social process. But there was no realisation — not even a dawning intuition — in this context that there might need to be an equal concern for the effects of uncontrolled competition upon the integrity of the biosphere as well as upon social justice.

The 'principles of political ecology' arise out of the sense of bewilderment of our own age, as stepping stones intended to assist in a reformulation and reconstruction not only of our social world but of relations between the social and natural worlds[2]. As in the case of political economy, theory does not precede practice but follows the early stages in the development of social and political movements intent upon bringing coherence into the response to inchoate perceived crisis; theory and practice thence interact and become a single process of development. It might be considered ironic that the 'critique of political ecology' should have been initiated well before even the earliest attempts at defining principles (Enzensberger (1974)). But then it can be argued that the correct procedure to address the ecological problematic is through dialectical critique of existing reality rather than through assertive didactic and, indeed, the following pages are in structure more a matter of dialectics than of the establishment of principles. The title of this book becomes no more than a play on words, a reminder that the ecological critique is one which fundamentally displaces the ideology of economics, the lifeless modern distillate of political economy, as the dominant political and intellectual movement of the early 19th century.

The main function of this introduction is merely to provide in summary a sense of the content of this book by way of a map with which readers can approach the content in a more structured way. However, although there is as yet very little literature under the title of 'political ecology' that might allow readers to approach the subject with any substantial previous knowledge, there is nevertheless a very extensive literature concerned with the general subject matter dealt with here and it is thus necessary first to explain in brief how this book relates to that literature and, above all, why certain subjects that might be considered to be of key importance are dealt with seemingly only in an incidental manner.

To the uninitiated it may be a disappointment, given the term 'ecology' in the title, that this book contains nothing of significance on biological questions. It should not therefore be assumed that the use of this word is incidental. Although this book is primarily about matters relating to humanity — human consciousness and human society and hence *political ecology* — it is also concerned to bring such matters back into a holistic perspective encompassing *all* natural processes of which the human is but a part. The term 'ecology' emerged in the early years of the positivist Dark Ages[3] as a marker for an absent recognition of the essential interconnectedness, the living, organic, creative dimension of nature that has been of so little concern to positivist science as handmaiden to a competitive, exploitative culture. The concept has a complex and interesting history (Worster (1979)) involving: the development of ideas about nature that justified conservative political attitudes towards nature; attempts to bend the concept to serve the requirements of liberalism and economic development; and, of most interest here, the opening up of the concept, under the titles 'human ecology' and 'cultural ecology' to use as a holistic framework incorporating sociology and geography (Park and Burgess (1921); Bews (1935); White and Renner (1936); Zipf (1949); Quinn (1950); Hawley (1950); Park (1952)) and latterly for the analysis of the interaction between human societies and natural ecosystems (Steward (1955); Stapledon (1964); Vayda (1969); Shephard and McKinley (1969); Ehrlich et al. (1972); Bennett (1976); Campbell (1983); Hawley (1986)). It should become clear to readers working their way through this book that its primary concern is with the establishment of a way of thinking and acting which is congruous with an understanding of the natural world, through the framework of ecology, that is contemplative and empathetic in the first instance and physically interactive, such as to sustain human systems, only secondarily.

A second omission which may cause disappointment is the lack of any but the most cursory review of the environmental problems which we face. As will soon be evident to readers, our ecological crisis is taken as given. Political ecology starts from an acknowledgement of the environmentalist warning that our cultural trajectory is potentially catastrophic. There is now a very extensive literature on the nature of these problems. Many authors dealing essentially with the social, political and cultural ramifications of these issues feel it incumbent upon them to spend at least one chapter and perhaps a third of their book justifying environmentalist views. In Chapter 2 the environmentalist perception of emerging problems — termed the ecological problematic — is defined and it is pointed out that there cannot be any definitive proof of these contentions until after the fact; but no attempt is made to justify belief in the validity of these concerns and readers are pointed in the direction of certain key references for further information and explanation.

A third concern that might be deemed to be inadequately dealt with here is the question of relevant philosophy. There is now a very extensive literature on 'ecophilosophy' and 'deep ecology' (Davis (1989)) that purports to address in particular the ethical and, to a lesser extent, epistemological problems thrown up by our ecological crisis. In practice readers will find reference made to some of the key texts from this debate in the course of the argument which unfolds in the following pages. It is, however, useful to state at the outset that this whole debate, far from having the expansive terms of reference implied by the term 'philosophy', has been rather narrow in focus and, although useful ideas have been forthcoming, they cannot be said to be systematic in extent in a way which one might expect of analyses which refer to themselves as philosophy.

A major problem from the standpoint of the approach to analysis of the ecological problematic taken in this book is the shortage in the ecophilosophical literature — this being an incipient problem in any attempt at philosophy — of clear directions with respect to practical activity that might effectively take us in the direction of solving the practical problems which we face. The importance of ideology, of the role of perception and understanding as a necessary part of addressing our ecological crisis, is stressed throughout this book. However, the forms of interconnection between theory and praxis must be developed at all points in the analysis. It is all too easy for theory and praxis to fall apart, for theory to be but a cover for contradictory, and worse, unreconstructed praxis; and the lack of practical purchase within much of the ecophilosophical and deep ecology literature can be seen as potentially constituting a major problem with regard to the requirements of political ecology aimed at changing cultural practice with respect to nature. This argument is further extended at relevant points in the following chapters. These principles of political ecology are not intended to be philosophy as such;[4] they have more modest aims that are short of total coherence but hopefully of greater immediate practical value.

Finally, 'ecosocialists' and in general those coming to this analysis from the political left, will be expecting blame for our problems to be placed upon 'capitalism'. An argument (unfortunately it cannot be elevated much above this) has arisen between 'green Greens' and 'red Greens' as to whether the ecology movement should see 'industrialism' or 'capitalism' as its main opponent. Greens of all kinds generally focus attention on the importance and extent of manufacturing industry as source of pollution and the over-exploitation of resources; they wish to see — in Bahro's phrase — an 'industrial disarmament' that will both reduce our overall reliance on industrial production and simplify processes and products so that they are more robust, last longer and are easier to maintain, and which make less use of sophisticated and potentially polluting materials. Ecosocialists focus their attention more on the social processes which spur on the increased elaboration of industrial production, seeing this as the central problem which we face.

In practice there is no fundamental contradiction between these views. If we are to de-escalate our ecological crisis then it will be necessary to restructure productive industry along the lines envisaged by the Greens. But it is also true that any headway in this direction will be made over the dead body of capitalism: the very soul of capitalism is the requirement for economic growth and the substitution of less profitable for more profitable means of production regardless of environmental or social consequences. So the ecosocialists have a point when they say that 'green Greens' are unrealistic in focusing their attack on industrialism rather than the social motive force that impels the industrialisation process. However, ecosocialists, indeed socialists in general, fail to penetrate much beyond laying blame for our ecological crisis at the door of capitalism. It is quite remarkable how even the most thoughtful and least obviously orthodox of socialist writers (eg Raymond Williams (1983) and David Harvey (1989)) still feel that their criticism has reached its goal once 'capitalism' has been identified as the villain. There the argument ends as a kind of black box of negativity, to be exorcised, without further effort at intellectual deconstruction, following some future proletarian revolution as the consequence of assumed contradictions between capitalism and the industrial working classes.

Green Greens have no faith in this scenario. The industrial working class as a sectional interest is not seen as revolutionary but, on the contrary prima facie, as supportive of capitalist interests in the drive to increase production, because this is seen as maintaining industrial employment. The road to the destruction of capitalism is seen from the perspective of political ecology in a very different light. Capitalism is, in practice, no more than a set of attributes specific to European cultural evolution. In so far as it has made inroads into other cultures — and it is notable how limited these have been in spite of the crushing efforts of European cultural imperialism — these have been due to a lack of any alternative option available other than assimilation of capitalistic practices into existing culture or simply standing witness to the destruction of indigenous culture effected by means of legal and/or military force on the part of Europeans. It is a poetic irony how successful Japanese culture has been at assimilating and reproducing European culture, including capitalism, such as to colonise Europe and North America in reverse.

The point at issue here is simply that it is not good enough to rest the analysis upon the identification of the concept of capitalism as the cause of environmental destruction. Capitalism has to be dismembered, intellectually, into its cultural components as part of the process of its destruction, by way of a preliminary to rebuilding our culture upon ecologically benign lines. Thus although the term capitalism will be found from time to time in the analysis which follows, it is not seen as being in itself of importance, as some kind of analytical resting point or category of pronounced significance. The intention is to penetrate beyond, to the roots of European attitudes and practices, as an essential part of building a new approach to social critique and praxis in the context of political ecology and of the growing ecology movement.

So following this explanation of what political ecology — at least as dealt with in this book — is not, it is now necessary to move on to an explanation of what it is. Prior to summarising the content of each chapter, a few remarks regarding the intentions of the book as a whole are in order. Principles of political ecology, as should be evident from the foregoing paragraphs, comprise an assemblage of theory, addressed to the particular needs of the moment in the development of the ecology movement. They are aimed at assisting the establishment of a sound basis for a new social and political settlement that resolves problems of security and control arising out of the current cultural crisis, but more significantly one that involves an inherently benign, sustainable relationship with nature as a whole. The analytical procedure which is adopted throughout is one of dialectical critique aimed at unearthing the roots of present-day attitudes and actions. The main branches of our cultural roots can be traced back through history to Christian, Greek and Judaeo-Mesopotamian origins and revealing these becomes an important function of the body of the text. But the historical interpretation in this book is focused above all on a critique of the legacy of that period of European cultural development from the mid 17th to the early 19th centuries known as the Enlightenment.

In my youth, I came across a cartoon (it must have been in the *News Chronicle* or the *Manchester Guardian*, around 1951) which left a deep impression. A tortoise, labelled 'social progress' or some such was looking dolefully into the sky which was rent by a jet aeroplane labelled 'technological progress'. The sense was of a great disparity between the willingness of our society to accept and promote (certain kinds of) change based upon the natural sciences but an unwillingness to accept social change on an equal footing. The notion of progress towards enlightenment has come to dominate not only the European cultural imagination, but has latterly swept the whole of humanity into its orbit. The conclusion to the ecological critique of enlightenment contained in the following pages is that it has far overshot its need to know about the inner structure and forces of nature whilst fatally procrastinating with regard to the need to create a form of society that is able to use this knowledge of nature with sufficient wisdom. It may already be too late to rescue the situation: symptoms of collapse of aspects of the biosphere both regionally and globally are rapidly materialising in a situation where progress towards even the beginnings of an awareness of the urgent need for effective social and political change is desperately weak, and where there is virtually no sense of the direction in which appropriate change might lie. On the contrary, during the 1980s we have seen a significant move in the direction of the political right which insists on recreating class distinctions — in the British case we have seen a renaissance of private education enculturating a whole new generation onto structured class culture — and which will certainly render any subsequent efforts to create a more rational, participative social decision-making process more difficult to achieve.

This brings a further image to my mind: of driving at night, some years ago, through the Arabian desert when suddenly a group of camels loomed in the headlights as they crossed the road, blocking our passage. In the event, deft and undignified movement on the part of the animals obviated disaster on both sides. But the roadsides, regularly displaying the corpses of dead camels and the wrecks of cars, were testimony to the fact that often enough evasive action was too late. My own view at this point in time is that we will not avoid ecological catastrophe and that within one or two hundred years from now — a mere moment on the time-scale of evolution — the biosphere will be utterly changed and, from the point of view of human survival and that of much of the genetic richness and sheer volume of biomass, radically degraded; it may no longer support humanity at all and nature's self-consciousness will vanish as a dramatically failed turn of evolutionary events, perhaps for millions of years, perhaps forever. This may already be a foregone conclusion, in that global destructive processes (such as the loss of the ozone layer) with as yet unknown final consequences, are already well under way. If this is the case, then the efforts that have gone into these principles are of no consequence (I should add, however, that the work has been interesting!). Or it may simply be that the inertia of technological change, currently in progress within the framework of capitalism, proves to be too great to deflect in the time available, particularly if this is coupled with an inadequate deftness on the part of our society to become conscious of the profundity of the problems and to take the necessary steps towards the implementation of genuinely effective change.

A further problem lies in deciding which way to jump once the nature of the problem has been identified. An essential aspect of the analysis in this book is to make clear the way in which our culture has deluded itself with respect to its capacity to discover the ultimate truth about life. Whilst this analysis is designed to loosen our insistence on continuing to pursue the millenarian trajectory which has possessed our society in recent centuries, on its own such a conclusion could lead to fatal inaction with respect to solving the urgent problems in hand. The particular direction out of these problems which the Green movement has chosen, and which they refer to as 'bioregionalism', is also subscribed to within this text. There is a growing sense amongst those most deeply involved in developing solutions that radical political decentralisation to regions which can be effectively run as ecological and politically self-managing entities provides an adequate basis for rescuing us from self-destruction. This does not pretend to represent in any way some 'ultimate truth' or ultimately correct direction but is a pragmatic — nevertheless sufficiently radical — response to meet the challenge. The situation does not call for 'strong leadership' but for the participation of everyone in a commitment to changed perceptions of their social role and a willingness to change lifestyles. It is a matter of us all agreeing on a practical way forward in a tight situation; as in the case of the camels: deciding on tactics and then acting decisively!

Finally it is necessary to stress that there is no ultimate reason why it should matter whether we leave a world fit for our grandchildren to live in or not. If humanity does become extinct within two or three generations then there will be no thought as to what might have been, no hope for the future, no memory or aspiration left to regret what has happened. Problems arise only in a situation where a dangerous and degraded world is left behind for a depleted and miserable remnant of humanity. But, as is made clear in the final chapter of this book, such a scenario should not be used as justification for a coercive programme of social and political change: it is precisely the coercive nature of our social arrangements that has constituted the chief impediment to enlightened social change, and it is through the dissolution of this coercive framework that solutions must be sought. Coercion begets irrationality in the sense that attempted evasion encourages the devising of counter-strategies that can lead to random changes in direction and loss of control or justified sense of direction. 'Progress' in such circumstances is fate rather than conscious organisation. One of the central objectives of this text is to arrive at non-coercive means to the organisation of social life as a prerequisite for conscious control of our relationship with the rest of nature, and beyond that as a means to making life a happier affair for everyone. Mutualistic libertarianism in the anarchist tradition is presented as the political paradigm through which we *can* solve the problematic which we face.

The chapter which follows this introduction is mainly descriptive. The novelty of the approach and the mix of material which goes into the subsequent analysis and the compilation of principles of political ecology necessitates a preliminary stage where the basic material is laid out for inspection. This involves in the first instance a review of previous attempts to analyse and bring intellectual coherence to political ecology and the Green movement using conventional tools of academic analysis. This leads on to a discussion of the possibilities of using Marxist methods to the same ends, culminating in a review of the writings of political ecologists who have progressed out of Marxism in directions suggested by the requirements of political ecology. Finally, some pointers are made with respect to the methodological approach to be employed in the subsequent analysis.

Chapter 3 concerns itself with the issue of methodology but necessarily strays into philosophical questions. It emerged in the course of attempting to compile principles of political ecology that the basic tools provided by our intellectual traditions were simply inadequate for the job and it is in this chapter that the background conditions to any effective theory of political ecology are established. The three subject areas, each of which flows into the next, are: rationality, ideology and alienation. The argument around the issue of rationality is simply concerned with calling for the abandonment of the notion that there is any one Truth revealed by a 'correct' scientific method. The resulting relativistic approach to analysis does not, however, have to abandon structure: this simply becomes contingent to the needs of the analysis, itself aware of both the immediate and general purpose with which it is associated. Leading out of this, the analysis of ideology exposes the way in which all human action is based upon mental constructs and that there is no legitimacy to the notion that one ideology — be it 'scientific' or otherwise — is somehow inherently superior to any other. But the conscious construction of ideology — and as an essential aspect of this semiotics and aesthetics — is a necessary part of the creation of a self-consciously created world. Finally, the heading 'alienation' provides the focus for an understanding of human nature and the human condition; this is viewed here from a perspective that is coherent to, and facilitates, the development of a consistent set of principles of political ecology.

Chapter 4 focuses on the dimension of time from a methodological and a philosophical viewpoint. Social change and in general the cultural history of humanity is a highly structured process. But this cannot be simply understood in a deterministic way. Above all, whilst there might only be a limited set of possible directions out of which our society might move beyond the immediate present, the future will nevertheless in part be the consequence of conscious decisions made by us. This idea of the future as being open to design is embodied in the notion of Utopia and the second part of Chapter 4 is concerned with establishing the possibilities for moving towards a more consciously formulated process of social change within the framework of Utopianism.

Chapter 5 moves beyond the establishment of methodological and philosophical ground rules to initiate the critique of enlightenment from an ecological perspective. Three key subjects are discussed here: science, progress and individualism. Earlier chapters are concerned with deflating the pretensions of science to possess a fail-safe methodology for arriving at the Truth. The analysis in Chapter 5 aims at discovering the origins of our belief in science and at throwing this into some relief with respect to possible interpretations of the Truth about nature and the human predicament. The discussion of progress which follows is equally one which focuses on our surrendering to a blind faith in fate to take us to some undefined better life. The faith in progress, in the efficacy of revolutionism and evolutionism alike — and beyond that our insistence on the pursuit of 'economic growth' — is a specifically European cultural mythical belief in progress deriving directly from the Judaeo-Christian tradition. The impetus of change, though now acted out in terms of exogenously determined physical processes, derives its inner life from a particular ideological predisposition; the deconstruction of this mythical framework is a prime task for political ecology. Finally, the construction of a holistic ecological vision and a coherently organised social process finds its most intractable ideological and practical obstacle in individualistic modes of thinking and action which are deeply embedded in our culture. The complexity of the structures of individualism precludes dealing adequately with the subject in just one section of one chapter of this book, but a set of markers and pointers are established around which further development of principle and initiative might be structured.

The final chapter brings the threads of the analysis together. It is here that the principles in question are spelled out. This is accomplished under five headings, although the argument as a whole is cumulative. Firstly it is necessary to recognise the importance of the inertia of existing ideas in providing structure to our everyday lives. But at the same time we must be sensitive to the availability in the social subconscious of a reservoir of alternative ideas available to reconstruct our ideological universe — and from the point of view of political ecology this means seeking out concepts and ideas which will provide the basis for a social process that will establish a benign relationship with the rest of nature. Secondly it is necessary to realise that all our knowledge is influenced by, and in certain respects gains its essential structure from, the configuration of social structure and intercourse. Whilst being conscious of the way in which this guides and sets limits on the direction and rapidity with which we can change life around us, we need to come to an understanding of the configuration of society which will allow us to live our lives in a more consciously responsive and, in the end, a more pleasurable way. This having been achieved, the aim must be to change our lives through social praxis to conform with these models. The ecological society is one which is decentralised such as to enable participation in all of life's important decisions. But the will to participate presupposes egalitarian and mutualistic modes of social organisation that have overcome the suspicions and psychoses of our competitive and individualistically organised society.

Thirdly we need to acknowledge the influence of the particular environment in which our culture has arisen as informing the kind of culture which it is. Technology has allowed us to change the environment which we inhabit, and the reformulation and reconstruction of our culture in response to the ecological problematic must take this into account. But in so far as we eventually seek philosophical understanding of our predicament, this must respond to the particularity of the micro-environment, which might involve quite small regions. Fourthly, we must look for appropriate means to address the problematic of morality, ethics and aesthetics in an ecologically reformulated and reconstructed culture. The argument in this section, which goes back over the history of enlightenment aesthetics, puts forward the notion that in an egalitarian, mutualistically organised society, morality has no place and ethics becomes a subset of aesthetics: life is lived in the pursuit of love and beauty. Finally it is necessary to initiate the process of devising Utopian models and strategies. This is a matter of using whatever tools are immediately to hand, including technocratic planning procedures as well as fictional and speculative visions of an ecological future, together with a gathering of strength of the Green movement to tap new intellectual, analytical resources and beyond that experimentation with lifestyles and political strategies to raise general awareness and move in a structured way towards the Green utopia.

In concluding this introduction, one point needs to be underscored. Readers will rapidly become aware that these principles are offered not in terms of a definitive argument but rather as an exploratory exercise on several levels. Firstly there is an urgent need to establish a foundation for serious theorisation with respect to political ecology. A start has been made elsewhere in Europe and North America and one of the intentions of this exercise is to plant seeds for theory indigenous to Britain, whilst contributing also to the consolidation of initiatives elsewhere. Secondly, we should not expect any one or even a small clique of theorists to hand down a fully formed theory of political ecology. In the very nature of political ecology, theory must be developed as a process of agreement and in relation to practice. We do have to be concerned for coherence and consistency: in the end we are going to have to move in the same general direction. But the research that has gone into this exercise — which has involved as much participation and discussion within the ecology movement as the reading and analysis of textual references — is a conscious attempt to express the current state of thinking in the movement as much as it is an abstract process of theorisation by one individual. Finally, the content of this exercise is set out with the express aspiration to leave open ends, to provide purchase for extensive debate and for others to use the material for other arguments and for new lines of investigation. If this performs no other function than to increase the coherence and extensiveness of the debate then it will have succeeded. But it can only be made in terms of an offering to the ecology movement.

Notes

1. Marx conducted most of his life's work under the general heading of 'a contribution to the critique of political economy'. This became the subtitle of his massive work on capital and also a title appended to other unpublished writings.
2. The first 'principles of political ecology' were laid out by Heberle (1951a). His approach to the phrase was, however, via the school of sociology that sprang up in the early years of this century in the University of Chicago under the title of 'human ecology'. In Herberle's analysis, 'political ecology' concerned the locational influences on voting habits.
3. Referred to under the title of 'the economy of nature' throughout the 18th century

and up to the mid 19th, including by Darwin, developments in biology in the second half of the 19th century suggested the need for a more succinct title for the interconnective and interactive dimensions of nature. Various titles were suggested (Kormondy (1976: ix-xi); Allaby (1971: 86)), with Haeckel's term 'Oekologie', coined in 1866, eventually winning the day.

4. Hegel (1975a: 11–12) had the following remarks to make that are pertinent to this question: 'In England this (i.e. empirical science) is still the usual signification of the term philosophy. Newton continues to be celebrated as the greatest of philosophers: and the name goes down as far as the price-lists of instrument makers ... Surely thought, and not a mere combination of wood, iron, etc., ought to be called the instrument of philosophy!' He then elaborated in a footnote: "In connection with the general principles of Political Economy, the term 'philosophical' is frequently heard from the lips of English statesmen, even in their public speeches ... Differences there may be between English and German philosophy: still, considering that elsewhere the name philosophy is used only as a nickname and insult, or as something odious, it is a matter of rejoicing to see it still honoured in the mouth of the English Government." Whilst there is a real need for a philosophy adequate to an ecologically sustainable polity — and the possible scope of this is sketched in Chapter 6 — we must not imagine that a mere set of principles of political ecology might be elevated to the status of philosophy.

2 Laying out the ground

Although the term 'political ecology' has been in circulation for at least 20 years, few people have heard of it. It may immediately conjure up certain notions — when mentioned in lay company it often elicits the query: 'You mean Green ideas?' — but what this might comprise is completely unknown to most people. Furthermore, even amongst those who use the term, there is no agreement as to what it denotes conceptually, what it should cover and what is not relevant; it is not a matter of there being any dispute over the term, it is simply a question of the concept having been, as yet, little explored.

The purpose of this chapter is therefore to bring together and present various materials aimed at helping to orient the reader to the subject matter. Most readers will be familiar at least with some of the material but there will be few who are familiar with it all or who will expect to find this particular grouping of material. It must be stressed here that the aim of this chapter is neither to theorise, nor to analyse but to describe in outline salient analytical approaches that have been attempted in relation to environmental concern and political ecology, and then to point in the direction of the approach which subsequent chapters take to the subject.

The first task of this chapter is to spell out the 'environmental problematic'. Political ecology has arisen out of a conviction that our current way of life is unsustainable, and that if our grandchildren are to inherit a world worth living in then we are going to have to radically change the way we live and the way we relate to the rest of nature in general. But political ecology is not the same as environmentalism or conservationism so the chapter then goes on to clarify the relation between these concepts and the role which political ecology plays in this context. The advent of environmentalism and the environmental movement stimulated academic attempts to theorise various aspects of this phenomenon and thus potentially to provide material that could be of use to political ecology itself. The next part of this chapter critically reviews these academic developments, identifying the problems which conventional approaches to theory have had in providing any very useful insight into the concerns of the environmentalists and of political ecology.

The chapter then goes on to explore the possibilities of applying a Marxist analysis and from there to outline the main attempts at more coherent approaches to political ecology that have grown out of the ecological critique of Marxism. This focuses on the writings of André Gorz, Rudolph Bahro and Murray Bookchin. The chapter ends with a number of pointers regarding the general theoretical approach to be taken in subsequent chapters prefaced by consideration of the impediments to adopting this approach which lie within our cultural inheritance. In particular the appoach taken emanates from a phenomenological understanding of the form and purpose of analysis, and to provide preliminary input to this, salient aspects of the analytical approaches of the sociology of knowledge and Feyerabend's 'anarchist theory of knowledge' are outlined.

It has been of concern in this chapter to present all of this material in an approachable form, especially to readers unfamiliar with it. Readers who feel they are already familiar with one or other aspect of the material might wish simply to skip relevant sections. It must, however, be emphasised, that subsequent chapters will assume that this chapter has been read. Readers may be sceptical of the environmental problematic, unconvinced as yet that we really are facing insurmountable problems with respect to the way in which our society is organised and functions; and that 'capitalism, inventive as ever, will find a way out' or that improved government and international managerialism will be adequate to the task. The analysis, particularly as it comes together in the final chapter, cannot be adequately understood unless this environmentalist conviction is accepted at least as hypothesis by the reader; references are given to analyses which argue the environmental problematic in detail and no attempt is made to do so here.

As for the final section of this chapter concerning phenomenological — or 'hermeneutic' — approaches to analysis, this may be very familiar to many academic social analysts (though far from generally accepted) and the brief exposition may appear somewhat simple. However, there are few environmentalists who have any knowledge of this approach to analysis and it is to this sub-readership that this material is primarily directed. Once again, although subsequent chapters argue more forcefully for the adoption of such an epistemology as background to scientific and social praxis, it is important that readers accept this point of departure — if only by way of hypothesis — for the subsequent analysis to make adequate sense.

The environmental problematic and political ecology

There are various versions of the 'conventional history' of the kind of environmental concern, that came to be termed environmentalism, that arose in the early 1970s (Allaby (1971: Ch.1); Sandbach (1980: 29–30); Worster (1979: 341–342)). In the wake of the euphoric days of 1968 and as the first signs were emerging that the long post-war economic boom was drawing to a close, the public were suddenly exposed to an intense debate in the media over 'the environment': arguments were presented for and against the contention that our way of life and in particular that 'economic growth' — the continued accumulation in material wealth — could not be sustained for too much longer without bringing about increasingly intractable environmental problems that would sooner or later radically and violently reduce our material well-being. With, in 1970, the celebration of 'Earth Day', the passing into law of the Federal Environmental Protection Act and the creation of the President's Council on Environmental Quality, these concerns seemed to be making a substantial impact in the United States; with the organisation of a world conference on the environment by the United Nations in Stockholm in 1972, these concerns seemed to have become universal. However, following the 1973 oil crisis and the ensuing increasing international economic problems, environmental issues were eclipsed.

Behind and beneath the media attention there lay a process of gestation, culminating in a broad analysis of the environmental problems which we face and there also developed a sketch of the kinds of directions in which fundamental and effective solutions to these problems might lie. There were two strands out of which this environmental concern evolved. On the one hand, the testing of nuclear weapons in the early 1950s was found to be leading to significant rises in atmospheric radioactivity and this precipitated a campaign aimed at highlighting the problem and seeking appropriate solutions (Commoner (1966: 101–9)). On the other, in 1962, the biologist Rachel Carson published a book in which she identified the massive detrimental impact which pesticides were having on the ecology of areas where these had been introduced. In the course of the 1960s, this concern for the environmental impacts of modern processes was married to older concerns over the detrimental impact of exponentially growing world population (Borgstrom (1965, 1969); Ehrlich (1972)) and the depletion of both non-renewable and, through mismanagement, renewable resources. It is of more than passing interest that all the major contributors to the development of these environmentalist views were biologists or ecologists.

Between 1970 and 1972 a series of books appeared, attempting to bring the various strands together into a single analytical framework and to demonstrate the urgent need for fundamental changes in social and economic practices and it was these which fuelled the media attention to environmental issues at that time. Before laying out the synthesis that was generally achieved in these analyses, it is useful to give at least a brief impression of the approach which the main contributors brought to the problematic in order to show how multifaceted it was but at the same time the extent of agreement on the general nature of the problematic.

Paul and Anne Ehrlich first published their massive textbook *Population Resources Environment* in 1970 (Ehrlich and Ehrlich (1972)). Although the first edition was clearly informed throughout by an insistent concern with the global population problem, it nevertheless addressed a wide range of issues including resource limitations, pollution and ecology. Problems in these areas were then linked back to social, economic and political factors and the underlying institutional framework and systems of belief. The conventional presumption in favour of economic growth was severely criticised and in its stead, redistribution of resources from the 'overdeveloped' to the 'underdeveloped' nations was called for. A broad but also very specific programme of radical reforms was proposed, to be carried out in the context of increased international co-operation. Over the 1970s new editions of the book were produced, with John Holdren joining in the editorial work, under the title *Ecoscience*; these de-emphasised the population problem in relation to other dimensions.

Barry Commoner, who had played a central role in the campaign to stop atmospheric testing of nuclear weapons in the 1950s and who, in the 1980s became deeply involved in environmental politics in the United States, standing as Presidential candidate, published his synthesis of the environmental problematic in 1972, under the title *The Closing Circle* (Commoner (1972a)). He initiated this analysis with descriptions of four major cases of deteriorating environmental conditions in the United States. The subsequent analysis focused on the way in which economic forces are bringing about major structural changes in the way in which nature is being exploited and degraded. This analysis was the culmination of research which Commoner (1972b, 1972c) had been carrying out into changes in materials and products in circulation. This showed clearly that increased amounts of energy and more environmentally damaging processes and products were being substituted for hitherto existing ones so that environmental damage was increasing independently of increases in per capita consumption or population growth. Commoner was more direct than the Ehrlichs in criticising capitalism for these growing problems and in calling for collective political action to overcome them.

Undoubtedly the greatest impact on public consciousness was made by the publication of the report entitled *The Limits to Growth* (Meadows et al. (1974)), describing the outcome of a study undertaken for the Club of Rome, an international grouping of industrialists, academics and senior civil servants who were concerned to bring the environmentalist message to a wider audience[1]. The study did not start from any single problem factor but rather used a computer programme that modelled the interaction of several factors through time. Thus the relationships between population change, capital accumulation and depreciation, changes in food and non-renewable resource supplies and growth in pollution were estimated and projected into the future on the basis of past trends. The model initially showed increasing growth in population and economic activity up to a point of sudden crisis and collapse some way into the 21st century. Adjustments were made to the model to take account of the implementation of policies aimed at amelioration and an equilibrium was produced on the assumption of the implementation of major policy initiatives designed to stabilise population and economic activity and to curb pollution. Although *The Limits to Growth* openly declared that major policy changes would be required, it did not in any way prescribe these, leaving this open to public debate.

Already two months prior to the launch of *The Limits to Growth*, *The Ecologist* magazine published a special issue entitled *A Blueprint for Survival* (Goldsmith et al. (1972)) which attempted to sketch out a programme of political, social and economic changes designed specifically to avoid the environmental denouement about which the Club of Rome had warned. Edward Goldsmith, the proprietor of the magazine, drew together a group of people, known for their environmentalist views, who proceeded to lay out a Utopian sketch. Material generated by *The Limits to Growth* study had been received in advance by the group and this, together with other environmentalist analyses, formed the background. It was stated that current trends, if allowed to persist, would lead to the breakdown of society and the disruption of the global life-support system and that to avoid this it will be necessary to create a new social system. The aim was to achieve a 'stable society' within the next one hundred years and a programme was devised to achieve this. Such a society would involve radical decentralisation of social and economic organisation so as to rely on local and regional self-sufficiency and self-management. As a mechanism to start to move towards implementing the necessary changes, the Blueprint called for the formation of a 'Movement for Survival'.

These analyses and proposals were far from isolated. On the one hand certain scientific work (eg Committee on Resources and Man (1969); SCEP (1970)) provided useful sources of evidence and numbers of other books and studies, not necessarily so directly prescriptive, provided tacit support (eg Fraser-Darling (1971); Ward and Dubos (1972); Schumacher (1973)). Nor, it must be noted at this point, did the dying away of media interest curb the accumulation of this literature. On the contrary, as the years went by, both developments of the analysis of the problematic and evidence to support the contentions of these analyses — particularly in the form of general environmental degradation in Africa and Latin America and the occurrence of a number of large-scale industrial accidents — appeared in increasing numbers. Notable examples include *The Global 2000 Report to the President* (Council on Environmental Quality (1982)), the ongoing publications of the Worldwatch Institute, especially their annual *State of the World Report* (Brown (1984–1990) and publications of the World Resources Institute (1986–1990). However, in the immediate wake of the initial texts and in particular following the major media attention accorded *The Limits to Growth*, there was a substantial wave of academic criticism both of the details of the analyses and of the environmental problematic as a whole (eg Maddox (1972); Cole et al. (1973); Kay and Mirlees (1974); Beckerman (1974)). But the fact remained that definitive proof would have to await the denouement. The question was, rather, whether the contention and the way in which it was being presented to the public consciousness was convincing enough to command effective action and in the first instance it clearly was not.

In spite of certain differences in approach — in the case of the Ehrlichs and Barry Commoner, breaking out into public acrimony (O'Riordan (1981: 65–68)) — it can be said that in general an analysis, in the form of a scenario and a prescription, with certain well-defined contours, emerged from the environmentalist literature of the early 1970s and it is this which is referred to throughout this book as the 'ecological problematic'. The following paragraphs provide a summary which might be employed, for the purpose of the subsequent analysis, as a kind of definition:

• World population is growing exponentially, without any counter-trend within immediate sight. This is placing increasing pressure upon the resource base which, whilst clearly somewhat extendable through astute technological intervention is, in the final analysis, finite.

- The kind of economic processes currently under way are increasing the pressure per individual upon the resource base. 'Economic growth' has meant that the average citizen in the 'developed world' makes a massive impact upon the resource base which cannot ever be available to the population of the world as a whole even now and population growth makes this prospect recede ever further.
- Changes in the structure of resource use currently in progress are tending to increase the pressure on resources and the environment per unit of output, thus working to exacerbate problems arising from population and economic growth.
- Subject to this exponential demand upon it, the renewable natural resource base is becoming over-exploited and the non-renewable element mined out without forethought for future needs. Under these circumstances, at some stage economic growth must go into reverse and human misery and degradation result.
- But the limits of resource exploitation are not in the end those associated directly with the stock, but of the degradation of resources that comes from the production and dispersion of waste from the social production and consumption process. The increase in scale and sophistication of the means of production is generating increasingly sophisticated pollutants threatening to degrade and render the ecosystem unusable, even uninhabitable, on a massive scale; nuclear power epitomises the problem.
- To head off this complex of problems, radical changes are needed in our institutions. This is not just a matter of new laws and taxes but of changes in the general structure of social and political organisation and of lifestyles, effecting not only changes in patterns of production and consumption but also the way in which society works, such that the social decision-making process is coherent to the source of the problems.
- But institutional change is unlikely to come about, and even if it does, unlikely to be effective, without a radical change in outlook. This means a change in ethics and the way we understand what life is all about.
- The radical nature of the necessary changes goes beyond the scope of existing operations of government and it is therefore necessary to initiate a new political and social — even ethical — movement aimed at establishing a basis for the changes being called for.

We can hardly speak of an 'environmental movement' as existing until about 1972 (Allaby (1971)). The early environmentalist texts spoke to 'leaders' and to the population at large. But in time, a number of organisations and initiatives arose specifically concerned to disseminate the message and promote the proposals of the environmentalists and in this way to develop the means to bring about the required changes in the world at large. It is, of course, this development of environmentalism as a political movement that takes it out of the realms of an exercise in technical forecasting and exhortation into what is here denoted as 'political ecology' and the following paragraphs aim to help bring this better into focus.

Political ecology is both a set of theoretical propositions and ideas on the one hand and on the other a social movement referred to as the 'ecology movement' or, latterly, the Green movement. It presents us with the confluence of two social and perceptual phenomena which can be easily demonstrated to have recurred in the history of the European peoples from time to time over the past 400 years. Firstly we can identify periods in which concern has arisen over environmental problems including both crises in resource availability and problems arising from severe pollution. Nicholson (1972: Ch.7), Merchant (1980) and Thomas (1983) all traced the origins of the environmental movement back at least as far as John Evelyn in the late 17th century who wrote about crises both in the depletion of timber in Britain and the major problem of air pollution in London. But Thomas goes back even earlier to the late Middle Ages whence the origins of the term conservation (originally 'conservacy') which became the concept with which to promote management of river quality in the Thames and during which period draconian measures were resorted to in efforts to reduce air pollution in London. Conservation movements of this sort became more frequent with the advent of modern industrialisation; we should include here the public health movement of mid-Victorian Britain which gave us the kind of municipal government which was characteristic of this country until recently. Conservationism could be said to have been endemic in the United States during this century, with repeated waves starting in the so-called 'first conservation movement' of Theodore Roosevelt's government (Hays (1959)), with a less pronounced event during the 1930s dustbowl. A major resurgence occurred in the 1950s (Vogt (1949); Osborn (1948; 1953); Sears (1953); Ordway (1953); Brown (1954); Political and Economic Planning (1955); Brown et al. (1957)) and then again in the form of the environmental movement of the 1970s.

The second source of political ecology lies in radical political ideas and movements of the past of the kind that later in this book are referred to as Utopian. The kind of decentralised, self-managed polity that we can see sketched out in the *Blueprint for Survival* is typical of a wide selection of writing and practice generated by the ecology movement in recent years (Atkinson (1991)). The diggers and levellers in the English revolution, the French and English Utopians of the 19th century and many less well-known movements, together with a vary large selection of political writings and projects (Manual and Manual (1979)), have been over this ground and present us with what amounts to a coherent political paradigm quite distinct from the conservatism, liberalism and socialism which today are commonly seen as defining the limits of the political spectrum.

Conservation movements of the past, whilst including an element of ethics — even, if we think of Thoreau or John Muir, of spirituality — have nevertheless commonly been concerned with improved resource management and the politics of managerial reform. They have generally married a romantic attitude to nature — and also the legacy of historic buildings and places — with improvements in technical management of natural and man-made environments. In political terms conservationism is at best liberal but the body of its following tends more to conservatism, respectful of existing social arrangements and concerned to conserve environments as confirmation of the stability of the *status quo*. The environmental movement was in the first instance apolitical and references to environmentalism are by and large about technical problems with respect to the management of nature. The difference between conservationism and environmentalism is that the former comes naturally with a belief that ethical vigilance and political reform will be enough in themselves to overcome the problems that have been the cause of the rise of the movement; these problems are seen as being relatively local in extent. Environmentalism came replete with the belief that the environmental problematic was global in extent and that the solutions would need to go well beyond the kinds of reform deemed by conservationism to be adequate.

Environmentalism has informed ethical and political movements in two directions. On the one hand there has been a massive increase in conservationist initiatives. The interest in 'environmental ethics' and ecophilosophy can be seen as an extension and attempt to deepen the romantic and ethical writings of, in particular, American writers of past conservation movements such as Thoreau, Muir and Aldo Leopold. Meanwhile there has been very extensive reform of government and industrial methods and techniques with respect to resource and pollution management. Both of these can be seen as essentially conservative interpretations of the environmentalist message.

Meanwhile, however, environmentalism[2] has informed a steady growth of ideas and initiatives that can be interpreted as — and are certainly understood by those involved to be — pointing towards radical changes in the political and social settlement as a whole. It is this side of environmentalism that is referred to as political ecology and with which this book concerns itself. It must be immediately said that the lines distinguishing political ecology from the managerialist side of environmentalism and, indeed, from certain aspects of conservationism, are not so easily drawn. Many environmentalists who are convinced political ecologists, nevertheless, do involve themselves in 'reformist' environmental management initiatives and are confronted with a dilemma whereby these efforts hide the radical insights of political ecology from wider public view (Dobson (1990: 205–213); Young (1990: 165)). The fact is that even in a world that has been transformed into a Green Utopia, environmental management will have an important place and so it is necessary to be involved in these efforts as part of the process of getting there.

Also, the line between a conservative environmental ethics and a coherent theory of political ecology is by no means clear cut (Engel and Engel (1990)) and at several points in this book it becomes necessary to clarify the relation between these two ideological outlooks. This having been said, a significant problem with the academic attempts to analyse the environmental movement has been a fundamental lack of understanding of the overall shape of this phenomenon: thus, in the Kuhnian sense discussed later in this chapter, confounding incommensurate paradigms of conservationism and political ecology. It is nevertheless necessary to look at this literature as a preliminary to focusing on political ecology as such.

Analytical approaches to political ecology

The advent of environmentalism as, firstly, a major media event, secondly, an apparently momentous political message and finally, the beginnings of a new kind of social movement, presented the conventional intellectual debate with some very severe problems. Compartmentalised disciplinary specialisms had grown out of a relatively stable set of post-war social and political arrangements and adopted a set of interrelated methodological approaches to knowledge — empiricism, behaviourism and pluralism — that could not easily come to terms with this new phenomenon. In the first instance the reaction was inevitably one informed by the poverty of disciplinary narrowness. Thus it was that although the biologists and other scientists who were at the forefront of generating the environmentalist view were often keen to shed light on the implications for aspects of life and knowledge other than that with which their discipline was normally concerned, their views of social and political issues were generally seen as extremely naïve.

In the first instance, the economics profession was almost universally condemnatory of the environmentalists, seeing itself as threatened by these attempts of natural scientists trespassing on their disciplinary territory (Beckerman (1974); O'Riordan (1981: 53))[3]. However, gradually a subdiscipline of environmental economics arose which adopted a firmly managerialist approach to resources and pollution problems (Edel (1973); Kneese (1977); Baumol and Oates (1979); Pearce et al. (1989)). There was a much more muted response from economists potentially sympathetic to political ecology (Daly (1973)) that proliferated, accelerating in the course of the 1980s (Ekins (1986)), but which failed to establish any unified new approach to the subject, tending rather towards the debate on environmental ethics, in its attempts to criticise the fundamentally individualistic epistemology upon which all conventional economics is based or wandering off into discussions of practical and political issues.

Political scientists also showed an early interest, on the whole not at all antagonistic in the manner of the economists. Initially these analyses were firmly within the framework of the debates of the times concerned with whether politics merely involves the representation of pluralistic interests or if it is necessary to acknowledge and analyse the mechanisms whereby issues are raised or suppressed and hence some interests fail to gain representation (Lukes (1974)). This debate had already seen environmental issues as an important case for debate (Crenson (1971)). However, the nature of the issues remained secondary to the question of who it was who was expressing them; environmentalists simply became another set of interests within a polity that went unquestioned. The more extended analyses (Rosenbaum (1973); Nagel (1974); Enloe (1975)) also looked at the ways in which government mechanisms were adjusting to environmentalist pressures.

A few sociologists also found environmentalism to be a useful new field of enquiry. On the one hand a number of analysts undertook to collect case studies of particular environmental conflicts and debates, focusing particularly on objections to major new construction projects (Gregory (1971); Kimber and Richardson (1974); Brookes and Richardson (1975);

Brookes et al. (1976); Caldwell et al. (1976); Sewell and Coppock (1977)). On the other hand, attention was focused on environmental groups, within the well-defined method of pressure group analysis (Alderman (1984)), describing who they are comprised of and how they organise themselves with respect to their internal functions and their relationship with the outside world. Particularly industrious with respect to the analysis of environmental groups in the UK was Philip Lowe working with various associates (culminating in: Lowe and Goyder (1983)) but in general this work failed to distinguish between conservation and ecological groups, mainly because it maintained a low level of interest in the concerns and ultimate objectives of the groups.

The reality of the environmental problematic was widely accepted within the disciplines of geography and biology and such views have come to be woven into basic classroom textbooks. New courses on environmental management have almost all grown out of these disciplines. But with few exceptions, the message of these courses is strictly environmentalist and although there are often contradictions between the radical message — that intractable problems are in the making — and the mild recommendations, focusing exclusively on improved technical management, these emerge naturally from the configuration of the disciplinary boundaries that preclude any very structured view of social and political process that lies at the root of the problems.

The most substantial sympathetic contribution concerning the radical message to environmentalism from within academia came from disciplines concerned with ethics and theology (Davis (1989); Engel and Engel (1990)); indeed, the only English language academic journal concerned specifically with environmentalist issues to be established within two decades of the advent of the environmentalism, other than those dealing with the technical management of environmental problems, was *Environmental Ethics*, aimed at servicing the thriving debate on this subject. Whilst, as already noted, this debate can largely be classified as conservationist rather than an aspect of political ecology, it has nevertheless developed some lines of argument that are of interest and which are taken up in Chapter 5 of this book. This literature is largely concerned with debates on ideological questions and with exhortation, independent of any analysis of the social and political process within which ideology operates and becomes effective. Whilst it involves many very interesting and fair arguments, its functional value remains fundamentally in question.

Meanwhile, a few academics were concerned in the immediate presence of the environmental debate of the early 1970s to overcome disciplinary fragmentation and initiate the process of synthesis. Attempts within the conventional framework achieved no more than compendia of entirely disparate articles (Roos (1971); Burch (1972)) that said more about respective methodologies and the narrowness of disciplinarity than about the nature of the environmental crisis and approaches to understanding it, let alone to achieving coherent action.

Somewhat apart from academic developments, a significant stream of more radical analyses appeared (Ridgeway (1971); Weisberg (1971); Hall (1972);

Rothman (1972); Coates (1972); Barratt-Brown et al. (1976)), emanating from long-standing populist traditions in the United States and from a re-emerging Marxism both in Europe and the United States. These approaches were more effective in linking the analysis of environmental problems to social and political causes and hence able to identify more realistic avenues along which solutions might be sought. Many of these were directly connected with the early organisations of the ecology movement — Ridgeway and Weisberg serving to disseminate information on environmental campaigns and the Coates' collection comprising an important contribution to the establishment of the Socialist Environment and Resources Association (SERA) in the UK. Of interest, but in the end less successful (Rüdig and Lowe (1984)), was the attempt in the late 1970s by Alain Touraine (1981) (Touraine et al. (1983)) in France to integrate theory and practice within the anti-nuclear movement, seen explicitly as the spearhead of the ecology movement as a whole. In the anglophone world, articulated sympathy for the ecology movement waned as Marxism became more extensively adopted by academic social science and other than expressing a positive acknowledgement of the ecology movement as one of the 'new social movements', there remained suspicion, bordering on hostility, towards political ecology on the part of Marxists. Political ecology itself failed to develop within academia in Britain. This contrasted sharply with the *rapprochement* and the creative dialogue which arose between Marxists and the growing ecology movement in the Federal Republic of Germany and to some extent also in other continental countries.

Virtually all the academic analyses of environmentalism carried out in the anglophone countries during the early 1970s (and, as becomes evident below, many of the more speculative analyses around the turn of the decade found it difficult to shake off this approach) were underpinned by empirical analyses aimed at verifying the existence of the environmental movement in statistical terms in relation to general descriptors such as 'social group', 'amount of media coverage' and 'degree of expressed concern'[4]. In prefacing a substantial bibliography of these 'empirical studies of environmental concern' (Dunlap and van Liere (1978)) Riley Dunlap — the most prolific analyst in this genre — commented that there "has been (a) proliferation of *ad hoc*, and often poor, measures of environmental concern, and this in turn has created a situation in which it is often difficult to compare the results of different studies". The difficulty clearly lay in the then prevalent assumption that theoretical questions require little forethought but can be simply taken off the shelf in terms of official definitions of social categories or adopted in isolation *qua* 'hypotheses'. Thus the whole question of 'class' at that time undergoing intense debate amongst one group of, mainly Marxist, sociologists (Poulantzas (1973, 1978); Westergaard and Resler (1976); Wright (1978); Giddens (1981)) was trivialised amongst the analysts of the environmental movement who concluded almost unanimously that the movement was 'middle class'[5] without further elucidation as to how this might relate to social theory as a whole, or what its significance might be for the movement and society in general. On the other hand, the meaning of 'environmental concern' became enshrined in the analytical technique itself, the more so as the procedure moved beyond the simple question of asking people directly whether they were concerned about population, resource and environmental problems to more indirect questions, the responses being 'factor analysed' into variables, the names for which were provided by the analysts. The latter procedures were accompanied by some quite elaborate *ad hoc* theory building.

The mid and late 1970s saw a decline in the environmental movement in terms of a variety of (but not all) empirical measures which was, however, in contrast to an increase in both the volume and sophistication of the analytical literature (Dunlap and van Liere (1978:2)). An uncharitable analysis might see this as a case of an academic group having developed a 'speciality' which it refused to allow simply to evaporate. On the other hand, this process of change needs to be related to a general shift in the nature of social investigation which had its origins in some disciplinary areas well back into the 1960s, which was more 'interdisciplinary' and speculative/theoretical, not to say eclectic, in approach than had hitherto been the case. No longer did social scientists see themselves strictly as describers of an empirically given world, but as possessing at least some responsibility to contribute more substantially to the social process. In the case of the analysts of the environmental movement, there was at least some element of commitment to the basic solving of problems and hence a disinclination to let the public forget potentially serious issues simply because they were no longer fashionable (Downs (1972)).

Seminal in broadening out the analysis of environmentalism in Britain in a manner informative of political ecology was the publication of an extended essay, entitled 'A Critique of Political Ecology', by Hans Magnus Enzensberger (1974) originally published in Germany in 1973. This Marxist analysis saw the environmental movement as comprising three distinct groups within the larger society. The first he designated 'technocrats', comprising those within business and government whose role it was to find and implement technical fixes. These were the welfare economists with their 'pollution pricing' and 'resource depletion theories' and the new administrators of 'environmental impact analyses', both intent upon the 'quick technical fix'. More equivocal in terms of their social interests were the second group, labelled 'concerned and responsible citizens' (or in Germany *'Bürgerinitiativen'*). Belonging to the middle class — the 'new petty bourgeoisie' — Enzensberger nevertheless saw within them 'the seed of a possible mass movement' (Enzensberger (1974:8)). The extreme wing of the movement he designated the 'eco-freaks' who, by departing from organised society to live in rural communes, had marginalised themselves in relation to the ongoing political process. Although he saw the environmental texts as being methodologically extremely confused he nevertheless believed the overall ecological message to be in general correct and presaging the need for important changes in the socialist project. He foresaw a long process of clarification as being necessary and that this would involve politicisation of the movement along radical lines in conjunction with the development of relevant theory and method.

Throughout the following decade, a number of academic researchers in Europe, the United States and notably Australia, attempted to develop theory aimed at understanding, and to a certain degree also promoting the ends of, the ecology movement. The following paragraphs outline the structure and conclusions of the main British contributions.

1976 saw the publication of two major attempts in Britain to provide the environmental movement with a theoretical framework tying it into the broader social process. Stephen Cotgrove (1976) published a substantial essay looking at the environmental movement as representing a Utopian movement in the context of Mannheim's (1936) rendering of the sociology of knowledge. The claim of the movement to Utopian (ie socially critical) status lay in its rejection of 'the primacy of economic goals'; however, Cotgrove was aware that conservationists are not critical of conventional values in this way and that a distinction must be drawn amongst those conventionally seen as environmentalists. The body of the essay was concerned to set up a number of distinctions between different sets of attitudes prevailing amongst Utopian environmentalists as a preliminary to engaging in a wider research project. The main distinction which Cotgrove drew was between 'traditionalists', who see the medieval village community as the solution to the environmental crisis and the libertarian anarchists whose answer lies in changed attitudes and lifestyles. He was not, however, able satisfactorily to classify the alternative technologists.

Tim O'Riordan's (1981) major contribution to the analysis of environmentalism, originally published also in 1976, amounted to a classifying exercise based upon a review of over 2,500 references. Chapters concerned themselves on the one hand with the major concerns of the environmental movement, the possible means to operationalise these concerns and on the other hand with analysis of the movement itself. In each case, models were suggested to indicate the main varieties of view, set of machinery and so on. As it were the 'master model' was that which classified the environmentalists themselves; in the postscript to the second edition, environmentalists were seen as ranging from 'deep environmentalist' 'ecocentrists', through 'self-reliant soft technologists' and 'accommodators' to 'cornucopian' 'technocentrists': the latter two categories being not environmentalist at all, but rather expressions of the conventional view that economic growth is right and good. Whilst the analysis provided an excellent quarry for other researchers interested in the environmental movement, the methodology rendered it of little assistance to improving the intellectual and social coherence of the movement.

The next substantial attempt to come to grips with environmentalism was that published by Sandbach (1980) which attempted various methods of analytical approach. He defined two poles within the movement along somewhat different lines to those adopted by Cotgrove involving on the one hand ecological systems and in general scientific brands of environmentalism (including all the environmentalist texts outlined earlier in this chapter), and on the other the critiques of technology and society embodied in the alternative technology movement and counter-culture. He then used this dichotomy, as relating to a contrast between pluralist and radical (in this case more specifically Marxist) analytical perspectives, to review various aspects of society — in particular its structure and the use of technology — and the environmental movement. The study culminated in a view of the interaction of environment and society under socialism, avoiding the use of the Soviet Union which had hitherto been quite generally used to discredit the notion that socialism might have a more benign impact upon the environment (Goldman (1972); Pryde (1972); Daly (1973: 23); Komarov (1980)), and using China instead.[6]

Following the publication of a number of papers (Cotgrove and Duff (1980, 1981)) developing on his earlier ideas, Cotgrove (1982) published a full-length analysis of the environmental movement which ranged over a series of issues and attempted to piece together a comprehensive sociological view of environmentalism. A distinction was made at the outset between 'new' or 'radical environmentalism' as opposed to the re-emergence of older forms of conservationism. Surveys which he conducted had clearly indicated that members of conservation organisations sat at the opposite end of the political spectrum from those active in the new environmental organisations (Cotgrove (1982:19–20))[7]. The former possessed views on a range of issues that were similar to those of a sample of industrialists whilst the latter had views which correlated better with those of a sample of trade union officials. The subsequent analysis had two chief concerns. On the one hand Cotgrove was interested to be able to place environmentalists in class terms in the wider society and concluded that they did, indeed, come from a rather narrow range of occupations generally at some distance from the processes of production. On the other, he was concerned to understand where their ideas fitted into the general ideological spectrum and concluded that they do, in practice, form a discrete 'paradigm' quite distinct from conventional idea clusters.

The last major contribution to the analysis of environmentalism to emerge in Britain in the early 1980s was David Pepper's (1984) investigation into the ideological roots of environmentalism and of the dominant ideas which political ecology is concerned to attack. The first and larger half of the book ranged widely across the history of European ideas, focusing in particular on the genesis of science which was subjected to a radical critique of the kind which is clearly required by political ecology seen from the standpoint of the sociology of knowledge. The second half of the analysis, not obviously related to the first, concerned itself mainly with a Marxist analysis of environmentalist ideas and interests, which were then sorted into the categories of 'ecosocialist', encompassing anarcho-communism, Utopian socialism and their modern counterparts, and 'ecofascist', characterising a certain undertow of some analyses, rather than any specific coherent manifestations.

Thus by the mid 1980s it could be said that a small number of researchers had carried out some useful exploration of the structure and content of political ecology in Britain; further such research had been pursued in other countries. However, these attempts were very isolated and on the fringes of academic debate as a whole. Discussion was more or less restricted to the seminar rooms of the few departments where the research was being undertaken, spilling out in only a very small way into the developing movement. There were no specialist journals to widen the debate; articles coming out of the ongoing research were scattered thinly across a wide spectrum of disciplinary journals. On the other side, debates raged around Althusserian structuralism and thence the work of the latest French and German intellectual gurus; around the fine points of Marxist interpretation of modern society; around sociobiology, the rise of the New Right, the changing structure of capitalism and many other subjects: but in all of this the concerns — even the existence — of political ecology remained entirely unacknowledged.[8]

No new analyses appeared in Britain in the second half of the 1980s. It seems rather odd in retrospect that across this period in which the 'Green movement' and Green political parties became much more visible and acknowledged by the general public, where the media came to pay considerably more attention to environmental concerns, that there was no significant response from within academia, no serious attempts to explain these phenomena in terms of ongoing academic preoccupations. Indeed, the few studies which did appear to be primarily concerned with political ecology were in fact directed at defamation and denigration of the aspirations of political ecology from orthodox political left and right positions respectively (Frankel (1987); Mellos (1988); Bramwell (1989)).

In 1990, however, Andrew Dobson made a contribution to academic debate on political ecology which comprises the first genuine attempt in the UK to understand and empathise with the viewpoint of political ecology itself, rather than imposing pre-existing academic analytical models, and to appraise both its internal coherence as well as its relationship to subjects and ideas current in wider public and academic debate. Areas covered in Dobson's analysis included a discussion of the literature of ecophilosophy and environmental ethics followed by critical reviews of environmentalist proposals for a 'sustainable society' and the strategies proposed to progress towards such social arrangements. Finally, Dobson compared and contrasted ecological ideas and projects with those of socialism and feminism indicating the degree to which a common project might be envisaged but also where these do not concur. Written in the wake of the massive increase in public awareness of environmental issues that arose at the end of the 1980s, Dobson stressed the crucial difference between the kinds of environmental managerialism that is now very widely accepted and the Utopian project of political ecology (which he referred to as 'ecologism') which still remains in the shadows of political and academic debate and analysis.

Some theoretical considerations

In the late 1970s a noticeable shift took place in particularly the analytical literature of the environmental movement in the United States. This had two aspects to it. Firstly in the context of a broader social science debate concerning the emergence of a 'post-industrial' society (Bell (1973); Touraine (1974)), Ingelhart (1977) suggested the simultaneous abandonment of 'materialist', in favour of 'post-materialist', values amongst the population at large. Based on massive social survey work throughout the United States and

Western Europe, it was contended that the particular social experience of the current generation was leading to changing views which would lead to 'basic social reorganisation' (Inglehart (1977:190)). Whilst a coherent outlook had yet to emerge (Inglehart (1977:372)), a 'silent revolution' was found to be in progress. *The Limits to Growth* was seen in this context as 'one of the most significant books of the 1970s'. This analysis was subject to some academic debate and criticism amongst analysts of the emerging environmental movement (Lowe and Rüdig (1986:2–13); Rüdig (1986a:17–26)). It is perhaps useful to re-evaluate this debate in the light of the more recent emergence of the massive debate concerning 'postmodernism' which is further referred to in the final chapter of this book.

Secondly, the cautious use of theory as an instrumental adjunct to the dominant pluralist-functionalist-empiricist form of social investigation, as conforming to positivist strictures, loosened up and analyses become more speculative. Some of the bolder analysts of environmentalism now found a millenarian style to match that of the original environmental texts (Catton (1982); Milbrath (1984)). This metamorphosis coincided with the discovery in the social sciences of Thomas Kuhn's (1970) theory of scientific revolutions which had already for some time been debated as a counter-theory to that of Karl Popper (Lakatos and Musgrove (1970)). His notion of a 'paradigm', as comprising a coherent set of ideas, incommensurable with alternative such sets, fitted well the conceptualisation of the environmental movement towards which the analysts had been groping and which had previously been handled under the rather cumbersome term '*Weltanschauung*' (Black (1970:20); Schwab (1972:56)). Thus the term 'paradigm', or 'NEP' (New Ecological Paradigm), became common currency in American environmental analysis and Cotgrove adopted this usage in Britain. Riley Dunlap (1980) edited a set of essays in this vein that had been brought together from various social science disciplines, analysing — but simultaneously promoting — environmentalism. Ranging over a wide literature and giving consideration to many possibilities, these essays were in agreement that a common set of paradigmatic elements which might form a coherent theory of environmentalism, subsuming ecological and social process, had yet to be devised.

The disappointing results of these attempts (O'Riordan (1981: 379–380)) can be partly attributed to the inappropriateness of the empirical investigations, carried out in the earlier phase, to inform the substance of theory. That is to say that the 'new paradigm' was assumed to be about social and ecological process, whereas the empirical material merely indicated, in the main, the extent to which the population at large, divided into analytically unuseful subgroups, might adhere to such a paradigm: useful market research for the sale of a 'new paradigm' perhaps, but of little use for constructing it. A second reason for the disappointing results lay in the comparative naïvety of the analysts with regard to understanding the role of theory in relation to analysis and prescription. Positivism, in particular in the form of the empiricist programme, defines the analyst's role in such a way as to obviate the need to ask such questions and thus encourages such naïvety. In Popper's (1965: 176–281) version, analysts should not indulge in broad generalisation but stick to incremental hypotheses and then spend their time attempting to refute even these: this was very much a normative programme directing analysts away from investigating the wider social causes and consequences of their activities. Kuhn's (1970) contribution was to note that whether or not 'scientists' proceed in this manner, the net result of their work is a series of revolutionary changes in the understanding of the structure of the world. In fact Kuhn thought that most analysts (practising what he called 'normal science') spend their time devising and carrying out experiments to confirm rather than refute theories, but that their work has a habit of turning up ever more insistent anomalies. Scientific revolutions are major changes in theory which subsume existing theory and at the same time account for the accumulated anomalies.

Kuhn's theory was not prescriptive in the same way as Popper's but more like a rediscovery of Adam Smith's (1976:456) 'invisible hand': scientific revolutions happen whether you want them or not. For the environmentalist social analyst followers of Kuhn, however, the notion of the paradigm presented something of a route to freedom from the puritanical strictures of positivism. There was, nevertheless, a serious misunderstanding of the case: Kuhn had noted that new paradigms emerge as full-fledged theory designed to make sense out of anomalous data; the environmentalist analysts were merely pointing to what they construed as something akin to anomalous data, namely a suicidal society. Their role was thus not 'scientific' but more analogous to the millenarian (or perhaps merely 'cheer leader'). It involved a strong element of advocacy, calling for the need to build a new theory.

There is no intrinsic reason why social scientists should not be involved in advocacy. There are relatively few today who would assert the extreme positivist doctrine that social science will one day attain the status of the 'exact sciences' and that it is merely a question of time'. If social investigation is inevitably inexact because it is 'up to its eyes in values' (Cotgrove (1982:68)) then the proper question becomes: what role should values play? What is of interest about Kuhn's theory is its striking resemblance to Hegel's basic notion of the dialectic, wherein life progresses through the appearance of contradictions which are reconciled into an ever more comprehensive framework. Writing before the hegemonic rise of positivism, Hegel was little concerned with any theoretical distinction between description and advocacy, and saw his philosophy as covering simultaneously scientific investigation and social action. Indeed, it was in process of making sense out of his commitment to the French Revolution and its relation to German political life of the times, that he constructed his philosophy (Lukács (1975:23–26)). For a short period after Hegel's death, a heated debate took place in Germany over the best way in which his philosophical system might be forged into a more earthbound social programme (McLellan (1969)), and it was, of course, the insights of Marx and Engels which eventually proved to be by far the most influential. As has already been noted, some British analysts of the environmental movement appeared to consider Marxism to be adequate as an analytical-prescriptive framework for the movement. Some American analysts on the other hand assumed a Marxist framework to be inadequate and called for the formulation of a new and more appropriate theoretical framework of the breadth and type forged by Marx and Engels (Inglehart (1977: 372); Rodman (1980: 74)).

The acceptability or otherwise of the Marxist framework in analysing the environmental movement depends crucially on two things. Firstly, is the Marxist scenario, encompassing social structure and dynamic, believable in relation to the ecology view and movement? Taking Cotgrove's (1982:93–97) analysis, which clearly contains much of value relating to this issue, at face value it would seem that such a reconciliation would be extremely difficult to achieve. But then Cotgrove was making no attempt to match his material to a Marxist framework. Sandbach (1980:21–41), in realigning the various elements of the environmental movement, was explicitly trying to sort out what in Marxist terms might be seen as 'progressive social elements' or 'social subject' within the movement: who, in other words, is going to bear the chief responsibility for bringing about the necessary social changes. However, in discussing the explicit relationship between the movement and the social process as a whole he presented a somewhat simple view of society which recognised only in passing the existence of the debate concerning modern social structure and hence failed to illuminate the incoherence between political ecology and the Marxist social scenario that insists on proletarian revolution to bring about real change. Pepper (1984:196–201), whilst characterising ecosocialist initiatives well in terms of Utopian socialist strategies, did nothing to help locate these within the Marxist scenario. It is therefore necessary either to elaborate Marxist ideas of society to incorporate the ecology movement adequately or, as Marxists, to belittle, reject or ignore environmentalism as being of marginal relevance, which is precisely what many Marxists do.

Secondly, there is the question as to whether Marxist theory is capable of handling adequately the 'environmental problematic' or in general the question of ecology. Notwithstanding assertions that Marx and Engels were at heart ecologists (Parsons (1977)), there has been some debate about the adequacy of Marxist (and more specifically Engels') theories about nature (Schmidt (1971:182–196); Burgess (1978)). In major respects these have been found wanting, without any specific substitute coherent to Marxism having been devised. As noted on the frontispiece to this book, Marx did specifically reject the possibility in the mid 19th century of creating a coherent single theory encompassing Humanity and Nature although he saw such a theory as being an integral part of the culmination of human evolution (Marx (1975: 355)). There has been an abundant critique of technology (the interface between social process and nature) amongst Marxist and generally leftist sympathisers in recent years (Ellul (1964); Dickson (1974); Harper and Boyle (1976); Boyle et al. (1977); Winner (1977, 1986); Slater (1980); Norman (1981); Albury and Schwartz (1982); Bellini (1986); Zerzan and Carnes (1988)) — which was a central part of Sandbach's (1980: 138–182) treatment of environmentalism — and this has often been explicitly critical of Marx's assumption that technology is 'value neutral'. But that is not the same as an adequate ecological critique of society (Schmidt (1971:167)) which is, presumably, a central requirement of the 'new paradigm' which the political ecologists are calling for.

Loosely speaking, based upon the foundation of Hegelian philosophy, Marx constructed a 'paradigm' for social change. Perhaps a better word to use is 'heuristic' in that it was not (and, being concerned with the social realm, could not be) merely a theory about what is, but incorporated a view of what might be, if society (and particularly certain elements of it) consciously worked its way towards it. The heuristic had profound effects on the course of history although many of these were clearly quite other than intended. But the world is now a very different place than it was when Marx devised his theory and whilst the Hegelian-Marxist approach might still be of value, the specific Marxian scenario is, according to the political ecologists, now obsolete, requiring either radical modification or supersession. It may well be argued that the growing profusion of Marxist analyses over the past few years *qua* 'normal science', may lead in time to the hoped-for NEP. However, not all normal science leads inevitably to changes in paradigm and where social questions are at stake there may well be built-in avoidance of genuinely radical views. There is no obvious reason why current 'Western' Marxism should not be as barren as much of Soviet Marxism during the Stalinist era (Schmidt (1971:165–196)). The point is that when science fails to produce a new paradigm it is not the end of the world; but if we fail to produce a new social configuration, so the political ecologists say, then we are likely to be faced with just that. But the NEP is not simply out there waiting to be discovered, it is in large measure something that we have to invent and then live by.

Marxism and political ecology

Developments in social analysis out of Marxism have been considerably more fruitful outside Britain, where the tendency has been either to embrace orthodoxy or to reject or avoid Marxism altogether. As a branch of these developments, a relatively rich offering of attempts to construct a political ecology evolving out of Marxism and attempting to redeploy Marxist concepts is already to hand elsewhere and it is useful at this juncture to review a selection of these. Central examples are taken from France, Germany and the United States.

An explosion of Marxist social analysis took place in France in the late 1960s and subsequently the writers involved took various routes which do not relate to what in UK academic debate would be considered to fall within distinct disciplinary boundaries. As this analysis proceeds reference will be made to many of these writers. Two of them, Alain Touraine and André Gorz, identified ecological issues to be of particular salience and the ideas developed by Gorz are considered to be useful to the discussion developed later in this book so an outline of these is presented here.

Gorz has been involved in 'criticising Marx' (some write that he has long ceased to be a Marxist) since the early 1960s. His main focus was initially on the question of labour organisation, but he also — in common with many French analysts — swung with the fashion. Thus in the early 1960s he was the great champion of syndicalist 'autogestion' (workers' self-management)

(Gorz (1964)), only to vehemently reject it in later work. In the late 1960s he was carried along by the enthusiasm for 'student revolution' (Gorz (1969)). Then with the advent of environmentalism he wrote a number of essays on this theme. Since the end of the 1970s his concern has been with the long-term consequences of technological unemployment and more generally a return to his earlier preoccupation with meaning and methods in work. Nevertheless, his contribution to a restructuring of Marxism as a contribution to political ecology has been generally acknowledged as useful.

His chief direct contribution to the environmentalist debate comprised a collection of essays edited into a book, translated as *Ecology as Politics* (Gorz (1980)). The first essay, 'Ecology and Freedom', outlined the main argument. Growth-orientated capitalism and its socialist counterpart are finished. In the face of the environmental problematic (which Gorz outlined), both conventional and Marxist economic theories are irrelevant, and capitalist and state socialist practices are incompatible with ecological necessity. Although there can be no 'ecological ethic', ecology must be of primary concern: better a non-nuclear capitalism than a nuclear socialism. But capitalism is inevitably growth-orientated and increased consumption, far from solving social problems, only exacerbates them. Abolition of social hierarchy (presupposing changes in education) is a prerequisite to the necessary basic change. The essay ended with a Utopian sketch involving a society which worked but did so in decentralised work places, bringing consumption and production to a greater extent into the same arena, was educated more and produced via organic farming and the application of soft technologies. Subsequent essays mainly involved critical discussion of specific areas of production and consumption: automobiles, nuclear power, health care.

Gorz (1982, 1985) then contributed two short books of a rather polemical nature focusing on the problem of technological unemployment which were complementary and together presented one well-elaborated thesis. They also clarified certain propositions put forward in a rather general way in *Ecology as Politics*. Gorz's basic proposition here was that automation is bringing about a permanent abolition of work, precipitating a dualisation of the economy between those involved and those marginalised through lack of work; the potential negative consequences of this must be confronted with an alternative. This highlights processes of class change that have been taking place for some time, above all abolishing the industrial working class, which clearly represents a crisis for Marxism. The development of productive forces (of 'progress') has reached a point where these are inhibiting social development: organisation of work is now on a national or transnational basis, so that no significant decisions are taken at the level of the plant. This means that 'workers' self-management' can no longer be considered as the way forward; and in any case, industrial labour has been absorbed into the logic of capital.

Class society today is best described in terms of a dominant 'neo-proletariat', or a 'non-class of non-workers', or individuals and fragmented groups that wish only to escape from 'socialised labour' into individual self-realisation. It has become necessary to push the economic realm into the background, but this can never be eliminated: a dualistic production system is inevitable, comprising on the one hand a highly efficient system of production of necessities and of the means to individual emancipation, planned and managed by the state and termed 'heteronomous', and on the other an 'autonomous' system of production by individuals or small groups at the local level. Gorz attacked the notion of local or regional autarky and the social proposition of the commune as focus of social organisation (Gorz (1982:Ch 9, 1985:63)). The social mechanism around which such a production system would be organised involved a 'social wage' or basic income for all, paid by the state and in exchange for which everyone participates for a short period in the 'heteronomous' economy. The political mechanism for bringing about such a system was seen in terms of a pluralist political system.

Following his retirement, Gorz gathered together his views on the problem of work and produced a more academically substantial analysis (Gorz (1989)) under the title *Critique of Economic Reason*. He confirmed his contention that the capitalist 'Utopia of work', that is in general terms shared by Marxism, is in a state of collapse because there is a diminishing amount that can be validly attributed to production. The immediate consequences are an increased dualisation whereby some are inside the economic system and some excluded, in a socially and materially disadvantaged condition. This allows the inner impulse of the system, driving towards its own social and ecological dénouement, to continue unchecked. In looking for solutions, Gorz confirmed his view that the 'heteronomous' economy cannot be subsumed by the 'autonomous', although some development of autonomous activity at the level of the local community, particularly with respect to services previously the responsibility of the welfare state, is possible and should be encouraged.

In clarifying the theoretical underpinning of this view, Gorz went on to assert a liberal individualist epistemology over against one that considers psychological attitudes to be primarily socially determined: throughout the analysis Gorz maintained a sharp distinction between the 'functional integration' of the individual through the heteronomous system and the 'social integration' that grows out of the individual's own proclivities and with this a pessimistic view of the ability of the individual to empathise with and take control of structures beyond those in his or her immediate proximity of experience. His suggested strategy to head off the social and ecological denouement ahead is in general to liberate ourselves from the ideology of work. Tactically we should work towards the redistribution of work, reducing working hours without reducing wages and encouraging a sharing around of heteronomous, coupled with an expansion of autonomous work, mainly in a more balanced sharing of work in the household and immediate neighbourhood.

Gorz's concept of an irreducible dualism (which appeared in a different guise already in his interpretation of 1968 (Gorz 1969)) is not Marxist at all but is a very clear reinterpretation of the French philosophical tradition from Descartes to Satre: that life involves a struggle between an irreducible human essence and the dead machinery of the world around us. Byrne (1985) noted how Gorz's model of social structure consisted of a restatement of liberal individualism rather than any development of Marxism; furthermore, this model is quite incompatible with the epistemology developed later in this analysis. Indeed, both Bahro (1984:197n) and Bookchin (1980: 289–313), whose work is analysed in the following paragraphs, have been severely critical of Gorz and it is thus probably best to characterise Gorz's work as having raised key issues for debate for political ecology, rather than that he has moved closer to clarification.

The development of political ecology out of a Marxist and in general leftist milieu has been far more extensive in West Germany than anywhere else (Rüdig (1986b)). However, relatively little of this has been translated into English and hence entered anglophone debates, the one major exception being the work of Rudolf Bahro (1978, 1982, 1984, 1986), which has been extensively translated. In fact, whilst the richness and nuance of the broad debate might be of interest here, it is deemed adequate to present in outline Bahro's approach, both because it is more extensive in scope than other contributions and because it probably also represents the most radical stance. Before proceeding to outline his position, it is useful to note his own view of where he stands relative to Marxism (Bahro (1984: 218–220)). His major work, originally entitled *The Alternative* (Bahro (1978)), was written in the German Democratic Republic (DDR) and published in West Germany. This earned him a prison sentence and then expulsion to the West. He professed that writing in the DDR inevitably involves adopting a Marxist stand: that is simply the context of all intellectual work. His critique was therefore not seen in those terms but when he arrived in West Germany he claimed no longer to be a Marxist but that Marx's work should be used 'as quarry', and his work continued to make extensive use of Marxist terms and concepts.

Although *The Alternative* was not written as a contribution to political ecology, it nevertheless presented a path to what clearly is an ecological future. Once in West Germany, Bahro joined the Green Party and the same arguments became explicitly ecological. It is therefore useful to present his ideas as set down in *The Alternative* as these come in a more systematic form than his subsequent work. The latter is then presented below by way of an assessment of Bahro's development.

It was in the third part of *The Alternative* (albeit almost half the book) where Bahro presented his revision of a Marxist strategy. The first chapter of this section was pivotal. This called for a return to Utopian modes of thought, followed by a denial that the proletariat were relevant any more to spearheading change: it is necessary, rather, to form an 'eclectic consensus' of interests to work towards change. The environmental problematic was then laid out as the fundamental problem which we currently face and this was followed by a call for an anti-consumerist social restructuring process aimed at addressing basic psychological needs. The elements of this 'restructuring of the human subjectivity' were outlined in some detail and included a redivision of labour so that all participate in many facets of life; an unrestricted access to education; an unconstrained process of child development; a restructuring of community life; and a socialisation of knowledge and decision-making. Two chapters followed, one a critique of the current situation in the DDR relative to this call and the second aimed at outlining the means to move towards these goals, seen as inevitably proceeding by stages. A 'League of Communists' must be formed to spearhead a cultural revolution; this would not be a conventional party — any attempt to reconstitute social democracy would be anachronistic — but more in the nature of a multi-structured movement.

The final two lengthy chapters then outlined 'The Economics of the Cultural Revolution'. The key to change is to attack the economic system and above all abolish the vertical division of labour. This must be a slow process, but can be started by liquidating bureaucratic corruption and privileges, abolishing economic incentive systems, ensuring management also participate in process work and pay scales be adjusted in the direction of an equalisation. These were all seen as lending the psychological confidence necessary to launch further stages of the cultural revolution: this must be a process of emancipation *from* economics. Five paths were outlined for the all-round development of human beings: to integrate production and education as a unified process of human development; to optimise conditions for individual socialisation (satisfying needs); to adapt production to natural cycles (ecology); to locate value in the individual rather than in things; and to organise on the basis of an association of communes.

Of particular interest here are the details of the third of these, where Bahro called for rebuilding and maintenance rather than competitive innovation, a radical prevention of environmental damage and a reduction of raw material and energy requirements. But the section on organisation is also of interest. Whilst eschewing 'decentralisation', he nevertheless called for an increase in small-scale production at the local level and discussed at length how the commune must be the central locus of all social, including economic, decision-making. 'Commune', in German, refers to local authority and although Bahro clearly meant much more than what is generally construed as a local authority, his model of commune was at this scale.

Upon arriving in West Germany, Bahro immediately joined the Greens and launched a propaganda campaign around his ideas. Inevitably these acquired a polemical edge and some of the ideas were sharpened in the process. Thus, his critique of the usefulness of the working class as chief protagonist of change was further developed, together with a critique of attempts at economic reflation and employment generation (Bahro (1982: 62–74, 112–121; 1984: 205; 1986: 12–13)). His call for a multi-front approach involving coalitions became more concrete as he worked with the Greens and attempted to draw in all manner of disparate elements from the political left and right and including the churches. He called for a re-examination of the whole European theoretical inheritance and himself moved towards religious ideas. His critique of modern industry was conjoined with a critique of the military situation — he became involved in the rebirth of the peace movement — and elaborated into a complex concept of 'exterminism' (a term originally coined by E. P. Thompson to denote the nuclear arms race) denoting a kind of death-wish built into the current socio-political dynamic. His solution involved a more forthright embracing of decentralised production (Bahro (1986: 13–15)). He then became involved with the communes movement in Germany (Bahro (1986: 86–98)) and his earlier focus upon the commune adjusted to a call for communal experimentation — he made no distinction between the secular and the religious. In June 1985, after having served as a Green member of the German parliament, he resigned from the Green Party following a series of disagreements in which he — designated a fundamentalist in the spectrum of views developing within the Party — could no longer tolerate the *'realpolitik'* that had come with access to political power. It needs to be emphasised in conclusion that Bahro's writing has a pragmatic and practical edge to it relative to 'orthodox Marxism', with its bottomless faith in one scenario, but on the other hand insists on consistency between faith and action. In this sense, it is 'mid-level theory' rather than involving any thorough-going epistemological enquiry.

In the United States, in addition to the more strictly academic analyses already referred to above, there have been numbers of more 'committed' analyses/syntheses of the ecology movement, including those of the essentially conservative William Ophuls (1977) and the liberal Allan Schnaiberg (1980). Arguably the most important theorist from the point of view of the political ecology has been Murray Bookchin. An academic coming from a 'Marxian intellectual training' (Bookchin (1982: 1)), Bookchin became concerned with the environmental problematic already in the early 1950s and his intellectual position shifted to that of an anarchist. Before looking into his development of ecological ideas, it is useful to present his relationship to Marxism, particularly as his work has continued to make extensive use of Marxist concepts.

In 1969, Bookchin published an essay criticising the New Left and hence stating his position *vis-à-vis* Marxism; a further essay was written in response to Marxist critics (Bookchin (1969, 1970)). Modern Marxists, he wrote, adhere too rigidly to the original ideas of Marx and Engels, seeing things from a mid to late 19th-century position. They are thus backward rather than forward looking — which Marx certainly would not have endorsed. Bookchin also criticised the new academic Marxism in so far as it was divorced from praxis. His own position was one which no longer believed the industrial working class to be salient to revolutionary social change. Co-opted by capital, they suffer centrally from an adherence to the work ethic which must be abandoned; many other groups in society are moving towards such a rejection and these are the new revolutionary forces. The class system is rapidly evolving so that the industrial working class are no longer the majority, nor in any important relation to the political system. By defending predominantly the position of the industrial working class, Marxists are reactionary. Bookchin then criticised the notion of a centralised party as representing the way forward and suggested that anarchism (which does not mean no organisation) provides a richer basis for social development, emphasising the need to recover Utopian thinking. The New Left, he wrote, has not grasped the revolutionary potential of ecology. Analytically, he thought the Marxist concepts of class and exploitation need to be replaced by the more generic concepts of hierarchy and domination. Like Bahro, Bookchin (1980:242n) has regarded the works of Marx and Engels as a kind of quarry of ideas, and clearly found the work of the Frankfurt School of use.

Bookchin's early interest in environmental issues led to the publication of two books concerned with the 'syntheticisation' of modern life (Herber (1952, 1962)). These were followed by a series of articles of which two, written in 1965, presented in outline all the salient concerns of the ecology movement of the late 1970s and 1980s; it was these which establish the importance of Bookchin to the movement. In 'Ecology and Revolutionary Thought', Bookchin (1965a) was concerned to show that ecology, as an integrative science, is critical beyond political economy. Man's parasitism, involving a regressive simplification of the environment to the detriment of ecosystems, is best criticised through ecology. But man's domination of nature is but a function of man's domination of man so that the social problem is encompassed by the ecological. Anarchism and ecology are at one; decentralised social structures, along the lines defined by William Morris and Kropotkin need to be pursued to overcome social control by experts.

'Towards a Liberatory Technology' (Bookchin (1965b)) had a broader scope, starting from the view that social progress is bound up neither with technological progress, nor with a radical rejection of technology but that a truly liberated society requires a technology to match. Previous Utopias have been constrained by the necessity of work, but now technologies can be implemented to make the Utopian project a reality. Capitalism is concerned with whether it pays, not with what it could do for us; Marxists and liberals have relied on the State to mediate a transition towards the realisation of the potential, but only through a decentralised communitarian lifestyle (the creation of 'ecocommunities') can the project be realised. The essay analysed in a little detail the technological possibilities, including a section on renewable energy technologies and another on the breakup of what are considered to be necessarily large-scale industries, and the relationship between communities and 'the agricultural matrix'. 'Self-sufficiency' was not at issue, but a shift in the centre of economic power from the national to the local scale. We could then reject the social democratic babble about 'jobs for all' and embrace the dadaist demand for unemployment for all. We need technology, but not bureaucracy; nor do we need centralised institutions or consumerism. How idiotic it would be if we bring our shoddy civilisation down in a Wagnerian *Götterdämmerung*.

Bookchin continued to develop these themes in detail in further essays and also to develop other lines of analysis including the writing of a definitive history of the Spanish anarchist movement (Bookchin (1977)), the question of urban planning, including its history and potential for Utopian planning (yielding two books as well as a number of essays (Bookchin (1973, 1974b, 1978, 1986b, 1987))), an increasing interest in questions of ethics (Bookchin (1982, 1986a)) and an interest in immediate possibilities for the re-empowerment of local community politics, in which he himself became deeply involved (Bookchin (1983)). In the late 1980s he became concerned with what he saw as major problems arising out of the one-sidedness of the ecophilosophy and 'deep ecology' debates as promoting a fanatical anti-humanism. This generated both a popular summary of his views as a whole (Bookchin (1989)) and a series of philosophical essays (Bookchin (1990)) concerned with developing a 'dialectical naturalism', rooted in Hegelian dialectics that overcame any collapse into either ecologism or humanism promoting, rather, a time-oriented dialectic between society and nature. Bookchin's most extensive attempt at an integrated theory was written during the late 1970s and early 1980s and published under the title of *The Ecology of*

Freedom (Bookchin (1982)). A summary of this is deemed to be useful to understanding his thesis as a whole.

It is difficult to summarise the almost 400 pages of fine-grained argument presented in *The Ecology of Freedom*. The project in general was to carry out a fundamental critique of 'civilisation' and establish the ground rules for a future ecological society in line with Utopian traditions. The first chapter outlined the concept of social ecology — developed from the ideas originally presented in 'Ecology and Revolutionary Thought' — which included a critique of the European focus of epistemological speculation that separates human thought and action from the reason and functioning of nature as a whole. Over half the book was then given over to a detailed account of social evolution, from 'organic societies' without hierarchy and at one with the ecosystems they inhabited, to our own society. The argument was at pains to separate out concepts of social organisation and thought as they emerged and the unity of these in any one context. On the one hand there emerged hierarchy, domination, the State and religion and on the other hand there developed ideas of alternatives to these: notions of freedom, the millennium and Utopia; specific renderings and movements that arose around these were analysed. Later chapters then focused on technology. These charted the narrowing of the Greek concept of 'techne', embodying art and craft, to the modern utilitarian and instrumental concept. The emergence of modern abstractions of work and commodity were juxtaposed to a concept of human labour as just another facet of the functioning of nature. This line of argument culminated in an appeal not to reject reason, science or technology but to rescue these from their misuse in modern society. The final chapters were concerned with clearing the way conceptually towards the construction of an ecological society by rescuing certain ancient social habits, rejecting practices of social hierarchy and domination and moving towards the establishment of decentralised ecocommunities (communes) and an ecological ethics. The world, Bookchin concluded, deserves better than what the future currently seems to hold.

In the writings of Gorz, Bahro and Bookchin it is already possible to understand in outline what political ecology is concerned with. These are beginnings, upon which the authors in question continue to build, illuminating different aspects of the theory and practice of political ecology, not always in agreement over what is most salient or even what is the correct view. But between them — and as this book proceeds it will be clear that there is already to hand a significant literature that is directly or indirectly of substantial use in developing political ecology — these provide a common framework and outline of that set of views, that way of understanding life, which answers the requirements that emerged from the identification of the environmental problematic in the early 1970s. Although these authors are not heavily referenced in the text which follows, it should be stressed at this point that their contribution to foundations of political ecology has already been considerable and that the rest of this book should be understood as a further contribution to the construction of an ecological world that is the explicit purpose of these authors and of the ecology movement and political ecologists in general.

Methodological foundations

Nevertheless, although political ecology and the ecology movement have been in existence for over twenty years, although the environmental problematic is increasingly recognised as a genuine problem for humanity and modern culture, there is still a very meagre theoretical literature upon which to construct an adequate political ecology. There is a common view amongst some active political ecologists that we are less in need of theory than effective action and it is clearly true that in the final analysis it doesn't matter what we think but what we do that will bring about or obviate the ecological denouement. But it is extremely naïve to suppose that 'common sense' and an eclectic choice of theory from amongst that immediately available in the universities and public libraries might be sufficient intellectual guide to the kinds of radical social and cultural reorganisation which the ecological problematic — and indeed the environmentalist literature — suggest will be necessary in the immediate future.

The intention of this book is to attempt to contribute additional impetus towards a more coherent formulation of relevant theory (the practical side of this I have then developed in a further text (Atkinson (1991)). However, before progressing into the discussion proper, it may prove useful to focus upon a few background issues relating on the one hand to the reasons why progress in developing political ecology has been so slow — and what might be done about this — and on the other to the general approach to theory which has been adopted in the body of this book.

It was noted earlier in this chapter that in the course of the 1970s a shift took place in analytical procedures and the use of theory on the part of academics studying the various manifestations of environmentalism. This attempting to break away from positivism was not, however, restricted to analyses of the environmental movement but affected the social sciences as a whole. Not only, as previously suggested, were real world changes in the social subject matter suggesting the need for new analytical approaches to be adopted, but the situation of the academic analysts was a powerful shaper of the scope of analytical enquiry. This included the configuration of the local academic environment, the nature of the international debate on the analysis of social issues and national analytical traditions and their foundations in national culture.

In general there has been a thaw in the empiricist-positivist-behaviourist straightjacket into which the analysis of social questions was forced both in this country and elsewhere, under the discipline of economics and behaviourist psychology, from the years following the First World War into the 1960s and even the 1970s. In recent years, the 'critique of positivism' has become the subject of a number of analyses, given a big initial push on the continent by Habermas (1987a (1968)) and associates already in the 1960s and eventually taken up by numbers of British social theorists (Giddens (1977); Halfpenny (1982); Bryant (1985)). It now forms a standard adjunct to many studies of particular topics. This should not, however, be overstressed in that words are regularly mistaken for content. The education, and as discussed further below the cultural tradition, of academics leads easily to misunderstanding of methods other than those with which they are familiar and hence to analyses that are *de facto* positivist in spite of declarations to the contrary. (Perhaps this is why there is some confusion as to whether the influence of Karl Popper upon anglophone social analysis has waned (Outhwaite (1987: 17)) or remained dominant (Aronowitz (1988: 281))).

There is no need here to present in any detail the alternative methodologies and epistemological positions that have been espoused in the area of social analysis in recent years. Suffice it to note that the dominant influence in the UK was ostensibly Marxism (Outhwaite (1987: 3)). 'Ostensibly', because there has been much leeway, in terms of what is salient in Marxism, with respect to the analysis of particular issues.

The initial fashion involved an ardent pursuit of French structuralism — as illustrated in a very widely read collection of articles edited by Robin Blackburn (1972). This could be interpreted not merely in terms of the liberation of a suppressed Marxist tradition in Britain but also a rebellion against the reductive British empiricist tradition, fleeing to the equally reductive French rationalist tradition, of which structuralism is a clear descendant (Geertz (1973: 356)). This flight (or flirtation) was relatively brief[10], terminating in Edward Thompson's (1978) very widely read 'The Poverty of Theory', which insistently reasserted the value of 'the empirical idiom' of British intellectual traditions. The third major stream of the new Marxism — until very recently more referenced than actually studied and assimilated — was that of the 'Frankfurt School': of Horkheimer and Adorno, Marcuse and latterly Habermas.

Moving into the 1980s, other analytical strands began to emerge both independently and in terms of a *rapprochement* with Marxism. These included a re-evaluation of the methods of Durkheim and Weber, taking a more independent line on methodology with attempts to define and apply a more consistent realism, hermeneutics and critical theory (Outhwaite (1987)) and the sociology of knowledge was consciously adopted by some analysts. Very marked in recent years has been an appraisal of methodology flowing from 'post-structuralist', 'postmodernist' and other recent emanations of French theory. Practically all of this is, however, of a tentative and self-conscious nature and displays a methodological eclecticism, rather than any conviction that any consistent methodological revolution is at hand.

It is important to relate these developments back to the academic context which has produced them. The meteoric rise and subsequent cooling of the wave of Marxism relates directly to the millenarian atmosphere of the 1960s and the events in the universities in 1968. The feeling that radical social change was imminent (without any significant concrete notion of what, in a technical and organisational way, this might result in) infected the generation of students then graduating, particularly those in the social sciences, and Marxism — with its orientation towards revolutionary social change — was seen, prima facie, as the most appropriate off-the-shelf methodology to make sense out of what was happening. This generation, upon attaining academic positions, proceeded to adopt this methodology as their approach to social analysis.

However, the residue of 1968 in terms of changes in the organisation of academic life — the relationship between the generation of theory and esoteric knowledge in the social realm and the actual structure and function of the social organism as a whole — was virtually nothing. The seats of higher learning retained their position as portals in the walls of the social structuring process. Hence there was a massive disjuncture between the Marxist theory espoused, and the actual function of the academics who adopted it. This was initially reflected in terms of a lack of consistency in the application of the methodology itself — the abdication of praxis and the attempt to force a particular scenario of social change, formulated in relation to 19th-century society, upon a social organism which had since undergone quite fundamental changes. Subsequently this generated disillusionment and cynicism in the face of a social reality that insisted in disregarding the views of these academics (and, indeed, which initiated an attack on their protected lifestyle) and which showed no signs of succumbing to the expected scenario of revolutionary change.

Marx was not an academic and his approach to social questions is deeply incompatible with the way in which knowledge in our society is generated and controlled from within academic institutions with their stable, well-defined — and thoroughly conservative — social role. The triumph of positivism earlier in this century can be understood in terms of a homology between social structure and function, on the one hand, and the analysis and presentation of this, as ideology. In particular it was compatible with the privileged position which academics occupy and which their approach to analysis would generally be expected to reflect. This was well-understood by Leszek Kolakowski (1972: 244) when he wrote:

Positivism so understood is an act of escape from commitments, an escape masked as a definition of knowledge, invalidating all such matters as mere figments of the imagination stemming from intellectual laziness. Positivism in this sense is the escapists design for living, a life voluntarily cut off from participation in anything that cannot be correctly formulated. The language it imposes exempts us from the duty in speaking out in life's most important conflicts, encases us in a kind of armour of indifference to the *ineffabilia mundi*, the indescribable qualitative data of experience.

Given the lack of change in the role of the 'seats of higher learning' following 1968, it was inevitable that academic Marxism would not develop creatively from the point of view of Marx's chief aim of wishing revolutionary change upon society, but that it would, rather, tend to adopt an inner structure compatible with the institutional and social framework which sustained it. It is in this context that Marxist structuralism — the adaptation of Marxist terminology to a much older French academic tradition — and what amounts in Britain to a Marxist empiricism and functionalism (Banks (1972:38)) became the academic residue of the high hopes of 1968.

Within this context, however, a second set of forces might appear to have the effect of generating some creative tension towards changes in focus and methodology within academia. This is the drive to establish individual careers and attain high position. On the one hand this encourages research in ever new areas and thus the uncovering of 'facts' but also the generation of alternative methodologies. The great expansion of the universities in the middle years of this century proliferated the numbers of academics and with it the impetus towards the generation of new material. Recent developments in methodological debate are clearly a further product of this. However, it is worth bearing in mind Mary Midgeley's (1979) remarks concerning the way in which academic disputes, deriving from internal ambitions, are often over insubstantial questions and false polarisations and promote fragmentation of knowledge rather than any deeper insight into issues with any practical social value.

Turning now to a further issue of some importance in this context: it is of more than academic interest that different national cultures, within the overall framework of European intellectual traditions, have generated significantly different approaches to knowledge, which have been held within their respective cultural boundaries over long periods. The importance of introducing this subject here is to confront and head off an a priori application of a particular set of thought processes and to reveal in brief how these arose and how they are sustained. In the first instance the English reader, steeped in empiricist traditions, is addressed. However, these traditions are necessarily contrasted with equally one-sided thought processes which are brought to bear by readers of other European cultures.

The main point here is to stress the way in which methodological — and beyond that philosophical — approaches are not somehow either mere convenience or personal foible (although it is argued later in this analysis that ultimately there is no methodology, to be discovered outside of human social relations, that represents 'The Truth'). A consistent approach to knowledge which connects through to aspirations towards radical social change, such as is deemed by those political ecologists who recognise the importance of sound theory to be urgently needed, necessarily requires the adoption of methodology, epistemology and ontology lying significantly beyond what is immediately to hand by way of conventional indigenous, or other off-the-shelf, approaches.

In the opening lines of one of his interventions in the current European debate concerning methodology, Ernest Gellner (1985:4) wrote as follows:

It is a curious and indisputable fact that every philosophical baby that is born alive is either a little positivist or a little Hegelian. It is also interesting that, philosophically, Europe has remained in the eighteenth century, as it was prior to the diplomatic revolution: there is an Anglo-Austrian Alliance, facing a Franco-Prussian one. Muscovy and the states and principalities of the Mediterranean area tend to be aligned with the Paris-Berlin axis, whilst the Scandinavians side with the opposing camp. Poles of distinction have fought on both sides.

Whilst glossing over a whole world of complexities (and there are certainly other interpretations concerning the relationship between the various European intellectual traditions[11]), this statement nevertheless says two things of some significance. Firstly, it is of great importance to realise that the totality of European thought has no centre, but comprises, rather, a tension between approaches to thought which are quite alien to one another at a basic level. The best of European philosophical debates, when they have managed to escape from mere expedition into the deserts of scolasticism (which has been all too rarely the case), have attempted to transcend this polarisation and achieve a comprehensive philosophical system; German philosophy in particular has aspired to this.

The second insight from the foregoing quotation by Gellner which is also of interest is that the dominant national philosophical positions held today were arrived at already in the course of the Enlightenment, stretching from Hobbes and Descartes in the mid-17th century to Hegel in the early 19th. Subsequent attempts to dislodge these ways of thinking, which inform in an extraordinary way the approach which the population of each country takes as its understanding of meaning and purpose in the everyday world, have failed.

Gellner is also right to point towards an essential political dimension to this which subsists as a distinct facet of the cultural. It might be said that the partiality — in both senses — of these various intellectual cultures is bound up with the whole nature of Europe as a set of polar political and cultural entities within a common cultural cosmos and the transcendence (we might say with Hegel, '*Aufhebung*') of these partial views is necessarily bound up with the supersession of a Europe of nation states.

Subsequent discussion throughout this book focuses on further details of the way in which this tension between partial views, and between the various European political and cultural entities which they inform, has worked itself out in terms of the evolution of European ideology as a whole. However, no attempt is made at this point, beyond this sketch, to provide any further overview of the origins of the differences and the interaction between the political and the ideological.

The main point is to note that any attempt, from whatever European cultural base (and the problems are, of course, magnified when the approach is from a more distant culture), to progress ideological debate in the direction of developing a consistent political ecology at the theoretical and philosophical level, will have an arduous road to travel simply to leave behind the one-sidedness of its origins. A consistent political ecology is not the negation of any particular European intellectual tradition, but of the tradition as a whole.

To arrive at a radically new, ecological, philosophical position that provides a comfortable and confident centre of gravity of thought and is not always achieved with effort and pain, requires in the first instance a major effort of the imagination and intellect. Seen from the point of departure of English culture, the Hobbesian view, reinforced again and again through English intellectual history by Mandeville, Hume, Adam Smith, Malthus, Darwin, and incorporated by almost every lesser theorist and analyst as the basis of views on every subject of intellectual endeavour, is not overturned in a day's ratiocination.

One might go so far as to say that empiricism and every sort of individualism — methodological, humanistic, even eschatological — peaks out from behind every word of the English language. These philosophical assumptions pre-define, a priori, where people brought up in the context of British, and to a large extent right across anglophone, culture expect ideas to come from and provide the framework within which all ideas tend to be ordered and given meaning. Hence ideas that emanate from a different set of assumptions and that are concerned to build a different kind of world become the subject of all manner of confusions and misinterpretations that easily lead to suspicions and accusations that the individual holding these ideas has evil, fascistic, even satanic, intentions that must be radically resisted. Minds are closed off from even attempting to understand and the aspiration to transform attitudes to facilitate the ecological revolution remain empty sentiment, devoid of intellectual and hence of any substantial and workable content.

The ideas presented in the chapters to follow are not designed in themselves to add up to any systematic 'ecophilosophy'. They are intended more as stepping stones in that general direction. The argument will have succeeded in terms of the aims of the analysis if advances have been made on the following three fronts. An attempt is made to subsume and thence exorcise the partial and hence distorted paths to knowledge which dominate the various European cultures. An attempt is made to approach knowledge from points of view which are homologous with the long term ecological order and hence which obviate the corrosively destructive approaches to knowledge with which our culture presently approaches the life process. As Josef Bleicher (1982: 1) put it:

Never before has the fate of mankind been so precariously balanced. Its destiny seems intimately bound up with the questions of whether and how it can cope with accelerating scientific advance and channel its potential away from human self-destruction towards socially useful ends. The problems posed by science and technology had, therefore, best be seen as a challenge to the socio-cultural framework of society in the form of requiring us to understand their cultural significance and to create the social conditions in which their misuse — which seems to be programmed into our political order — can be avoided.

Finally, the type of 'theory' developed aims to be handmaiden to effective praxis. The scolasticism of the great corpus of European philosophy must be de-escalated in favour of transparency of ideas that allow for the participation of the average intellect in the substance of the discourse as an adjunct to action in the everyday world. In the first instance this remains an intractable task but if it is possible to point to areas where whole branches of 'knowledge' may be abandoned as lost causes, then this analysis will have made headway.

The approach to these problems of knowledge which has been taken here should became evident in the structure and content of the text itself. But it is worthwhile to note that it does build upon European traditions of thought with a long history and, indeed, despite their lack of roots in British thought, are amongst what are currently being referred to as the 'new philosophies' (we might do better to refer to them more as methodologies) of social science (Outhwaite (1987)).

The first and most important aspect of the approach developed is that it abandons the absolute distinction which is made in positivistic science between the objective and subjective and beyond that the elimination of consideration of subjectivity which is then effected. A critique to which an earlier manuscript of this book was subjected concluded that the aim of the book was 'subjective and polemical' and with these words it was dismissed as a serious contribution to knowledge.

The extreme case for subjectivity as a valid contributor to knowledge as a whole was made by Husserl whose phenomenological approach to reconstructing the foundations of science aimed to (Luckmann (1978: 9) '...*describe* the *universal* structures of *subjective* orientation in the world, not to explain the *general* features of the *objective* world.' The dismissal of the manuscript on the assumption of its subjectivity was based upon an a priori assumption, lying at the foundations of British intellectual culture, that subjectivity is necessarily arbitrary (and in this sense 'irrational') and individual; that subjectivity is unique to each individual.

The point which phenomenology makes in this context is that subjectivity and the whole of conscious human life is in the first instance a structured, intersubjective totality of social and cultural phenomena (Schutz (1940: 134–135)). The very existence of objective knowledge and beyond that the particular aspects of the phenomenal world on which we choose to focus our attention obtains its animus for the life process as a whole and it is through an interpretation of the subjective that any measured understanding of the meaning of knowledge and the human situation — particular or general — can be obtained. The horror of the situation in which humanity currently finds itself, on the verge of self-destruction, can be traced rather directly to the radical separation of the objective and subjective where objective knowledge is supplied to the unbound forces of struggling social power relations, no questions asked. Phenomenology provides a basis for the creation of a framework whereby the intentionality and meaning to the subject can be considered in direct relation to objective knowledge, to make whole again and to bring some wisdom back into the process of organising knowledge and organising human life.

Looking upon modern phenomenology as a reinterpretation of the so-called hermeneutic tradition, we can see that it relates back to forms of medieval intellectual method that were eclipsed by the rise of empiricism and rationalism, universalised in the Enlightenment (Mueller-Vollmer (1985)). In Germany this approach to knowledge was never entirely eliminated and in the late 19th Century, through the efforts of Dilthy in philosophy and Weber in sociology, it became one of the chief bases for the humanities and social science — the *Geisteswissenschaften* — in Germany. However, a largely independent line of development of related method and epistemology evolved in the United States, originating in the work of George Herbert Mead (Berger and Luckmann (1967); Luckmann (1978: 17–24); Benson and Hughes (1983: 44, 54)). This included the symbolic interactionist approach to sociology and anthropology originating in the Chicago School of human ecology and subsequently the development of ethnomethodology out of the confluence of the earlier American work with German influences, particularly with the emigration of Husserl's student Alfred Schutz to the United States (Benson and Hughes (1983)).

An important further line of development out of this same tradition has been the sociology of knowledge. This is the only line which has had any significant influence in Britain until very recently and that has been extremely limited. British intellectual susceptibilities in this respect are well illustrated in the contrasting fate of the ideas of two Germanic refugees who settled into the London School of Economics in the 1930s. On the one hand, Karl Mannheim pursued the development of the sociology of knowledge but made very little impact on British intellectual life. Karl Popper on the other hand, developing a severely rule-dominated method, with an insistent subject-object separation (and an extreme anti-Marxism) became the dominant theorist of postwar British social science; it will be necessary to say more on this theme in subsequent chapters of this book.

In recent years the sociology of knowledge has become somewhat more widely applied, particularly as interpreted and disseminated by Berger and Luckmann (1967). This can be understood as a practical approach to ensuring that anything considered as 'knowledge' is not only understood in terms of its inner structure and relation to the empirical manifestations of its object but that it is also understood in terms of its relation to the social process: who produced it and what the overt and implied use and meaning of that knowledge might be in this context. In other words it insists on the importance of understanding the dialectical relationship between 'objective' knowledge and the knowledge generation process on the one hand and its broad subjective context on the other. Whilst the sociology of knowledge clearly evolved in general from a hermeneutic approach to knowledge, its immediate origins lie in Marx's (1975: 425) insight that "(i)t is not the consciousness of men that determines their existence, but their social existence that determines their consciousness" (Berger and Luckmann (1967: 17). Hermeneutics is not necessarily a 'critical' approach to knowledge, but it can be adapted to such purposes and it is useful to note the fact that Marxism itself finds its roots in part in, and lends itself to being evolved out of by reference to, hermeneutic method, in contrast to the incommensurability which it faces in relation to positivist method.

It should be added at this point that whilst, in the very separation of *Geisteswissenschaft* from *Naturwissenschaft*, hermeneutics has been assumed to refer only to method in the study of social phenomena, nevertheless this has radical implications for the understanding of method and meaning in the natural sciences and beyond that for the understanding of the dialectic of nature and culture which is the ultimate focus of this book. By way of indicating the way in which this should be understood and so pointing the reader at least in the direction in which s/he should expect to be travelling, over the chapters to follow a few words are in order concerning the approach to the natural sciences which hermeneutics suggests.

Reference was made earlier in this chapter to Thomas Kuhn's view of the process of scientific knowledge accumulation as advancing through the formulation of successive 'paradigms' that account for anomalies arising in relation to the practical or experimental use of earlier paradigms. This basically hermeneutic theory of science as social subjective mental process suggests strongly that 'objectivity' possesses an irreducible relativity, that objectivity within the framework of one quite workable paradigm might be substituted for another version of objectivity within the framework of another paradigm. Criticised for raising the spectre of irrationality and relativity, Kuhn (1970: 198–207) responded with an assertion that although later paradigms are not necessarily better representations of what nature really is, nevertheless, he himself is a convinced believer in scientific progress measured, it seems, in terms of appropriateness to its social purpose.

Kuhn's analysis, whilst far and away the most influential, was but one among a whole genre of re-evaluations of the scientific process conducted in the United States, France and Germany (Kuhn (1970: v–xii)). The most consistent exposition of the line of analysis pursued by Kuhn was that of Paul Feyerabend (1978) who, under the title of *an Anarchist Theory of Knowledge*, argued fundamentally against the notion that there is or should be any one method defining the scientific process, asserting that 'anything goes'. He noted that not only was the 'rationality' of one scientific theory 'irrational' from the point of view of a competing theory but that successive levels of 'higher rationality' which might be expected to resolve the incommensurability between theories eventually terminate in language which is not a *rational* framework but a *cultural* one. Theories of knowledge and within that particular ways of approaching knowledge of nature are manifestations of cultural evolution and hence the product of more general attitudes to knowledge in the context of cultural mythologies and religions. The criteria for scientific progress are thus (Feyerabend (1978: 223–224)) 'aesthetic judgement, judgements of taste, metaphysical prejudices, religious desires', themselves the product of their own evolutionary and historical process of accumulation.

Although argued with great consistency and widely footnoted, Feyerabend's proposition concerning the subjective cultural wellsprings, the cultural relativity, of science has proved to be unacceptable within mainstream philosophical debate, he being dismissed as a 'philosophical joker' (Naughton (1982: 375). The importance, however, of his insight to political ecology should become evident as the argument of this book unfolds. Above all, it is the decisive way in which he argues against the messianic universalism and absolutism of the ideology of science in the context of the European cultural project as a whole, mindlessly aggressive as it is towards other cultures, towards nature and in the context of modernism (Berman (1984a)) towards itself.

The phenomenological and hermeneutic modes of analysis comprise a broad stream of approaches to understanding and knowledge and not simply a 'new method' amongst methods (Mueller-Vollmer (1985: x)) for conducting 'social science'. As such they are fundamentally at odds with the positivist methods which, whilst in process of dissolution, nevertheless continue to inform the 'natural' way that much academic work is undertaken in Britain and to a lesser extent in other anglophone and continental countries. The foregoing paragraphs have attempted to provide an outline understanding of the scope and approach which hermeneutics in general takes and it is hoped that these will prove to be useful in illuminating the reasoning — the sensibility — that lies behind the structure of the argument which unfolds in the text to follow.

Notes

1. Aurelio Peccei, the president of the Club of Rome, made no secret of the fact that the modelling exercise described in *The Limits to Growth* was not intended as some kind of 'scientific proof' of the validity of environmentalist concerns but rather as a means to broadcasting the message. Already in 1969 Peccei had published a book in which he had attempted to raise the issues. Then, according to Gillette (1972): "for two years Club members had plodded quietly from Moscow to Rio, from Stockholm to Washington, seeking out political leaders, appraising them of the dangers ahead." At the official launch of *The Limits to Growth* in March 1972, Peccei stated that "Our message was received with sympathy and understanding but no action followed. What we needed was a stronger tool of communication to move men on the planet out of their ingrained habits. This is the reason for the MIT study and the book."

2. An older generation of geographers and perhaps other social scientists will recall that earlier in this century the term 'environmentalism' had a very different meaning from that generally understood today (Platt (1948); Tatham (1957); Harvey (1969)). An elision of 'environmental determinism', it referred to a commonly expressed view in the late 19th century that social attitudes and practices are environmentally determined and furthermore that the superiority of Europeans had been determined by the superior environment in which their culture had developed. This theory clung to 20th-century geography like the blood on the hands of Lady Macbeth, such that the term environmentalism came to be seen as representing attitudes and views that must at all costs be rejected. Whilst the current meaning of the word was coined in all innocence of its previous meaning, there can be little doubt that many an academic suspicion of the new movement was rooted inchoately in its connection to the older meaning of the term environmentalism.

3. Clark and Cole (1975: 10) remarked: "The bitterness of much of the criticism seems to stem from the perhaps understandable resentment that work of such ambitious scope (viz *The Limits to Growth*), attempted on such a flimsy data base, could have such an impact, while economists themselves have spent many years developing techniques and accumulating data for much more limited objectives." One of the most extreme criticisms (Kay and Mirlees (1974: 141, 151) referred to *The Limits to Growth* as 'useless models for illegitimate ends', adding: 'when research is congratulated on the importance of its subject, beware!' Kaysen (1972: 663) arguing the economist's case in contrast to that of the physical scientist's wrote: "Resources are properly measured in economic, not in physical terms.... new mineral resources can be created by investment in exploration and discovery."!

4. Sandbach (1980: 2–10) reviewed and summarised a substantial number of these. See also Trop and Roos (1971) and McEvoy (1972). Vernon Richards (1981: 122–123) commenting in the magazine Freedom on a sit-down held by the Committee of 100 on 10 December 1961 wrote: "How should we go about assessing last Saturday's sit-down and other demonstrations organised by the Committee of 100 and its regional counterparts? By the total number of supporters who attended? By the number of arrests, by the numbers who refused to give their names or be bound over? By the numbers jailed, by the reactions of the Press as well as the publicity received? To our minds, these are poor yardsticks at this stage in the development of the loose movement which supports the activities of the Committee, by which to assess such demonstrations, and those of us who take part must be the first to insist that the Committee should not be tempted to encourage the assessment of the success or failure of any

demonstration by a counting of heads, of arrests, of people kicking their heels in jail".

5. E.g., Trop and Roos (1971: 53); Buttle (1975: 54); Cotgrove (1976: 33); Sewell and Coppock (1977: 80). There were voices questioning the notion that the 'lower and working classes' are not so conerned about the environment as the 'middle and upper-middle classes': eg Kimber and Richardson (1974:2), Buttle and Flinn (1978). However, these, too, came with inadequate social theory to indicate what meaning or use such class designations might possess. Van Liere and Dunlap (1979) reviewed the whole question of the social bases of environmental concern by reference to the findings of the various empirical studies. Substantial analyses in the 1980s continued to refer, without further explanation, to the movement as 'middle class' (Lowe and Goyder (1983:10–11); Pepper (1984:173)).

6. In general, sympathetic analysts wishing to indicate the potential benignness of socialism with respect to the environment pointed to the Chinese example: Weisberg (1971: 149–156); Enloe (1975: 17–21); Sandbach (1980: 183–199). A major challenge to these views was mounted by Smil (1984).

7. It is interesting to note as an aside that Sklair (1973: 254–256), in attempting to construct a sociology of science and technology, saw 'techno-economism' as 'the ideology of our times' and as being under attack from all sides. He clustered the critics into two groups: a reformist 'environment and resources lobby' and the reactionary 'primitivists' (conservationists). He thought that a potent attack on the ideology *should* have come from Marxists but had failed to materialise, thus robbing society of any truly radical critique of its dominant ideology.

8. In so far as the anti-nuclear movement could be understood as a facet of the ecology movement, this did generate a small stream of articles in the early 1980s (eg Spence (1982, 1983); Rüdig (1983)). This linked in with a broader critique of technology as part of an academic interest in 'technology and society'. Whilst this had links with the 'alternative technology movement', it was not seen in academic circles as a dimension of any broader political ecology and this became explicit in Sandbach's analysis.

9. Kuhn (1970:207), in confronting the positivist and Popperian views of 'scientific progress' was quite explicit not only in rejecting the possibility of separating the 'normative' from the 'positive' ('is' and 'ought') but even the desirability of attempting to do so: "A few readers of my original text have noticed that I repeatedly pass back and forth between the descriptive and the normative modes... 'Is' and 'ought' are by no means so separate as they have seemed ... The preceding pages present a viewpoint or theory about the nature of science, and, like other philosophies of science, the theory has consequences for the way in which scientists should behave if their enterprise is to succeed". Feyerabend (1978: 167) summed the situation up in a simple aphorism: "Progress can be made only if the distinction between the *ought* and the *is* is regarded as a temporary device rather than as a fundamental boundary line".

10. Contributing to the cooling of structuralist ardour in Britain was the difficulties into which it was getting in France. On the one hand it was suddenly confronted in the late 1970s by the trenchant anti-Marxism of the 'New Philosophers' (Dews (1980)). Meanwhile, Marxist structuralism was losing some of its chief ideologues, notably Lucio Colletti and Manuel Castells who abandoned structuralism, and more dramatically, Louis Althusser, imprisoned for the murder of his wife and Nicos Poulantzas, who committed suicide!

11. The French physicist and philosopher Pierre Duhem put his interpretation of the differences in the following manner (Harding (1986: 234)): there are two kinds of scientific mind, "on the one hand, the abstract, logical, systematizing, geometric mind typical of Continental physicists, on the other, the visualizing, imaginative,

incoherent mind typical of the English." Johan Galtung (1981) undertook an analysis of national intellectual traditions — saxonic, teutonic, gallic and nipponic — that is of considerable interest. The following chapter looks in some detail at the way in which various regional intellectual traditions contributed to the totality of what became modern science.

3 Some philosophical considerations

Having in the foregoing chapter looked in some detail at existing approaches to the analysis and conceptualisation of structure and tasks of political ecology, ending with a pointer in the direction which this analysis aims to take, this chapter is devoted to following out in more detail important questions which this approach poses for the further development of political ecology. Starting from the requirement for an adequate methodology, the analysis inevitably leads into certain epistemological questions and in the last section to certain key aspects of ontology. As pointed out in the Introduction, the intention is not to found a new 'ecological' philosophical system as such, but to contribute to the construction of foundations — simultaneously theoretical and practical — for political ecology to proceed to a further stage.

Rationality

Since the Enlightenment, all aspirants to the status of knowledge have been increasingly eclipsed by whichever doctrines and disciplines that succeeded in acquiring the label 'scientific'. Science, in both the educated and the popular imagination, was seen as a method for attaining the one and only Truth, sorting out real knowledge from the counterfeit, the rational from the irrational. It has been commonly supposed that, although the products of science might be captured and used by the forces of evil just as much as by the forces of good, this was a separate issue from the value of science itself: this was — and continues largely to be — seen as absolute rational knowledge, free of human attributes or aspirations.

Of course it is a vital pragmatic necessity that in everyday life we believe that our knowledge of our immediate environment is irrefutably real. Without this confidence we would suffer vertigo with every step we attempted to take and with every attempt to pick up or manipulate objects in the world around us. There is, however, a tendency to extend this confidence into broader and more general beliefs about the structure of the environment — natural, social and metaphysical — and to believe that our way of viewing things represents the one and only Truth. As Lévi-Strauss put it (1972: 3):

Every civilisation tends to overestimate the objective orientation of its thought and this tendency is never absent. When we make the mistake of thinking that the Savage is governed solely by organic or economic needs, we forget that he levels the same reproach at us, and that to him his own desires for knowledge seem more balanced than ours...

The object of this section is to argue that science is essentially a cultural project. Nature can be described, classified, analysed or ordered in an infinite number of ways. The way this has been done in practice by science accords with the particularities and idiosyncrasies of the European pattern of cultural evolution. The trajectory has been essentially instrumental with respect to the working out of tensions internal to the social process and now we are faced with this trajectory — of knowledge interwoven with social dynamics — emerging as lethal to the continuation of that — indeed perhaps of any — social process. This section aims to provide an analytical framework — forthrightly synthetic and contingent — designed to understand the nature of the scientific 'knowledge accumulation process' in such a way as to provide a basis to diffuse the lethal dimensions of this project. In Chapter 5, further argument is presented aimed at assisting in the understanding of the evolution and derivation of our belief in science as a means of apprehending nature and designed to provide some footing for the construction of alternative approaches, compatible with an ecologically sustainable future. In the final chapter, the framework constructed here is used to provide the structure for the principles of political ecology.

The natural sciences have presented the most convincing case for the existence of a 'bedrock' of truth and rationality and so rather than confront this head on, a more accessible route can be taken, via the critique of the social sciences. By way of prolegomena, it is useful to note that right across the history of science, there have been indications of a realisation that all knowledge is moulded and hence influenced by the structure of language. In the early years of the Scientific Revolution Bacon (1960: 56) wrote: "For men believe that their reason governs words; but it is also true that words react on the understanding." Vico put this more clearly thus (Berlin (1976: 42)): "minds are formed by the character of language, not language by the minds of those who speak it." Mannheim (1936: 74) put the case more generally as follows:

The word and the meaning that attaches to it is truly a collective reality. The slightest nuance in the total system of thought reverberates in the individual word and the shades of meaning that it carries. The word binds us to the whole of past history and, at the same time, mirrors the totality of the present.

This has been reflected in a debate in recent years about the necessity, if science is to be truly objective and value-free, for the existence of a 'universal observation language' that would not contain a priori values and perspectives on the world which science wishes to focus on. It takes little reflection to realise that this represents an impossible task and that language has, indeed, continuously shaped the scientific project. The whole scientific project has been shaped by the structure and values that lie within the languages that provided the basis upon which to enter into the project in the first place.

Whilst this is by no means the end of the story, already it becomes apparent that the scientific project does not provide any absolute truth but is circumscribed by an essential contingency. And as the linguistic philosopher Edward Sapir wrote (Lyons (1968: 432): "The worlds in which different societies live are distinct worlds, not the same world with different labels attached."

The point at which the assertion of the absolute rationality of scientific knowledge has been most vulnerable is in relation to the analysis of societies and cultures in time and space: whether there are 'lawful' structures to the social process that lie beyond human volition and whether the ideas about truth and knowledge, held by societies other than ours, are truly inferior to science. The following chapter looks in some detail at the question of rationality and 'lawfulness' in history. Here it is useful to look at how and why the essential relativity of different societies that emerges from the analysis of anthropologists has been pushed aside by an insistence on the superiority of scientific knowledge over all other contenders.

Before looking closer at the debate it is essential to note that the focus of attention has shifted substantially over time with three distinct eras being discernable. It is generally accepted (Garbarino (1977: 25, 43–44); Burrow (1966: 75–76)) that the impetus to the founding of anthropology as a discipline in late 19th-century England was the fact of colonialism producing substantial cross-cultural contact and conflict and requiring some kind of rationalisation with which to apprehend and control it intellectually. The initial solution lay in an evolutionary framework (Burrow (1966)) which purported to demonstrate in detail how society evolved through increasingly superior stages, culminating in European science, and hence justifying the colonial destruction of 'outdated' indigenous cultural manifestations. The ultimate expression of this era was Frazer's (1957) monumental *Golden Bough* which, *inter alia*, involved a concerted attack upon 'irrational' modes of thinking and action, and in particular upon 'primitive' magic[1].

The combination of the rising socialist movements and the Marxist interpretation of evolution, which gave self-congratulatory evolutionism a whole new twist, was largely responsible for motivating the wholesale rejection, as established doctrine, both of social evolutionism and of the more extreme parochialism and the cultural and racial prejudice so openly flaunted throughout the 19th century. The structural-functionalism in England[2] and relativism and diffusionism of the United States (Sahlins and Service (1960: 1–2); Garbarino (1977: 45–55)) which emerged from the rejection of evolutionism predominated even into the 1970s.

The hallmark of this era was a studied empiricism (Leach (1957)) involving massive data collection exercises in the face of a dwindling source of empirical material. Interpretation remained highly circumspect and diffuse. In the United States theorisation was virtually proscribed, although the faith in an eventual inductive science provided a general context (Garbarino (1977: 48, 52)). British structural-functional anthropology, however, whilst calling for participation in the cultural subject, nevertheless indulged in substantial rationalist interpretation based upon the assumption that all aspects of a social system serve some instrumental purpose towards system maintenance.

That there might be a radical theoretical contradiction hidden in the method — not to mention violent insult to the subjects involved — did not surface in the theoretical debates surrounding this practice. In general these debates attempted to find some happy mean between the rejected radical rationalism of Frazer and an extreme phenomenological rejection of commensurability as between the social and cultural systems being studied and the investigative tools of the 'social scientist' (Lukes (1970)).

The potentially radical relativism harboured within these debates, with implications well beyond the boundaries of anthropology, was not drawn out and certainly there are indications that this related to a half expressed realisation of the dangers which such insights posed to triumphal scientism (Barnes and Bloor (1982: 21)). Neither 'bourgeois' nor Marxist social scientists wanted to know.

However, in the course of the 1970s the possibility of a radical relativism emerged in tune with the general relaxation of intellectual constraints and the efflorescence of international social and political movements pressing home the incommensurability of alternative social and political projects. Bryan Wilson (1970) gathered together a group of essays concerned with these issues and then in 1982 a further set, some contributed by the same authors, was edited by Hollis and Lukes. It is of some interest to note the shift in views that was in process of unfolding over that period. Whilst more recently it has become acceptable to express radical relativistic views (Bauman (1991)), there nevertheless remains an unhappiness, amongst most writers who address the issue, of departing in the final analysis from some notion of there existing at some level a core of absolute scientific truth (Hollis and Lukes (1982: 14); Brown (1988: 114)).

Looking now at salient details of the debate it is useful to start by identifying the two divergent ways of coming to terms with alien social systems, generally labelled respectively 'understanding' and 'empathy'. The extreme case of empathy involves a conviction that social systems (or historic conjunctures) are incommensurable and that coming to terms with any system means participating in its activities and using its terms with no relevance to any other system (as implied in the aphorism of Sapir cited above). The extreme case of understanding involves translation of terms and actions into the categories of 'social science'.

Given that no commonly accepted set of anthropological categories or typologies have yet emerged[3], the relativists accuse the rationalists of simply exercising their cultural prejudices. The rationalists, on the other hand, insist that without some 'common core' of rationality to form a 'bridgehead' spanning between alien social systems and our own (Hollis (1982: 73); Horton (1982: 260)), it becomes impossible to 'translate' between the two systems and hence they become incomprehensible to one another. The relativist rejoinder (Barnes and Bloor (1982: 37–39)) is that it is not at the level of *theory* but of *practice* that translation is effected[4]; initially this is verbal and by analogy and in depth it involves demonstration and participation.

There is no inherent or abstract call or basis for translation; it all depends on why you want to do it, on motivation and intention. Barnes and Bloor (1982: 47n)) conjectured that the reason academics are concerned to maintain the notion of one rationality relates to the fact that its loss would call into question the whole social scientific endeavour and hence their role and status in society. To acknowledge that your views are less than The Truth clearly represents a devaluation of those views in the context of our society and ideology. However, the continued insistence upon the need to render other cultures in 'rational' terms certainly continues the insistence upon European cultural superiority[5] as well as the superiority of the intellectual classes. Bauman (1988) has also come to focus on this issue and considers the sudden concern with the 'postmodern condition', discussed in more detail in the final chapter, to be informed by a 'status crisis' of the intellectuals arising out of the growing recognition of, or capitulation to, the validity of relativistic modes of perception.

The question of the relativity of scientific knowledge has not been wholly restricted to the area of anthropology but has been raised from time to time in relation to more general debate on the philosophy of science. The intellectual traditions of the United States have in general allowed for more leeway in investigating non-central lines of philosophical reasoning, under the general heading of pragmatism and thus relativism gained a certain credibility at least in anthropology in the earlier years of this century.

Thorstein Veblen (1969) wrote of science as representing in our age aspects of what mythology has represented in other eras. Whilst he was convinced that it presents a true — a matter of fact — picture of nature, this is not to say that it necessarily represents a better or worse leading cultural expression. Indeed, it could be construed as particularly problematic in so far as it has systematically diverged from a pragmatic approach to the organisation of society. Above all, Veblen wished to establish science as a creation of culture and not as representing some standard of truth lying beyond and above culture. It is indicative of the decades which followed his efforts that Veblen's views on science — as on other subjects — whilst commanding respect in intellectual circles, remained on the margins.

German approaches to the analysis of science have generally broken it into two disciplines — *Geisteswissenschaft* and *Naturwissenschaft* — which has allowed for an attitude that accorded the former a more contingent status and the latter an absolute status. The sociology of knowledge, within its premises, promised to overcome this dualism and to 'relativise' natural science in the course of establishing the social origins of positivism.

Mannheim (1936), however, in mapping out the content of the sociology of knowledge, was not able to find the intellectual strength in the face of the impregnable status of natural science, to adopt a forthright relativism. On the one hand his critique of positivism (pp. 146–153) simply aimed at divesting it of its hold over the conceptualisation of social and political matters but left it inviolate in relation to knowledge of nature. He was then (pp. 253–254) at pains to dissociate himself from any unstructured — or for that matter well conceptualised — relativism in the social and political sphere, defining his position as one of 'relationism' wherein 'it lies in the nature of certain assertions that they cannot be formulated absolutely, but only in terms of the perspective of a given situation.'

Of course the sociology of knowledge grew out of Marx's (1975: 425) assertion that 'It is not the consciousness of men that determines their existence but, on the contrary, their social existence that determines their consciousness.' This was not, however, a clarion call for the relativisation of science: Marx was a hard-line believer in one absolute knowledge represented by science and saw this as extending across the social as well as the natural spheres; in this he was in agreement with positivists, such as J. S. Mill and the positivist social science community of the 20th century, who see social science as being 'inexact', 'immature' or 'young', in process of achieving exactitude and via this the absolute universality of the natural sciences.

This attitude has been reflected by Marxists across this century who have tended towards espousal of a mechanistic connection between social interests and interactions on the one hand and the holding by those interests of particular ideas. However, there was an assumption that whilst some of these ideas — particularly in so far as they involved social and political analysis — were contingent upon social interests, those which emanated from the natural sciences were somehow free from the influence of interests. This attitude is to be found in the writings of Lukács.

More recently Habermas revived the debate specifically aiming an attack at positivism. Whilst this intervention (Habermas (1987a: Appendix)) triggered a wide-ranging debate, it is necessary in this context to note that his rejection of positivism was incomplete. He suggested that there are three forms of knowledge in currency. One relating to the empirical sciences which is rooted in nature itself — and hence remains an absolute form of knowledge; one relating to the 'historico-hermaneutic sciences' and which proceeds through a phenomenological understanding of the inner connections of events; and the third relating to the 'critique of ideology' or the 'sciences of social action' (referred to, when detached from the notion of praxis, as social sciences). So Habermas, in conformance with general practice, maintained the conviction that some areas of European thought represent absolute and universal knowledge.

Somewhat at a distance from the theoretical debate, recognition of the socially-bound nature of the natural sciences has nevertheless been accumulating in the form of essays on scientists and their work. Robert Merton's (1970) seminal analysis of the development of science in 17th-century England, first published in 1938, initiated a wide-ranging debate which was followed by many other historico-sociological analyses of science. Whilst these provide a clear basis for a theoretical critique of scientific absolutism, they have so far rarely been used to that effect.

Clear exceptions to this are to be found in the writings of Barry Barnes and David Bloor (and it should be added that such views are becoming more common (Aronowitz (1988: Ch.10)). Barnes (1974,1977) writes from a consistent sociology of knowledge (and acknowledging an affinity with ethnomethodology, symbolic interactionism and in general phenomenology) concerning the culture-boundedness not only of scientific activity but of scientific knowledge itself. All knowledge is accepted belief, not correct belief; no particular set of natural beliefs represent 'The Truth'. There is no set of rationality criteria that is more than a set of conventions and, as Kuhn has demonstrated, there can subsist at any one time a variety of interpretations of any set of observations. Nor is there any one set of methodologies. What there is, is a culture, or set of subcultures or communities of scientists with their own baseline of normality and contextual continuity; there are always peripheral contradictions within the beliefs of these subcultures and more seriously between the subcultures.

Whilst science represents in our time a highly developed and high status cultural element with its differentiated disciplines and roles, esoteric clusters of activity and characteristic artifacts, it is nevertheless only an aspect of that culture in terms both of function and output. In so far as it provides services to the culture as a whole, these can face in different direction — say attacking 'metaphysics' or curbing the spread of disease or following out aesthetic investigations in pursuit of fundamental innovation — and in doing so employs entirely unrelated standards and models. This implies that the terms of reference of science generally emanate from within society. This is, on the whole, demonstrably the case albeit that the connections are often complex. Furthermore, new directions always start from a base of existing conceptions, facts and artifacts so that 'social determination' becomes an orientation rather than an alternative source of absolute value in contrast to the notion that science gives us the absolute truth about nature.

In conclusion to this argument, Barnes (1977: 24) writes:

It is never unambiguously clear that existing theories could not have reasonably been maintained, or that yet other theories might not have been produced with just as much to recommend them....The diverse real universals postulated at different times and in different cultures and contexts, should be regarded alike as inventions of the mind, sustained to the extent that they are instrumentally valuable in the settings where they are found.[6]

Barnes (1977: 25) goes on to note that:

It is sometimes felt that such arguments must be rejected simply because they represent a concession to relativism. Relativism is often opposed in sociology as a matter of passion and commitment, even by those who recognise the lack of any good arguments for their case. It is felt that to do otherwise is to provide a license for any kind of nonsensical thought, and to display a lack of interest in what the world is really like.

Bauman (1988: 228) expressed the same sentiment in the following manner: 'For well neigh three centuries relativism was the *malin génie* of European philosophy.' However, adopting a relativist position requires an analysis to answer the question at the outset: 'relative to what?'; the answer 'relative to culture' remains at a level of generality with insufficient purchase by way of analytical purpose. But it is perfectly possible both in a relatively generalised way and in a way specifically oriented to the needs of particular aspects of knowledge, to answer this question in a clear manner.

For instance, in the introduction to their collection of essays on rationality and relativism, Hollis and Lukes (1982: 11–12) set out five variables that might provide the basis for relativistic analysis. These were: the natural environment, psychology, social context, language and 'some all-embracing context'. The position adopted here is that particular problems require the adoption of particular standpoints and that in most cases a number of different standpoints, taken in succession, will provide enriched insight. Fernand

Braudel's (1972) seminal work on the Mediterranean in the 16th century used just such an approach. The analysis of the development of science in Chapter 5 of this book also adopts this device, looking initially at the way in which science emerged as the reconfiguration of pre-existing ideas, then looking at the way in which changing social forces influenced that reconfiguration and finally discussing aspects of the way in which the physical environment impinged on this process of ideological transformation.

The principles of political ecology laid out in the final chapter of this book are advanced in the framework of a set of viewpoints in the sense that has emerged from the foregoing discussion. It is therefore useful at this point to present these viewpoints and to discuss the way in which these are seen as representing a balanced set, appropriate to the requirements of the principles in question.

Of the viewpoints suggested by Hollis and Lukes, two are acknowledged as being of great importance: the influence of the natural environment and that of society. The latter, of course, represents the perspective from which the sociology of knowledge proceeds. Whilst language has already been discussed as an important influence upon the way in which ideas arise and evolve, this is not adopted here for further development (albeit this is acknowledged as representing a significant issue).

The viewpoint of psychology is also not further followed out here, although the last section of this chapter discusses some of the background necessary to any use of this variable. In sum, it is held that individual differences in psychology are, in our society, greatly overrated as an influence upon social action. The dialectical interaction of individual psychologies in the social process is judged to be of significance but this is best subsumed into a generalised social viewpoint in keeping with the sociology of knowledge, as outlined by Berger and Luckmann and discussed in the previous chapter. The view taken here is analysed in some detail in the last section of this chapter.

Three viewpoints not identified by Hollis and Lukes are also adopted here. Firstly it is essential to look at the way in which ideas are derived from other ideas in a process of historic evolution and diffusion. This is what Barnes referred to when he wrote of all scientific ideas growing via the reconfiguration of pre-existing ideas[7]. This is the essential territory of the 'history of ideas'. Secondly there is an important question of the aesthetic qualities of ideas — and indeed of actions of everyday life — and the way in which these make coherent and intelligible the relationships between otherwise incoherent and even incomprehensible notions, facts and conjunctures[8]. Whilst this has until recently been a systematically neglected dimension of modern science and social analysis, it has nevertheless made some headway in the form of symbolic interactionism and particularly semiotics as further discussed in the following section of this chapter.

Finally, it is useful to view the development of ideas from the vantage of the future. This might sound prima facie absurd: the future remains unknown. However, in practice, all ideas, social, political or scientific, arise in society in relation to some assumption about its temporal status. In a society existing in an equilibrium state, this dimension will be of no consequence (indeed, 'new ideas' as such will occupy a very meagre place). But in our society, assumptions about the future impregnate our every thought and all ideas presuppose particular futures. Although it might be conjectured that the inability of functionalist analysis to account for social change (Atkinson (1991, Ch.3)) is the consequence of a studied refusal to look at the consequences of current social dynamics for the future, the reality of social science is that it has, in fact, adopted priorities, particularly in reaction to Marxism, which assume a particular scenario to be unfolding. The classic case concerns the emphasis (and in some cases the studied de-emphasis) of social class which gains its importance by dint of a scenario which sees the working class as being the chief instrument of social change. Of course the environmentalist scenario requires a thorough reorientation of priorities which is, indeed, the central function of this book as a whole.

What is of importance here is that in a situation of *de facto* rapid change it is simply foolish to avoid making assumptions about the future and testing the present against them. Furthermore such assumptions must be made conscious and necessarily contain an element of normative aspiration. Although the building of future scenarios has in recent years proliferated into an immense industry of fiction and technocratic fact, social studies, *qua* 'science', have largely refused to accept the validity of this activity (one thinks of the disdain with which such analyses as Alvin Toffler's (1973) *Future Shock* have been held in academia). As a consequence, social scientific analyses have contained implicit scenarios which operate by way of a teleology — an unexamined belief in a necessary future. The positivist notion of a process of secularisation and economic progress as being under way is one such teleology and the Marxist scenario concerning the inevitability of proletarian revolution is posed by way of an explicit teleology. This is a key area where 'social science', so keen to remain 'objective', dissolves into faith.

A proper attitude to adopt is to uncover what constraints and opportunities exist in the current situation with respect to the achievement of particular future states; the forward projection of existing dynamics is in itself insufficient above all because it remains blind to aspects of the social process which are currently recessive but which could rise to prominence in the future. It also pays too little heed to the role of volition, both individual and institutional. Of course *in practice* assumptions about the future play an important part in the way that individuals, groups and whole societies confront everyday life now, and the existence of the ecology movement, invoked as a reaction to the 'environmentalist scenario', is an excellent illustration of this. The importance of this issue dictates that it be analysed in considerably more detail and this is accomplished in the following chapter.

To end this discussion of viewpoints relevant to a relativistic analysis, it is useful to relate this back to current theoretical debates. There has in general been a dispute as to whether ideas in science are 'internally' or 'externally' determined (Barnes (1974: Ch.5); Harding (1986: 209–215)). These can be identified with positions that relate respectively to the subdiscipline of the 'history of ideas' or to the 'sociology of knowledge' (or, in the latter case, to a Marxist analysis). Internalists tend to focus on the evolution of ideas in relation to pre-existing ideas and to disregard, or even argue against, the influence of social, economic and other external influences. Externalists, on the other hand, minimise or disregard the origin of ideas and how these gain the particularities of their internal form.

It is necessary to state forcefully that all ideas and actions have multiple causes which involve both internal and external factors. It can be seen that amongst the viewpoints listed above, two are 'external', two are 'internal' and the final one cannot be easily classified in this manner. It should be noted that there is nothing new about the suggestion that multidimensional analysis is necessary to an adequate interpretation of the world: this was clearly laid out in a seminal essay, entitled *Fundamental Problems of Marxism*, written by G. V. Plekhanov in 1908 which set a precedent for a significant stream of Marxist analyses. Nevertheless it has been necessary to assert the point again forcefully into an intellectual arena which all too easily avoids this insight[9].

Finally it is useful to add a note to the effect that beyond the structuration processes of ideas and actions lies the motivations and intentions of the human subjects. Whilst these remain inchoate in the absence of accepted frameworks, it is nevertheless the beliefs attaching to these frameworks and the essential processes of human life that inform the processes of everyday life and of change. This, too, requires attention and receives it in the final section of this chapter.

We can summarise the foregoing argument in the following manner: there is no ultimate rationality but only contingent ways of understanding the world and our actions which is more or less tacitly accepted as a social and cultural project. Things gain their meaning in general by their relationship to other things and are understood in their relationship back to coherent and consistent structures. Potentially there is a large number of relevant structures which might have a bearing on a given analysis but here it is deemed helpful to the argument to present five structural dimensions which inform subsequent parts of the discussion and to which the analysis returns, in full, in the final chapter. These dimensions are:

- Our actions and our understanding are informed predominantly by ideas inherited from history that have their own inertia and present definite channels to any aspiration to change.
- The structure of society and social relations have a similar constraining and channelling effect not only on our actions but on what we might so much as consider; they define the whole tenor and orientation of our thinking as well as our actions.
- Nature is not a mere passive background to our social and cultural projects but, in a similar manner to social relations, inspires particular approaches to fundamental problems of epistemology as well as praxis.
- Human activities and understanding are deeply informed by aesthetic structures: purpose and meaning arise out of a sense of coherence and beauty attaching to thought patterns and lived procedures. The essentially social life of human beings can be summarised as comprising a series of interlinking dances encompassing intellect and action.
- An essential aspect of our social condition is its future-orientedness: *de facto* change built upon a progressivist ideology generates a sense of anticipation that demands an implicit or explicit structured view of the

future.

None of these dimensions is in an abstract sense more important than the others to analytical endeavour. Whilst acknowledged as contingent, their choice and focus is nevertheless made on the basis of their usefulness to the project in hand: the outlining of a set of principles of political ecology and the furthering of the requirements of the ecology movement.

Having discussed the basis and validity of a purely relativist approach to understanding or conceptualisation of social and natural structure and function[10], it is useful to refocus on the motivation behind the tenacious assertion of rationality against which relativism stands in opposition. In Chapter 5 it is revealed how science came of age as a particular moral stance towards nature that was practical in intent. It is further pointed out how this practicality, in practice, involved an instrumentalism — a polarisation of means and ends, cause and effect — whereby nature is used by some social interests to maintain hegemony over others within the overall framework of an ideology of progress. The process has been analysed under the general rubric of 'technological rationality' by the Frankfurt School (Horkheimer (1974); Adorno and Horkheimer (1979); Marcuse (1964)) and recently extended to encompass the notion of 'exterminism' (Thompson (1980, 1983); Bahro (1984, 1986)) which borders on a fatalistic vision of the process as lying beyond any structured political intervention.

The social system of 'civil society', involving class and cultural conflict, pushes into the background the aesthetic and playful structures of human co-operation and insists on an instrumentality to hold it in place on the one hand by inducement, represented by an ever increasing and more exotic flow of commodities, and on the other by coercion, made possible by ever more sophisticated and effective means of force (Bauman (1988: 221)) and so effectively supported by those ideological structures which suppress criticism of power and the powerful (Lukes (1974)). The 'secularisation' of thought processes is not some natural process of enlightenment but is forced by dint of an ever more instrumental real world (Kavanagh (1980: 170)). Social science — whether positivist or Marxist — as ideological adjunct to this social and political system, acts as legitimation of instrumentalism: its 'discovery' of the 'function' behind non-instrumental cultural manifestations represents a simple hegemonic denial of the validity of other cultures or non-instrumental cultural attributes. In other words, *all* forms of rationality comprise *our* cultural prejudices — a kind of fanatical Judaeo-Christian based millenarian self-righteousness — insisting on instrumentalism as the only validator of culture. Adorno and Horkheimer (1979: 4) characterised the situation in the following terms:

What men want to learn about nature is how to use it in order wholly to dominate it and other men. That is the only aim. Ruthlessly, in despite of itself, the Enlightenment has extinguished any trace of its own self-consciousness. The only kind of thinking that is sufficiently hard to shatter myths is ultimately self-destructive. In the face of the triumph of the factual mentality, even Bacon's nominalist credo would be suspected of a metaphysical bias and come under the same verdict of vanity that he pronounced on scholastic philosophy. Power and knowledge are synonymous.

Marcuse's (1964: 154–166) contribution included the following:

...when technics becomes the universal form of material production, it circumscribes an entire culture; it projects a historical totality — a 'world'... In view of the internal instrumentalist character of scientific method.... a closer relationship seems to prevail between scientific thought and its application, between the universe of scientific discourse and that of ordinary discourse and behavior — a relationship in which both move under the same logic and rationality of domination.... The point which I am trying to make is that science *by virtue of its own method* and concepts, has projected and promoted a universe in which the domination of nature has remained linked to the domination of man — a link which tends to be fatal to the universe as a whole.... Thus the rational hierarchy merges with the social one.

Of course political ecologists, feminists, peaceniks and increasing numbers without label see the march of instrumental and technological rationality as disastrous — and there are social scientists who both see this and at the same time deny their part in the responsibility for it, for instance Gellner (1985: 92) who maintains a faith in absolute rationality:

The self-destruction of humanity, through nuclear or other war or ecological disaster, is perfectly possible and perhaps probable in the post-scientific age, whereas previously mankind did not possess the power to destroy itself, and, owing to its dispersal, was virtually certain not to face destruction by any outside force. So if truth were equated with that which increases the probability of survival, then science would certainly be untrue.

To divert and diffuse this horrendous machine requires both thought and action. Replacing rationalistic modes of social and cultural interpretation with relativistic ones, that encompass local social and ecological conceptualisation within a single framework, provides a different foundation for thought processes that could move in a benign direction. But for this to work effectively it is also necessary to change the way in which the social organism functions. Banks (1972: 41ff)) noted that attempts to innovate socially have a general tendency to run up against unintended and unanticipated reactions and side-effects within the social organism and insisted that we must discover the system lying behind these tendencies. The system, however, is simple: one person's rational innovation is another person's irrational ploy in a situation where competition between classes of various definition and beyond that between individuals is encouraged — or worse, comprises a basic belief about 'human nature', underpinning the structure of society — and hence lack of trust and insecurity become systematic and endemic. The 'irrationalism' of fascism, instrumentalism and exterminism is nothing more than the fragmentation of reason into inherently conflicting interests and hence aims.

The 'egalitarian mutualistic' social system which clearly represents something of a logical opposite to the conflictual modern social organism is manifest in the political realm by anarchism (no leaders) which has both a substantial intellectual and political history. It is no coincidence that radical relativism, upon gaining a concerted philosophical statement by Paul Feyerabend, should have been subtitled 'An Anarchist Theory of Knowledge', and it is flagrantly inconsistent for Feyerabend then to have so vehemently denied the homology between his epistemology and the political theory of the same name (Feyerabend (1978: 21, 187ff)). The view taken throughout this analysis is that political ecology, informing the praxis of 'Green Utopianism' is basically an anarchist political philosophy and that this is essentially informed by a relativistic epistemology of the kind laid out in the foregoing paragraphs. The analysis developed in subsequent parts of this book are grounded upon the presumption that it is only on the basis of a radical extension of an adoption of relativism and of its homological cultural expression that we can expect to be able to avoid the ecological denouement ahead (Dumont (1974); Maruyama (1976)).

Ideology

The foregoing demolition of the notion that there is a class of ideas which possess the status of absolute truth was not carried out for its own sake or to score academic points. It must always be borne in mind that the purpose of this analysis is to promote the ends of the ecology movement in its bid to head off the destruction of the biosphere. So the next question of interest is: what is the role of ideas in the maintenance of our society and social evolutionary trajectory, and what is the potential role of ideas as a means to changing these? Questions of particular interest are: where do ideas come from? What, in general terms, is important about ideas or particular structures of ideas? Are ideas simply phenomena, there to be studied, or can we decide what we want to think? Above all, we are interested in the connection between ideas and actions: in the end, it is not ideas but the way we act upon and within nature that will decide whether the biosphere will continue to support human societies. It is useful to state at the outset of this discussion that the position of this analysis is that ideas and ideologies, under whatever title, serve a vital function in changing the direction and nature of society. It must be acknowledged that it is necessary to steer a careful path through terminology — such as the term 'ideology' — that already evokes complex ideas and feelings and to clarify the particular meaning adopted in a situation where various interpretations are possible. It is thus to be made clear immediately that the term 'ideology' is here used in a general, and not a critical, sense as denoting sets and systems of ideas which inform social actions and processes. Science is, in this context, an aspect of ideology.

Several discourses, more or less loosely connected, within society at large have some significant bearing on this discussion. These include the educational process itself, with its in-built assumptions about the status of ideas. It also includes religious teaching and beyond that the teaching of comparative religions and philosophy (in particular epistemology). However, the focus of the discussion here is more narrowly concerned with discourse on the history of ideas and above all sociological debates around — and social action founded upon — ideology and related concepts.

Whilst societies cohere and reproduce themselves with the aid of self-justificatory notions, ideas and theories, these are not seen immediately as a coherent whole. As discussed later, these are in many respects manifestly fragmented and contradictory and yet, when set against contrasting social outlooks and practices, they can also be seen to sum to a whole — that has been referred to in phenomenological discourse as a 'Weltanschauung': a set of shared cultural assumptions which form the common ground upon which arise the conflicts and particularities of social classes and subcultures. Concerted efforts to change society, however, are always accompanied by consciously formulated and structured ideas. We inherit from the ancient world the notions of religion and philosophy as terms applying to systematic attempts to comprehend and often, in the first instance, to change the way in which the social world functions.

Recent analyses of social change have adopted a variety of general terms for the frameworks of ideas which movements for social change formulate and adopt to justify and direct their efforts. These include such terms as 'constitutive ideas' (Heberle (1951b)), 'Generalised beliefs' (Smelser (1962: 79ff)) and 'ideational superstructures' (Larrain (1979: 50)). Far more widespread in usage and far more contentious and fought over in terms of its meaning and content is the term 'ideology'. Before proceeding with a discussion that concerns itself with the general content of this area of discourse — under whatever terminology — it is necessary to make a few background remarks about the concept ideology.

The original, self-confessed 'ideologues' were a group of prominent participants in the French Revolution, intent upon establishing revolutionary society on the basis of a coherent historical and social theory which they termed 'ideology' (Lichtheim (1967)). Initially embraced by Napoleon, in consolidating his power he pushed the ideologues aside and, although some elaboration of their ideas continued, this had no further influence on political developments. (Stuart Hall (Centre for Contemporary Cultural Studies (1978: 10)) wrote of this episode: 'Their fate constitutes a salutary warning for all ideologues.'!)

Marx's adoption of the term was in line with his general approach to the Enlightenment. Whilst the revolutionary bourgeois had succeeded in casting off the mystification of religion in their conception of the worlds of nature and society, they nevertheless developed partial theories and views of society, distorted by the misshapen nature of the society of which they were now masters; Marx was always insistent, as has already been noted here from time to time, that the social existence of people determined the nature of their thinking. His own 'scientific' analysis of capitalism was aimed at revealing the true picture and at the same time pointing the way to the creation of a classless society in which the whole of society would become master of its own destiny and no longer the servant of the blind forces of nature and history. Initially Marx used 'ideology' as a term of abuse against his immediate rivals amongst the group of radical followers of Hegel, the 'Young Hegelians' (and in particular the anarchist individualist Max Stirner) (Marx and Engels (1970)). But in time it came to denote bourgeois social theory in general[11] oriented, as it was and remains, towards maintenance of existing social structures and relations.

Already around the turn of the century followers of Marx were employing his terminology in new ways and Lenin, following Bernstein's 'revision' of

Marx and Engels, asserted that each social class possesses an ideology through which it attempts to enthral society in general. Thus the 'historical materialism' of Marx and Engels was seen as the ideology of the proletariat, informing the praxis of this class in its struggle against bourgeois political power and its ideological underpinnings.

In this same period, the foundations of modern 'social science' were being laid in the form, largely, of a 'struggle with Marx' (Berger and Luckmann (1967: 17–18); Hughes (1959: 42)), displacing 19th-century 'bourgeois' social theory where this might lend tacit support to Marxism. Durkheim initially directed the concept ideology to the analysis of religion and thence broadened it out to encompass the full range of ideas informing the way in which society functions. For him this was not a critical concept — Durkheim saw religion in approving terms as 'social cement', giving guidance to the individual and maintaining the unity and viability of society — but he nevertheless contrasted it with science. Sociology, as a science, was an additional form of knowledge which could bring rationality to society in parallel, not in competition, with ideology.

German social science, on the other hand, particularly in the hands of Weber, developed explicitly separate from the natural sciences — as 'Geisteswissenschaft' as distinct from 'Naturwissenschaft' — and with a distinct methodology, hermeneutics, derived from phenomenology. Although positivism — the aspiration to encompass all knowledge within scientific principles — made considerable headway in Germany, nevertheless, the followers of Weber and related schools of thought (Dilthey, Scheler and others) remained influential and were happy to develop their ideas as explicitly other than scientific in the positivist sense (in the sense in which it is used in the English language); whilst their analyses were concerned in great measure with the role of ideas in society, they had little use for the term ideology or the concept which it denoted in Marxist discourse.

Mannheim (1936), however, in developing his interpretation of the sociology of knowledge, explicitly embraced, in the first instance, Marx's use of the concept ideology as a critical term, earning himself the title of 'bourgeois Marxist' (Hall (1977: 13)). Ideology is accepted ideas in the cause of maintaining the social and political status quo. Mannheim did not, however, accept Marx's notion that there is only one, truthful, scientific alternative. Contrasting sets of ideas, aimed at changing society, Mannheim referred to under the title 'Utopia'. The de facto relativisation of ideas implicit in this approach, and Mannheim's difficulty in acknowledging this, was noted earlier in this chapter.

In reviewing the development of the critical role of ideas in society, La Piere (1965: 292n) concluded that attempts throughout the first half of this century had failed to bring any effective systematic view to bear. Of course this related directly to the way in which academic sociology shied away from acceptance of the fact of social change, constructing functionalist models that presented society as a fixed object, implicitly unchanging and so inured against the aspiration to build any other kind of society. In such a situation, ideas had little role to play. The term ideology stood as a marker for the absence of Utopian thinking in an ideologically embattled world. As Drucker

(1974: 140–141)) came to express it, Western society was rent by conflicting political beliefs, each of which interpreted the role of socially effective ideas in a different light: to socialists, ideology comprised bourgeois modes of thought; to liberals, ideology was any intolerant system of thought; and to conservatives, ideology was the title appended to any set of ideas that might encourage social change. In all cases, ideologists, formulators of socially creative ideas, were taboo. There appeared little milage for academics to engage openly in this struggle. On the whole, however, academia stood firmly on the side of conservatism and during the 1950s, in the context of the cold war, went so far as to declare the advent of the 'end of ideology' (Waxman (1968); MacIntyre (1971: Ch.1)).

No sooner declared dead, than attitudes began to change. In the course of the 1960s, it became apparent that social analysts had been avoiding a central aspect of society in the 20th century. Banks (1972: 9) noted the contrast between the absence of analysis and the fact that this has been:

...a century which has experienced two world wars, frequent violent revolutions and a continuous clash between advocates of numerous social doctrines, of which socialism, communism, fascism and nationalism are only the most manifest — is above all the century of social movements, as well as the century of sociology.

The thawing of self-imposed restrictions on academic investigation on social issues in recent years, and in particular the growth to respectability of Marxist analysis, has encouraged debate around the term ideology and more generally the role of ideas in social change; the latter part of this section is designed to engage with this debate. However, as an aside, it is useful to raise the concern, expressed at the outset of this chapter, regarding the influence of national intellectual traditions on the choice of subject matter and approach taken to analysing it, in the context of the discussion of ideology. In particular it is necessary to draw attention to the roots of the substantial difference between the approaches which British and French analysts have taken to this issue.

Social theories in Britain and France do not merely grow out of differing theoretical traditions, they actually fulfil different functions within the overall structure of the culture of these societies. In attempting to use social theory for purposes other than those which it has traditionally fulfilled theorists constantly risk being dismissed a priori. Readers are confused and irritated and perhaps beneath that disturbed by unfamiliarity in the structure of arguments. On the whole, they expect variations on a particular plot, not an altogether different story. But political ecology must succeed in transmitting the urgency with which it is necessary for our society to reformulate its purpose at a quite fundamental level but in a way which leads to and supports fundamental changes in social practice. For that reason, it must be prepared to adopt and promote new roles for social theorisation.

British inductive social theory — the English ideology — has its roots in the efforts of Hobbes and Locke to contain social change; written in times of overt social disaffection, they were designed to define new walls within which society would operate. Social theory, in the British setting, attains the status of a serious contribution if it traces a dour and arduous road through a sea of detailed empirical evidence and argument to achieve a new commitment to truth. The truth is always a traditional, common sense truth, never a striking new proposition — although the writers might present it as if it were. And this truth always confirms the belief that life is inevitably unpleasant. For some. The aspiration to change society is anchored down by sheer weight of facts and intellectual speculation is severely discouraged.

Thus we see Hobbes confirming the need for power and authority over the claims of democrats and anarchists, by reference to a notion of 'human nature' that sees men as inevitably selfish and vicious[12]. Locke, the 'father of modern empiricism', was concerned to limit the scope of speculation to things which already exist and so curtail any tendency to question the virtue of existing reality. This position was confirmed by the sceptic, Hume, who insisted that reason is and should be the slave of the passions, not to be trusted as a basis for altering the way that things are. In the calm of the late 18th century, Adam Smith turned the Hobbesian and Humean assumptions concerning human nature into the practical discipline of economics[13]. In the face of the French Revolution, out of which arose alternative, optimistic propositions about human nature, and revolutionary movements concerned to demonstrate their practicality, Malthus insisted on the inevitability of the Hobbesian model. Finally, by direct reference to Malthus, Darwin extended the Hobbesian model to the whole of natural creation and so, by reflection, lent the weight of science and inevitability to the old contentions. Of course 'sociobiology' represents a further variation on this theme, moving on from Darwin[14].

Modern French social theory is rooted in the speculative tracts of the 18th-century Enlightenment. These works were not averse to the promotion of social change, albeit in favour of bourgeois ascendancy over the claims of Monarchy, but above all, they laid the foundations of a tradition of social theorising as an adjunct to acceptable cultural debate. Whilst this certainly gave birth to a current of genuinely critical (Utopian) social theory that came to rest as the foundations of modern positivism, there has remained about the mainstream of French social theory a dimension of unreality and irrelevance to the potential requirements of movements for social change. French deductivism is inherently speculative and has encouraged flamboyant theory-building — Foucault and Baudrillard immediately spring to mind — as not much more than an esoteric expression of high culture. Creative intellectual brilliance — but disembodied from the subject of its speculation — commands a high respect in France; but it remains largely in the control of a traditional intellectual élite (Bourdieu (1988)).

This willingness to embrace creative thought, together with an optimism concerning the possibilities for social change — perfectly expressed in the contrasting meaning of the word 'Revolution' in France as opposed to Britain — provides useful ingredients for collaboration between French and British theorists in the development of theory adequate to the task of helping the growth to effectiveness of the ecology movement. (We would, of course, expect a Europe-wide collaboration to be most fruitful in the full development of relevant theory.) The situation is, however, one in which British and French theory finds relatively little purchase one in another and this is not merely a question of adequate translation. Mention was made at the outset of this chapter of the brief flirtation amongst British intellectuals with structural Marxism. In spite of the rapid retreat, some fruitful traces of the exchange remained. In the recent development of the analysis of ideology, there have been further attempts to integrate French ideas into the developing British discourse, in particular in the work of Stuart Hall and collaborators. There have also been some useful attempts to introduce German and Italian approaches to analysis into play and all of these have a salutary effect of drawing British social analysis into more fruitful paths.

But it remains necessary to guard against retreat into the traditional model. One of the extraordinary manifestations of recent British intellectual history is the way in which a 'Marxist' history of Britain has been written, with very many participants contributing to the whole, in which the working classes are shown in minute detail to have been effectively weaned of Revolutionary ambitions. This history has been reinforced by 'Marxist' sociological and cultural studies which reveal in great detail the self-reproducing sense of subservience and internal maintenance of subcultural conformity which has been the hallmark of the English working class since the second quarter of this century. Certainly it can be argued that amongst this material there are strands that are useful in assisting in the creation of an ideology aimed at constructive social change (Atkinson (1991)). However, these analyses do not, themselves, put forward any clue as to the way in which the information they generate might be used for the purposes of reconstructing society. Reading these analyses, Marx, as *practitioner* of social change, would long ago have abandoned the working class as vehicle for promoting social change and, indeed, those serious political ecologists coming from a Marxist background *have* abandoned this vehicle, as outlined in Chapter 2.

Even more disturbing than the lack of consciousness of the flagrant contradiction between the discovered reality of the working classes and the central purpose of Marxism — to push through to an egalitarian communist society — is the active efforts that have been made in some quarters to defend this contradiction. Edward Thompson's (1965) attack on Perry Anderson's (1964) attempt to raise pertinent issues concerning the structure and direction of British society falls into this category: 'correcting' generalisations with a weight of 'facts', embedded in an insistent methodological stance, that had the effect of confirming that nothing can be done about existing social reality. The same act was performed by Abercrombie et al. (1980) in attacking the 'dominant ideology thesis'. The lack of relevance of the modern British working class to any efforts to initiating social transformation was revealed, without any attempt being made to pose an alternative route. Meanwhile, a stance towards the genesis and usefulness of ideology, *qua* intellectual effort, was maintained in direct conformance to the Humean tradition, namely: don't bother, it's a pointless exercise. The general Marxist form of this stance has been referred to by Bourdieu as 'pessimistic functionalism' (Lipietz (1987: 4)).

Thus the worn out shell of the Revolutionary ideology of Marx and Engels — which really did transform the world, albeit achieving only social democracy (the programme of the Levellers and Tom Paine) rather than a true communism (the programme of the Diggers and Owenite Socialists) — has, in an extraordinary dialectical reversal, been distorted to confirm, yet again, the dismal English ideology which asserts that Reason — the conscious construction of ideology (or, as Marx would have seen it, a 'science' of social transformation) — can serve no useful purpose towards the improvement of society. The rest of this section is aimed at arguing that concerted effort to construct a coherent ideological system is essential to the project of political ecology — the creation of a society that is capable of regulating its relationship with the biosphere such as to achieve a sustainable symbiosis.

In the first instance, launched into the British intellectual milieu, with its inherent mental resistance to the very notion of optimistic social creativity, the effort for the British reader is arduous. It may therefore be helpful at this point to make the following assertion: the English common-sense assumption concerning human nature and the organisation of society necessarily embodying hierarchical relations that emerges constantly as the essential 'discovery' of British social theory, is no more than cultural prejudice reinforced by cultural prejudice. Other societies are organised around different cultural assumptions and history demonstrates regularly that change in assumptions and organisational arrangements does occur and is possible. If the project of political ecology is to be attained then changes in our outlook — that are optimistic about the possibilities for conscious organised social change and the fulfilment of human needs and aspirations — will be necessary. If the rest of this analysis is to be understood as intended, then in the first instance the reader will need to allow the possibility that the foregoing assertion might correspond with reality.

In the main the debate about ideology has been carried out at a very high level of generality and yet has centred on a very specific aspect of the genesis of socially functional ideas as a whole. The usefulness of Durkheim's approach to the subject was that it gave structure to the role of ideas at various levels of effectiveness. As Gramsci (1971: 324) put it:

We are all conformists of some conformism or other....The personality is strangely composite: it contains Stone Age elements and principles of a more advanced science, prejudices from all past phases of history at the local level and intuitions of a human philosophy which will be that of a human race united the world over.

In the first instance we encounter ideas, for the greater part never questioned, as informing the every practice of our daily lives. The bathroom and breakfast routines first thing in the morning, the breakfast that we eat and the clothes we decide to wear for the journey out into the wider social world: what kind of day is it, where am I going, what kinds of encounters can I expect? Or the complex sequence of events that surrounds an English Christmas: the very particular foods, the decoration of internal environments, the preparation for ritual exchange and the particular forms of gathering. And of great importance are the highly structured routines and relations of the work milieu. There is very little in life that does not conform to procedural norms around which ideas play only a facilitatory role. The heart of functionalist sociology was concerned with categorising and codifying such practices and anthropology to do the same for cultures other than our own.

But our daily practices are informed by a variety of intersecting contexts. As Therborn (1980:24) put it:

...one may be, simultaneously, a conscious US citizen, a Catholic, an Italian, a member of the working class, a resident of a particular neighbourhood, and a member of a particular kin group.

Of course there are many other contexts besides and although it is always possible to identify clusters of commonly held contexts and tendencies towards, or even social rules that coerce, conformity to whole sets of contexts, nevertheless, cross-cutting of contexts is, in our society, a common occurrence. Procedural norms of everyday life are, on the whole, associated with and dependent on these contexts but they, in their turn, also confirm and reinforce contexts. Much of the creativity of modern life grows out of the settlement, or attempted settlement, into new modes of practice that result from the contradiction of cross-cutting contexts.

The implication is that there is a hierarchy of levels of determination of cultural practices and accompanying ideological structures. Various attempts have been made to provide some kind of analytical framework that would allow this notion to be investigated more systematically. For instance, Gregory Bateson's (1964) enquiries into 'levels of learning' as psychological process, and Georges Gurvitch's (1971) diachronic and synchronic subdivisions of social activities and related conceptualisation as a contribution to the sociology of knowledge.

Such attempts are implicitly positivistic: academic exercises that assume that enquiry is good in itself and leads to the accumulation of facts and truths. They are unselfconscious concerning their own purpose in supporting (or challenging) the social life process. There can be little doubt that certain classes of ideas govern the existence and the form of others, in other words that some are 'strategic' whilst others are 'tactical'. But the importance of particular ideas or ideologies or classes of ideology is not an abstract question but is related to the totality of historically and geographically specific cultural forms. The role and structure of ideology amongst, say, African Bushmen, is not only utterly at variance with that in modern European society, there is little meaningful that can be said concerning any commonality of the very notion of ideas as between the two. Even when comparing 'religions' of 'civilized' cultures such as China and Europe in the 17th century (certain aspects of the latter being discussed in some detail in Chapter 5), it becomes apparent that the content of the ideology determines a different way in which the society as a whole operates such that ideology, as such, occupies a different meaning within the overall cultural organism.

In itself this says nothing. Knowledge is only of interest in so far as it satisfies human needs at some level. As stressed in the foregoing discussion, modern academic social analysis is implicitly instrumental (aimed in the functionalist case at social system maintenance) and Marx's analysis was an explicit instrument aimed at promoting social change in a particular way. In this context, the determination of what is important about ideology is necessarily an aspect of promoting certain ideological — and thence socially practical — ends. Marx acknowledged, to some extent, that ideology — even that the role of ideology — is culturally specific, when he wrote of 'modes of production' and their accompanying 'legal and political superstructure to which correspond definite forms of social consciousness' (Marx (1975: 425)).

But the importance to Marx of class ideology, as a specific type of strategic ideology, was a functional matter concerned with the specific role of the working class in precipitating specific social changes in 19th century bourgeois capitalist societies.

If political ecology has concluded that the working class is no longer salient to the process of bringing about relevant change in our society, in a situation where social change is urgently called for, then it is necessary to question the usefulness of focusing on class ideology at all. It may transpire that class ideology (indeed, specifically working class ideology) can be identified as one of the main constraints to the achievement of the kind of social change being sought, in which case it maintains a residual importance as something to be overcome. But there can be no doubt that the landscape of ideology with which political ecology is concerned is necessarily substantially different from that of Marx — and hence from both Marxists and conventional sociologists concerned, as they have been, to address the Marxist challenge.

So: is there some leading ideological factor or context which orients the attitude of political ecology towards socially effective ideas? Certainly not at present, although there are leading concerns on the part of political ecologists with respect to where intellectual efforts should be concentrated, and Chapter 5 focuses considerable attention upon these. But in looking for an adequate framework, there are certainly salutary lessons to be learned from Marxism. In retrospect there can be no doubt that Marx and Engels were extremely optimistic concerning the ease with which the working classes could be weaned of pre-existing ideas and attitudes. Steeped in high bourgeois intellectual culture, these two theorists were quite unaware of the subterranean workings of the average intellect and its intractability with respect to radical ideological reconstruction, even under the stress of systematic physical deprivation.

Gramsci (1971: 419–421), to whom many recent analysts of ideology have been turning, noted this problem, criticising Bukharin's attempt at a popular Marxist sociology. His view was that any attempt to change social attitudes must start from where people currently are, what he referred to as the spontaneous philosophy of the multitude, philosophy of non-philosophers or, simply, 'common sense'. It was his view that the principal elements of common sense are provided by religion, although in practice formal religion is made up of a multiplicity of contradictory views and elements, as it is interpreted by different social classes and elements. In Italy, Catholicism may well continue to occupy the commanding ideological heights. In Britain, however, it is possible to assert that secular thought has been triumphant and that the 'English ideology', as secular common sense, occupies those heights. It is important to note, at this point, the positive aspect of the recent British Marxist social and cultural studies of the working class, criticised above on another account. These indicate the richness of attitudes and notions harboured by the working class, from which strands might be developed to provide ideological guidance and inspiration to the broad population in our efforts to escape from our present cultural impasse (Atkinson (1991)).

The foregoing discussion places the task in hand within the framework of British social theory, which makes the functionalist assumption that ideology, like all other aspects of the functioning of society, can be dealt with in an instrumental fashion, but is then treated as an exogenous variable of no further interest. Clifford Geertz (1964) made an extremely useful contribution to the re-emergence of measured academic debate concerning ideology and the role of ideas in the functioning of society. He was critical of the one-sidedness of then existing English language theories of ideology which were all variations of 'interest theory' or 'strain theory'. It is not merely through the compulsion of following out one's interest or the effects of social stress that ideology is formed. These theories may be diagnostically convincing concerning the reasons for the generation of ideology but they say nothing about the specific tools and materials with and out of which ideological manifestations are forged. The creative aspect of ideology — in terms both of maintenance and invention — is not instrumental or directly functional at all, but aesthetic: resulting from the process of symbol formation and maintenance.

History gives us countless examples of the dysfunctional actions of people that has ended in tragedy. The tenacity with which countless ideas and ideals have been held or pursued, in the face of manifest contradiction with material interests, confounds any reasonable functionalist analysis; of course this is a problem — of 'reification' and 'false consciousness' — which Marxists have debated at great length at least since Lukács'(1971 (1923)) elaboration of the subject. Much can be attributed to the inner construction of ideas and relationships between these and the patterns which these impose on the physical and social world. Geertz (1964: 209) listed some of the tools as 'metaphor, analogy, irony, ambiguity, pun, paradox, hyperbole, rhythm'; of course beyond the verbal and into the visual, aural and tactile, further such tools are easy enough to identify: counterpoint, harmony, symmetry, proportion, elegance, consistency, coherence, juxtaposition and so on. The search for meaning by members of, and groups in, society, may well be coerced or cajoled into action by external, social forces, but it finds and expresses itself through symbols and myths that possess structures made up of such elements and relationships that are perceived as reality by those who adopt them. But we can also conjecture that a significant dimension of social evolution has arisen not through coercive forces at all, but through inventive and creative social processes having little to do with instrumentality.

Geertz's challenge (and more generally that of the symbolic anthropologists and sociological school of symbolic interactionists) to the social sciences to pay more attention to the tools of ideological construction fell largely on barren ground, gaining little more than the occasional footnote reference in mainstream British sociology. However, it is not hard to see, in the light of the earlier discussion concerning the English ideology, how it is that British social analysis not only remains blind to social forces other than coercion but — and more importantly — that it avoids the whole subject of creativity (and hence any analysis of the tools of creativity) within the social process. Social analysis with whatever critical pretensions cannot realistically hope to make any headway without possessing some notion of ideological reconstruction and hence some consciousness of the elements wherewith ideology as such is constructed. French social analysis[15] has been very fruitful in this respect over the years and it is therefore useful to turn to this to further the analysis.

Although it is, nowadays, regularly declared that structuralism is being left behind by new lines of analysis,[16] there is no denying that this approach to social and allied analysis dominated the post-war French intellectual world. Key to the development of structural analysis generally, but specifically in relation to the role of ideas in society, was Claude Lévi-Strauss. Although claiming some debt to American anthropology (Lévi-Strauss (1968: Ch.1)), his analytical approach derived in the first instance from the sociology of Durkheim and Mauss and more specifically from Saussurean linguistics. But his insistence on the primacy of ideas imposed upon the content to be analysed clearly reproduces classical Cartesian rationalism (Lévi-Strauss (1968: 21)):

In anthropology as in linguistics, therefore, it is not comparison that supports generalisation, but the other way round. If, as we believe to be the case, the unconscious activity of the mind consists in imposing forms upon content, and if these forms are fundamentally the same for all minds — ancient and modern, primitive and civilized (as the study of the symbolic function, expressed in language, so strikingly indicates) — it is necessary and sufficient to grasp the unconscious structure underlying each institution and each custom, in order to obtain a principle of interpretation valid for other institutions and other customs, provided, of course, that the analysis is carried far enough.

Concerned with the relationship between phenomena, rather than phenomena themselves, Lévi-Strauss has embraced a 'scientific' search for constant relationships amongst social phenomena, independent of cultural context. As will be clear from the arguments so far presented in the previous chapter, it is not this 'scientific' search for constants (which, in any case after many decades, shows no signs of revealing any significant results) that is of interest, but rather the related approach to defining what is to be considered as subject matter to be studied — ie what are the sinews that hold society together?

Of most interest in French developments over the past few decades, with respect to the role of ideas in our society, is the discourse surrounding semiotics or semiology. With Roland Barthes as its initial proponent but subsequently extending into a broad, international debate, Saussurean linguistics was taken in a somewhat different direction from that adopted by Lévi-Strauss, to investigate the way in which signs, symbols and images, elaborated into systems — or mythologies — give structure to our everyday lived world[17]. In Barthes' (1988: 8) hands, the ambition remains one of 'human science', to analyse the origins and structure of system-maintaining signs and mythologies. But it is a critical science (a concept which has no referents in established British discourse): 'Semiology must attack...the symbolic and semantic system of our entire civilization.'

In 'Mythologies', one of his earliest extended works of semiology first published in the late 1950s, Barthes (1973) laid out the ground through a series of more or less extended cases — including the world of wrestling, the antics of royalty, the meaning in toys, the status of wine, steak and plastics — illustrating the way in which social activities and objects obtain their status and meaning through their relationships and associations with other aspects of people's lived lives and with historically held assumptions and mythologies. At this stage he was at pains to present this material as forms of ideology in the Marxist sense, distorting the 'truth' of the situations presented. Myth, in this sense (p. 156):

...acts economically: it abolishes the complexity of human acts, it gives them the simplicity of human essences, it does away with all dialectics, with any going back beyond what is immediately visible, it organises a world which is without contradictions because it is without depth, a world wide open and wallowing in the evident, it establishes a blissful clarity: things appear to mean something by themselves.

Myth of this kind depoliticises. Barthes also attempted to argue that where right-wing politics is essentially about creating myth, left-wing politics, in so far as it is revolutionary, is not mythical. But — and here Barthes is arguing in a similar vein to Gramsci — left-wing attempts to enter the arena of myth, with their aspiration to change society, fail to take root in 'the immense field of human relationships' and hence remain 'inessential'. The Utopian is seen as living in a different world from the mythologist (p. 172). Of course this interpretation of the concept of mythology differs from that of Levi-Strauss who conceives of all forms of structured social ideology as myth — ie noncritically; this is also the interpretation used here.

The usefulness of semiology is the way in which it prepares a framework that allows us to focus on the way in which objects and routines are grasped and used by people and social groups as things in themselves, that have lives of their own only tangentially, or secondarily, or partially associated with particular functions. Saussure insisted that the forms of words are arbitrary in relation to the meaning which they receive in social use as means of communication. With the exception of onomatopoeia this is evidently correct. But already with rhymes we find words taking on meaning simply because they possess the same sounds. Few rhymes are only invented for their sounds: they generally possess other layers of meaning that might, as in many common nursery rhymes, derive from actual occurrences and beyond that political messages that have been long forgotten or reconstructed but which can nevertheless remain harboured as a hidden message in the rhyme and its process of transmission. The worlds of manufactured objects and social rituals present fabulously rich layers of meaning in this way. The point is that created objects may be remembered and transmitted through simple associations or ease of recall through aesthetic structures, but then bring with them or screen out whole other worlds. The inertia of such mechanisms clearly favours cultural conservation and conservatism, but these mechanisms also provide purchase for the incremental reconstruction of life. If we are serious about any project of social reconstruction, then it is a basic necessity to look at these structures, processes and relationships in the particular forms in which they present themselves and not assume a priori, as does functionalist analysis, that there is some obvious functional value to social phenomena and artefacts which exhausts their meaning.

Barthes' work presents us with a spectacle of the world as immediately perceived and lived by society and accompanies this with some striking assertions about its meaning. But he — and in general French analysis concerned with semiology — fails to construct more than ephemeral links back to the specific forms and functioning of our society in general. As Robert Hodge and Gunter Kress (1988: 1) put it:

'Mainstream semiotics' emphasises structures and codes at the expense of functions and social uses of semiotic systems, the complex interrelations of semiotic systems and social practice, all of the factors which provide their motivation, their origins and destinations, their form and substance.

Their own work (Kress and Hodge (1979); Hodge and Kress (1988)) attempts to interpret the functioning of society through the use of semiological tools[18]. Subjects of interest to them are the relationship between the acceptance of 'truth' and 'reality' and the status of person or organ that is putting it forward; and more generally the way in which contexts are flagged and projected as mechanisms for holding down given interpretations of reality, through the development of visual and verbal language and discourse. However, antilanguages, antiworlds and dialects amongst subcultures, co-exist with mainstream culture, resisting incorporation and providing purchase for the development of alternative realities. They look in some detail at two key aspects of the creation of social reality: the 'cultural capital' of societies and its anchoring of truth in the interpretation of history, and the family, as the basic forge of social reproduction through the inculcation of language in many planes, but in itself also a language.

The two latter subjects are of particular importance to any movement concerned to bring about social change, because unless alternative interpretations of these are formulated that recognise the depth to which current structures and interpretations are enculturated into society at large, and which propose routes to the realisation of the alternatives that build themselves systematically out of existing structures, then this will fail. But it is important to note that there are, in our time, already sharp contradictions between the everyday reality of family life for the majority of people and the ideal which our society holds. Whilst the conservative project is to bring reality into line with the ideal, the alternative project is to use this contradiction to create a new ideal through which the manifest disintegration of cultural values, characteristic of the 'postmodern condition', can be turned around into a project of social reconstruction.

A topic dealt with only briefly by Hodge and Kress, but nevertheless of great importance with regard to projects designed to bring about social change, is the question of 'cultural ruptures' and how these can be understood under the illumination of semiology. Their conclusion is that although culture clearly does evolve, with changes in the meaning of words and phrases and with ceaseless variation in visual styles which express differences across society, in practice this always takes place in an incremental way, building upon vast reservoirs of existing components. Their view is that 'cultural ruptures' appear in retrospect, as a consequence of history rewritten from the point of view of new hegemonic social groups or classes, erasing the complex traces of the past and submerging minority cultural manifestations, to establish a false simplicity. However, the current debate over the demise of 'modernism' and the emergence of a 'postmodern' era, discussed in some detail in the final chapter of this book, presents a view in which changes in cultural outlook possess a style component that is distinct from particular social interests. Social groups certainly do push their interests through particular ideological vehicles. But the 'believability' in the components of ideology is by no means always or inevitably linked directly with the possession of physical or economic power or any other social functionality. The aesthetic mechanisms that govern the attraction or loss of clarity of ideology must be understood as an important dimension in the overall task of social construction and reconstruction.

From the point of view of intellectual work aimed at promoting specific forms of social change, there can be little doubt that 'social semiotics' of the kind being developed by Hodge and Kress is distinctly useful. In the end, however, it is also necessary to possess a sense of the need for social change, together with a sense of what is specifically wrong with existing arrangements and some idea of the direction in which solutions to these problems are most likely to lie. At the present time there is little indication of such an approach being adopted within the context of academic discourse in semiotics or elsewhere in the 'social sciences'. So the tools will need to be adapted and honed elsewhere for the purpose of promoting the ends of political ecology.

In concluding this section, a few points arising from the foregoing discussion need to be brought out and underscored. Political ecology is an ideological project in the service of the ecology movement. It is concerned to develop ideas at all levels that promise to assist in the reconstruction of society such as to head off the destruction of the biosphere and create a society which is an improvement, for everyone, on that presently existing. It must therefore develop knowledge of the ideological life of existing society and, above all, the ways in which this attaches to and supports existing social practices amongst different sections of society. It is necessary also to discover the inner tensions and fissures within existing ideologies and the contradictions that have opened up between these and the practice which they ostensibly inform. These fissures and contradictions provide purchase for the development of alternative ideologies that can command social attention. Ideology construction on this basis is a necessary aspect of the project of political ecology as of any movement for social reconstruction (Bouchier (1978)). But there is a second approach which is also of great importance. It is not only necessary to put forward instrumental alternatives that can be promoted as reasons for practices to change. It is vitally necessary that the alternatives are seen as being attractive on an aesthetic plane, concerned with signs, symbols and mythologies. Alternatives need to appeal on both the rational and the aesthetic level to the perceived and felt needs of all social groups and individuals.

Alternative ideologies will not, however, penetrate far without being linked to alternative practices. It is all too easy for such ideologies to be hijacked by existing practices if these are not simultaneously seen to belong, unequivocally to alternative practices. 'Green consumerism' provides an excellent illustration of this, where a rapid growth in social commitment to the basic ecological message — that current industrial and consumer practices are destroying the ecosphere — are translated into a surface ideology that answers this social concern without requiring any significant changes in social practice. This therefore fails to address the roots of the basic contention of the ecology movement. So in this sense, the Marxist criticism of ideology remains valid: the call for social change at the level of ideology that is not linked with effective practice, results *de facto* in maintaining existing practice, precisely because the links between 'reason' and practice are not direct. Rather, ideas at the level of instrumental reason are generally confirmed in the practice within which they are conceived and have only a weak capacity to change practices in themselves. However, there are subterranean levels of ideology formation and maintenance where the battles are not carried out with any direct reference to rationality, but are concerned with symbols and myths, representing whole sets of ideas, attitudes and orientations and it is participation in these battles with which political ecology must come to grips. Changed practice — different ways of living and doing things — can play a major role in this arena because the dissolution of existing practices removes the worldly reinforcement of existing ideological attitudes and so weakens their power on the subterranean ideological battleground.

Alienation

So far in this chapter the discussion has revolved around 'culturalist' arguments that relate social attitudes and ideology back to the cultural context in which they arise. However, one basic question remains outstanding with respect to this discourse and that is the question of 'human nature'. Culture is, after all, the product of human beings who are not physically the product of culture. Somewhere there must be a line that separates culture from nature and it is important to any discussion with pretensions to surveying the human condition in general terms — and that is what this analysis finds itself having to do — to achieve some clarity concerning where this line is — or rather what is salient about the relationship between culture and nature. This section explores this question. The structure of the section is as follows: various concepts of human nature as presented by biologists are reviewed, in order to establish a view 'seen from the viewpoint of nature in itself' that is congruent with the arguments set out so far. A discussion of the evolution of the human species is followed by a 'cross-sectional' analysis in order to locate the human organism as middle term between nature, as ecological substrate, and consciousness, as the essence of culture in general. The philosophical debate concerning the concept of alienation provides a point of departure from which to obtain an understanding of the genesis and development of consciousness as a product of nature.

Whilst there coexist many elaborate views on what it is that is quintessentially human — the 'essence' or the 'nature' of Man — few of these are not informed by the residue of religious and philosophical notions from the past. On the one hand, we possess the Christian notion of the radical separation between Man and Nature, translated into modern discourse in Descartes' dualism of body, *qua* machine, and soul, *qua* essence. Elaborated and refined by the French Enlightenment and German Idealism, this position and the categories/methods which it has informed remain implicit in most modern 'social sciences', be they ostensible 'empirical' sociology or 'materialist' Marxism, and explicit in some cases, such as 'structuralism' (Geras (1983)). On the other hand, growing out of the empiricism of Hume, with its implied religious iconoclasm (being an association traceable back to William of Ockham at least (Saw (1964)), a further view has insisted that Man is not qualitatively different from the rest of the animal kingdom so that 'reason', in Hume's version, can only be interpreted through the 'passions', or, in its most recent manifestation, as 'ethology' and 'sociobiology' — through the 'genes' (Dawkins (1976); Wilson (1975, 1979)).

These two reductionisms have dominated the discussion of human nature even until today. The Gestalt and Behaviourist schools of psychology, clearly representing the two forms of reduction, generated a massive, yet barren, literature across the first half of this century. The sudden appearance of structuralism in the late 1960s and the intense debate around sociobiology in the late 1970s (Caplan (1978); Montagu (1980)), provided eloquent testimony to the continued survival of these reductionist views, fuelled indeed by the continuous extension of academic specialisation (Midgeley (1979); Barkow (1980)).

Yet the potential was always there to use the tension between these views in creative fashion to construct a more multidimensional view of human nature. In fact, such an approach was initiated by Kant (1953: 9) whose Rationalist 'dogmatic slumber' was interrupted by Hume. Out of this attempt evolved the dialectical approaches of Hegel and Marx: human nature is seen as multidimensional and interpenetrated with other dimensions of nature more generally. Under the constant shadow of reductionist explanations, on the one hand, and, on the other, the evaporation of explanation into mystical experience, a path has been worn by a minority insistent upon achieving a holistic, structured understanding of human nature as object and process. Two main approaches to this have been taken: an evolutionary approach (diachronic) analysing the emergence of Man and the development of human society and culture; and a cross-sectional approach (synchronic) analysing subsystems separately and then indicating how these interact (see Rose (1976: 30) for illustration). More sophisticated analyses use both approaches in combination (Campbell (1974)). The following paragraphs sketch a view taken via each of these approaches.

From available fossil records it is conjectured that the branch of evolution which yielded humanity broke away from the primate 'trunk' about 15 million years ago. *Ramapithecus* remains have been found in Africa and the Indian subcontinent, suggesting that this early hominid species already showed an ability to adapt to various environments so characteristic of the species as a whole; but insufficient remains have been found to say much about the complete form, let alone the lifestyle of this species.

Australopithecus is estimated to have appeared between five and a half and three and a half million years ago and been superseded between one and one and a half million years ago. This species appears to have developed all the basic physical characteristics, beyond which subsequent changes can be construed in gross physical terms as being extremely small. This species was already bipedal with hands possessing considerably enhanced powers of manipulation over its tree-living forebears, and this was reflected in the development of increasingly well-worked tools; and it subsisted on a omnivorous diet. Whilst the emergence of these characteristics must be seen as reflecting adaptation to changed environments — specifically, moving to the edge of the forests and then out onto the plains — this process is also discernable in other primates, notably chimpanzees and baboons, without yet developing these specifically human traits (Campbell (1974: 375); Crook (1980: 97)). Chimpanzees can walk on two feet and carry things, albeit awkwardly; and they do use, and even fashion tools, but do not make tools out of tools. It has been conjectured (Campbell (1974: 334)) that *Australopithecus* was already in the process of developing conceptualisation in terms of conceiving of 'thingness', that elements could be broken away from the continuum of nature and transformed into other things. It seems that this was associated with a highly elaborated social existence which included organised hunting, and perhaps gathering, which necessarily involves some means to working out strategies and specialised functions within groups.

Somewhat over a million years ago there emerged a transitional species, replacing *Australopithecus*: *Homo erectus* appears to have involved a 'cascade' (Crook (1980: 108)) of evolutionary change from which emerged *Homo sapiens* some 300,000 years ago. During this period the brain cavity doubled in size — though it had been growing prior to this and it is probable that the structure of the brain continued to evolve substantially even after its present average volume had been reached. *Homo erectus* came to control fire — and with this came cooked food and subsequent 'recession and reduction' (Campbell (1974: 244)) of the masticatory apparatus — and the form of the throat associated with speech emerged.

The latter is not to say that conceptual communication had not emerged considerably earlier, but the palaeoanthropological record gives no clues as to when or how this might originally have come about. Whilst, with considerable effort, a rudimentary system of conceptual communication has been drawn out of chimpanzees (Woolfson (1982)), it must be conceded with Chomsky (1968: 61), who has nevertheless subscribed to the notion that somewhere within the human organism there is an innate 'deep structure' to human language, that human language is qualitatively unrelated to other forms of animal communication. The perceived importance of language to the emergence of humanity has generated a substantial literature conjecturing its origin in terms of possible environmental stimuli and developmental steps (Woolfson (1982: Ch. 6)). What is clear is the close relationship between language and the process of conceptualisation. This in turn relates both to the production of tools and the broader process of utilising nature in a systematic way, hence to the whole question of the generation of human culture. It is this unique process of conceptualisation, of which language is the main communicational element, which allowed humans to form different kinds of society to deal with different ecological situations and to colonise virtually all parts of the biosphere.

Before moving on to a cross-sectional analysis of certain key aspects of human nature, a more general word about the mechanisms of evolution is in order. The traditional 'scientific' view of evolution based on Darwin's theory (Maynard Smith (1975)) is that the individual organism (or its genetic structure) is engaged in a 'struggle for survival', the outcome of which is the 'survival of the fittest'. Sociobiology represents an attempt to hold on to this reduction whilst acknowledging a degree of social organisation of the survival of species via additional mechanisms of 'altruistic' behaviour (Clutton-Brock and Harvey (1978)). It is contended here that all attempts to reduce evolution down to a 'scientifically' determined set of discrete mechanisms, starting with Darwin, represent no more than an attempt to lend ideological weight to a particular view of social morality (Washburn (1978); Montagu (1980: 4)). To say this is neither to deny that evolution does take place nor to impute any 'mystical' dimension, merely to say that evolution is a rich process of change and development containing an essential aspect of contingency: evolution is an opportunistic process (Gould (1990)). As the 19th-century naturalist Louis Agassis put it: 'The possibilities of existence run so deeply into the extravagant that there is scarcely any conception too extraordinary for Nature to realise.' Co-operation and conflict coexist (Kropotkin (1979)) and to say that the fittest survive is no more than tautology: the fittest are those that have survived, by whatever accident. As with human history, given circumstances in terms of organisms, social organisation and interaction, and environmental change, all provide the basis of equilibrium and metamorphosis[19]. What is deemed to be important in all of this — genes, the individual organism, the social unit, the niche, the ecosystem, or whatever — depends to a major extent on what this insight is supposed to achieve *for us* and, in the end, our 'explanation' can never wholly escape the caricature and the descriptive (the 'just so' story)[20].

Ecosystems certainly have a coherence to them and evolution produces the necessary range and mix of species, genera and so on to create this coherence[21]. Both environmental change and disruption from without an ecosystem can disturb its coherence and balance but, in the long run, this will be recreated in some new configuration provided the inorganic substrate continues to provide adequate purchase. The particular mechanisms whereby species come to occupy particular niches within ecosystems are many and varied, including, even in non-humans, an element of social adaptation but, in the longer run, involving genetic change that might include 'genetic drift', 'neoteny' or other mechanisms as yet unknown. Certainly, the concept of 'random change' is less than helpful in understanding these processes: in the end there are always specific creative mechanisms and contingencies.

Turning now to the cross-sectional analysis, three levels can be usefully scrutinised. The human organism is a physico-chemical system of vast complexity and sophistication. For instance, knowledge of the physiology of the human eye alone runs to 3,500 pages in the current standard British textbook (Davson). Differentiated in terms of organs, membranes and other subsystems and elements, the whole cannot be characterised in any simple way as hierarchical. The blood circulation system and, to an extent, the nervous system might be so characterised, but these are systematically interdependent with other elements. As a whole, the system is not mechanical, but empathetic: if (contingently) the cell is seen as the basic building block, then it can be shown that it participates in terms of reacting to changes in its general environment (involving temperature, chemical substances and electric impulses at a minimum) and in reacting on these. The totality of this internal environment can be construed as analogous to ecosystems: of participating organic systems and of physical settings; and like ecosystems, the 'normal' equilibrium situation can be characterised in terms of federation and coexistence, with an element of imbalance and 'struggle' involving diseases and other more or less systematic or far-reaching disequilibria.

Looking at the interaction of the organism with the outside environment as a second level, this must initially be characterised as possessing many disparate elements rather than as a system in itself. If skin or bone is broken then local mechanisms act to contain and heal the injury. Sensory information may also be dealt with locally through 'reflexes'. More elaborate reflexes are to be found in instinctive responses that might possess several iterative actions and reactions and involve learning, without yet making significant call on the brain. It is these mechanisms that have been of particular interest to the ethologists (Lorenz (1977)), who see them as being central to organism-environment relations and hence the 'essential nature' of the organism. There can be no doubt that all animals, including humans, possess both innate and learnable or influenceable action sequences stored in various locations within the central nervous system. The action of running or playing a piano piece, once learned, involve complex coordinated actions that call for very little thinking; and much that animals learn is encouraged by the direct connection of particular sensory inputs to such coordinated preprogrammed action sequences (Lorenz's 'Lehrläufe'). Indeed, even in humans, sensory inputs are taken apart and presented to the decision-making system in highly filtered and 'interpreted' form (Wickelgren (1979: Chaps 2 and 3)). In other words, our impression of the world outside is in no way the empiricist's notion of a direct presentation of information.

At this point it becomes essential to present some model of what it is that happened in the evolution of our species that introduced conceptualisation. The brain comprises three main elements (Rose (1976)). Relatively little is known of the structure of these or how they work, but certain features are known, as follows. At the base of the brain a number of glands and related protuberances go to make up the limbic system. This is the largest element of the brain of earlier species, and is referred to as the seat of the emotions. It has the main effect of secreting hormones and hence of adjusting the chemical environment of the body. A second element is known as the cerebellum and this is responsible for controlling the accuracy of muscular response. This comprises a major feature of the brain in tree-living primates, facilitating precision in moving about the tree-tops, and was passed on to humans by their tree-living forebears. This continued to develop, presumably as a function of developing manipulation and dexterity in tool making. The third element of the brain is the cerebrum. It is this which developed so rapidly in recent human evolution. The cerebrum is responsible for 'association', memory and language. It is clearly central to what we think of in the higher sense as learning, conceptualisation and consciousness.

The fundamental difference between the most primitive of animals and even the most sophisticated of plants is that the former must possess a tendency towards temporal as well as spacial unity. Whilst parts of the organism might perform their roles relatively independently, as a whole, the organism must be able to decide when it is going to ingest a particle of food and when to exit left or right. In the most primitive forms, the rules that govern such decisions will be simple, comprising quite basic reactions to a few environmental stimuli, and we need hardly conjecture the existence of any 'I'. As organisms become more elaborate, however, this tendency towards unity has a more complex job to fulfil in deciding what is and isn't important for the organism as a whole in a given situation. Whilst the 'I' never emerges, even in humans (*pace* Descartes), as a distinct object, nevertheless, as the centre of gravity of the decision-making process of the organism, it certainly finds a particular location in the brain, where come together the main lines of communication from the sensory organs and back to the motor mechanisms.

We can conjecture that the 'threshold effect' which marked humanity off from its forebears and from the rest of the animal world had something to do with the 'normal' location of this decision-making centre of gravity. Prior to humanity, it was at rest within the limbic system. The 'truth' of the animal organism was itself at rest. The development of the cerebrum provided ever more elaborate services to the organism: the capability to learn about aspects of the environment and to co-operate with its fellow organisms, thereby, it might be conjectured, bringing increasing flexibility and contingency into the process of cultural and social formation and by this means opening up new horizons for the colonisation of new ecosystems, new environments. Some time in the course of *Australopithecean* evolution, this centre of gravity crossed the threshold out of the limbic system and into the cerebrum. What had been a series of models and 'learning loops' was now the home of the essential 'I' and the organism lost its status as 'the truth' and became an alien object. Suddenly the limbic system was no longer at the centre of the system, but reliant upon the content of the cerebrum for its satisfaction, reduced to an alarm system that could be overridden by decisions emanating from the cerebrum (Campbell (1974: 267–268)).

So what would be the effects of this migration? This takes us to a third level of the operation of the human organism. Whereas in prior species, the process of learning could remain fragmentary and still satisfy the needs of the organism, this new situation would inevitably call for the creation of a complete and coherent model of the world: the organism could not operate until such a complete model were in existence and all actions held together via such a unified model. This would force the development of language with which to communicate with the outside world (no need for 'deep structure': it could be perfectly opportunistic and would tend towards reproducing the world itself, comprising first society and culture, and then the wider world of nature). The creation of a spiritual and religious world would, in the first instance occur automatically to fill in the contradictions between first appearances and complex reality: the inner structure of nature and, with the development of civil society, the structure of society itself. The 'proof' of such a conjecture lies in the processes of the individual consciousness (William

James's 'stream of consciousness'): the images and sounds which inhabit our waking lives and our dreams and which are nothing but the products of a socially created world, its language and its symbolism. Thus the organism is dragged about by the aspirations of the socially created model, of rules dictated by the world outside, translated by a subservient 'I' anxious, above all, that the model stay coherent and complete.

We move now to the concept of alienation. As used here, the concept has several roots, not all of them labelled 'alienation' in their original form. On the other hand, there are many recent usages of the term which are quite other than what is meant here by the concept and it is therefore necessary to sort through the terminological confusions that have arisen and in the process arrive at an understanding of the philosophical notion that squares with the foregoing discussion.

The usage of alienation adopted here can be traced back at least to Plato's notion of essences. Nature, Plato contended, exists in two forms: as contingent objects and material on the one hand, and as idealised, abstract forms of these objects and material on the other; there are many different actual tables, all of which relate to one essential 'tableness', many different dogs and types of dog, all of which relate to an essential 'dogness'. For Plato, this duality was a property of nature and he saw a progress towards goodness as residing in the movement of mind out of first impressions of the contingent into a knowledge of the essence of things. For him, the contingent was vulgar illusion, essences were reality, as wisdom and true understanding.

Saint Paul, in employing the term alienation, was bringing together Plato's philosophy of essences with older Judaic religious virtue: in his Epistle to the Ephesians (4: 18), he depicts men who live this-worldly lives as 'being alienated from the life of God through the ignorance that is in them'. Just as Plato saw wisdom as being achieved in rejecting the contingent and embracing essences, so Christ taught the rejection of the this-worldly in favour of the ultimate essence: God. Kaufmann (1970: liii) saw this as a major thread running through the Old Testament: exhortation to reject nature, society and the self, in exchange for the embrace of God. The radical nature of modern empiricism was the way in which it reversed the poles of this argument: essences were declared to be evil illusion and the contingent healthy reality. The Young Hegelians reversed this equation in the different way: religion was no simple illusion but, rather, a refuge from a malformed social reality. But this is running ahead of the argument.

The modern use of the term alienation originates in a reworking of the English legal term for the sale of property (Lukács (1975: 538)), particularly by Rousseau (1968: 54–70). He contended that alienation of freedom, by a man to his master or a people to their king, did not involve any quid pro quo and was therefore contrary to human nature. On the other hand, alienation of all men's rights and powers to the sovereign state, or representative of the General Will, in the form of a Social Contract, is the device wherein individual freedom could best be protected. Whilst Rousseau's arguments were far from unambiguous, the notion that men are capable of and, under certain circumstances, willing to part with their essential selves in constructing society was clearly enough expressed.

Hegel's adoption of the term alienation — that is, the two terms *'Entfremdung'* and *'Entäusserung'* — clearly descended in the main from Rousseau's usage. It makes its appearance in his *Phenomenology of Spirit*, at the point where the Enlightenment is being discussed, clearly linked with the notion of Contract. But, as Lukács (1975: Part IV, Ch. 4) put it, the concept which it embodied lay at the heart of Hegel's whole philosophical system. In earlier writings, the terms *'Entzweiung'* and *'Positivität'* had been used in process of working up the concept of alienation, and it is clear that the process which alienation denotes was described in many ways as Hegel's philosophy developed.

Hegel's whole philosophical system is concerned with showing how individual and social consciousness develop through one another as a historic, dialectical, process of unfolding. Engels, writing of the *Phenomenology*, put it like this (Lukács (1975: 468)):

One may call it a parallel of the embryology and the palaeontology of the mind, a development of the individual consciousness through the different stages, set in the form of an abbreviated reproduction of the stages through which the consciousness of Man has passed in the course of history.

The point was that the individual consciousness *is* the historic consciousness and its structure is centrally determined by the social developmental process through which human consciousness as a whole has passed; its current state is but a facet of the totality of the current social consciousness.

Alienation comprises the process through which consciousness is constructed. Becoming aware of a social and natural world of things and processes outside itself, the essential individual divides itself and one part migrates out to make connection with this external world. This process of self-alienation leaves the individual barren until its other half returns, laden with knowledge with which the whole becomes enriched through this experience. Perhaps the most concise description of this process appeared in the Preface of the *Phenomenology* as follows (Hegel (1977: 21)):

The immediate existence of Mind, *consciousness*, contains the two moments of knowing and the objectivity negative to knowing. Since it is in this element (of consciousness) that Mind develops itself and explicates its moments, these moments contain that antithesis, and they all appear as configurations of consciousness. The science of this pathway is the science of the *experience* which consciousness goes through; the substance and the movement are viewed as the *object* of consciousness. Consciousness knows and comprehends only what falls within its experience; for what is contained in this is nothing but mental process, and this, too, as object of the self. But Mind becomes object because it is just this movement of becoming an *other to itself*, ie becoming an *object to itself*, and of suspending this otherness. And experience is the name we give to just this movement, in which the immediate, the unexperienced, ie the abstract, whether it be of sensuous (but still unsensed) being, or only thought of as simple, becomes alienated from itself and then returns to itself from this alienation, and is only then revealed for the first time in its actuality and truth, just as it then has become a property of consciousness also.

Hegel then continued by broadening out this 'psychologistic' description to relate it back to philosophical debates; and it is this which relates the concept of alienation both forward to modern philosophies, dealt with below, and also into the notion of the 'I' dealt with in previous paragraphs:

The disparity which exists in consciousness between the 'I' and the substance which is its object is the distinction between them, the *negative* in general. This can be regarded as the *defect* in both, though it is their soul, or that which moves them. That is why some of the ancients conceived the *void* as the principle of motion, for they rightly saw the moving principle as the *negative*, though they did not as yet grasp that the negative is the self. Now, although this negative appears at first as the disparity between the 'I' and its object, it is just as much the disparity of the substance with itself. Thus what seems to happen outside of it, to be an activity directed against it, is really its own doing, and Substance shows itself to be essentially Subject.

Before proceeding with the discussion, two asides are in order. Firstly, the latter sentence, marking what Marxists would consider to be Hegel's 'idealist' failing, is an important principle in ecological thought: we should not imagine that our thought processes can be understood as detached from the on-going processes of nature and society themselves. The second point is that here Hegel is clearly defining the negative nature of his philosophy and how closely the concept of alienation is bound up with this. The profound contradiction between this and the attempts to insert the concept into positivistic sociology in recent years is discussed further below (Marcuse (1941: Part II, Ch.II, Section 1)).

The above quotation, concerned as it is more with the aspect of the development of individual consciousness, rather than the process of development of human consciousness as a whole, indicates also the way in which alienation is a necessary part of human existence, part of human nature. However, in dealing with the historic aspect, Hegel clearly saw the complete process of civilisation as proceeding through the self-alienation of humanity — in medieval religiosity (the 'unhappy consciousness') and the relationship of the master and bondsman — and the discovery by the alienated self of its other in Rousseau's notion of the General Will. The culmination of his philosophy lay in his assumption that the alien consciousness had returned to itself in the form of the constitutional monarchy of the Prussian State.

It is interpretations of Marx's views on alienation which have dominated debate on the concept in recent years. Generally these interpretations are quite unaware of the relationship between Marx's usage and that of Hegel. Indeed, there is a general problem concerning the philosophical derivation of many of Marx's concepts in that Marx never wrote a systematic philosophy but, rather, adopted and adapted existing views: whilst criticising views he disagreed with, he failed largely in indicating what he did accept. The massive exegetical literature on Marx includes many attempts to reconstruct his philosophy. Notable examples include Lukács (1971) and Avineri (1969); on 'human nature', Ollman (1971) and Geras (1983); and, specifically on alienation, Mészáros (1970) and Mandel and Novak (1970).

Broadly speaking, it can be said that Marx, in adopting Hegel's concept of alienation, was only interested in the historical side of the equation and not at all in the side concerned with the development of the individual human consciousness. Perhaps this can be traced to his belief, cited on the frontispiece of this book, that the time was not yet ripe for a single science that could embrace both the natural and the social and thus to his decision to pursue the social. Be that as it may, he certainly insisted that, as far as his interest was concerned, the individual *is* the social (Marx (1975b: 350)):

It is not only the material of my activity — including even the language in which the thinker is active — which I receive as a social product. My *own* existence *is* social activity. Therefore what I create for myself I create for society, conscious of myself as a social being. My *universal* consciousness is only the *theoretical* form of that whose *living* form is the real community, society, whereas at present *universal* consciousness is an abstraction from the real life and as such is hostile opposition to it. Hence the *activity* of my universal consciousness — as activity — is my *theoretical* existence as a social being. It is above all necessary to avoid once more establishing 'society' as an abstraction over against the individual. The individual *is* the *social being*.

And it seems that it is this early sketch of his philosophical position, without any counterbalancing view concerning man's *physical* nature, that has led many to deny that Marx believed that man has any fixed nature at all (Geras (1983: 50–53)).

Marx thus disregarded the mechanisms of alienation which Hegel saw as the driving force of *individual* and hence social consciousness and reinterpreted Hegel's view of the *social* history of consciousness. It was not constitutional monarchy, but communist society which would reconcile man's alienated self with his true self; the final reconciliation was not achieved through some theoretical path to knowledge or wisdom, but involved the supersession of private property as the historic embodiment of self-alienation (Marx (1975b: 348)):

Communism is the *positive* supersession of *private property* as *human self-alienation*, and hence the true *appropriation* of the *human* essence through and for man; it is the complete restoration of man to himself as *social*, ie human, being, a restoration which has become conscious and which takes place within the entire wealth of previous periods of development.

Marx elaborated on the term alienation (*Entfremdung* and *Entäusserung*) at greater length than did Hegel (see in particular Marx (1975b: 322–334)) and distinguished a number of facets of the phenomenon. Nevertheless, his concept was narrower than Hegel's. Under present circumstances, men are alienated from nature, from their essential species and from one another. However, this is indissolubly bound up with the existence of private property (Marx (1975b: 332)):

It is true that we took the concept of *alienated labour (alienated life)* from political economy as a result of the *movement of private property*. But it is clear from an analysis of this concept that, although private property appears as the basis and cause of alienated labour, it is in fact its consequence, just as the gods were *originally* not the cause but the effect of the confusion of men's minds. Later, however, this relationship became reciprocal.

Whether or not Marx would have conceded that alienation at the level of the individual organism would survive the supersession of alienated labour and private property remains a moot issue. What is certain, however, is that recent discussions of alienation based upon what Marx did write almost all fail to understand the broader underlying philosophical concept; and it is this failure that lies at the centre of the massive confusion over the meaning of alienation that arose during the 1960s.

Hegel's notion of alienation as a property of individual consciousness was not, however, lost to philosophy, but evolved along a route quite separate from Marxism. Kierkegaard (a student of Hegel) and Nietzsche developed protestant-based individualist moral philosophies which, combined with the phenomenology of Husserl led in the 20th century to the development of existentialism (Warnock (1970)). The root concern of existentialism, as developed by Heidegger and elaborated by Satre in particular, was the problematic of individual freedom. It involved a passionate call for the individual to shake off cowardly conformity and embrace the freedom inherent in the nature of the individual. Human existence was seen as a permanent battle against nothingness — that same void that Hegel had seen as the principle of motion — which is allayed by most people through adopting poses and other social conventions. But even though embracing freedom inevitably leads to anguish, a sense of absurdity and eventually nausea, it is nevertheless our central duty to ourselves to uphold it.

Heidegger and Satre both employed the term 'alienation', but neither in the same way as either Hegel or Marx, and not in a position central to their philosophy (Schacht (1970)). Both eventually migrated towards a more historically orientated philosophy — Heidegger through an evolution in his thought and Satre by embracing Marxism — and existentialism as a distinct philosophical school passed away. Nevertheless, some *rapprochement* took place between existentialism and Marxism (Kaufmann (1970)), without yet re-establishing any general framework for understanding the processes of alienation in the Hegelian sense.

Beginning in the late 1950s and peaking in the late 1960s, interest grew in the concept of alienation amongst academic social scientists. This was centrally related to the ascent into respectability of Marx's writings and a desire of social scientists with a severe positivist training and without any understanding of the background or method or praxis of Marxism attempting to move in a general way towards a *rapprochement*. A truly massive literature grew up and careers were forged out of the search for empirical evidence of alienation amongst industrial workers and in society generally. (Schacht (1970) surveyed this phenomenon, and Geyer and Schweitzer (1976) edited a representative group of papers including extensive bibliographies). However, the whole exercise was based upon a fundamental misunderstanding of even the Marxist case, let alone the Hegelian. Israel (1971: 204) attempted to sort out the confusion by referring to alienation as a 'macrosociological' concept that should not be interpreted in a positivistic manner. But the confusion was already rampant and, by the late 1970s, the whole literature was being quietly set aside, without any further effort at clarification.

As a prelude to re-establishing a concept of alienation in a modern context which encompasses the full extent of the Hegelian notion, it is clearly necessary to sort out the confusion involved in the recent existentialist and positivistic interpretations. The collapse of existentialism resulted from a growing awareness that it is pointless to imagine that the psychological characteristic of alienation can be meaningfully contemplated philosophically on its own without reference to the model of the world — hence the essentially social content — of the void of which it consists. The human brain is at no time an empty hole but, from the moment of birth on, is actively engaged in ingesting and making sense out of the world around it. There really is nothing to contemplate and attempts to do so inevitably lead to pointless despair — an extremely masochistic exercise. It should be added that the notion that such an activity might be worthwhile certainly stems from the 'individualist fallacy', so well developed in our culture and discussed in some detail in Chapter 5 below.

The central fallacy of the positivistic interpretation of alienation looks like this. Surveys of workers (an excellent example is the massive study of car workers carried out by Goldthorpe et al. (1968)), which fail to discover alienation, entirely miss the point. Alienation in this context refers to activities involving a radical divorce between means and ends of human *social* life. Medieval monks overcame their sense of alienation by embracing the socially given ideology of religion. This may well have made them happy, but the philosophical point is that religion is a surrogate solution to the fundamental problem of consciousness in nature. The alienated worker carries out his work (as the medieval monk carried out his religious rituals) in order to obtain peace of mind in the context of the socially given ideology of the 'puritan work ethic'. Today this is understood instrumentally as a means to earning money with which to buy the accoutrements of a reasonably comfortable life, but there are other ways of organising life. The workers having no control over what is being produced and to what ends, and thus relinquishing responsibility over this aspect of the way in which society is organised and nature exploited, is a strategic problem, not an immediate psychological one. When General Motors is 'restructured' and workers are thrown out of a job through the closure of factories, or when the whole of nature is progressively destroyed as a function of the workings of the automobile economy, then workers come to feel the impact of their alienation as a force that comes to them from outside. But it is, in reality, the consequence of their own acquiescence in relinquishing their powers as human beings. The 'solution' to this aspect of alienation lies in the organisation of society such that it is transparent to the average understanding, as is the process of exploitation of nature; above all, that everyone participates in the decisions and the multifarious actions through which this society and its productive processes operate. Such a situation would not entirely eliminate either the dichotomy of means and ends or the need for faith in abstractions. The point, however, is that these become negotiable and controllable through everyday social interaction.

It is now necessary to connect up the earlier discussion of human nature with the discussion of alienation. It was pointed out that animals antecedent to *Homo sapiens* certainly possess the ability for complex learning, for modelling of the surrounding world and of certain social functions. But there is no totality of historic consciousness in other animals to which these learning faculties link up: 'consciousness' in animals, if we think we can legitimately use the term, always reverts back to the individual organism and animal societies are almost entirely invariant for a given species because these are, from the point of view of the organism, no more than the interaction between individuals, as opposed to the human case, where society becomes a contingent construct of the permanently alienated — the communal — consciousness. We might think of 'animal consciousness' as involving a rudimentary form of alienation which, however, only embodies the one side, the individual, psychological aspect.

Alienation in the proper sense, as the ground upon which human consciousness as a social and historic process develops, is the product of human nature, or rather of human physiology. It is the consequence of the configuration of the human brain, creating a kind of void at the centre of the thinking function which the processes of the brain and the rest of the human organism then spend their time attempting to fill in. The result is the creation of human consciousness, through the evolutionary process of society as a whole. Each individual inherits the particular consciousness of her or his culture, age, society, class, family and so forth. But he or she is then part of the process of carrying the totality of consciousness forward through his or her actions.

Whilst the individual manifestation of alienation is a necessary prerequisite for the existence of consciousness — and hence of society and of any possible way of organising human activity necessary to sustain human life — there is no guarantee in the first instance that the model created, and the society and productive processes associated with this model, are in fact 'correct', or, shall we say, viable to the needs of human existence in the longer run (or we might set our sights lower and simply refer to a life of reasonable comfort for all). The point which Hegel and Marx were making with respect to the 'strategic' aspect of alienation was that there is some ultimate form of consciousness which *is* 'correct' in that it squares our understanding of social and natural process with the satisfaction of human needs, without major residue of unsubstantiatable belief or intransigent or unviable process.

The main point of the foregoing argument is simply this: in broad outline Hegel and Marx are correct in their supposition, although, as argued in detail in the following chapter, such an 'end state' is far more contingent and subject to conscious effort than is suggested by the grand historical models of these philosophers. And the key problems certainly are the propensity of humans to turn away from manifest reality (and so at the same time inure themselves against rational argument even in their own interests) and the concentration of strategic, organisational decisions in relatively few hands (be it through 'ownership of the means of production' or bureaucratic structures). But unfortunately, there is no guarantee that history will resolve all in our favour. At this juncture it seems very unlikely that we will ever push through to Utopia — the minimisation of 'strategic' alienation — prior to destroying the biosphere. But we owe it to ourselves to do everything in our powers to try.

Notes

1. It is worth spelling out the aggressive stance which Frazer took *vis-á-vis* non-scientific attitudes to knowledge; the following is a representative passage (Frazer (1957: 73)): "Yet when we have penetrated through the differences, which affect mainly the intelligent and thoughtful part of the community, we shall find underlying them all a solid stratum of intellectual agreement among the dull, the weak, the ignorant, and the superstitious, who constitute, unfortunately, the vast majority of mankind. One of the great achievements of the nineteenth century was to run shafts down into this low mental stratum in many parts of the world, and thus to discover its substantial identity everywhere....This universal faith, this truly Catholic creed, is a belief in the efficacy of magic....The dispassionate observer, whose studies have led him to plumb its depths, can hardly regard it as otherwise than as a standing menace to civilisation. We seem to move on a thin crust which may at any moment be rent by the subterranean forces slumbering below".

2. The origin and initial development of functionalism in British anthropology is generally attributed to Bronislaw Malinowski. Although his approach was severely anti-evolutionist and the abrasive parochialism of earlier anthropologists was discarded (to be replaced by an effortless superiority in the revelation of the true function — as only scientific Europeans could understand it — hidden in obscure primitive practices) he nevertheless displayed an abject reverence for Frazer as originator and inspiration for his interest in anthropology (Malinowski (1948: 93–95)): "The extended and deepened outlook of modern anthropology finds its most adequate expression in the learned and inspiring writings of Sir James Frazer."

3. Bryan Wilson (1975: 10) insisted on the necessary lack of absoluteness of social scientific categories and adopted an 'ideal type' system of analysis derived from Weberian methodology. Earlier in the century, Wissler (1923) had insisted — and been widely followed — on the existence of 'cultural universals' that are to be found in any social system. In practice these comprised little more than a jejune regurgitation of Enlightenment categories turned into dogma.

4. Already in 1974 Barry Barnes laid out the 'strong' case for relativism and, noting that incommensurability was not only a potential problem between societies but also within them through time, wrote (p. 39): "Inconsistency is continually appearing and being eliminated from systems of belief; it is never absent. To understand the process it is necessary to set beliefs in relation to *activity*. To consider the logical relationship between the elements of abstractly conceived belief systems is, on the whole, misleading. The sociologist should consider belief systems in terms of their functions in practical activity."

5. Gellner (1982: 200), subscribing to rationalism, as norm and empirically demonstrable, wrote: "Science needs one world. It does not need one kind of man (*sic*) within it. But one *kind* of man did make the single world. His historical situation may have been unique, his basic constitution was *not*. The single world seems to be gradually adopted by all of them, and appears manifestly accessible to all men." Geertz (1973: 20n) threw further light on this when he wrote: "So far as it has been reinforced the anthropologist's impulse to engage himself (*sic*) with his informants as persons rather than as objects, the notion of 'participant observation' has been a valuable one. But, to the degree that it has lead the anthropologist to block from his view the very special, culturally bracketed nature of his own role and to imagine himself something more than an interested (in both senses of the word) sojourner, it has been our most powerful source of

bad faith."

6. There is significant anthropological evidence illustrating, however, that aspects of knowledge, taken with peoples as they have migrated to other areas, or in cases where circumstances have changed, can leave a culture adhering to beliefs which are manifestly dysfunctional. Indeed, it is precisely the dysfunctional aspect of the scientific project that renders it so urgent that it be understood in the way presented here and thus divested of its epistemological status and opened up to rational criticism.

7. This is what Lévi-Strauss has referred to as 'bricoleur': the constant reformulation of culture using old objects for new purposes. Darwin put this beautifully in relation to natural evolution when he wrote (quoted in Ingold (1986: 201)):
   "Although an organ may not have been originally formed for some special purpose, if it now serves for this end, we are justified in saying that it is specially contrived for it. On the same principle if a man were to make a machine for some special purpose, but were to use old wheels, springs and pulleys, only slightly altered, the whole machine, with all its parts, might be said to be specially contrived for that purpose. Thus throughout nature almost every part of each living being has probably served, in a slightly modified condition, for diverse purposes, and has acted in the living machinery of many ancient and distinct specific forms".

8. The importance of the aesthetic attraction of science to scientists, and to a lesser extent the lay public, has almost totally failed to enter the analytical literature. And yet it has from time to time featured prominently in the utterances of scientists themselves working in the more abstract realms, as highlighted by Easlea (1980: 55, 66–67, 178, etc). In an interview in 1979, Nobel Prize winner Yang said: "What converted me (to a belief in Dirac's magnetic monopole) was the intrinsic beauty of the structure of natural laws, if there does exist this particle." The theory of the magnetic monopole utilizes global differential geometry which "is just incredibly beautiful, and it is one of the profound motivating forces of 20th century mathematics... Talk to any mathematician, they will tell you, with joy and with awe, their appreciation of this beauty." Dirac reasoned that "it is hard to imagine that nature does not utilize this possibility." Yang summarised his view by saying: "I don't believe nature, in her fundamental formation of fundamental laws of physics, uses non-beautiful pieces. I just can't believe that... The fundamental laws of nature are mathematically beautiful."

9. It is an essential attribute of the modern 'academic disease', referred to by Mary Midgeley and discussed above, that analyses insist on casting every other facet of explanation aside in order to highlight just one explanatory variable. As highlighted by Barnes (1977: Ch.2), Marxist analyses have a tendency to collapse the explanation of cultural change into one or other form of socio-economic determinism. Of interest to this analysis is the influential attack which Abercrombie et al. (1980) launched upon the growing debate concerning the function of ideology in cultural maintenance and change, insisting that it is (p. 165) "...not Protestant asceticism as the ideological belief system of workers and capitalists which provides ideal conditions for capitalist development, but the political and economic organisation of capitalist society." The following two chapters of this book are concerned to broaden out from such 'just so' functionalist reasoning and establish a more complex structure of explanation, oriented towards creative change.

10. Allegorically it might be said that the adoption of a consistent relativism is like the acceptance of the view that the world is a ball floating free in the universe. Science approaches knowledge from a flat earth perspective, on the assumption that

everything is built, like a pyramid, upon an infinitely solid foundation. A consistent relativism states that knowledge is a dynamic set of relations that cohere into a cultural ideology with no absolute referents, just like the spheres which inhabit the cosmos....

11. Academic Marxists, or Marxist sympathisers (eg Therborn (1980); Larrain (1979); Thompson (1986); McLellan (1986)) are generally unwilling to concede that Marx was so crude as to set his theories apart by a simple labelling device whereby *he* was scientific, and hence universal and correct, whereas *they* are ideological, and hence particular and incorrect. However, this is *de facto* the effect. Clifford Geertz (1964:47) encapsulated this attitude in the witty aphorism: "I have a social philosophy, you have political opinions, he has an ideology."

12. The success with which the dismal vision of Human Nature put forward by Hobbes has been so widely accepted in Britain since the English Revolution can be linked to the deep sense of defeat that followed the consolidation of autocratic power by Cromwell and which was confirmed in the subsequent return of the Monarchy, as analysed by Christopher Hill (1984) in his book *The Experience of Defeat*. There are clear instrumental reasons why established power would want to project such a dismal myth upon society as a means of justifying their power (which was precisely Hobbes' intention). The widespread acceptance of such a myth cannot, however, be so easily explained but for it being the ideological residue of actual political defeat of a popular movement that had high hopes of establishing society around an altogether more optimistic vision of Human Nature, a movement which intended to reorganise society based on co-operation (the Diggers and Levellers) and the direct expression of human sensibilities (the Ranters), rather then the brute power relations which still characterise our society.

13. When Adam Smith (1976: 456) wrote the following:
"...by directing that industry in such a manner as its produce may be of the greatest value, (the individual) intends only his own gain, and he is in this, as in many other cases, led by an invisible hand to promote an end which was no part of his intention. Nor is it always the worse for the society that it was no part of it. By pursuing his own interest he frequently promotes that of the society more effectively than when he really intends to promote it. I have never known much good done by those who affected to trade for the public good. It is an affectation, indeed, not very common among merchants, and very few words need be employed in dissuading them from it".
he was essentially saying: you can only really rely on yourself, investing trust or love in others is a vain enterprise that no right-minded individual indulges in. Seen for what it is, this is difficult to comprehend as anything but a miserable and inhuman view of life emanating from a miserable and inhuman society.

14. E. O. Wilson (1975, 1979), the 'moving spirit' of sociobiology, is, of course, American, rather than British and although there is a strong British contingent to the debate (eg Morris (1967); Dawkins (1976)), it has nevertheless been something of an international affair, with a major contribution also from ethology — essentially a Germanic discipline. This is partly a question of a tendency towards the internationalisation of academic debates generally. But as an aside it is noteworthy that for all the general bias of American academic culture towards the British model and the 'English ideology', there have been strains of some strength that have emanated from other European traditions. This is particularly true of American pragmatic philosophy on the one hand and sociology and anthropology on the other. Influences from Germany have been strong in these disciplines in the United States from the late 19th century to the present.

15. Although in his early work on symbolic anthropology Geertz made some reference to French anthropology — mainly of Lévi-Strauss — and saw the concept of culture to which he subscribed as 'essentially a semiotic one' (1964: 5), he nevertheless failed to interact in any structured way with semiotic theory under development at that time in France.

16. Just as British social analysts are tending to declare the supersession of empiricism (and hence the accompanying baggage of functionalism and a certain form of positivism) and yet continue to use much of the framework that produces *de facto* empiricist end products, so French social analysts continue within the traditional framework of French analysis which is *de facto* structuralist.

17. Although Saussure is universally acknowledged as the father of moderm semiotics, Hodge and Kress (1988: 17) wrote that, following its invention as a component of linguistic analysis, he then repressed its further development by excluding it (and in general the dynamic aspects of linguistics, intractable to positivist analysis) from the formal content of the discipline.

18. The analysis of Hodge and Kress follows, with regard to sociology, a general Marxist line. In France, a more hard-line Marxist 'social semiology', assigning language structure and various modes of cultural symbolism directly to social power arrangements, has been formulated by Pierre Bourdieu (1990).

19. It is important to realise that nature — and beyond that society — is not a region of fixed size that will not allow for expansion or reduction, but is dependent upon the richness and inventiveness or, conversely, poverty of the total structure to support life and activity. Prigogine and Stengers (1985:196) write: "However, in ecology as in human societies, many innovations are successful without such a preexisting 'niche'. Such innovations transform the environment in which they appear, and as they spread, they create the conditions necessary for their own multiplication, their 'niche'. In social situations, in particular, the creation of a 'demand', and even of a 'need' for this demand to fulfil, often appears as correlated with the production of the goods or the techniques that satisfy the demand."

20. Prigogine and Stengers (1985:189) put the general case well when they wrote: "Be it in biological, ecological, or social evolution, we cannot take as given either a definite set of interacting units, or a definite set of transformations in these units. The definition of the system is thus liable to be modified by its evolution."

21. An analogy is sometimes drawn between ecosystems and human cultures as discrete organic phenomena. The argument here would be that this is not merely a question of analogy: culture *is* a dimension of ecosystems. The problem we face is that out culture has outgrown the bounds which it initially possessed as being closely tied in with specific ecosystems. Our universalist culture has lost the characteristic interpenetration between culture and ecology and in doing so become aberrant and insensitive to its own ultimate requirements in terms of life-support systems. It has become like a disease upon the biosphere that is set to destroy the whole arrangement. The aim of political ecology is to re-establish a self-regulating relationship between biosphere and consciousness, between discrete cultures and ecosystems in bioregional arrangements. The key notions of decentralisation and bioregionalism which inform the strategy of political ecology are clearly compatible with the need to reconstitute culture at the level of the individual ecosystem.

4 History as process and context

For a society which has achieved a stable, self-reproducing relationship with nature, there is little purpose in historical awareness. As Carr (1964:132) put it:

> But history is meaningless in a static world.... History so-called can be written only by those who find and accept a sense of direction in history itself. The belief that we have come from somewhere is closely linked with the belief that we are going somewhere. A society which has lost belief in its capacity to progress in the future will quickly cease to concern itself with its progress in the past.

Information on the origins of creation and of natural and social evolution may occupy peripheral concern in rounding out the system of knowledge but this would remain esoteric; in 'pre-historic societies' — indeed, arguably, during most of the era of 'civil society' which is historically documented — this was the case.

Both infatuated and frightened by it, our age is dominated by instability and change. It is therefore time dominated, obsessed with history (Carr (1964:134)) and with its obverse, the future: what are the wellsprings of these convulsions through which we are living? Where is it all leading? The ecology movement is primarily concerned with bringing this infernal machine under conscious social control before it destroys the biosphere. Thus, whilst the movement wishes to overcome and set aside history, in the first instance it is vitally necessary to understand how the machine works. Only by mastering it can it effectively be dismantled.

Necessarily, from the outset of this book interpretations of history insinuated themselves into the approach to analysis. However, history is not necessarily one thing or discipline: there are many interpretations as to the use of history and the significance to be placed upon elements of its structure. Before continuing with this analysis it is therefore advisable to make clear in theoretical and methodological terms what overall interpretation is being made here of history. It is then useful to sketch out what is seen here as the essential structure of the historical process. Subsequent chapters look more closely at vital parts of the machinery which, through critique, it will be necessary to dismantle as a central activity along the path to the construction of Utopia.

There are three parts to this chapter. The first is intended to locate the approach taken here within the overall spectrum of methodological approaches to history. This necessarily involves some analysis of the origins of prejudices which hide within the debates about methodology and hence the underlying reasons why history is approached by various historians in the way that it is. The second part is concerned with the content of history in so far as it may possess a general structure. This is treated generically in terms of the concept of social evolution and the discussion focuses largely on locating the approach taken here to the 'historical materialism' adopted by Marxists. The final section is concerned not with the past but with the future: what are the steps that must be taken to dismantle the juggernaut of history, to resolve the matter in favour of Utopia?

The use and abuse of history

In different ages scholars and writers have investigated and written about past events and ideas with different purposes in mind. J. H. Plumb (1969:1) put it like this:

Man, from the earliest days of recorded time, has used the past in a variety of ways: to explain the origins and purpose of human life, to sanctify institutions and government, to give validity to class structures, to provide moral example, to vivify his cultural and educational purposes, to interpret the future, to invest both the individual human life or the nation's with a sense of destiny.

Reading about the past remains a popular pastime, albeit the locus of that popularity has little bearing on academic debates concerning the function of history and what should be deemed 'legitimate' in terms of methodology and structure: there is a strong tradition amongst historians of seeing their role as one of tutoring the public with regard to what history *should* be about (Finley (1986); Ferro (1987)). In fact, historians often append to their work some explanation of what has motivated them and hence why they have focused on particular persons and events and dimensions of those events (Stern (1970)).

Parallel with the actual investigation and writing of history there has grown up a distinct discipline of historiography and of the philosophy of history, focusing on the nature, meaning and purpose of history. This is often seen as originating in the attempts of the French Enlightenment (or more specifically Voltaire (Carr (1964:19)) to bring the study of history into the orbit of science. However, as is made evident in the following chapter, the structure of Enlightenment historiography was largely created in the English universities during the latter part of the 17th century (Tuveson (1949)) and contains within it a hidden agenda of Judaeo-Christian apocalyptic.

The philosophy of history, as pursued across the Enlightenment and into the early years of the 19th century, was predominantly concerned to discern from amongst the historical evidence whether there is any general internal structure to the historical process which could indicate what the future might hold. As the 19th century wore on, the emphasis shifted to a debate about approaches that should be taken to classifying and interpreting the increasing volumes of available evidence. In part this stemmed from a more equivocal attitude to the Enlightenment notions of progress, as Burrow (1966: 214) put it:

... it is now a sobered Enlightenment, harsher and more priggish, having lost wit and taste for indecency and acquired Malthus and Ricardo. But there is still the same sense of a new dawn for humanity — and the cliché is perhaps a more accurate rendering of the state of mind than a fresher metaphor would be.

However, this change in emphasis stemmed also in part from the genuine logistical problems of handling the rapidly increasing volumes of material. The empiricist approach to history, *qua* 'scholarly discipline' — concerned first with correct approaches to information collection and interpretation only subsequently and generally in relatively unpremeditated fashion — is often seen as originating in Leopold Ranke in the 19th century (Atkinson (1978: 14); Marwick (1981: 27)) but may be traced back as far as Bayle in 17th-century France (Cassirer (1951: 201–202)).

This shift in theory away from structure in history to methodological concerns continued in the 20th century (Gardiner (1974: 1–3)) to a point where mainstream academic historiography became largely critical of more than the most limited interpretation of structure in history (Plumb (1969: 135); Marwick (1981: 45)). It is of considerable interest, however, that the general public refused to restrict their tastes to those prescribed by mainstream academia. Plumb (1969: 136) noted that:

H G Wells, Oswald Spengler and Arnold Toynbee, who sought to mould history into a meaningful past, secured millions of readers but the almost universal condemnation of historians.

Marwick (1981:88) wrote in the same vein:

Toynbee has been acclaimed by the reading public and denigrated by professional historians. In general there is professional agreement that whatever Toynbee has written in 'A Study of History', it is not history.

It is important at this juncture to point out that Wells, Spengler and Toynbee are in practice only scapegoats serving to provide an intellectual context, warning historians to keep clear of certain territory. On the one hand, the traumatic events of the early years of this century shattered the Victorian illusion of history as a grand march towards an ever more glorious future (Carr (1964: 43)). But at the centre of this territory has lain a particular interpretation of history which academic historians and the dominant interests which they have served across this century have not wanted to hear: namely historical materialism. As E. P. Thompson (1978: 287) put it: 'Our intellectual culture is sensitised to Marxist concepts in a hundred ways.' This factor that already entered the analysis in the foregoing chapter, remains central to the rest of this chapter which aspires both to acknowledge the importance of the Marxist legacy of historical analysis but also to subject it to a critique relevant to the requirements of political ecology.

Whilst mainstream historiography has attempted to restrict controversy to methodological issues — penetrating, in the process, deep into the deserts of scolasticism — and the interpretation of the minutiae of particular events (Gardiner (1959, 1974); Marwick (1981: Ch.8)); some fruitful developments of historical interpretation have continued to be made, particularly in relation to Marxism and these are deemed to be of importance to political ecology and therefore pursued in some depth later in this chapter. But it is first necessary to make some sense out of the debate about methodology in history and via this to gain a better understanding of the theoretical bases of the method which we find embedded in run-of-the-mill history books. In this context, it is useful to look at two central issues with respect to the ordering of historical information and investigate briefly the way in which various schools of history writing relate to these issues.

On the one hand there has been an assertion that the writing of history should conform to the strictures of science and hence that scientific rules must be formulated against which the validity of approaches to the writing of history can be evaluated. On the other hand, and less forthrightly stated, there can be discerned a division between historians who accept that history is concerned with analysing and promoting social change and those who are more inclined to see history as an anchor, tethering the political process to existing social arrangements — and we should include in the latter the 'Whig interpretation of history' which, whilst embracing general meliorative improvement, nevertheless precluded any change in the ranking of social interests.

Taking first those historians anxious to be considered scientific and also concerned with the question of social change, we can see this field being dominated by Marxists. In its classic form, historical materialism — Marxist history — represents an approach to analysing the past which both wishes to be considered a science and which is essentially committed to promoting fundamental social change (Carr (1964)). Whilst rejecting the possibility of discovering any 'general historico-philosophical theory' for all places and periods in history, Marx, in laying the foundations of this approach to historiography, nevertheless claimed that 'inexorable laws' governing the movement of capital — i.e. of the structure of modern history — are there to be found (Marx and Engels (1975: 293–4)). On the one hand, the material transformation of the economic conditions of production could be determined with the precision of natural science. But these were seen as being overlain by legal, political, religious, artistic and philosophical forms which possess a more contingent, 'ideological', character (Marx (1975: 426)).

Of course the term 'science' possesses immense prestige in our society, denoting unrivalled, authoritative knowledge. During the 19th century the term was adopted by a broad range of approaches to the analysis of the natural and social world that differentiated themselves from theological approaches but which did not possess a common body of rules and principles. It was in the course of the 20th century, in direct relationship to Marxism, that the struggle over the validity of particular rules governing science in relation to social analysis came to a head.

The continued claim of Marxism to being a science relates to the way in which it asserts a specific structure to the process of social evolution and a set of analytical categories and tools through which this process is to be understood. Indeed for Marxism sociology and history are essentially one enterprise (Carr (1964: 66)). Nowadays it is freely admitted that the concept of 'laws', governing social processes, may well be inappropriate and also that there are clearly differences between social and natural science stemming, above all, from the inseparability of the subject from the object of study (Carr (1964: Ch.3)). But the central importance of the analysis of cause and effect, as tools in the effort to achieve beneficial change in the constitution of society, remains a scientific endeavour essential, amongst Marxists, to the maintenance of meaning and the usefulness of history.

Whilst Marx and Engels initiated the researching and writing of history from the point of view of historical materialism, a gradual accumulation of works emerged in conjunction with the growth of the socialist movement. In the past thirty years there has been a substantial extension of the adoption by historians of a historical materialist methodology, particularly in Britain, where a broad reinterpretation of British history from this perspective has been achieved (Johnson (1979); Kaye (1984)). Where the traditional focus was upon the activities and ideas of the ruling classes, now we have available a systematic view of history from the perspective of the common people and which analyses social movements amongst the common people and their role in historical change. This has significantly moved historical concern in a more general way beyond the description of particular events and personalities to focus more upon social process. The Marxist historians have also shifted the centre of interest within the general community of historians who are otherwise relatively unaware of the theoretical issues involved.

The second approach to historiography is concerned with those — mainly theoreticians — who have declared that history should be considered a science but who are also concerned to defend existing social relations. Reference has already been made in the foregoing chapter to the way in which intellectual life in Europe reacted to the rise of socialist movements around the turn of the century by thoroughly re-evaluating its premises and rules to inhibit the development of socialist ideas and ideals — with the basic intent of blocking specifically the kind of social change which socialism both anticipated and called for. 'Science' in this context involved a kind of ideological authoritarianism, particularly marked in the anglophone world, of Humean empiricism, inductivism, functionalism and behaviourism practised within a positivist philosophical framework, that cast its shadow right across Europe.

A central thrust of this intellectual practice was to define scientific knowledge in terms of a narrow set of rules and then to declare all other forms of intellectual activity to be illegitimate. This programme was extremely effective in confining the scope of the 'social sciences' of economics, sociology, anthropology and psychology. But with respect to history, the problem was that such an approach would exclude all history apart from the collection of information and yet it was precisely the interpretation of history which these ideologues of science were most concerned to curtail. The particular approach which became central to the effectuation of the positivist programme in relation to historiography was the so-called 'Popper-Hempel thesis'.

In its purely theoretical form, as the 'covering law model of explanation', this derived from the empiricism of Hume. It was Hume's view that (Day (1964: 352)):

we may be free, and yet another may be perfectly certain what use we shall make of our freedom.

He was convinced that all human activity would some day be amenable to analysis in terms of cause and effect. Hempel's intention was to frame rules within which causality might be discovered in history. But it was quite clear that these rules would be extremely restrictive in terms of allowing generalisation.

Karl Popper's (1961; 1966) approach was to insist that a hypothesis is 'scientific' only if it can be tested. He conceded that Marx's theory of social change *was* testable, and so scientific, but that it had been successfully refuted (D'Amico (1989: Ch.1)). It was Marx's followers who, in their attempts to rescue Marx's theory, had resorted to untestable hypotheses and so entered the realms of the unscientific. Popper (1961: iii) made no secret of the fact that his argument was intended as a frontal attack on the notion of 'inexorable laws of historical destiny'. His concern was both with theory and the political practice which this informs. His conclusions were that we can only speak of laws in history on a very restricted basis because there are few hypotheses that remain within the bounds of the testable. Related to this, Popper insisted that we should not indulge in Utopian schemes but only in 'piecemeal social engineering' because we cannot be sure of the results and so we must avoid making big mistakes.

Carl Hempel (1942; 1963), and the chief academic theoreticians of history who participated in this debate (Gardiner (1974)), avoided any analysis of the political context of their approach to knowledge. Popper, on the other hand, made relatively little secret of the motivation behind his polemic. Whilst his *Poverty of Historicism* was ostensibly a critique of fascist and communist doctrines, those references which were not Marxist were in no case fascist either. Marwick, himself a supporter of positivist approaches to history, wrote, perhaps somewhat disingenuously (1981: 189):

Karl Popper's polemical works, *The Poverty of Historicism* and *The Open Society and Its Enemies*, were powerful, and often highly emotional, attacks on the notion of their being meaning in history — in this case *meaning* meant Marxism.

It might be thought that the attempt to restrict the imputation of meaning and the drawing of generalisations from history on the part of historians has not been particularly inhibited by the esoteric methodological debate about 'covering laws' (Dray (1963:135)). However, the seriousness with which Popper's views have been taken indicates that the general strictures, of which the 'covering laws' are but the most refined form, have had considerable influence. This question therefore requires a little further analysis with respect to the problem which follows from this.

As has already been noted in the foregoing chapter, historians of the modern era who concern themselves with cultural and intellectual developments can hardly avoid comment on the profusion of theorisation on social issues which developed around the turn of the century (Joll (1976: 113)), particularly anxious to come to terms with and contain Marxism. Of this 'struggle with Marx' (Berger and Luckmann (1967: 17) referred to more decorously by some as a 'dialogue with Marx' (Bell (1973: 44))), Stuart Hughes

(1959: 42) wrote in the following terms:

To come to terms with Marxism, then, was the first and most obvious task confronting the intellectual innovators of the 1890s.

A feeling of the mood of the time in particular as it affected the question of evolutionary theory is given by the Italian socialist Ferri (1905: 1ff) who wrote of the biological congress in Munich in 1877 where the biologists Virchon and Haeckel debated whether of not Darwinism should be accepted, as a biological theory, on the basis of its social implications. Virchon rejected it on account of the potential support which it might give to social revolution. Haeckel, on the other hand, maintained that Darwin had proved that the lower orders were an inevitable social presence and hence that Darwinism was incompatible with revolution and so acceptable. There can be little doubt that the wholesale rejection of the massive corpus of 19th-century social evolutionism (Barrow (1966)) was strongly motivated by this concern to deny Marxism any purchase in legitimate social theory (Wertheim (1974: 18)). In looking back over the development of social theory in this century from the perspective of the 1970s, H.M. Drucker (1974: 97) wrote as follows:

There should be little question that the Marxist movement in all its various shapes is *the* social and political doctrine of our age. There are exceptions to this rule, of course, and there are divisions in the Marxist camp to be sure; but to a remarkable degree the serious political ideas of our day are either pro-Marxist or anti-Marxist .... Marxism commands the centre of the field .... liberalism and conservatism, are today .... primarily reactions against the progeny of Marxism.

Whilst this may represent an over-statement of the case — and certainly the 1980s saw a progressive relaxation of the divide — it is nevertheless necessary as a precondition for any attempt at social analysis today to understand clearly the importance of the struggle over Marxism even to analysis which makes neither reference to, nor appears to gain any theoretical content from, Marxism.

In practice, some fruitful analysis committed to perspectives emanating from Marxism did develop across the first two thirds of this century and even the reaction against Marxism — one thinks in particular of German social enquiry — has provided ideas which remain of significant use, as evidenced in the following chapter of this book. The most problematic reaction was that which insisted on creating an intellectual cordon sanitaire around Marxism that has amounted to a kind of mass intellectual neurosis on the part of both supporters of and detractors from Marxism. The ideological origins of this phenomenon can be traced to the philosophical and scientific methodological school of 'logical empiricism' that flowered in Vienna in the wake of the collapse of the Austro-Hungarian empire and from which both Hempel and Popper subsequently became refugees. Anglophone 'social science' and with it historiography was very badly infected by this neurosis, as noted by Perry Anderson (1969). Indeed, the very narrowness with which the term science continues to be used in British discourse (Carr (1964: 56–57); Marwick (1981: 104)) can be attributed in significant measure to the efforts of the theoreticians of history to deny the use of the term to historical materialism.

With the waning of the proscription on Marxist analysis from the 1960s on, this history has continued to provide problems in British social analyses. Firstly, this stems from the lack of a sufficient indigenous intellectual basis for Marxist analysis, resulting in a tendency to adopt, uncritically, approaches from elsewhere (the clearest example has been the rise and fall of French structural Marxism). Secondly, this is evidenced by the continuation of awkward disjunctures between Marxist and non Marxist analyses where the former remain fearful of moving creatively out of orthodoxy and the latter continue, albeit with less intensity, to avoid insights emanating from a general Marxist direction. The critique of historical materialist history in the following section attempts to overcome this problem.

The third approach to history concerns historians who are neither anxious to declare their efforts as scientific, nor interested in the uses of history towards the ends of social change. The majority of historians at work today, at least when we are considering the case of Britain, remain relatively theoretically unconscious and *de facto* empiricist in approach (James (1984)). The centre of gravity of this work is one which tends to use history as a tool to reinforce present arrangements by venerating what has existed and what exists now. This is done by presenting history as story and morality through particular heroes, places and events: history as spectacle[1]. Whilst recent Marxist history might have introduced some new heroes and events, the framework within which this is presented by the corpus of professional historians remains unreviewed and in general historians are discouraged from undertaking such a review.

Arthur Marwick's (1981:278) text on historiography which has formed the basis of many university courses on this subject in recent years put this general case relatively clearly in the following terms:

Am I too prosaic? Do I present too lowly a view of the potential of the subject when I speak of 'the industry of history?' Marc Bloch's *The Historian's Craft* and E. H. Carr's *What is History?* are both compelling personal statements about how, in the authors' views, history ought to be written. In more recent books, Gordon Connell-Smith and Howell A. Lloyd have demanded a history more relevant to the needs of a changing society and Geoffrey Barraclough has spoken passionately of history's opportunity to break into a new scientific dimension, incidentally criticising my own apparent conservatism and complacency in defending the modest advances which historical study has made over the years. I believe deeply in the importance of history, but I cannot share in the messianic fervour of these writers.

According to this approach, historians should avoid engagement with structured debates about the purpose of history and simply continue to collect information in unpremeditated fashion. Marwick (1981:242), following Popper, also warns historians off attempting to draw any very structured conclusions from the evidence:

Of course it is always open to a self-advancing extrovert, or misguided crank, to offer the world a startling new interpretation of certain historical events: should his work not be based on thorough scholarship, should it not be offered in good faith, the ever-ready police battalions of the historical guild will soon club his pretensions to jelly.

This censorship role of the run-of-the-mill historians, based on a priori assumptions, and not on any structured analysis, about the purpose of historical writing clearly plays an important role in determining in practice what historical theories are perpetrated and the way in which empirical material is mustered to support these. It is worth adding that the motivation of the historical fraternity in maintaining this attitude clearly relates back to the wider support for positivist approaches to knowledge as a whole, resting, as Kolakowski so eloquently put it and as cited in chapter 2, upon the privileged way of life of academics and the wisdom, as seen from this perspective, of avoiding engagement: life is fine, why rock the boat? The problem which this 'conventional wisdom' concerning the use and abuse of history presents to political ecology can hardly be overstated and will become evident later in this chapter. In particular, history, according to this approach, does not engage in any direct way with any open discussion of what the future might hold. History as an active ingredient of Utopian construction must reject fragmentation into events and personalities, must reject moralising and must adopt a direct commitment to the reconstruction of society along ecological lines, drawing on an analysis of the past.

The final category of historians to be discussed briefly here is neither Marxist nor empiricist, having maintained a recessive influence since the very beginnings of modern historiography, and is best described as phenomenological. Originating in the writing of Vico and Herder at either end of the Enlightenment, its chief philosopher was Hegel. Via this route, it can also be said to comprise one of the ingredients or foundations of Marxist history. Important impetus was given to it in the context of the turn-of-century 'dialogue with Marx', in particular by Wilhelm Dilthey and Benedetto Croce. This 'hermeneutic' approach was then introduced into English discourse by R. G. Collingwood who is considered by Marxist and non Marxist historians alike (Gardiner (1974:4); Carr (1964: 21)) to have made the most substantial contribution amongst English theoreticians of history even though his method is rarely followed.

The historical school of phenomenology has consciously eschewed the notion that history should be considered a science. As Hughes (1959: 199–200) put it:

After Dilthey historians no longer needed to apologise for the 'unscientific' character of their discipline: they understood why its methods could never be the same as those of natural science.

This approach to history generally understands it to be a social and cultural process, organic rather than lawful. Particular societies and cultures possess their own unique inner consistency and coherence to which individual participants and events relate back for their meaning. Change through time is an essential aspect of this process: Herder was one of the initiators of the notion of social evolution but rejected the idea that there were any laws underlying it or that there might conceivably be only one evolutionary path (Berlin (1976)).

The central idea which Collingwood (1946) brought to the study of history is that, unlike in the case of the natural sciences, 'facts' — events, the activities of people — are meaningless when divorced from the thought processes which lead to them and which inform them. The coherent whole of ideas, of the corporate mind of the community or the age, provides the only valid framework within which history can be meaningfully understood. History is essentially the process of the development of human consciousness, not a catalogue of events and heroes.

It should be clear from the foregoing chapters that the approach to history which is adopted in this analysis owes much to the phenomenological school — and, it might be added as an aside, warms in particular to the interpretation originating in the work of Herder (1968). Nevertheless, there is much both in the structure of historical materialism and in recent empirical history built upon this framework which is deemed to be of great value and has been employed extensively throughout this study. There is, indeed, a danger that this study will be interpreted, as a consequence of this reliance upon Marxist precedent, as accepting more by way of historical materialist methodology than, in fact, it does. It is therefore necessary, in the following section of this chapter, to clarify the distinction of approach.

History as social evolution

Political ecology is primarily concerned with achieving social and political changes in the short term in order to head off the current, suicidal social trajectory. It thus clearly accepts that society is amenable to change. Nevertheless, the ecology movement has learned over the past twenty years that it is not good enough in itself simply to point to the suicidal nature of the current social process and hope that things will immediately change. Society operates in very complex ways and effective intervention requires an understanding of the nature of this complexity. Sociology as social science has been overwhelmingly concerned to analyse society as artefact or a self-reproducing mechanism with very little interest in the possibilities for, and the machinery involved in, social change through time. As we have just seen, academic historiography has worked very hard to suppress insight that acknowledges the actuality of social change through time. So we are faced with very unhelpful intellectual tools if we look to the corpus of academic social analysis. It is nevertheless worth noting that anthropology has been more inclined to present material which might be useful to political ecology simply because of the great difficulty in denying that societies and cultures in various parts of the world manifestly are very different and that these are subject to change.

The concept through which we can most usefully approach this task is that of social or cultural evolution, bringing as it does a sense of coherent movement to the analysis of social phenomena. Few would deny that we live in a social and cultural world today that is radically different from that which existed five hundred years ago which is then different again from those existing five thousand and fifty thousand years ago. Whether we want to acknowledge it or not, society and culture have evolved. The problem is then to look at features of this process which might help us to understand the possibilities for the future both by way of understanding the structure of the evolutionary trajectory or constraints and opportunities and by way of understanding the possible role of conscious intervention, of human volition.

As is discussed further in the following chapter, the realisation in the course of the French Enlightenment that society is involved in a process of evolution, and the assumption then imputed that there is also constant improvement in the human condition, gained its initial impetus from the secularisation of the Judaeo-Christian apocalyptic in the late 18th century and it is possible to conjecture that this ideological underpinning continues to inform even recent forms of evolutionism. It is of more than passing interest that Rousseau (1964c) argued in the opposite direction out of an alternative tradition that saw modernity as a descent from a previous 'golden age'. The earliest approaches at attempting to discern the structure of social evolution already contained the notion of discrete types of social and political arrangement; these were then placed in sequence as representing steps through which human society in general has proceeded from the primitive to the modern. Typically there were just three or four stages — Adam Smith (1976) in *The Wealth of Nations* simply stated that 'The four stages of society are hunting, pasturage, farming and commerce' — but Condorcet (1976) conjectured a further nine stages through the present and into the future, following on from the initial four.

In spite of the equivocation with regard to the kind of unguarded speculation of the Enlightenment that entered into intellectual life particularly in Britain following the French Revolution, in the latter part of the 19th century evolutionism became the conventional structure for much of what passed at that time for social science (Burrow (1966); Sanderson (1990: Ch.2)). The impetus behind this came from the felt need to gain some theoretical perspective upon the multifarious other cultures with which burgeoning European colonialism was confronted and which required justification for the cultural destruction and rapacious exploitation which this process involved. A combination of Malthusian pessimism and Enlightenment progressivism enabled the Victorian social theorists to project Europeans as both at the forefront of an inevitable historic process and at the same time as having emerged from the benighted superstition that engulfed other cultures which it was the duty of European culture to actively destroy.

It has been overwhelmingly assumed that this social evolutionism, as 'social Darwinism', came in on the coat tails of Darwin's biological evolutionism. However, the facts of the case are that Herbert Spencer (1852), the prime mover behind the wave of social evolutionism, was publishing Malthusian social evolutionary views well before Darwin had published anything on evolution. Indeed, it was Thomas Huxley who had for many years been debating evolutionism with Spencer who, upon discovering Darwin's work, became Darwin's prime and tireless promoter (Spencer (1967)). There is ample evidence to assert that Darwin, with his insistence on applying Malthus to the whole of nature, was simply used by the social evolutionists to lend the weight of natural science to their ideological proclivities.

Marx and Engels evolutionism originated from the same Enlightenment

sources as that of the Victorian social evolutionists (Anderson (1970: 462ff))
although they vehemently rejected the Malthusian interpretation (Meek
(1953). Although the main elements of historical materialism were in print
well before the advent of Victorian social evolutionism, there was little
substantive interaction between the two. Marx and particularly Engels (1972)
followed developments in social evolutionism and were particularly
enthusiastic concerning the work of the American anthropologist Lewis
Morgan on primitive societies. Their response to Darwin was also one of great
enthusiasm; Marx wrote (Marx and Engels (1975: 115): 'Darwin's book is
very important and it suits me well that it supports the class struggle in history
from the point of view of natural science.' But they were scathing about its
Malthusian framework, Engels writing (Marx and Engels (1975: 284):

The whole Darwinist theory of the struggle for existence simply transfers from society
to living nature Hobbes' doctrine of *belum omnia contra omnes* and the bourgeois-
economic doctrine of competition together with Malthus' theory of population. When
this feat has been performed (and I question its absolute permissibility... particularly as
far as the Malthusian theory is concerned), the same theories are transferred back again
from organic nature into history and it is now claimed that their validity as eternal laws
of human society has been proved.

Reference has already been made to the way in which evolutionism in social
analysis was thrust aside in the early years of this century, to be substituted by
severe positivist doctrines of empiricism, functionalism and behaviourism.
A rather inflexible interpretation of Marxist evolutionism continued to
inform social studies in the Soviet Union and Gordon Childe (1951, 1964,
1965) and Leslie White (1959) continued to interpret new archaeological data
in accordance within a quasi-Marxist framework. From the mid 1950s on, a
new wave of social evolutionism arose independently in anthropology
(Steward (1955); Sahlins and Service (1960)), largely acknowledging the
Marxist framework and in sociology (Lenski (1970); Parsons (1971)) relating
much more closely to Spencerian meliorativism and the progressivist
scenarios of the Enlightenment.

Social evolutionary views cannot reasonably be restricted to conceptions
about the past and present without implications for the future. There is now a
wide range of views in print concerning the structure and content of social
evolution all of which more or less support the maintenance or development
of a particular future set of political arrangements. Thus functionalist
sociology clearly sees meliorative liberal democracy as adequate to future
needs. Much of modern anthropological evolutionism contains Marxist
implications, but there are also overtly feminist interpretations (Dobbins
(1978); Leacock (1981); Moore (1988)) and a significant stream of anarchist
interpretations (Montagu (1978); Barclay (1982); Bookchin (1982, 1987)).
There is also a significant anti-evolutionist backlash (Mandelbaum (1971);
Giddens (1982, 1984)) that is useful in so far as it sharpens the analytical side of
evolutionary thinking.

There are three key issues that can be usefully discussed at this point
concerning the structure of social evolution, namely the question of
'evolutionary stages', the mechanics of social and cultural evolution and the

issue of teleology (ie whether evolution is goal-oriented or has an externally-imposed structure to it). The main difficulty with the adoption of any particular set of social evolutionary stages is that there are always cases of particular societies and cultures that fit unhappily into any particular stage. Furthermore, particular cultures do not necessarily follow any obvious progression from a 'lower' to a 'higher' state: sedentary Indian farmers on the United States plains 'reverted' to hunting when horses became available and early European capitalist society 'reverted' to a slave society upon settling in the Americas. A further problem with the categorisations used by 19th-century evolutionists — and often adopted by their followers until quite recently — is the pejorative connotations of the titles appended to earlier and simpler societies and the casual ethnocentrism which this involves. Morgan's use of 'savagery', 'barbarism' and 'civilisation' for his three main stages — subsequently followed by Childe and the Soviet evolutionists alike — is a classic case in point: ethnographic field work indicates unequivocally that 'savage' peoples are incomparably less savage than the putatively 'civilised'! But if the processes of social and cultural evolution are to be rendered comprehensible then some form of categorisation does become necessary. It should be evident from the argument in the foregoing chapter that the answer to this lies in questions about the reasons why knowledge of evolution might be being sought in the first place. For the Victorians and many modern evolutionists, belittling other cultures is a central purpose of the exercise. Political ecology — which finds much relevant material in the work of cultural ecology and ethnomethodology — would choose categories that highlight the relations between culture and environment and which shed light on the aberrant growth of elaborate competitive culture. According to political ecology, evolution as an organic process of change may not be legitimately characterised in terms of 'progress' and nor may we define 'higher' and 'lower' stages in anything but contingent fashion. It must be acknowledged nevertheless, as highlighted by the almost simultaneous advent of organised agriculture in five or six separate locations (Cohen (1977)), that complex macroprocesses are at work and that systems of classification that are sensitive to such complexities require careful construction; we should not imagine that because we cannot arrive at more than contingent categories that these are therefore necessarily arbitrary. Further reference to macroprocess as it affects our predicament today is made later in this discussion.

There are essentially two approaches to the question of mechanism in social and cultural evolution, an 'evolutionist' or 'developmentalist' view that explains history in terms of a logical unfolding of a general set of mechanisms or even a preordained plan, and an 'evolutionary' view that explains change in terms of a series of discrete responses to particular conditions and requirements (Sanderson (1990: 16–17)). Spencer's famous definition of evolution as being "...definable as a change from an incoherent homogeneity to a coherent heterogeneity, accompanying the dissipation of motion and integration of matter" is a classic example of evolutionist thinking as is Parsons' notion of social evolution as being revealed in increasing differentiation and adaptive capacity of society. On the other side are the 'materialist' explanations, of population pressure, economic and technological determinisms. The predilection of political ecology is certainly towards the latter explanatory approach: the entire environmentalist literature takes this form. But, from the discussion in the foregoing chapter it must be evident that we should not over-rely on arguments concerning material forces alone: there is indeed no material influence on social and cultural life that is not mediated by ideological structures — to the point where whole societies can and do commit suicide for lack of an adequate material response to a material challenge and our own society may be involved in just such a dynamic. Political ecology should argue for dialectical modes of explanation and intervention and would certainly look to developing different explanatory configurations for different ages and places (i.e. 'increasing differentiation' and 'economic determinacy in the last instance' (Engels) are unuseful generalisations).

From the point of view of political ecology, teleology is the bane of evolutionism. The 19th-century evolutionists, following the Enlightenment thinkers and back into Judaeo-Christian apocalyptic origins, accepted openly the teleological assumption that evolution meant improvement towards some ultimate good. This was openly declared even by the recent sociological evolutionary theorists discussed above (Lenski (1970); Parsons (1971)). In all cases, this teleology is indissolubly linked to European ethnocentrism. It is the assumption that social evolutionism necessarily involves teleology that lies at the heart of the modern anti-evolutionist critique but, as discussed further below, this is not necessarily the case.

As with all aspects of Marxism, a massive exegetical literature has argued over whether Marx and Engels did or did not espouse a teleology. Many Marxist writers have not wanted to see Marx as having espoused teleology and have simply denied this (Hindess and Hirst (1975: 9)) whilst others have argued this case in more detail (Sanderson (1990: 54ff)). Elster (1985: 107), on the other hand was amongst those who have undertaken substantial analysis to arrive at the conclusion that 'There can be little doubt that Marx was indeed guided by a teleological view of history.' We might admire such non-teleological statements as the following (Marx (1973a: 147):

Men make their own history, but not of their own free will; not under circumstances they themselves have chosen but under the given and inherited circumstances with which they are directly confronted.

But then be confronted by statements of the following kind (Marx (1976: 929):

.... along with the constant decrease in the number of capitalist magnates, who usurp and monopolize all the advantages of this process of transformation, the mass of misery, oppression, slavery, degradation and exploitation grows; but with this there also grows the revolt of the working class, a class constantly increasing in numbers, and trained, united and organised by the very mechanism of the capitalist process of production. The monopoly of capital becomes a fetter upon the mode of production which has flourished alongside and under it. The centralization of the means of production and the socialization of labour reach a point at which they become incompatible with their capitalist integument. This integument is burst asunder. The knell of capitalist private property sounds. The expropriators are expropriated.

And in the case of Engels this mode of expression becomes even more explicit as in the following (Engels (1976: 364–67)):

But if, upon this showing, division into classes has a certain historical justification, it does so only for a given period of time, for given social conditions. It was based on the insufficiency of production; it will be swept away by the full development of the modern productive forces. In fact the abolition of social classes presupposes a level of historical development at which the existence not merely of this or that particular ruling class but of any ruling class at all, and therefore of class distinction itself, has become an anachronism, is obsolete .... This point has now been reached .... The conditions of existence environing and hitherto dominating humanity now pass under the dominion and control of humanity, which now for the first time becomes the real conscious master of nature, because and in so far as it becomes master of its own social organisation. .... The objective extraneous forces which have hitherto dominated history now pass under the control of man himself. It is only from this point that man will himself make his own history fully consciously, it is only from this point that the social causes he sets in motion will predominantly and ever increasingly have the effect he wills. It is humanity's leap from the realm of necessity into the realm of freedom.

Whilst the kind of society which Engels has in mind as emerging from the dénouement of class struggle may possess significant attractions to political ecology (and the final chapter of this book goes further into this question), the point at issue is that the teleological assumption which this form of words embodies is simply unrealistic. We might argue that Marx and Engels were in themselves aware that life is not preordained but found it contingently useful to make confident exclamatory statements that would make more impression upon the political process than more honest equivocation. If this is the case, then political ecology still cannot endorse Marx and Engels' teleology and in the final chapter it is argued why such coercive modes of discourse are counterproductive.

The position of political ecology on the question of teleology is that it is entirely possible — even probable — that the macroprocesses under way will end peremptorily in the very near future in the radical curtailment of the capacity of the biosphere to support human life. But the route which such a scenario might take is unlikely to be foreclosed even yet and the possibility is still there to transform society to obviate this scenario altogether. The possibilities for human societies and culture in the future are manifold and whilst, as Marx would have it, our actions are to a degree circumscribed — there are, that is, only a discrete number of paths which we can follow out of our present predicament —there is, nevertheless, a vital dimension of conscious decision-making that will go into determining what kind of future, if any, will be available to our descendants. Political ecology is above all about maximising the coherence and effectiveness of the decisions which we are able to make in the immediate future with respect to the salvation of the biosphere.

Most literature referring to itself as social evolutionary is involved almost exclusively with the grand overview and more specifically with the main stages of development and hence with times which, to the man-in-the-street, seem very distant indeed. Many of the anthropologists who are developing these arguments (for it is they who have made this their disciplinary niche) are in the main very close in spirit to political ecology, being acutely aware of the apocalyptically destructive tendencies of our society and pointing to the manifest benefits of the kinds of mutualism which was practised by 'primitive' societies as possessing essential lessons for us today. But this mode of argument makes no effective engagement with the common understanding of the immediate social process.

As discussed earlier in this chapter, the analysis of current social process in the framework of social evolution is very considerably more contentious than any argument derived from the analysis of distant times or places. It is in this context that we see the majority of historians who concern themselves with the past few hundred years of European history — and in particular analyses of events within living memory — subscribing to a rather narrow set of politically conservative, liberal or social democratic views and kept in line by the censorship role of the professional fraternity of historians and their academic masters. In so far as any distance from the immediately descriptive and functionalist explanation is allowed, this falls into the framework of liberal meliorativism. It is notable how the influence of Marxism in historiography has been overwhelmingly one of simply extending the scope of hopes for melioration and (essentially liberal) freedom of movement and expression to a wider segment of the population; the notion of social transformation within the kind of forthright evolutionary framework with which Marx and Engels concerned themselves has been all but squeezed out of the intellectual arena. The massive exegetical debates about the interpretation of the minutiae of Marxism which continue in the interstices of academia are of very little value to political ecology, having little possible bearing on the vital issue of effective praxis. Of more interest are the debates on social and economic structure for although they have also lost their orientation towards social change of the kind which political ecology believes to be essential, they nevertheless do address some very relevant background issues.

But before engaging with these debates, it is useful to take one step back and look at what serious, structured views are in currency with respect to the question of social evolutionary mechanisms and scenarios in our own time. If we brush over the approach to evolution, epitomised in the work of Teilhard de Chardin (1964), which takes religion as its centre of concern, as having relatively little to say about the material side of social and political structural change, then we can roughly divide modern evolutionist concerns into those emphasising technology and technical questions and those emphasising social variables.

On the technological side we have pessimists and optimists. The extreme case of technological pessimism — and we might do well to include here the 'exterminist' and Frankfurt School 'technological rationality' arguments — is that elaborated by Ellul (1964) which leaves no room for active resistance: technological evolution has a dynamic of its own which works against human interests but which precludes organised or conscious social intervention. However, there are also technological pessimists (Jungk (1954, 1977); Winner (1977); Norman (1981)) who are concerned to warn us of the problem of the technological domination of current social life — and who note the serious lack of coherent analysis of the relationship between recent technical and social change (Winner (1986)) — but who allow for the possibility of social and political intervention to bring technics within the ambit of social control (Elliott and Elliott (1976); Harper and Boyle (1976); Boyle et al. (1977); Collingridge (1980)). Many of these authors have been or have become associated with the most concerted attempts of the ecology movement to develop and promote alternative technologies and lifestyles (eg Boyle and Elliott; also Jungk and Müllert (1980)). Against this we can contrast the technological optimists (Toffler (1981); Simon and Kahn (1984)). In so far as problems are acknowledged with respect to recent technological evolution, these latter analyses are insistently sanguine about both the capability and the probability of future technical measures to improve the human lot. These do not acknowledge the environmentalist problematic — indeed Simon and Kahn's compendium is an explicit attack on environmentalism.

Turning to the question of socially-defined futures, it is useful initially to define a three-way division of views: liberal meliorative, Marxist and anarchist-Utopian. Liberal meliorativism can be seen at once to be the dominant 'common sense' vision of the age which is, however, largely unanalytical with respect to the future of society. Resulting from an intellectual culture that has actively resisted social structural change, it continues to be unthinkingly ethnocentric and embody at least hopes of continued meliorative change into the future. But in so far as it fears that these might be unrealistic — and the spread of environmental concerns is fuelling such an outlook — liberalism has no analytical machinery with which to approach the question of social change, demanded by these concerns, in a structured manner. The technological optimists join the social ideologues of an optimistic liberal future such as Daniel Bell (1973) in attempting to assert that a realistic future is possible — either by a return to fundamental liberal roots or through concerted government intervention at ever more comprehensive levels — without the necessity of fundamental change in social structure and process.

The dominant alternative social vision is that of Marxism which, as noted by Drucker quoted above, has come to influence and orient thinking across the complete spectrum of analyses about the social present and especially concerning possible social futures. Because of this interaction and because there have developed many interpretations as to what is salient about the Marxist scenario, it becomes difficult to make any summary pronouncements that will not be seen as contentious by one tendency or other. It is nevertheless necessary to enter this field of debate in order to be clear as to the suppositions against which the critique which follows, and which is continued into the final chapter, is conducted.

The heart of Marx and Engels' vision about the future can already be seen in the two quotations provided on the immediately preceding pages. Although later in life they acknowledged evidence to the effect that pre-civil societies were mutualistic, it was indicative of their preoccupations that the opening sentence of the Communist Manifesto should exclaim that: 'The history of all hitherto existing societies is the history of class struggles.' The future, as the above quotation from Engels clearly indicates, is about the abolition of social rank differentiation as such and the instrument of this process of abolition would be the industrial working class. As Marx (1975: 256) wrote at a very early stage in the development of his analysis:

So where is the *positive* possibility of German emancipation? *This is the answer.* In a formation of a class with *radical chains*, a class of civil society which is not a class of civil society, a class which is the dissolution of all classes .... A sphere which cannot emancipate itself without emancipating itself from — and thereby emancipating — all the other spheres of society, which is, in a word, the *total loss* of humanity and which can therefore redeem itself only through the *total redemption of humanity*. The dissolution of society as a particular class is the *proletariat*. The proletariat is only beginning to appear in Germany as a result of the emergent *industrial* movement.

The concern of Marxist analysts and activists has thus been to discern and promote awareness of signs and mechanisms that would indicate and facilitate the development of consciousness amongst the industrial working class of their central role in achieving emancipatory ends not only for themselves but for society as a whole; as it were to promote the enlightenment and organisation of working class interests as a preliminary to the abolition of particular interests as such. Although this project might be interpreted in various ways by modern Marxists — and there are many statements within the copious writings of Marx and Engels that allow for different interpretations — in the final analysis a Marxist is only such if she or he remains faithful to the notion of the primacy of the working class as particular interest and by whatever definition (and in modern discourse this has been reduced down to the term 'social subject'!), to bear the responsibility for transforming society as a whole into a mutualistically organised entity.

The anarchist-Utopian vision of the future is also one that is concerned to establish mutualistic social relations. Since before and during Marx's time, anarchists have presented alternative routes to that put forward by Marx and Engels and have also been concerned not only with the process of establishing the ground rules for mutualistic society but also of defining some of the content of such a society: process and content cannot, for anarchists, be so rigorously separated out. Thus although the self-activity of the working class — most evident in the turn of the century anarcho-syndicalist movement and the early stages of the Spanish Civil War — has always been seen as important by anarchists, they have also been concerned with the actual machinery of operating mutualistic society. This can be seen not only in the schemes of the Utopian socialists and Kropotkin (1974, 1985), but also in modern anarchism. Thus it is that although many of the critics of technology discussed above are influenced by modern Marxism, they are much more clearly associated with the modern anarchist movement.

Having sketched the main positions with regard to consideration of future society in general, it is necessary to engage in a critique of the Marxist approach to the future as a preliminary measure to a more extensive discussion of Utopianism as representing an important dimension of the approach of political ecology to the question of the achievement of a sustainable future society. There are three points which need airing here. These are: what is the role of class in preventing or promoting the achievement of egalitarian mutualistic society? what can we say that is of use about periodisation of recent history and, perhaps, about the future? and what status should we attribute to the construction of Utopian models?

Concerning the question of class, it must be categorically stated at the outset that ours is a hierarchically differentiated society with different levels of privilege, freedom and access to power, wherein very extensive proportions of the population of all societies are necessarily limited in the control which they can exercise individually or socially over essential areas of their lives by these status structures. Furthermore, as is argued more extensively in the final chapter, this situation is fundamentally problematic to the implementation of any principles of political ecology. However, at risk of stating the obvious, it must be acknowledged that Marx's scenario of class polarisation and immiseration of an ever growing working class has not come to pass and is not in immediate prospect: it is at the initial years of their creation that the working class exhibit revolutionary potential (Mann (1973: 41); Kumar (1976); Abercrombie et al. (1984: 167)) and managed welfare capitalism in the 20th century has put the possibility of the materialisation of Marx's scenario far behind us. The lumpen Marxist notion, expressed in so many analyses of the ecology movement, that because it is not a movement of the working class it is therefore somehow of diminished value is completely meaningless. Mass immiseration — already clearly visible in some Third World countries — may become a generalised phenomenon during the next century but rather as a prelude to the extinction of humanity rather than a revolution to establish an egalitarian, self-regulating society. Class analysis — including analysis of racial, sexual and any other exploitative social structuration processes and also including an understanding of how middle and ruling classes function — is an important dimension of consciousness of social process in general which political ecology must develop. But, as Uwe Becker (1989: 152) put it: 'The lines of class demarcation are also always determined by the purpose of the analysis...' The complexity of modern society is part of the problem which political ecology has to confront and solve and an understanding of how it works and the weak points around which relevant transformation might be built are vital.

There are, of course, all manner of views regarding the most appropriate way to periodise modern history. Marxism separates off bourgeois capitalism from feudalism and then concerns itself little with the interstices of capitalism in that this is assumed in most essentials to be of a piece, to be transformed only following proletarian revolution; nevertheless, some expositions have looked at the cycles of capitalism from an economic standpoint (Baren and Sweezy (1968: Ch.8); Mandel (1978: Ch.4)). What is of particular interest to political ecology in respect of periodisation is points at which Utopian speculation and experiment have arisen and the new ways that have been devised in order to suppress these Utopian aspirations. Elsewhere I have taken a longer view over this question (Atkinson (1991)); here it is only necessary to look in a little detail at the structure of the most recent phase. But a preliminary word is in order with regard to the general process in question and about modes of social and political control.

The dynamic nature of post-medieval European society has led to periodic crises in political power relations and hence in the perceived legitimacy of political authority (Habermas (1976)). In the course of these crises contending social interests have rejected the pre-existing rules of social peace and attempted ideologically and practically to reconstruct the social and cultural organism. In many cases the most radical elements have attempted to abolish the very framework of antagonistic social relations through a wide range of Utopian proposals and strategies. In each case they have failed and the essential heart of the system has been held in place and a new political and social settlement has been built around it. However, the mechanisms used to preserve the core ideological, social and political structures have changed radically over time, with the effect that different settlements have created what amounts to a different kind of society and certainly a different relationship between society and nature; these have involved much more than new technological and productive initiatives which are the focus of Marxist periodisation within capitalism.

Classically there have been two main mechanisms holding antagonistic social relations in place. Religion — and as is pointed out in the following chapter, aesthetics as well — has provided both justification for prima facie unjust arrangements and other-worldly compensation for exploitation in this world. Where this has failed, repression has provided disincentive and, in the breach, violent restraint upon attempts to achieve redress in the here-and-now. Social caste built these elements into the social interstices of many pre-capitalist societies and Monarchy represents the heart, and the most tenacious residue, of such arrangements extending, as effective ideological restraint on Utopian aspirations, even throughout the development of modern bourgeois capitalism.

Bourgeois capitalism, inventive in its means of self-defence as it has been in other aspects of its self-development, introduced new mechanisms. What is of some interest is the way that different societies within the same general system have, per force, adopted significantly different *combinations* of measures. The relative lack of repression at home, which has often been admired as the hallmark of the British manifestation of bourgeois capitalism, has been achieved in particular through the development of a rich and varied process of 'externalisation'. The settlement of religious dissenters and traders in America; settlement in Northern Ireland and Cromwell's Irish expeditions; the opening up of plantation economies in the West Indies and Asia and the plunder of India; the capture of the slave trade; the system of 'transport' of 'criminals' to Australia; the development of nationalism and jingoism directly as methods of social control and the use of war abroad as a means to achieve social unity at home. Other modern societies have also used this technique though not as effectively or consistently.

The point was to open up possibilities whereby those elements of society who felt dissatisfied with the political settlement at home could, and would be encouraged or forced to, change their social status by acquiring dominion over others and acquiring property and wealth at the expense of others. This effectively undermined social tensions and put off social confrontation and by this means successfully defended the essential structure of ideology and political power at home. In the end it proved sufficient merely to introduce an underclass into the society (the Irish, the '*Gastarbeiter*') to give the lower classes an impression that they were not as badly off as they might be. Perhaps the processes of suburbanisation and above all the frantic travel mania of the late 20th century, with its obsession with automobiles, should also be viewed as yet another manifestation of this flight from — or safety valve with respect to — social engagement. But the generation of an 'enemy' without and the regularity with which wars have been fomented particularly by the United States — but the British polity has also been partial to this — can clearly be seen as a means not merely, as Marxist analyses have seen it, to justify the 'permanent arms economy' but also, and arguably more importantly, as a means to securing social and political cohesion around existing ruling interests in a contradictory situation of the ongoing 'modernising' destruction of any more tangible sense of community.

So from the point of view of political ecology, focusing upon the changing arrangement of mechanisms of social and political control and legitimation, how can we usefully understand recent periodisation? Since the mid 1980s it has become common currency to acknowledge that we find ourselves situated in some kind of 'post-industrial', 'postmodern' transition. Whilst this has been anticipated by incidental analyses as far back as the late 1960s (MacIntyre (1968); Touraine (1974)), and there is some consensus on certain aspects of this 'postmodern condition', little attempt has yet been made to formulate a useful analytical framework that might help lend perspective on the meaning of this situation within a broader social evolutionary framework. One of the problems with respect to understanding the present from a Marxist perspective is the way that it has lived in anticipation of a particular scenario emerging and thus has failed to attempt any very useful structural understanding of the era through which it could be deemed to be the leading political ideology. From the mid 19th century to the present unfolded like a telescope becoming ever more extended but under the assumption that the only real changes worth analysing were those relating to economic structures. Simple bourgeois capitalism became welfare capitalism which became organised capitalism and then late capitalism and eventually advanced welfare capitalism and even disorganised capitalism! Of course neither conservatism nor liberalism can at any time admit the fact that significant dimensions of society do in practice change. One of the most extraordinary phenomena of recent political history is the utter transformation of what is meant by the term 'liberalism', in the desparate attempts of liberal political interests to avoid relegation to irrelevance, from the political ideology of forthright *laissez-faire* individualism to pioneer of state intervention and welfarism, without ever admitting that it had undergone this change; today we see institutionalised socialism traversing this territory in reverse!

From the point of view of political ecology it becomes evident that a momentous revolution happened throughout the world of European culture between 1880 and 1920. (I have discussed the issues involved in more detail in Atkinson (1991).) European culture of the 19th century was qualitatively fundamentally different from that of the 20th century. Whilst we can certainly see in retrospect the seeds of the 20th century developing in the 19th and also the lingering of aspects of 19th century culture into the 20th; whilst we can find substantial variations in the particular form of development of 20th-century culture from one country to another with respect to structures of social regulation: in general there is a great divide between an era in which economic and political control were incipiently unstable and dependent upon religion and overt authoritarianism and one in which control has been exerted primarily through the orchestrated extension of welfare measures and the constant increase in material wellbeing made possible through organised industrial development. The putative great divide between Soviet communism and American liberal democracy was, by contrast with 19th-century culture, nothing but a massive smoke screen behind which a common culture — which, following Lipietz, we can refer to as a whole as 'social democracy'[2] — unfolded. It is necessary to add that the current postmodern 'transition' in which we find ourselves is far from wide open: the assumptions of social democracy, of an increasing flow of material wellbeing which has become the expectation of the broad mass of Europeans and one which has lost in large measure any sense of the process whereby this requires conscious management, not only persist but have taken on dimensions bordering on the religious. To political ecology this is immensely problematic because the continuation for much longer of this 'transition' in its current form may well turn it into a transition to extinction unless a feasible and truly sustainable 'next stage' is rapidly developed and implemented.

Finally concerning the question of the status of Utopianism: we can say with some certainly that one of the major effects that Marxism has had in dominating the radical wing of European enlightenment politics during the 20th century is the suppression of Utopianism. Radical politics has, under these circumstances, been an almost entirely discursive milieu concerning itself with process and leaving the field of imagery and the aestheticisation of social and political life almost entirely to the forces of reaction. Political ecology, in the tradition of Utopian socialism, is concerned to build the future out of the present in real terms, not following an instrumental revolutionary process. This being the case, it is necessary to discuss at some length the way in which Utopianism can and should become integral to the process of social and political analysis, thus recovering the origins of modern social analysis in Utopian socialism and correcting what amounts to the massively distorting influence of the battle between Marxism and its enemies.

Utopia: the end of history

Marx and Engels wrote as if Utopia would imminently come into being via the *deus ex machina* of history and as if the content of Utopia could only be of one kind[3]. Unfortunately, as argued in the foregoing section, the historic cannot be legitimately understood in terms of teleology and nor does the history of Utopian thinking immediately lead to one solution. It is therefore not merely the *process* of precipitating Utopia that requires thought and engagement but also the *content* of Utopia. The following analysis therefore looks at some concepts of Utopia which have arisen historically with a view to laying out options for debate. It should be noted, however, that the debate in question is not one simply to satisfy the intellect. It therefore looks to the practical and political in preference to the literary, conjectural and spiritual, without wishing to suppress these important aspects of Utopia from the longer term debate; the intention here is to give priority and set initial terms of reference for a debate on the practical aspects.

Through much of the 20th century, those with Utopian aspirations largely fell in behind the working class movement, relinquishing attempts at any very coherent formulation of Utopia as goal; a significant degree of the blame for this can be attributed to Marx and Engels whose relationship to Utopianism is well summarised by Ruth Levitas (1990). Indeed, it is necessary to return to the early 19th century to find richer material that might form the basis of a more structured debate. Nevertheless, the notion of Utopia never entirely died and much of the deeper discussion today starts from the analysis which Karl Mannheim (1936) put forward in the 1920s. As noted in earlier chapters, Mannheim conjectured that there are two basic kinds of political ideas: ideology and the Utopian. Ideology constitutes those ideas which contribute to the preservation of existing power relations and Utopian ideas are those which aim to destroy them. His concern was with the necessity of Utopianism to the health of society in the face of the rise of fascism. He illustrated, by reference to Utopian movements of the past, how Utopian thought and action has constantly arisen to effect the renewal of society. Nevertheless, it became evident within his analysis that in practice the two types of ideas cannot be self-evidently classified, self-conscious Utopian attempts as often ending up contributing to the maintenance of existing social and political arrangements as overturning them.

In recent years there has been a revival both in Utopian thinking and practice, and in analytical approaches to the construction of Utopian aims and strategies, which has brought out the multifaceted nature of Utopian thought and practice. The following paragraphs provide an initial typology in terms of four distinct components, derived from the detailed analysis of English 16th and 17th-century Utopias carried out by J. C. Davis (1980) (though it should be noted that Davis' conclusions are relatively unsympathetic to a consistent Utopian ideology of the type elaborated later in this chapter).

Firstly: Utopia is above all about the fulfilment of the desirable life for everyone in the here-and-now (Levitas (1990)). The classical myth of Arcadia, involving a life of eternal love and beauty (of a kind portrayed by William Morris (1891) in *News from Nowhere*), and the medieval myth of Cockayne (Morton (1969)), involving a more earthy conception of direct sensual pleasures, both describe the ultimate aim of Utopia. Whilst writings in these genres might act in the short term as consolation and hence deflect from the construction of Utopia as lived reality, nevertheless, any Utopian scheme which does not promise pleasurable ends is not worth considering.

Secondly: Utopianism necessarily has to confront the material aspects of life in a coherent way. Rules, laws, administrative arrangements, productive processes and technology, social health, welfare and education, land use and architecture, and other functions besides need to be considered. This may take the form of a radical constitution or manifesto or a more literary or analytical form, but in the end, such constructs are an essential aspect of Utopianism proper.

Thirdly: whilst the 'there' of Utopia might constitute a moving target in view of the possibilities opened up by the realities of today, it remains vital that consideration be given to the connection between now and then. The tradition out of which this side of Utopian thought has evolved, as a facet of progressivism and ideas of social evolution, is the Judaeo-Christian apocalyptic, already discussed earlier in this chapter and elaborated upon in the next. Of course it was this aspect — how to get there from here — that became the exclusive concern of Marxism and Marxists, who have always accused Utopians of being unrealistic on account of their emphasis of the 'there' and hence their apparent other-worldliness or lack of engagement with the difficulties of changing the direction of the present[4]. Clearly Utopianism needs to develop strategies to get from here to there in as serious a fashion as it attempts to formulate the structure of Utopia itself.

Finally: there remains a question as to whether reform is compatible with Utopianism. Certainly there has in the past been close collaboration between Utopians and reformists — though often of a more or less furtive nature, wherein reformers remain suspicious of any but limited goals and Utopians attempt to radicalise the reformers. Certainly most of the radical demands of the Levellers, Tom Paine and Condorcet were implemented through reform (in particular in the form of social democracy). But, as outlined below, the core concerns of Utopianism have, hitherto, stubbornly remained beyond the sights of reformers.

Once it is accepted that history is essentially made by human agency, as has been argued in the foregoing section of this chapter, then the way is opened up to Utopian speculation and design. Conversely, experimenting with Utopian ideas and activities relativises history and the future for others. Indeed, as Goodwin and Taylor (1982: 21–28) make plain, the future is a more or less covert battle ground to which few concerted schools of social theory do not lay claim. Conscious Utopianism merely raises the level of consciousness of the battle. Furthermore, whilst social theory remains largely the esoteric province of academe, it is literature and other aesthetic media which are far more effective in broadcasting the underlying notions to society at large.

For instance these are some of the mechanisms through which the battle has been joined. Hobbes used a hypothetical past to justify the present with the aim of preventing change and Rousseau used a different hypothetical past to criticise the present in favour of change. Modern liberal theorists such as Rawles and Nozick use an idealised present to justify the actual present. *Gulliver's Travels* and Samuel Butler's *Erewhon* used inversions of the present to open up present arrangements to criticism. On the other hand Huxley's *Brave New World* and Orwell's *1984* present worse futures that justify the defence of the present (Kumar (1987)).

Of course the Utopian novel has again and again popularised social theory aimed at change, as in William Morris's *News from Nowhere* and Edward Bellamy's *Looking Backward* which, through the Garden Cities movement and the suburbanisation bandwagon of the 1920s and 1930s had an incalculable effect on lifestyles and environment in the UK, albeit not perhaps that of which the authors would have approved. Today science fiction provides a framework through which social theories are soft-sold to very extensive readerships. The genre remains on the whole, by implication, conservative of existing arrangements but there are also widely read Utopian contributions such as Ursula LeGuin's (1975) *The Dispossessed* and, more seriously, Marge Piercy's (1979) *Woman on the Edge of Time*, as well as Ernest Callenbach's (1978) more directly Utopian *Ecotopia*.

There is no guarantee that any one mode of entering the battle will be more effective than any other and thus aspiring participants can only be enjoined to be inventive. Nevertheless, in the end there are many hard, technical questions that need to be confronted which, in the first instance, are inaccessible to all but a narrow public. Whilst Mannheim's rejection of literature as representing a genuine form of Utopianism might be called into question, nevertheless it must be agreed that if the debate remains at this level, short of a more coherent engagement with the broad spectrum of social and economic functions — and here the massive oeuvre of Ernst Bloch (1986) springs immediately to mind — then it cannot be deemed a serious contribution towards the solution to the kind of problematic with which this analysis is concerned.

Reviewing the history of overt and conscious Utopian thought in Europe (Mumford (1922); Berneri (1982); Negley and Patrick (1971); Morton (1969); Manuel and Manuel (1979)), it becomes evident that, whilst key elements of a more permanent solution to the 'human condition' recur, there has nevertheless been a distinct evolution of Utopian thought. This can be traced back to the dialectical role which Utopianism has played in relation to existing social reality and preoccupations. Thus the emphasis with respect to what is important in Utopia has changed radically despite a discernable common set of goals.

Coherent Utopian ideas and strategies first emerged in modern Europe in the 16th century. Ancient Greece and Rome had produced what has often been deemed to be Utopian thought (Finley (1967); Ferguson (1975)) — Plato's *Republic* is often included in anthologies of Utopian thought — but this lacked most of the elements which we would today consider to be essential dimensions of the Utopian (Kumar (1991)) and furthermore, with the fall of Rome, Europe came under the iron ideological grip of Christianity which fundamentally denied the possibility of any this-worldly solution to the human condition. Norman Cohn (1970) has shown that the thousand years following the fall of Rome saw innumerable millenarian attempts and movements, including peasant rebellions and migrations of truly massive proportions. However, although some historians have put forward the notion that some of these possessed an important political dimension — for instance, the European upheavals of the late 14th century, including the English Rebellion of 1381, have been seen by some as the beginnings of secular revolution — the consensus is that Christianity, with its insistence on other-worldly rewards rather than any possibility of a this-worldly social and political solution, undermined the possibility of any coherent Utopianism emerging.

Although ancient Greek and Roman literature had been seeping into European intellectual life from at least the 10th century, it was only in the 16th century that this emerged as something other than an adjunct and adjustment to Christian teaching. As discussed in more detail in the next chapter, the

Renaissance, born of greatly increased economic activity centred upon rich city states and a new capitalist class with no immediate allegiance to the Church, rediscovered independent secular thought. Initially this involved simply absorbing classical thought, but it soon gave way to independent speculation on nature — as the birth of modern science — and society. The ideological crisis which this precipitated resulted in the Reformation and then the Counter-Reformation. This ferment initiated both the first clearly secular attempts at Utopian thought — Thomas More's (1965) *Utopia* first appeared in 1516 — and Utopian movements. The German Peasant Rebellions around 1525, and Thomas Münzer's role in these (Mannheim (1936: 190ff)), and then the extraordinary Commune of Münster of 1534–35 (Cohn (1970: 256ff)), produced key features of what are seen as modern, secular Utopian social movements, even though they remained strongly circumscribed by Christian millenarian beliefs.

The 16th and 17th centuries saw numbers of crises that produced Utopian movements, such as that in southern Italy at the end of the 16th century which produced Campanella's 'City of the Sun' and, above all, the mid 17th-century English Revolution which produced a massive outburst of Utopian thought and social movements. It is possible to interpret this as having constituted a fulcrum within a steady process of secularisation of Utopianism. Thus, social change, although still seen as being achievable in one momentous convulsion, emerged as implementable in the political sphere without any other-worldly intervention. But it was initially seen simply as a new place, or way of organising life, rather than a more complex result of on-going change.

It was in the course of the 18th-century French Enlightenment that rationalistic thought on the possibilities for social change began to see Utopia as being not just a potential goal, but the necessary result of a social evolutionary process. The schemes of Turgot and Condorcet, which looked back across history and saw a coherent evolutionary process from which, in the future, a better world would inevitably emerge, were constructed in parallel with a continued refinement of idealised futures such as those of Morelly and Mably.

The French Revolution encouraged attempts to turn speculation into practice and the Industrial Revolution transformed the possibilities for Utopia as a life of relative ease. The first half of the 19th century produced multifarious attempts at both Utopian theory and practice both in Britain and France; it is above all the French Utopian socialists who have provided the richest reservoir of Utopian ideas relevant to the recent Utopian revival (Manuel (1962)). Seen from our current predicament, much of the speculation and activity seems naïve. However, it has yielded both the foundations of much of current unquestioned ideology — Saint Simon must be acknowledged as 'grandfather' to both Marxist and non-Marxist sociology — as well as a massive store of experimental social conjecture and practice. Indeed, given the success with which Utopianism was inhibited from 1848 until very recently, modern Utopians may find that there is still much to be learned from the writings and practices of the early 19th-century French Utopians.

In general, the early 19th-century Utopians attempted to combine a social evolutionary scheme with an account of what the Utopian end product should include. The universal failure of the revolutions that broke out right across Europe in 1848 (in England this was the final attempt of the Chartist movement to make an impression on the political process) signalled a retreat of Utopianism, or rather a shift almost entirely into its millenarian manifestation. Whilst Marxism became the dominant strand of Utopianism extending beyond the frontiers of Europe to become one of the 'world ideologies' of our day, it is notable that other Utopian streams, such as anarcho-syndicalism, adopted a similarly 'time-dominated' model of change, focused almost entirely on *means* with only a perfunctory concern for *ends*.

It is useful at this point to summarise the main points of difference and debate between the various 19th century Utopian schemes. What attitude to take to nascent industrialism was an important issue which finds resonance today in the ecology movement. There was also divergence over the issue of private property with Godwin and Saint Simon accepting it and Owen and Cabet rejecting it (of course for Marx the whole problematic of 'alienation' revolved around private property and its abolition under communism). From the late 19th century on, radical movements came largely to accept some form of common ownership or social sanction over the private use of property. The role of religion in Utopia was a further issue producing divergent views. However, across the 19th century, Christianity was on the retreat and although there have continued to be some attempts at radical Christian reformulation (such as Anthroposophy) and the adoption of Oriental religion, Utopian movements on the whole increasingly adopted a trenchantly secular stance. The degree to which this secularisation is, in fact, free from mythological and ideological content of mainly Christian origin is further discussed in the following chapter.

The distinction between revolutionary and evolutionary (or piecemeal) routes to Utopia was less important in the early 19th century than later: Owenism, for instance, was prepared to adopt any mechanism that might show promise. Revolutionism became dominant only after the decanting of Utopianism into 'secular millenarianism' after 1848. Although Saint Simon, and of course Marx, were predominantly concerned with the metamorphosis of the state, on the whole, the 19th century Utopians envisaged a radical decentralisation of power to the community and focused attention on the structure and function of small scale communities. Finally, and centrally, there was, amongst 19th-century Utopian models and movements, a tension between democratic and authoritarian modes of political decision-making (Fourier proposed a precise reformulation of social class). Although Godwin and Owen were concerned to eliminate class and gender discrimination, on the whole it is during the 20th century that this concern has come to dominate Utopian thought.

This brief review of 19th-century Utopian thought should make it clear that a single form of Utopia cannot be taken for granted as the outcome of some teleological historical process. Utopia involves choices. But in the end it has to present a consistent and workable set of ideas and proposals. By reference to the historical debate and the outcome of radical movements over the past few centuries, but particularly by reference to more recent debate, a conceptual outline of Utopia has been produced which is set out in the following paragraphs. This provides background for the development of the principles of political ecology with which the last chapter of this book is concerned.

Utopia is not a disorganised, chaotic world like the one we live in, but is defined by a relatively simple, controllable and controlled order — political ecologists refer to this in terms of a 'steady state' or of a 'sustainable world'. It is governed by rules, perhaps even laws, but these are not determined or controlled by lawyers (professionals) but by an altogether more participative social process. Utopia is a communitarian world without commerce or money; all but the immediate property of the individual is owned and managed in common. The means of management are debatable — experiments include co-operativism, community business and notions of electronic systems to facilitate distribution — but these are details rather than principles.

Utopia is egalitarian in the anarchist sense of possessing no leaders and no social hierarchy. Modern ecologists, feminists, communitarians and so on are sensitised to the question of leadership even if they have not already found ways of dispensing with it. Much of the preoccupation of the more concerted Utopian attempts today is with devising and implementing egalitarian decision-making mechanisms and social relations. Utopia is concerned with minimising the distinction between means and ends, and to structure life directly upon the sensual and the aesthetic. The instrumentality and alienation of our existing world gives way to a world where love and beauty guide the social process.

Utopian programmes are centrally concerned with devising the correct structure for education and health. Utopian education must be a socialisation process which encourages the direct satisfaction of individual needs whilst simultaneously enhancing the social whole. The aspiration to promote good health becomes the basis for devising much of the system of production in Utopia. Work in Utopia is not a means to any end but an end in itself: the fulfilment of creative capacities. Even Utopians writing in the era before industrialisation remarked of the possibility of radically reducing the total number of hours worked and, with modern technology, virtually everything could be automated. The main decisions with regard to production in Utopia revolve around what tasks we wish to dispense with and what tasks we wish to continue to do manually, and then to organise life accordingly.

Utopia is, relative to today's social norm, a frugal society, but one which is efficient in terms of the way it manages resources. There is no longer any social call for conspicuous consumption and the proliferation of individual belongings. Nature and the things of the earth are treated with respect and modesty, and society is seen as an integral part of the metabolism of natural systems. Whilst the elevation of 'ecology' to a key position may appear as a new aspect of Utopianism following the dissolute abuse of nature by modern industrialism and consumerism, in fact respect for nature has always constituted an important principle of Utopian thought and action.

Utopia promotes the appropriate use of science and technology. Whilst critics of Utopia have often accused Utopians of being reactionary in turning away from science and technology, this has almost always amounted to misrepresentation, as often as not intentional. Utopians have generally embraced the promotion of certain kinds of scientific knowledge but have rejected specific technologies in favour of alternative technologies to be developed. The centre of gravity of Utopian thought focuses on the arrangement of the physical environment. This includes the size and structure of urban areas and the arrangement and use of the land. An important strand throughout the history of Utopia is the aspiration to abolish the antithesis between town and country.

To conclude this analysis of Utopia and Utopianism, it is useful to return to the question of 'ideological struggle' with which this chapter began and to focus on the opposition which Utopians face in their attempts to formulate and launch their ideas into the wider society today. A number of recent analysts of Utopia have remarked on the relative poverty of modern Utopian thought and George Kateb (1963) therefore enquired as to who or what are the enemies of Utopia. The conclusion is that, although there exists an appearance of conflict today between three well-articulated political ideologies, conservatism, liberalism and socialism, in practice *all* of these oppose Utopian thought. Recent analyses, such as that of Levitas (1990), that see Utopianism merely as an adjunct to liberal, Marxist — or even conservative — political outlooks are committing a profound error in that they are likely to hinder the development of Utopianism of the kind which they ostensibly support.

Conservatism is clearly opposed to Utopianism above all because it is against any kind of change in basic social relations. Its political style is anti-intellectual and it opposes Utopianism by proscribing any structured debate about the way in which political life functions, let alone how it could or should function. When conservatism appears to adopt structured political programmes, these in general address issues other than those which they are designed to defend or promote; a successful conservative strategy is one which uses concepts that succeed in reinforcing prejudices through society and hence consolidating adherence to existing social practices. (It has been suggested that 'New Right' attempts to re-establish conservative values be considered as a variant of Utopianism.)

If anything, liberal democracy is even more opposed to Utopianism than is conservatism: this is one of the main conclusions of Kateb and other analysts of Utopia's enemies (Goodwin and Taylor (1982: Ch.4)). The roots of this opposition lay in the liberal dislike of any structured view of the future (this came out strongly in the discussion in the foregoing section on social evolutionism). This is seen as restricting the potentialities not only for society in general but for all individuals. As the freedom of the individual is the foundation of all liberal thought, so Utopianism is seen as necessarily authoritarian and assumed by many liberals to be totalitarian. Liberal ideologues are generally blind to the fact that freedom for some, in any social context, results in unfreedom for others. They disbelieve in the possibility of arriving at mutually acceptable social solutions to problems that fully satisfy human needs and insist, instead, that 'human nature' is inherently wayward and suspicious of the motivations and aspirations of others. Although, politically, liberals are assumed to be tolerant of others, this tolerance reaches its limits where it meets solidaristic and communitarian ways of thinking and acting.

Earlier it has been remarked how Marxist and related forms of modern socialism de-emphasised structured thought about Utopia at the expense of strategies to promote revolution. 'Actually existing socialist' societies, as Rudoph Bahro termed the states of Eastern Europe, inherited this Marxist attitude and put forward the notion that they are in the process of realising Utopia (communist society) without deeming it necessary to attempt any definition of what this might mean. That Bahro was imprisoned for publishing an attempt at a Utopian programme for Eastern Europe indicates the degree to which such modes of thought have been not merely de-emphasised but proscribed within socialism, as generally understood in conventional political debate.

It would be nice to think that Utopianism involves a mechanism that any political ideology would want to adopt in order to make the process of forging a better — or indeed any viable — future a more rational one. The sad conclusion, however, is that Utopianism represents one competing political ideology among many. Although it may appear quite senseless to Utopians that society reproduces so much frustration and pain, generation after generation, in a situation where the possibilities for resolution seem so close at hand, in the end it is necessary to accept that opposition is real and powerful and, therefore, to focus not only on what we want to achieve but also how this opposition is to be overcome.

As a political ideology Utopianism is anti-individualistic and therefore, in the political sense, illiberal. It is concerned with achieving a social system which is free *from* want and *from* the frustrations and indignities of a class-divided, racist and sexist society with its harrowing extremities of alienation. Utopianism is in an essential sense apolitical, concerned with ending the social debate and, indeed the very concept of morality. This necessarily involves severe contradictions in its confrontation with existing political ideologies, all of which rely on instrumentality — the separation of means and ends — as the basis of social cohesion and political structure. To the Utopian, if we all adopted Utopian attitudes and ways of living, then the social problematic would simply evaporate; we should remind ourselves here of Marx's words quoted earlier: 'The individual *is* the *social being*.' The fact that people manifestly do not adopt Utopian attitudes, necessitates the working out of some instrumental means to take us to Utopia. But *any* such instrumentality involves some kind of capitulation to existing political processes: history shows all too clearly how political means have a way of formulating their own ends that stubbornly remain this side of the borders of Utopia. But history also shows that society *does* change, and that aspects of yesteryear's Utopias *are* realised; and it is these rays of hope which must be grasped by Utopians as they pragmatically devise their way towards Utopian strategies. It is this process with which the final chapter of this book is primarily concerned.

A corollary to this is the fact that Utopianism is an environmentalist political ideology, that is to say that it sees the social and, beyond that, the natural environment as mediating 'human nature': humans can be many things and if Utopia is to work in the ways expected of it then it is necessary to construct it right. Existing society, with all its problematic tensions and conflicts, is the result of the natural circumstances in which it arose, together with the inertia of its own inner dynamic and structure. The social and economic 'world system', together with the apparently conflicting political ideologies within which it operates, make up a consistent and coherent whole: ideas generate practices which reinforce the ideas. But it is a system on the move: a train travelling along a particular set of tracks. Utopianism is about creating a consistent and coherent *alternative*, not only putting the train on another set of tracks, but removing the tracks completely and converting the train into another kind of apparatus altogether.

Above all, it is about the destruction of the 'world system' as such and the recreation of the centre of social gravity at a very local level. Decentralisation, as the key to much of what Utopian organisation is about, means the construction of a world which is of a scale that can be grasped by the majority of people and is controlled by them within manageable organisational systems. It is the introduction of responsibility, as a *social* attribute, into an environment where conscious decisions can be taken to actually control the general structure of social activity and its relationship with nature. It is the only political strategy that can remove the fate of humanity from the realm of faith to the realm of choice and so head off what the political ecologists, and, indeed, a growing proportion of society, increasingly see as the suicidal trajectory of existing reality.

Notes

1. Collingwood (1946: 221) wrote: "The false view of history as a story of successive events or a spectacle of changes has been so often and so authoritatively taught in late years, especially in this country, that the very meaning of the word has become debauched..."
   When Habermas (1987a) in his seminal *Knowledge and Human Interests*, separated out positivism, as the methodology practised by natural scientists, from 'historical-hermeneutic' methodology practised by historians and others in the humanities, he was pointing to the way in which natural science is used to assert control over nature but history is used to maintain social control.
2. Lipietz (1986), writing of the emergence of ecological politics, had the following to say: "En ce sens là l'alternative a les mêmes ambitions que les libéraux du XVIIIe siècle, les radicaux, ou les socialistes de naguèrs. Si, comme force politique, elle sait qu'elle ne sera jamais toute la France, elle entend proposer à tous un nouveau 'paradigme', un nouveau genre de vie en société. Je crois même que c'est le seul paradigme à opposer pour le XXIe siècle, sur les *ruines du paradigme social-démocrate*, au paradigme liberal-productiviste.... Ce modèle s'est imposé aprés 1945 sous la pression des rooseveltiens ou des sociaux-démocrates, sur la base de la défaite de l'alternative fasciste, et en rivalité avec l'alternative soviétique. Mais il a pu être géré par des forces politiques conservatrices ou démo-chrétiennes aussi bien que sociales-démocrates, avec ou sans l'appui des communistes. C'est en cela qu'il a constitué un 'paradigme hégémonique' s'imposant à tous, *tout en méritant le nom social-démocrate*." (Emphases added)
3. Searching for guidance on the shape of communist society in the works of Marx

and Engels is a notoriously disappointing exercise. On the one hand there are numerous rhetorical abstractions such as reference in *Capital*, Volume 1, (Marx (1976: 739)) to communism as 'a society in which the full and free development of every individual forms the ruling principle' or in the *Critique of the Gotha Program* (Marx (1972: 17)) where the ruling principle of 'higher phases of communist society' would be 'from each according to his (*sic*) ability, to each according to his needs'. On the other hand there are a number of vague references scattered across the writings of Marx and Engels (eg *Capital*, Volume 1 (Marx (1976: 173)), Volume 2 (Marx (1978: 390)), Volume 3 (Marx (1959: 261; 440)), *Anti-Dühring* (Engels (1976: 366))) hinting that communist society would involve a planned economy, without money, co-operatively owned and run. Little more than this appears throughout this massive oeuvre!

4. In her important discussion of the forms of social self-construction and maintenance, Mary Douglas (1973: Ch.9) came to focus upon the millenarian tendency in social movements which can become a vortex of anti-ritual that destroys *any* attempt to construct either a new set of social forms or even a means of moving practically beyond the existing forms of social structure and self-expression. Much of modern protest, from the 'ban the bomb' movement through student protest to much that has been justified by Marxism (ie a teleological assumption about social evolution and in particular the inevitability of the eventual triumph of the proletariat), has been drawn into the vortex of dysfunctional anti-ritual that not merely rejects Utopian formulation but also — perversely — accuses Utopians of being impractical.

5 A critique of enlightenment

Chapters 3 and 4 have dealt, in some detail, with the attitude with which political ecology must confront knowledge and specifically dealt with the problematic of social change in our time-dominated culture. This has contained implicit and explicit criticism of prevailing attitudes and theories with a view to creating an appropriate epistemological foundation for political ecology. This chapter initiates the ecological critique based upon this framework. The fundamental nature of the ecological critique means that there is little about existing social and cultural reality about which political ecology has nothing to say. The question is where to begin: what are the central issues out of which the critique must proceed?

Three issues are addressed in this chapter. They have been chosen by reference to the importance which they have been accorded by the existing literature of political ecology and in debates within the movement. The intention is to open up and extend existing debates by reference to the methodology presented in the foregoing chapters. Of chief concern has been to clarify the way that certain ideas have developed in European thought and how these have underpinned approaches to economic and political organisation. The emphasis has thus been upon the history of ideas. However, the way in which these ideas have been reinforced, and indeed selected, because of the ways in which they supported the cause of particular social interests, and beneath this the impact of the physical environment on the selection of ideas, has also been touched upon. It should be emphasised that the whole analytical enterprise presented in this chapter is of a tentative nature, designed to stimulate further development in research and methodology.

The three issues analysed here bear the titles science, progress and individualism. Each of these represents a concept which is, in general, highly valued by our society. And yet each of these possesses a substantial content of ideas and related activity which ecologists see as highly problematic, directly contributing to the lethal trajectory of our society. It is not a case of political ecology being anti-scientific or retrogressive or even anti-individualistic: these terms all cover extremely complex ideas and *something* is salvageable from them all. However, political ecology is concerned to unearth the problematic aspects within these concepts and the practices which they inform and to displace these with concepts which will be supportive of radically different social practices and a radically altered relationship between society and nature.

Science, as understood both generally and by mainstream 'philosophy of science', defines the main lines of modern social practice with respect to nature and it is for this reason that it takes first place in any ecological critique. The concept of progress has taken on many forms historically and today finds its most important manifestation in the idea, and more importantly in the practice of, economic growth. As political ecologists have focused much attention on the criticism of economic growth, it was therefore deemed important to contribute towards the extension and deepening of this critique within the framework developed in the foregoing analysis. Finally, the critique of individualism is addressed as a prolegomena to the development of holistic ideas and social praxis. Ecologists have made reference to this project without yet having come to grips with it in any very structured fashion. It is hoped that the critique of individualism presented here will initiate a broader debate, leading to an understanding of the human condition that is truly holistic.

Science

The key distinguishing feature of radical ecological views is the centrality given to the concept of nature and the way in which modern society uses and, above all, abuses the concrete reality which the concept describes. In investigating the wider historical background to the ecology movement and its concerns it is therefore only right that we start from this central position. The complexity of the concept 'nature' (Passmore (1980: 5n, 207)) makes it advisable to approach the subject from several angles and to build up a general picture useful to subsequent discussion rather than attempting any simple definitional analysis. Political ecology has, in fact, already adopted approaches to the subject and after scrutinising these the subsequent analysis then follows out several potentially fruitful further lines of enquiry.

The foundations of a historical awareness within the ecology movement is generally traced to a short essay published by Lynn White (1967) entitled 'The Historical Roots of Our Ecological Crisis'. Reissued in a number of anthologies (Anderson, Walt (1970); de Bell (1970); Barbour (1973)) this essay generated a very substantial debate and was described by Keith Thomas (1983: 23) as 'almost a sacred text of the ecologists'. White, who had established a position as an authority on the development of technology in medieval Europe (White (1960)), was convinced that Judaeo-Christian teaching, particularly in its Latin form, was primarily responsible for the aggressive exploitation of nature characteristic of Western European culture. Nevertheless, he also identified a 'recessive' tradition in Christianity, epitomised by Saint Francis of Assisi, which might be tapped such as to deflect current tendencies.

In practice, White's essay was simply the widest-read contribution to a debate on 'environmental ethics' which had already been under way for some years, involving primarily theologically inclined scientists and scientifically inclined theologians (Barbour (1972); Partridge (1981); Pepper (1984: 44-46); Engel and Engel (1990: 2–5)) and as the environmental movement blossomed, so the debate broadened and deepened. John Black (1970) expanded over the territory covered by White under the concept of the 'dominion of man over nature'. His Christian exegesis drew out the ambivalence of biblical references with respect to the ways in which humans should develop their relationship with nature and he then went on to exhort for the adoption of an attitude of 'stewardship' of nature which he saw as one of the strands of Christian teaching[1].

John Passmore (1980) took up the argument where Black left off and drew a number of conclusions based upon a broader reading of philosophical texts. Firstly he noted that 'Western' attitudes to nature are grounded in Greco-Christian rather than Judaeo-Christian ideas and that the radical separation of man from nature, which environmentalists saw as the cause of aggressive Western exploitation of nature, has indeed featured as a leitmotif through this intellectual tradition. However, far from being oriented towards encouraging exploitation of nature this attribute of Christian teaching was designed to effect a rejection of this world and a striving towards other-worldly ends; furthermore this separation of man from nature, Passmore noted, is by no means exclusively Christian. He concluded that modern exploitative attitudes to nature originated in the 16th-century scientific revolution rather than in antiquity.

Certain lines of criticism within this debate went further than Passmore in suggesting that Christianity merely 'created the ballpark' but not the game (Montcrief (1970)) and White (1973: 56) also went on to admit that 'the understanding of a society's value structure must be based less on what that society says about itself than what it actually does'. However, he still insisted — and this squares with Gramsci's position noted in Chapter 3 — that every culture is shaped primarily by its religion, overt or otherwise.

The problem with this debate, taken as a whole, lay in the high level of generality at which it was conducted and its discovery of religion as the source of the problem clearly related to the a priori adoption of ethics as the field of resolution. An abundance of texts have moved on from Passmore's philosophical approach and sketch, particularly with respect to 'ecophilosophy', 'deep ecology' and environmental ethics which are not further discussed here. Rather, it is deemed useful simply to cover certain limited aspects of this territory in some detail as they bear on the immediate issue of interest.

In the first place it must be stressed that ancient Judaeic and Christian texts say virtually nothing about what we, today, conceive of as nature (Barfield (1957: 111–114); Roszak (1973: Ch 4); Turner (1983: 31–47)). By contrast, the intellectual residue of ancient Greece is immensely rich in attempts to conceptualise nature. The great age of Christianity from Saint Augustine to the Renaissance was, in so far as it was interested in nature at all, concerned with assimilating ancient Greek thought, as it filtered into Western Europe from various sources, in terms of Christian concerns and terminology. With

Augustine, neo-Platonism entered Christianity, to be elaborated into a complex and contradictory cosmology termed the 'Chain of Being' (Lovejoy (1936); Koestler (1964: 87–117)) and in the 10th century a significant shift in emphasis occurred in response particularly to an influx of Aristotelian philosophy.

But intellectual effort was predominantly directed towards contemplative, theological ends with relatively tangential implications for social practice and interacting in only peripheral ways with the practical exploitation of nature (Montcrief (1970: 512)). Exploitation of nature was, of course, overwhelmingly the responsibility of the common people on the land and to a much lesser extent in the towns. There is good evidence to suggest that prior to the Reformation knowledge of Christian teaching was extremely limited amongst the common people (Thomas (1973: 189, 196)) and that their lives were given intellectual structure primarily through a complex of magical, spiritual and astrological notions and practices of predominantly pagan origin (Thomas (1973: 27–57)). Whilst the Catholic Church disapproved of such practices in theory and actively attacked them in their more aggressive manifestation (White (1967: 1206); Thomas (1973: 53)) it nevertheless interacted with them symbiotically at the level of the parish (Thomas (1973: 57)). The fact of the matter was that for the rural majority Christian teaching bore little relevance to their everyday lives whereas vernacular beliefs had grown up or been adopted in response to directly perceived needs. Indeed, such beliefs remained strong even in the 19th century and were finally overcome rather by changes in lifestyle (above all industrialisation and urbanisation) than any unmediated ideological influence (Thomas (1973: 798))[2].

There is really very little evidence that the exploitation of nature in medieval Europe was particularly aggressive or that an aggressive attitude might be peculiar to Christianity (Glacken (1967: 494)). In so far as the development of technology indicates such an aggressiveness it is necessary to point out that there is much dispute amongst historians as to when, in the course of the Middle Ages, European technological prowess came to exceed that of other complex cultures and particularly that of China (Needham (1954–1971); Landes (1969: 27)). It seems, rather, that technical advance proceeded on a piecemeal basis, encouraged or inhibited by specific local social conditions, the growth of particular trade patterns and the specific configuration of nature with which the various communities and the sub-continent as a whole were confronted (Merchant (1980: 42–68)).

Superficially, the scientific revolution seems to have thrown up a conception of nature which owes nothing to Christianity. The framework for this new conception was provided by ancient Greek science (Bacon (1960: 69); Leiss (1972: 139)) and vernacular magical and astrological traditions provided clues with respect to analytical method (Thomas (1973: 272, 770)). The Church, whilst remaining suspicious of the enterprise (White (1901); Draper (1927)), was not effective in opposing its rise and herein might appear to lie the truth with regard to the role which the Judaeo-Christian tradition played in helping to define modern attitudes to nature: it provided a permissive context (Merton (1970: 75)). However, this explains little and it is necessary to look more closely for explanation at the specific events accompanying this manifestation.

There are two important aspects to the scientific revolution which are really quite separate. Firstly, it brought into the foreground the concept of nature and a practical concern for nature which had hitherto occupied a relatively minor (or, if we consider the vernacular traditions, an underground) position in relationship to European thought as a whole. Secondly, it involved a fundamental shift in the focus of the concept of order in nature from a concern with external framework to a conviction that there exists an inner, hidden framework the discovery of which is an important human concern (Koyré (1957)). Science proved to be of relatively little practical value for some two hundred years after it had attained a position of ideological pre-eminence[3] so that simple functionalist explanations of why it should have arisen cannot be reasonably justified (Thomas (1973: 794)). However, with the marriage of science and technology in the mid 19th century, seemingly vindicating those who had from the beginning seen it as fulfilling a practical role, science attained an unassailable position of pre-eminence in the European ideological pantheon. In the form of a simplistic positivism, involving a conviction that in time not only our understanding of nature but also of society and the most inchoate of human aspirations would be reduced to sets of simple axioms and laws, science swept all attempts at philosophical critique aside to be relegated, together with religion, to the sidelines or underground of intellectual concern.

In recent years, however, a critical literature has been accumulating which has returned again and again to the events of the scientific revolution in attempts to make sense of science both as ideological process and in relation to the wider social process. This literature has been fruitful in identifying a number of positions or perspectives on the subject which it is useful to briefly summarise.

In the late 1950s Arthur Koestler (1964) published a substantial history of the Copernican and Galilean revolution in astronomy in support of an attack on the positivist notion of the triumphal march of scientific progress, concluding that science regularly takes cul-de-sacs, moves backwards and by no means moves in a straight line even when it is 'progressing'. He continued, nevertheless, to hold to the idea that science could lead to a more rational world view. About the same time, Alexandre Koyré (1957) published a history extending from Copernicus to Newton as the culmination of several previous studies on individual contributions to science. He saw the scientific revolution as having accomplished a profound change in the whole structure of European thought tantamount in one sense to a religious conversion and in another to the replacement of one fundamental aesthetic conception by another, writing (Koyré (1957: 2)) that in this process Western European man:

...lost the very world in which he was living and about which he was thinking, and had to transform and replace not only his fundamental concepts and attributes, but even the very framework of his thought.

Thomas Kuhn (1970), who built upon the analyses of Koyr, the early work of Feyerabend and others to produce what became the classic of this approach to the critique of positivism, took an even longer view of the history of the development of scientific ideas through which he expressed his notion of science developing through progressive supersession of incommensurable paradigms. It is significant that when attacked by his detractors on account of appearing to embrace relativism he insisted on asserting that he remained a convinced believer in scientific progress (Kuhn (1970: 206)).

It remained for Paul Feyerabend (1978) in the mid 1970s to cut the gordian knot and declare there not only to be no fixed criteria for scientific method but that there is no a priori justification for belief in the superiority of later scientific paradigms over earlier ones. Whilst Feyerabend gained no following amongst natural scientists his analysis nevertheless had the effect of robbing science of its totemic quality and thus allowing it to be viewed as just one aspect of the totality of social and ideological reality[4].

Several authors, including Theodore Roszak (1973), William Leiss (1972), Brian Easlea (1980), Carolyn Merchant (1980) and Fritjof Capra (1982), have moved into this analytical space and traversed yet again the events of the scientific revolution, taking with them a specific commitment to ecological — and in the case of Merchant also feminist — concerns. This ecological concern involved a view that whilst science as abstract search for knowledge might be a benign undertaking, in practice it has become a central aspect of a world dynamic which is lethal. This literature has generally acknowledged both the origins of science in the reconfiguration of pre-existing ideas (the 'history of ideas') and the significance of social and economic change as contributing to the selection of ideas and the orientation of the whole.

A common interpretation of the recent history of European attitudes to nature and the structure of our society amongst political ecologists is one involving degeneration from notions of organic, sentient unity to those of utilitarian and manipulable mechanism. In attempting to clothe this model in the material of history, Merchant (1980: 68) obscured important dialectical complexities which are worth drawing out. As has already been discussed, medieval intellectual life, dominated as it was by the Church, had little interest in nature. The hierarchical order which nature was assumed to possess — itself a clear reflection of the rigid feudal social order (Leibnitz acknowledged this by noting simply that: (Lovejoy (1936: 206) 'If equality were everywhere requisite, the poor man would set up his claim to it against the rich man, the valet against his master') — far from being conceived of by way of organic metaphor, was seen rather as the mere soulless residue of the overflowing goodness of God (Lovejoy (1936: 54)).

The organic metaphor, so pervasive in the 16th and early 17th centuries (Merchant (1980: 72)), was overwhelmingly the child of the Renaissance. It hardly needs repeating that the Renaissance obtained its name from the insistence of all intellectual endeavour in 15th and 16th-century Italy to revive the remains of antiquity. This amounted to a forthright paganism which constituted a massive assault on Church doctrine from the alteration of liturgy in the name of architecture (Pevsner (1957: 134); Wittkower (1962: 2, 10)) to the metamorphosis of God from distant judge to immanent soul of nature. It is quite clear that this ideological revolution was closely associated with a substantial growth in urban economic surplus in search of a more grandiose and exotic outlet for expression which was largely satisfied in a magnificent display of art, and the discovery of antique science and philosophy could be construed as an incidental side effect to the discovery of antique arts and engineering.

It was primarily the Renaissance revival of neo-Platonism and more specifically Hermeticism (Thomas (1973: 267)) which dragged the concept of nature into the forefront of European thought and laid the foundations of the scientific revolution (Cassirer (1951: 41)). The central tenet of this outlook was that the world, indeed the universe, was organic sentient being imbued with a soul; the medieval dualism of creator and creation was abolished and the intellectual eye was deflected from its eternal gaze into the infinite to focus upon living nature. Nature was no longer a wearisome riddle that might lead the faithful to God but was God in person.

Hermeticism was, however, a mystical and contemplative philosophy which would not, despite the aspirations of its advocates (Thomas (1973: 267)), yield any very practical results and it was the particular way in which the Counter-Reformation reasserted Christian doctrine which provided the context for the growth of a scientific outlook.

The relationship between the Renaissance and the Reformation was complex and evades precise or concise definition (Chadwick (1972: 30)). There is a sense in which each can be seen as a region-specific manifestation of a general set of underlying economic and social changes and another sense in which the Reformation was a reaction to the Renaissance. An interest in the past was fostered by a desire to find means of expressing new found wealth but also to find secure foundations against unsettling social change. Italy thus discovered the splendours of antiquity; Northern Europe found only the Bible and the primitive Church, initiating a process of progressive — and in times of social stress frantic — fragmentation into sects resulting from the search for the 'true' Church and then broadening out into 'true' beliefs and latterly the 'true' political creed[5].

Analyses of the emergence of modern science generally posit simple connections: a general drift from organicist to mechanistic thinking or the connection between Protestantism and empiricism, for instance. However, the actual process of emergence was subtle and complex, and such simplifications serve only to gloss over the rich causality underlying major ideological shifts. Focusing at this point on the connection between religious struggles and the emergence of science, it is possible to discern three main steps, each of which was essential to the eventual construction of the Newtonian synthesis.

The Reformation did not attack Renaissance neo-Platonism directly; indeed, this remained an intellectually respectable position amongst Puritans (Weber (1976: 168, 249)) and Hermetic doctrines spread throughout both Catholic and Protestant Europe. The vital middle step towards a theoretically adequate practical scientific outlook was not, in fact, the product of Protestantism, but came in the form of a Jesuit Counter-Reformationary attack upon English (Protestant) Hermeticist Robert Fludd (Merchant (1980: 192–205)). This attack, by Marsenne and Gassendi, consolidated by Descartes into a consistent dualistic rationalism, can be interpreted quite directly as a selective reassertion of Christian attitudes to nature, shifting from an organismic to a mechanistic interpretation amounting to the re-establishment of the independence of the creator and the creation[6]. Nature, that is, was not to be interpreted as an organism, imbued with (essentially unanalysable) mystical life force, but as a giant clock — which might have been built by men and certainly was open to analysis and manipulation by them — set in motion by the creator at the beginning of time[7].

The third step was already to hand. Francis Bacon, putting forward an empirical programme for science, simply rejected neo-Platonism and assumed that scientific advance could be made on the basis of empiricism alone. As discussed further below, an empiricist programme is closely connected with Protestantism and emergent capitalism, but on its own provides an inadequate framework for effective scientific work. It is important not only to note the necessary conjunction of Cartesian rationalism with empiricism to the development of a workable science, but — perhaps crucially — that Newton, who achieved the necessary synthesis, was also the product, educationally, of the final flowering of English neo-Platonism (McGuire and Rattansi (1966); Manuel (1968: 73)) and that it was a marriage of these three avenues of thought that provided the theoretical foundations of modern science.

Thus modern, practically oriented, demystified science, at first enclosed in a more general rationalist philosophy and veiled in theological terminology (Merton (1970: 79)), emerged in the guise of a return to essential Christian doctrine but was in practice the offspring of the creative tension between mystical nature-worship, inherited from antiquity, and the severe world-renouncing ('objective' (La Piere (1965: 307); Roszak (1973: 125–130, Ch. 5); Turner (1983: 176))) medieval Christianity: it was *the* paradigmatic dialectical synthesis which reshaped the foundations of European thought and which infuses our every idea today (Berman (1984b)). However, to grasp the *ideological* origins of modern science provides only a very partial explanation of present-day attitudes and practices in relation to nature.

Ideological structures can remain in place over long periods of time and then over a short period be subject to considerable modification or wholesale replacement. Whilst an element of 'random walk' may appear to guide this evolutionary process, a considerable degree of explanation can be attributed to the influence of economic and social changes. As already pointed out, a simple functionalist explanation of the coming of the scientific revolution is inadequate; nevertheless the receptivity of European culture to ideological change after the 14th century and the particular orientation of this change can be attributed in a general way to the revelations and requirements of the economic and social changes then in train. Social explanations of the genesis of science had always attracted a following, particularly amongst Marxists (Dobb (1946); Bernal (1969); Needham (1969)) but this is currently undergoing a thorough reworking at the centre of the stage of 'philosophy of science' as the 'sociology of science'. Marx's suggestion that men's social existence determines their ideological orientation remains a useful explanatory insight.

From this perspective the scientific revolution appears as just one step in the multifaceted process of the demise of feudalism and the rise of capitalism. It is not necessary to trace this whole process in order to understand the role of the scientific revolution though it is useful to highlight certain background features. The key aspect of this process was the way in which economic and political power shifted over several centuries out of the hands of rural, agricultural based interests into those of urban, trading and manufacturing interests (Dobb (1946)). This was not a question of massive rural–urban migration but of a gradual transfer of dominant economic and political decision-making powers.

The medieval economy can be characterised as a profusion of largely autonomous, self-sufficient agricultural units with a small surplus being syphoned off to maintain essentially conservative, static-tending monarchical and ecclesiastical structures. Capitalism introduced a dynamic dimension into the process of surplus accumulation and distribution which opened up and re-oriented the rural economy such as, eventually, to integrate it into national and international systems of production and trade. Monarchical and religious structures both competed with and fettered the growth of capitalism and it was therefore to be expected that capitalist interests — in the form of the rising urban bourgeoisie — would attempt to wring changes to these structures.

The process was long drawn out and although it possessed a systematic dimension it is easy to over-simplify, in retrospect, the way in which it unfolded. Maurice Dobb (1946: 99–100, 121)) showed how changes wrought in the economic and social structures of towns in Italy, Flanders and the Rhineland in the 13th to 15th centuries were not immediately followed up but that in achieving this transformation in Holland and England over a century later the process took on a more concerted form. In part this can be explained by the undermining of the land trade routes to the Orient by the new sea route and in general the effect of 'the discoveries' in shifting the focus of European trade from the Mediterranean to the Atlantic. But the effects of changing class differentiations and alliances as they acted themselves out in different regions clearly played a crucial role.

It was mentioned above in passing that the Renaissance unearthed the intellectual heritage of antiquity as a means to giving adequate expression to new-found urban wealth. This at once provided the gravity of historical precedent but also the necessary element of rebellion against existing institutional and inherited ideological constraints. Ben-David (1971: 60–64) pointed to the way in which the Renaissance academies, where neo-Platonism flourished as an albeit relatively minor aspect of this intellectual flowering, were a conscious reaction against the established universities. In the case of late 16th-century Naples this intellectual rebellion, involving at once the roots of science and the modern Utopia, was intertwined with social rebellion (Merchant (1980: 115–117)). However, the stagnation of early capitalist developments in urban Italy saw simultaneously the relative stagnation of intellectual development as well represented by the failure of Galileo to free intellectual enquiry from the controlling influence of the Church. The Catholic — constitutive rather than fragmentive — line of intellectual development then moved to a more economically powerful France.

It is generally contended that it was in 17th-century England that science — and in general the modern understanding of the concept Nature — was transformed from a relatively esoteric idea into a socially important institution (Ben-David (1971: 75)). The way in which this transformation was tied in with revolutionary social change was thoroughly investigated by Merton (1970) and has been subject to extensive controversy; more recently Hill (1980) looked at the general relationship between intellectual and social change in 17th-century England.

What emerges fairly clearly from this literature is a link between utilitarian and empiricist ideas identified with science on the one hand and that cluster of practical and ideological forces encompassing Protestantism and nascent capitalism analysed by Max Weber[8]. What is important about this process of institutionalisation of science is not its failure to produce practical results but that it represented, in the minds of those who championed it, a practical ideology in sharp contrast to the pre-existing dominant transcendental ideological systems.

Bacon was a poor scientist and blind to the real scientific achievements of his own time (Hill (1980: 85–86)). But the eloquence and clarity of his advocacy of science and the enthusiasm with which it was taken up after his death are testimony to its felt relevance (Eurich (1967: 144ff)). Again, although 16th-century science achieved very little of practical value[9], Merton (1970: 137–198) showed clearly that much of the effort of scientists was in fact oriented towards the solution of practical problems facing nascent capitalism: increasing production from mines (investigating scientific problems related to pumping and ventilation), increasing navigational skills (investigations into mathematics and astronomy) and increasing military efficiency (investigations into ballistics).

It is important to underline the way in which science was established as part of a complex of ideas which saw an urban, rather than a rural, practicality[10] as being morally superior to contemplative religious or artistic pursuits (Weber (1976: 168–169)); and from this it follows that nature from this point on was a practical, not a contemplative object. Nature was there to be conquered, as Bacon never ceased to proclaim; whilst the conquest of men was seen to be a dubious undertaking, the conquest of nature was seen as a noble aspiration (Bacon (1960: Aphorism CXXIX)).

Leiss (1972: 137ff), building on the analyses of the Frankfurt School — Horkheimer, Adorno and Marcuse — analysed how this complex of ideas contained an elision which obscured from view a contradiction which today urgently requires unravelling. The concept of the conquest — or domination or mastering — of nature encompasses two distinct ideas. On the one hand it refers to the activities of science in understanding the inner construction of nature and on the other hand it refers to questions of ownership — of property rights. The first can be seen as a form of contemplation which, however, is oriented towards practical exploitation; the second is concerned with the actual use of nature encompassing technology and control in the social sense.

The fatal deception in Bacon's (1960: 116) thinking — and one which has been carefully maintained down to our own time — concerns the notion that science can and will be used for the benefit of all mankind (Eurich (1967: 266)). But science was from the beginning a tool with which to advance the interests of certain individuals, classes and nations (Merton (1970: xxi–xxii); Young (1990: Ch.4)) — and in the end a particular culture — against all others. Indeed, the formulation of the most abstract of scientific theories is motivated at root (to put it crudely: paid for) by the machinery of competitive social structures. As C. S. Lewis (1947: 40) put it: 'From this point of view, what we call Man's power over Nature turns out to be a power exercised by some men over other men with Nature as its instrument' [11].

It is possible from the foregoing argument already to discern what must be deemed an important third dimension informing the transformation of European attitudes to nature around the 17th century, namely the influence of place. Mention was made of the way in which the opening of ocean trade routes undermined the role of Italy as entrepôt for Oriental trade with Europe. Fernand Braudel (1972: Vol. I 25–352) in his massive study of the Mediterranean in the 16th century pioneered an approach to understanding historical processes in terms of the constraints and possibilities opened up by specific features of the local environment: the dialectic between culture and place.

Such an approach recognises the role of terrain, land suitability and natural resource availability in facilitating, under given technological conditions, the development of certain economic structures which in turn influence the development of social and ideological structures. The very shape of Western Europe, having influenced the way in which particular social conjunctures came to settle and relate to one another (Landes (1969: 31); Anderson (1970: 428)), eventually played an important, even crucial role in facilitating the development of 'the capitalist world system' (Wallerstein (1974)). Then again, the extraordinarily rich mineral resource base of England in contrast, say, with France or Holland, can be seen as an important — though clearly not the only — ingredient determining why the Industrial Revolution was pioneered in Britain.

More controversial than the notion that the development of capitalism was nurtured by the geography of Europe is the idea that more deep-seated cultural attitudes have been conditioned over long periods by environmental factors. In fact, as Glacken (1967) went to considerable lengths to demonstrate, belief that geography and climate are important influences on the pattern and composition of culture has a history extending from antiquity right up to the 19th century and was an important ingredient of 18th-century Enlightenment social theory. So why should this be so controversial today?

Anthropological theories — only without the title — were elaborated by several Enlightenment writers using such 'case material' as was available from travellers' tales (and the key theorists Montesquieu and Adam Ferguson actually possessed considerable first-hand experience). A complete theory of the interaction of culture and ecology was put forward in outline. Montesquieu's (1949) *De l'Esprit des Lois - Book 1* and Adam Ferguson's (1767) *An Essay on the History of Civil Society* — especially Part III, Section I (p. 165 *et seq*): 'Of the Influence of Climate and Situation' were the key contributions in France and Britain respectively. Condorcet (1976: 293) in outlining a future programme for science, in his 'Fragment on the New Atlantis', saw the most important task as comprising an investigation into 'the natural history of man' which would include a detailed enquiry into the relationship between effects of climate and environment upon the physical constitution and socio-economic organisation of mankind. Rousseau (1964b: 203–213) laid out a clear — and arguably the first systematic — programme for anthropology in a lengthy footnote (j) to his 'Discourse on the Origin and Foundations of Inequality' of 1754. This was envisaged as investigating the causes of social difference in (p. 203) 'The Diversity of Climates, Air, Foods, Way of Life, Habits in General'.

This programme and its sketchy first conclusions were inherited by Hegel and Marx. It is of considerable interest to note that it was the 'idealist' Hegel rather than the 'materialist' Marx who wrote (Hegel (1975b: 191)) that: '...just as nature is the basis of history itself, so also must it be the basis of our study of history' and who went to considerable lengths to illustrate the relationship between social practice and environmental constraints, opportunities and sundry influences (Hegel (1975b: 152–196)). Marx did not make any major reference to this literature but followed its general tenor in occasional passages (eg Marx (1973b: 486; 1976: 649)); in *Capital* Volume 1 we can read:

Where nature is too prodigal with her gifts, she 'keeps him in hand, like a child in leading-strings'. Man's own development is not in that case a nature-imposed necessity. The mother country of capital is not the tropical region, with its luxuriant vegetation, but the temperate zone. It is not the absolute fertility of the soil but its degree of differentiation, the variety of its natural products, which forms the natural basis for the social division of labour, and which, by changes in the natural surroundings, spurs man on to the multiplication of his needs, his capacities, and the instruments and modes of his labour.

Followers of Marx continued to explore the influence of nature on processes of social and economic development right into the 20th century (Labriola (1908); Plekhanov (undated)).

However, the implication already in Montesquieu was that the European environment made for superior cultural attributes although a great respect was also shown for Chinese culture. By the time Hegel received this line of thought it had become associated with grotesque expressions of cultural prejudice. With respect to climate he wrote in passing (Hegel (1975b: 155)) that:

The torrid and frigid regions, as such, are not the theatre on which world history is enacted. In this respect, such extremes are incompatible with spiritual freedom. All in all, it is therefore the *temperate zone* which must furnish the theatre of world history.

Looking at different continents he (1975: 163) opined:

America has always shown itself physically and spiritually impotent .... Even the animals show the same inferiority as the human beings.

Furthermore (Hegel (1975b: 190)):

anyone who wishes to study the most terrible manifestations of human nature will find them in Africa.

Hegel was, however, no exception. Instead of the balanced anthropological programme proposed by the writers of the Enlightenment, what emerged, in tune with the post French Revolutionary bourgeois paranoia referred to earlier in this text, was a consistently bellicose nationalism and racism, upon the interpretation of the relationship between culture and place which came to constitute the conventional wisdom even of many trenchant critics of the era including Marx. Following the First World War and the Russian Revolution, such attitudes became more circumspect — although they were still reasonably common in the context of European colonialism until its collapse after the Second World War (Myrdal (1968: 677ff)). The growing criticism of these attitudes, however, did not attempt to refocus the concern for understanding the relationship between environment and culture but rather to label the whole debate 'environmental determinism' — thence shortened to 'environmentalism' — and, as noted in Chapter 2, proceed to proscribe *any* reasoned consideration of the issue.

The everyday fact of racial prejudice and the casual ranking of nations and cultures that is constantly presented by the media today demonstrates clearly that the attitudes inculcated in the course of colonialism, to which the environment-culture debate was so central in the formative years, are still very much with us. Academia, however, has attempted to exclude such prejudices at least from within its domain. But in practice it has merely locked the skeleton away and simply engages in the performance of an act of seeing and hearing no evil. The point that has to be made here is this: the influence of environment, including climate as well as geography, has been crucial in the formation of different cultures. In the case of European culture this ingredient becomes an important dimension in the explanation of our aggressive attitudes to nature and towards other cultures. If we are to succeed in abandoning the trajectory that is inexorably leading us to destroy nature then we are going to have to face up to this problem and exorcise it in short shrift. Far from the European environment and culture being 'the best', it is absolutely catastrophic not only for other cultures but for its own good as well.

Returning to scrutinise the genesis of the scientific revolution, this time from the point of view of the influence of nature upon culture, it is useful to focus again on Max Weber's analysis. A central concept which emerged from his study of Protestantism was the notion of 'worldly asceticism' — what has become known as the 'Puritan work ethic' — which he contrasted with world-renouncing ascetic systems of other religions. Weber (1976: 158–175) developed a complex argument concerning Puritanism which saw hard, continuous bodily or mental labour, as an approved ascetic technique in sharp contrast to oriental and monastic asceticism, as comprising the basic purpose of life ordained as such by God. This 'worldly asceticism' turned with all its force against one thing: the spontaneous enjoyment of life and all it had to offer. Hard work, however, was likely to yield a harvest of wealth in this world; but this was not frowned upon so long as it did not lead to idleness and uninhibited — sinful — enjoyment of it. The good Protestant, acting as an acquisitive machine, had a duty to his possessions to which he subordinated himself as an obedient steward. When the limitation of consumption is combined with this release of acquisitive activity, the inevitable practical result is clear: accumulation of capital through ascetic compulsion to save. Scientific utilitarianism and empiricism were clearly mere facets of a more general orientation towards productive activity as an expression of worldly asceticism.

This thorough dialectical reversal of world-renouncing asceticism makes good sense in the context of cultural attitudes nurtured by the necessities of agricultural life in a Northern European setting with its demand for complex annual cycles of planning and work and hence necessarily elaborate engagement with the environment. The way in which this became a spontaneous outlook on life is well-illustrated by a phrase penned by a London merchant in 1669, appended by Marx to the paragraph in *Capital* quoted above:

Nor can I conceive a greater curse upon a body of people than to be thrown upon a spot of land, where the productions for subsistence and food were, in great measure, spontaneous, and the climate required or admitted little care for raiment and covering.

How eloquently this expresses the deep strain of masochism which informs the Protestant work ethic — the reverse face of which comprises the deep sadistic aggression which Northern European men have meted out on nature, foreign cultures, women and, where they get the chance, their fellow men, and which is reflected also in their 'objective' interpretation of nature: 'red in tooth and claw'. Where, coming out of more benign environmental circumstances — notably in the case of Renaissance Italy — increased urban surplus might simply encourage more elaborate channels of consumption, in Northern Europe the deep-seated fear born of long and bitter experience of dire consequences following any uninhibited enjoyment of increased surplus can be seen as providing impetus to the construction of the 'spirit of capitalism'.

However, the transfer of the necessities of rural life, as a deep-seated orientation ever expectant of hardship and travail, to an urban economic setting, transformed a defensive strategy towards a demanding nature into an aggressive strategy which lies at the heart of the 'ecological problematic': it is first and foremost this nightmarish, quixotic, endless struggle against the ghost of a long-since vanquished Nature, and only secondarily the Judaeo-Christian tradition, that lies at the heart of (Northern) European aggression towards Nature. Bacon's programme to 'master nature' and with it the whole elaboration of the scientific paradigm makes all too clear a sense in this context. Furthermore the self-righteousness of ascetic attitudes necessarily led Northern Europeans to the view that cultures which did not possess such attitudes were immoral and hence must be actively destroyed — most recently through the mechanisms of universalistic 'economic development' (Young (1990: Ch.2)). Science, and in general an aggressive stance towards nature, released the means to destroy all other cultures except in instances where cultural and environmental conditions were receptive to the adoption of equivalent aggressive attitudes and structures — notably in Japan.

Whilst the Newtonian synthesis provided the foundation for the dominant modern view of what nature is — or rather how we might discover what nature is — this certainly has not remained unchallenged in the intervening period. All Newton, in fact, did, was to demonstrate in several key areas (astronomy, ballistics, optics) how nature could be 'taken to pieces' empirically and reconstituted through mathematics and geometry. Bacon (1960: 33) had already warned against premature assertion of the way in which nature works and it was a group of Dutch scientists at the end of the 17th century who generalised from Newton's point of departure (Cassirer (1951: 55)) such as to promote scientific work on the basis of, in Whitehead's (1926: 4) words, 'a widespread instinctive conviction in the existence of *Order of Things*, and, in particular, of an *Order of Nature*'. In fact Whitehead was himself firmly of the view that this attitude had been forged in the Middle Ages. If this is conceded, then it reinforces the foregoing argument concerning the subtle and multifarious ways in which 'the Judaeo-Christian tradition' informed the foundations of the scientific programme.

Thus the question of ontology (and by the late 19th century the question of epistemology as well) was cast aside in favour of methodological issues concerned overwhelmingly with how best to harness the powers of nature to the ends of men. The attempts of d'Holbach and la Mettrie, in the course of the French Enlightenment, to assert a mechanistic description of nature in defiance of religion were anachronistic (Cassirer (1951: 55)) (and Engels' (1954) attempt a century later to construct a 'Dialectics of Nature' succumbed broadly to the same fallacy[12]). Modern science is no more than some tools and an attitude towards nature animated by the social (or anti-social) purpose to which it might be put; science is fundamentally destructive of ecological systems to the ends of conflictual social interests. And yet the assumption came to prevail that somehow science, in the form of the positivist programme, would reveal all the answers to the questions traditionally posed by philosophy and attempts to reassert philosophy in its completeness were relegated to the cultural margins.

Two general paths have been taken to formulate attitudes towards, and practice in, nature other than via science, informed by constructive inclinations. The first of these can be termed the romantic and the second the ontological (or philosophical).

Keith Thomas documented in detail the way in which our modern romantic attitudes towards nature, as being something beautiful to be contemplated and tended as a thing in itself, developed over a 300-year period. There was no 'love of nature' in medieval Europe: whilst Saint Francis of Assisi may have recently been declared patron saint of ecology by the Pope, his teachings were heretical in his own time. The romantic idea of nature has origins concurrent with the origins of science: in the radical distancing of nature from man in the Cartesian dualism and on the practical distancing of nature inherent in the adoption of urban lifestyles (Thomas (1983: 181)). These attitudes contain a sense of loss. Far from being a radical force, however, this sentimentality served largely as an apology and an escape from the reality of the deepening instrumentalism towards nature and was associated in particular with the idea of value not as a higher good or thing in itself but as a means to display higher wealth and status: the possession of a large house in a country setting, and the possession of horses and dogs informed social attitudes towards nature at all levels of society (Thomas (1983: 240)). Of course, it would be wrong to write off the modern 'love of nature' as just another form of instrumentalism: the growth of a concern for preservation of wilderness and of species variety and even the growth of vegetarianism (Thomas (1983: 278ff)) can be seen as more radical initiatives stemming from romantic sources, from a feeling that our use of nature is fundamentally at fault. Indeed, this romanticism is an essential ingredient in the development of modern conservationism and environmentalism and the copious literature on environmental ethics that has emerged in recent years.

What was missing from Thomas's analysis — and was better developed by Leo Marx (1964) in his seminal book *The Machine in the Garden* — was a drawing out of the dialectical nature of the development of romantic attitudes to nature. Romanticism towards nature in this framework, and as a collective experience, is a form of regret towards the Faustian bargain which our society has made by the adoption of positivistic science. Seen in this light, it can never be an unequivocally radical force and will always obscure the epistemological and ontological bases not only of its own existence but, more seriously, the reality of our *social* relations with nature.

However, truly radical attempts to establish an alternative understanding of the meaning of nature for us and of our place in nature at the philosophical level have repeatedly surfaced over the period since Newton arrived at his synthesis, and salient developments are worth brief reference. In the course of the 18th-century Enlightenment, both Diderot and Stahl criticised the emerging scientific programme insisting on the wholeness, the organic interconnection of nature as process.

The most serious challenge unfolded round the turn of the 19th century through the agency of what became known as the '*Naturphilosophen*' — the German philosophers of nature — constituting one aspect of the development of German idealist philosophy in general. Kant had accepted and built into his broad philosophical system the attitude to nature developed by science: nature consists of 'noumena' (a realm of the unknown) until such time as brought into the realm of human knowledge as 'phenomena'. Deemed by a new generation of philosophers to be an unsatisfactory explanation of nature for a project intended to be an all-encompassing philosophy, Kant's system underwent a series of critical examinations and reconstructions. Three names are central to these developments. In general it can be said that Fichte attempted first to overcome Kant's dualism by extension of the concept of the human spirit; Schelling on the other hand attempted to overcome it through the notion of the organic unity of nature and man; and finally Hegel produced his grand synthesis that resolved the dualism by focusing on the process of development (Coppleston (1965)).

Schelling is of particular interest here in that he attempted, and with considerable success in his own time, to revive an organicist view of life and knowledge that clearly (Lovejoy (1936: 317–326)), and in some respects consciously (Coppleston (1965: Chs.5–7)), revived Hermeticism and medieval mystical teachings regarding nature, but did so in the context of developments in practical science. Nature was seen as a unified self-developing super-organism within which man represented nature's knowledge of itself; Schelling accepted the notion of biological evolution. (Neither Kant nor Hegel accepted this and it was not until a half century after Schelling's time that evolution became acceptable scientific doctrine and then only in the distorted form of Darwin's notion of universal struggle.) Developments in science were themselves seen by Schelling as part of this evolutionary process of the development of nature's own self-consciousness. Schelling took an uncritical interest in these developments: after all, from the perspective of his age, it would have been difficult to envisage how eventually developments in science might become central to the destruction of nature.

Hegel's system brought together Fichte's and Schelling's one-sided attempts at a unified philosophy into one synthesis. On the one hand he developed a philosophy of human consciousness as developing through the process of history; on the other he developed a philosophy of nature as the 'antithesis' of consciousness. These fed into a 'synthesis' concerned with Reason, as reflected in social and political life. His philosophy of nature abandoned Schelling's mysticism and focused predominantly on the process of scientific discovery. It was thus organised round the process of human understanding of nature rather than structure in nature itself, and his rejection of natural evolution reflected this perspective.

Schelling and Hegel developed their philosophy just at the point at which science was beginning to come effectively into conjuncture with practical developments of technology and of industry. Their attempt to envisage the unfolding of the process whereby science and nature would engage with one another over the ensuing years therefore had little evidence to guide it and subsequent developments left their attempts behind as comprising a *mélange* of inspired insight and irrelevant detail interspersed with mistaken interpretation (Collingwood (1945: 121–132); Stace (1924: 315)). Whilst elements of Hegel's philosophy generally survived and developed, his philosophy of nature faded into the background (Engels (1976: 13n)).

Across the 19th century numerous attempts were made to systematise science, understood as 'materialist' philosophy, and most of these have been long forgotten (Coppleston (1965: Ch.18)). Comte's positive philosophy, however, proved to be in tune with the trajectory of reductionist science and hence remained acceptable and, to a certain extent, influential in the course which scientific developments took. In spite of their failure, certain more radical attempts at philosophy in the 19th and early 20th centuries, that strove to redefine the role of science within a more holistic or organic framework, are worth noting.

The development of phenomenology, centring on the writings of Edmund Husserl, presented a philosophy based upon a certain interpretation of science which, in practice, as briefly discussed in Chapter 2, redefined science as a systematic view emanating from human subjectivity. In one sense related to Fichte's attempt to resolve philosophy through the unifying effects of the active human consciousness, phenomenology, particularly in the form of hermeneutics, has proved a powerful tool in the analysis of social issues but failed to make headway in the realm of natural science. Current developments under the title of 'chaos theory', discussed at the end of this section, may perhaps, however, admit extension of phenomenology into the area of natural science.

Further attempts were made to reintroduce and develop organicist and holistic philosophies that would reintegrate nature and the human condition.

These include, notably, the writings of Henri Bergson, Jan Smuts, Alfred Whitehead and Arthur Eddington. Bergson's approach attacked the physical and mathematical sciences broadside, seeing the universe as being informed by a unifying life force (*'élan vital'*). Nature is to be understood through evolution in which life develops structure in matter as creative process, bounded neither by mechanisms nor teleology. The mathematical and deterministic sciences are concerned only with space, defining time as nothing but a subordinate aspect of space. But time is of the essence of life and hence central to the comprehension of nature and meaning. Bergson was given short shrift in the hands of the scientific fraternity (Prigogine and Stengers (1985: 293)). Whitehead and Eddington, on the other hand, were more circumspect in their confrontation with triumphal physics, accepting the generally given framework and attempting to adjust the ground rules. Whitehead's (1920) central concern was that the dissociation which positivist science performs between matter and time be overcome by focusing on 'events' as units of analysis. He sketched out (Whitehead (1926)) an organic philosophy of science in place of the prevailing emphasis on matter and insisted that aesthetics and ethics be brought back into conjunction with science. Unlike Bergson, who used material from the sciences as adornments to his resonant narrative (Russell (1961: 762) suspected that this was all largely erroneous and confused), Whitehead's argument remained at all times respectful of historical precedent and current debate, providing his own commentary and views almost as an afterthought. Nevertheless, many of his conclusions speak clearly to current criticisms of reductive science, for instance (Whitehead (1926: 194, 244)):

It should be the task of the philosophical schools of this century to bring together the two streams into an expression of the world-picture derived from science, and thereby end the divorce of science from the affirmations of our aesthetic and ethical experiences.

The two evils are: one, the ignoration of the true relation of each organism to its environment; and the other, the habit of ignoring the intrinsic worth of the environment which must be allowed its weight in any consideration of final ends.

The problem with these attempts to confront high science in its reductionist mode at the level of theory and ideas was that they failed to recognise the vital underlying connection with the political settlement. Reductionist science had been shown to work: it took nature to pieces and offered it up to social forces to do with as they pleased, to be resynthesised in the image of human desires. Organicist philosophy might be 'true' in some ultimate aesthetic sense, but the material results of reductionist science were so much more engaging at the immediate level of political and inter-personal expediency. Atomic bombs, television sets, aeroplanes and pharmaceuticals and the profits and power that could be derived from these proved the practical worth of reductive science.

Meanwhile, however, the internal processes of theory building within science regularly threw up anomalies of its own quite independent of any external critique. In Kuhn's analysis, this would form the basis of 'scientific revolutions' of which Einstein's relativity theory provides ideal illustration. But unfortunately when it came to potential inconsistency between different disciplines, there was no need for revolutionary conflict and resolution: positivist philosophy had provided for this by dividing science into disciplines which could be expected to produce different — even antagonistic — results (Prigogine and Stengers (1985: 104–105). And the truth, as revealed by the sociology of science already discussed (Barnes (1974)), is that 'science' is made up of many communities and ideas oriented towards different ends within the social and political arena. In this way they pass one another in the night, avoiding conflict in areas where they are saying different things about the same subject to satisfy different constituencies and aims.

Thus science remained a conflictual and fragmented process in which lines of research unwelcome in the political sphere were easily rendered innocuous. 19th-century biologists, for example, seeking a general framework for their subject, came again and again to the conclusion that species interaction with one another and their environment must be studied as a whole. But the discipline of ecology, adopted to further such an investigative programme, remained in the shadows until well into the 20th century and developed in very one-sided ways, specifically on the backs of ambitious ecologists, keen to submit their discipline to positivist rules — viz devise a reductive, instrumentally effective programme — so as to gain scientific acceptability and with it more elevated social and political status (Worster (1979)). A further programme in biology was developed by D'Arcy Wentworth Thompson (1961) to research the general morphological characteristics of biological species across the complete spectrum. Acknowledged in many a footnote as fine work, this nevertheless remained at the margins of biology. The mainstream was concerned to take organisms apart, to study physiology, cell structure, chemistry and molecular constituents, to yield knowledge usable by industry and all too often for war.

From the outset, fundamental conflict revealed itself between the general laws of physics, concerned with inert matter, and those devised to cover energy, which possess an irreducible connection with real time (Prigogine and Stengers (1985: Ch.IV)). Whilst the question of reversibility of physical properties was axiomatic to classic dynamics, thermodynamics insisted on energy changing states irreversibly through time. The suicide of Bolzmann, putatively as a result of his failure to bring energy into the mainstream of physical theory and in spite of his attempts at compromise, is one of the notable dramas of scientific history[13].

But in the early years of the 20th century, conflict entered into the very heart of physics in the confrontation between relativity and quantum mechanics. Positive science is informed at its foundations by an assumption that beneath the complex surface everything in the universe has simple causes which it is the job of science to discover. As the French chemist Laplace put it early in the 19th century (quoted in Powers (1982: 138)):

We may regard the present state of the universe as the effect of its past and the cause of its future. An intelligence which at a given moment knew all the forces that animate nature, and the respective positions of the beings that compose it, and further possessing the scope to analyse the data, could condense into a single formula the movement of the greatest bodies of the universe and that of the least atom: for such an intelligence nothing could be uncertain, and past and future alike would be before our eyes.

Already in Einstein's formulation of general relativity, violent objections had been put forth by the traditional materialists, disturbed by the notion that measures of quantity might be dependent upon the frame of reference adopted, as relations between observer and observed; the observer cannot stand outside the system but is an integral part of it. Quantum mechanics pushed beyond this insight to a view that the relations between physical entities cannot be measured without the measurer influencing the state of the entity to be measured: the more precisely we locate the object to be measured, Heisenberg argued, the less precisely we can measure its properties and vice versa. The 'Law of Universal Causality' was overthrown and indeterminacy acknowledged to be an essential property of our relationship with the physical world. As is well known, Einstein never accepted this, asserting that 'God does not play dice' and despite the general acceptance of the premises of quantum mechanics, the quest for a Grand Unified Theory (GUT) continues today.

Of course non-acceptance of indeterminacy in mainstream physics relates to the underlying political importance of maintaining a determinist programme. The physicist Edwin Schrödinger (1952) expressed concern that the increasingly esoteric nature of the physics debate, admitting only a tiny circle of initiates to participate as it delved ever further into the ultimate micro and macro limits to the universe by appending ever more refined mathematical tools, would result in its ossification and death as a consequence of drifting away from its cultural context. But there appeared until very recently little hope of this in the face of the faith residing in the ultimate practical value of this work, in 'conquering the universe', capturing the energy of fusion power and perhaps as yet unimagined and unimaginable benefits (for some people) yet to emerge, in line with past experience. And the continuing vast flow of resources sunk into technologies — accelerators, fusion reactors, space probes and so on — and accompanying bureaucracies to support these suppositions and the activities of this fraternity is eloquent testimony to this.

However, starting in the 1960s, coming together in the late 1970s and emerging as a flood in the course of the 1980s, a new assault on determinism came into being amongst the scientific community, loosely bound together under the title of 'chaos theory' (Gleick (1987)). Of particular interest is the way that it was initiated in many corners of science quite independently and has had the effect of bringing together mathematicians and physicists, chemists and meteorologists, biologists and even analysts of social phenomena around what appears to be a common research programme.

Chaos theory amounts to a radical refocusing of scientific enquiry onto macroscopic, real-time phenomena. It is concerned with the structure of complexity in nature, with process rather than state, establishing a science of becoming rather than being. 'Morphological' issues of this kind had occupied the fringes of the 'social sciences' and biology going back into the 19th century. The work of D'Arcy Thompson and the programme of ecology were mentioned above; concern for morphological mathematics in nature and society were investigated further in various directions by Matila Ghyka,

Görgy Kepes, Walter Christaller, George Kingsley Zipf, Nikolas Rashevsky and Herbert Simon to name but a few.

Certainly ecologists played a special role in giving birth to chaos theory. Gleick (1987: 59) put it like this:

> In the emergence of chaos as a new science in the 1970s, ecologists were destined to play a special role. They used mathematical models, but they always knew that the models were thin approximations of the seething world. In a perverse way their awareness of the limitations allowed them to see the importance of some ideas that mathematicians had considered interesting oddities.

But its origins, from the point of view of 'hard' science, lay in the unsatisfactory way in which science managed to disregard perturbation and change in physical systems. Determinism could continue to be used in spite of its theoretical unsatisfactoriness by reference to the concept of approximation. That nature never conformed perfectly to any natural law could be discounted by reference to 'noise' in the experiment; statistical tools could be used to iron this out. Radical discontinuities could be overlooked by focusing only on stable states and avoiding transitional states and processes.

Chaos theory purposely focuses attention on these problem areas, looking for order amongst phenomena labelled by classic science as chaotic. And everywhere evidence appeared of complex structures and systems that can be described mathematically, but which are incompletely deterministic: small perturbations can lead to large changes in system functioning and there is more than one direction which systems might take depending on contextual and contingent variables. Whilst the point at which turbulence arises in water falling from a tap or smoke rising from a cigarette can be determined, the subsequent path of the water or smoke cannot because it is presented with alternatives which oscillate according to contingent circumstance.

Changing states beyond thresholds and the interactions of variables and states at such points required a new approach to mathematics of non-linear equations, 'fractal geometry' (Mandelbrot (1977)) and catastrophe theory (Woodcock and Davis (1980)). But it also involved a wholly new approach to the question of time in science and hence reopened the possibility for a dialogue between science and organicist or process philosophy and this has, indeed, been emerging.

On the whole, scientists, even those working on esoteric and theoretical questions, remain wary of any very concerted engagement between their scientific practice and broader political, social and philosophical questions. There has generally been a popular assumption that the latest scientific theories are also socially and politically progressive and it is well-known that Einstein and other major participants of the fraternity of high physics held generally socialist and/or progressive liberal views. Adherence to relativity theory became a highly contentious political issue with debate around the question of whether or not it could be interpreted as falling within the framework of dialectical materialism and, in the case of Nazi Germany, it being rejected a 'Jewish science'. It has also been presumed somehow to lend support to and/or be generated by the general progressive drift of the surrounding culture. Chaos theory, Gleick (1987: 116, 229)) noted, is seen by those developing it as consistent with a revulsion against modernism in the cultural sphere. But the diffidence of the scientific fraternity regarding the relationship between their science and the wider issues of the world makes inference in this respect difficult. Certainly, centre-of-the-road chaos theorists maintain their distance from the renewed attempts at process philosophy which aspires to use their findings in a new context. Gleick (1987: 195), who himself excluded Prigogine — who is a Nobel prize winner in one of the major areas of Chaos theory and also aspires to the development of a wider philosophical view — from his own survey of the field gives a flavour of the situation when he writes:

The mathematician who refuses to endorse an idea until it meets the standard of *theorem, proof, theorem, proof*, plays a role that his discipline has written for him: consciously or not, he is standing watch against frauds and mystics.

In the mid-1970s, Erich Jantsch and Conrad Waddington (1976) brought together a series of essays, under the title of *Evolution and Consciousness*, aimed at contributing towards a new process philosophy. Besides contributions from the editors, articles by Magoroh Maruyama, Ilya Prigogine and 'transdisciplinary' essays in ecology, systems theory and socio-cultural evolution were included. Establishing connections back to Whitehead, Bergson — and even Jacob Boehme and Hermetic philosophy — these essays were concerned to pull together emerging scientific (not to say scientistic) debate on 'emergent' and systemic properties in nature and human culture, implying a new philosophical basis for science itself. The exercise included an exuberant generation of new terminology. Waddington (1977), at that time in process of generating his own 'philosophy for the people' aimed at generating tools to combat what he saw as a civilisation in crisis, died at this time without completing his work. Jantsch (1980) who died a few years later nevertheless went on to produce a complete statement of his philosophical outlook under the title *The Self-Organising Universe*. In it he developed the theme of the dynamic connectedness of man and an unfolding universe in which 'autopoiesis' and 'autocatalytic' process acted to generate growth and change from within in natural, biological and human systems alike. Prigogine (1980), with co-workers in Brussels and Austin, Texas (Prigogine and Stengers (1985)) continued to develop both more strictly scientific ideas in the areas of thermodynamics and broader ideas that brought turn of century organismic philosophy up-to-date, putting 'time' and 'becoming' at the centre of his system. Maruyama (1976) continued to develop radical anthropological theories aimed at promoting symbiotic, mutualistic social relations.

In conclusion, it is necessary to stress two points. Firstly, the existence of significant debate in the region of organismic, process philosophy, and the development of related scientific work on 'chaos theory', says little about its importance. The fact is that so far these have made very little headway even into more generalised intellectual debates: details of the debates remain largely unknown even in the universities and almost entirely unknown to the population at large. By contrast, the existence, if not the content, of conventional scientific theory, and the main projects with which it is engaged, are common knowledge across a wide spectrum of society. This is reflected also in the resources available to each. It can therefore be asserted — in the spirit of this literature itself — that we are witnessing the beginning of a change in paradigm which, in the foreseeable future will transform our whole way of thinking and with it the way in which society and our relations with nature are organised. Or it is possible to dismiss the whole subject as an insignificant growth at the edge of our intellectual culture.

There is no way in which either view can be proven or denied a priori. But it is — and this is the second point — necessary to outline the potential relevance of these recent intellectual events to the requirements of an 'ecological society'. There can be no doubt in general terms that the 'truth' of an ecological society is an organicist philosophy and that deterministic, reductive science has to go: this has been declared right across the early literature of the political ecology and hardly needs arguing. The problem is, however, that there are many variants of organicist philosophy and it will be all too easy to climb out of the frying pan into the fire. With respect to social arrangements, there are clear contradictions between the various essays in *Evolution and Consciousness* and it is worth remembering that in the past such philosophies have been associated particularly with what today are generally considered as reactionary (hierarchical and even fascist) social and political arrangements and ideologies. In most of this literature terminological gymnastics hide, rather than clarify, the implications of vital elements of the putative new synthesis.

But above all, there reside strong millenarian implications both in the philosophy and in chaos theory. Waddington (1977) did express a concern for the growing ecological crisis and stressed the need to adapt social decision-making processes specifically to manage change in a prudent fashion. Jantsch, however — and the implication is prevalent across the whole literature — remained impatient of any attempt to bring any conscious control to bear on the development of society. Thus Jantsch wrote (Jantsch and Waddington (1976: 2)):

In this perspective, any attempt to stabilize structures by imposing boundaries — the *ultima ratio* of the machine syndrome — cannot but become counterproductive in two ways. First, a stabilizing control imposed *upon* the world and interfering with processes of self-transformation and self-organisation is inevitably bound to end up with dictatorship; equilibrium is synonymous with social and cultural, and ultimately physical, death. Second, if the human world cannot be put to death in such a way — and I believe that no religious, political or scientific zealot will ever totally triumph over life — enforced stabilization and equilibration will amount to but a temporary halting of the processes of life, which will ultimately break through with vastly increased explosive and disruptive power, just as a boiler will burst if it is expected to contain in the same structure water transforming into steam. The false paradigms and expectations of stabilization are becoming a serious threat as our century enters its last quarter. Therefore, this book also tries to convey a certain sense of urgency, *an appeal to trust in the evolving gestalt of life* (emphasis added), rather than in lifeless form.

There is very clearly stated a strong element of mystical belief that somehow, regardless of what we do, everything will turn out all right. The idea of the sudden, unpredictable qualitative break in social, political and conceptual systems, for which no meaningful preparation can be made, remains a powerful image right across the literature of process philosophy and is implicit also in chaos theory. Political ecology, whilst building upon the organismic ecological paradigm, must certainly avoid such millenarian sentiments.

The idea of progress

There are three reasons for discussing the idea of progress at this point. In the first place it is, after a concern with nature, central to the thinking of the ecology movement. That is to say that much of the environmentalist literature has taken as its primary role the critique of 'economic growth' (Daly (1973; 1977); Lacomber (1975, 1979); Henderson (1978; 1981); Daly and Cobb (1990); today, economic growth is the *sine qua non* of progress and any thorough-going critique does well to know its adversary in some depth. Secondly, although modern attitudes to nature were thoroughly aired in the previous section, the growth of science and technology over the past three centuries cannot be fully understood without understanding the role of the idea of progress (Merton (1970: 232ff)). Finally, it is through the idea of progress that it is possible to see most clearly that dimension through which Judaeo-Christian theology informs modern secular ideology; indeed it can be simply argued that it is via this route rather than in any more direct way that the Judaeo-Christian tradition has conditioned modern attitudes to nature (Black (1970: 105–108, 124)).

The modern idea of progress has its roots in millenarianism. Although this term is derived from biblical references to the second coming of Christ — being a period of a thousand years in which the righteous will live in peace and harmony under the direct rule of God — it has become something of a technical term in anthropology to describe a phenomenon that has arisen from time to time in many cultural milieux, quite unrelated with Christianity, involving extreme social agitation accompanied by beliefs in imminent radical changes, classically upon contact with modern European culture (Wilson (1975)). It is useful here to note simply that millenarianism is thus defined as a movement of sudden social agitation or revolt involving an intense, unreasoned belief in imminent salvation and which arises when a whole culture or society senses itself to be under external threat.

On the whole the complex and systematic 'world religions' take as one of their functions the task of regulating social relations over a wide spectrum of changed circumstances and of deflecting the possibility of social unrest. It is therefore something of an anomaly that the Judaeo-Christian religion is not only based on an apocalyptic eschatology (doctrine of heaven and hell) but also incorporates a number of texts which encourage the apocalyptic expectation of sudden and radical transformation; the main texts in question are: the Book of Daniel, Chapter VII, the Book of Revelation and the Sibylline Oracles (Cohn (1970: 19–36)). The circumstances which produced these texts were those which anthropologists would immediately recognise as encouraging millenarianism: in this case the confrontation between Jewish culture and, respectively, Mesopotamian, Hellenistic and Roman expansions. However, having been built into the religious system this element has had the effect of justifying movements of social destabilisation throughout the history of those peoples who have adopted the religion.

The Gospels of Matthew (Chapters 24–25), Mark (Chapter 13) and Luke (Chapter 21) all contain passages of a similar (in places identical) kind in which Jesus advises of the circumstances of His return in the future — making specific reference to the Book of Daniel. These passages, known together as the 'Synoptic Apocalypse', led in the early years of Christianity to a general belief in His imminent return and the salvation of His flock. As the religion spread, so an interpretation surfaced which saw the millennium — the thousand years in which Christ would reign on earth — as becoming an extension of the earthly Roman Empire (Manuel (1965: 21–22)). As time elapsed without His return and with the collapse of the Roman Empire it became necessary to radically adjust these doctrines if Christianity was to survive and this was accomplished in the main by Saint Augustine (Manuel (1965: 22); Pollard (1968: 4)). Important among Augustine's accomplishments was a demotion of the millenarian texts and a systematic denial of the possibility of any worldly salvation.

Augustine's doctrines served well the institution of the Christian Church in the West and it was almost a thousand years before the possibility of earthly improvement emerged again into approved intellectual debate, as an aspect, that is, of the Renaissance (Tuveson (1949: 75)). However, the millenarian texts formed throughout this period a source for voluminous 'underground' interpretations and innumerable social movements (Cohn (1970)). By far the most important of the texts was the interpretation of Joachim of Fiore, a Calabrian monk of the late 12th century. His notion of history as an ascent through three stages — of the Father, the Son and the Holy Spirit — not only lent form to subsequent millenarian outbursts but survived explicitly into the social evolutionary schemes of the Enlightenment, the German Idealist philosophers (with a residue clearly extending into historical materialism) and Comte (Cohn (1970: 108–109); Berlin (1976: 116); Manuel (1965: 44); van Doren (1967: 78–80)).

The idea of the possibility of progress which arose in the Renaissance was little more than doubt cast upon the hitherto prevailing doctrine of the degeneration of the world from a 'golden age' and might be attributable in part to the tendency in any age to see progress where signs of progress are clearly to hand (Pollard (1968: ix, 1)). As Thomas (1973: 510) put it:

The reason for the replacement of this cyclical view of history by a linear one is one of the great mysteries of intellectual history. But one may hazard a guess at the answer, by saying that what is most necessary to produce a sense of change is the fact of change.

However, in the first instance, Renaissance historical theory in general adopted the cyclical notions of antiquity, with the Renaissance representing an upswing, rather than any more far-reaching progressivism.

It is often stated that the modern concept of progress starts from the propaganda for science of Bacon, Descartes and the era of the scientific revolution. There is, however, little textual evidence for this, where these early scientists iterated little more than a faith that systematically pursued science could 'relieve man's estate' and it is to developments in theological doctrine that we must turn to understand the way in which the elaborate modern idea of progress came into being (Tuveson (1949)).

As might be expected of the Reformation, interpreted as a manifestation of millenarianism, the biblical apocalyptic texts were revived as a major aspect of theology and used by Luther as justification for his reforms (Tuveson (1949: 24ff)). The peasant revolt to which Luther was opposed and the Anabaptist Commune of Münster which followed immediately upon the first signs of reformation (Cohn (1970: 251)) were more explicitly millenarian and indeed the process of fragmentation of the Protestant Church which continued across subsequent centuries has been closely bound up with interpretation of the apocalyptic texts.

Tuveson (1949: 71ff) traced carefully the way in which the apocalyptic became woven into secular intellectual doctrine particularly in the English universities through the 17th century. Whilst the introduction of Protestantism into the universities did not immediately bring with it apocalyptic or progressivist notions, but rather adopted Renaissance models, as the 17th century progressed a complex shift in views took place. This must be seen against the background of the English Revolution which, once again, sired — indeed can be interpreted as in part being sired by — a massive outburst of popular millenarianism (Toon (1970); Thomas (1973: 79, 165, 202, 485); Capp (1972); Hill (1975)). A growing interest in science coupled with a reinterpretation of the apocalyptic texts merged with a temporalised interpretation of the neo-Platonist 'Chain of Being' (Lovejoy (1936: 242ff)) led to a series of theological books emerging from English universities in the late 17th century which laid the foundations for the secular evolutionary theories of history, society and, indeed, nature which emerged in the course of the 18th century. The main exponents of this synthesis were Mede, Cudworth, Burnet and Henry More, but they were clearly part of a broader process of intellectual metamorphosis incorporating the rise of science. It is worth noting that Newton, as the founder of the scientific strain which emerged from this synthetic milieu, also wrote copiously — albeit privately — on interpretation of the Christian texts with a view to understanding chronology (Manuel (1968: Ch 17))[14].

From this point on the European millenarian tradition divided into two main branches, the 'premillennial' and 'postmillennial', both of which found textual justification in Christian theology (Harrison (1979: 4)). Premillennialism saw the world as degenerating to a point of crisis at which Christ (or some immediate precursor of Christ) would emerge to lead His flock to salvation, followed by a thousand years of beatific existence for the righteous. Postmillennialism saw the millennium beginning with little or no overt signs and consisting of a process of progressive improvement culminating in the judgement. Premillennialism became the ideology of the oppressed and of secular revolution and postmillennialism the ideology of the ruling classes and of secular progress.

A very substantial literature analysing the secular notion of progress has grown up since Bury's (1932) seminal work of 1924 and two classificatory dimensions have been used in attempting to bring some order to this complex issue. The first of these looks at the different areas of intellectual effort into which progressivism has penetrated and where it has lent structure and the second looks at the way in which the emphasis of interpretation has shifted through recent times. However, the universality — despite perennial fears to the contrary (Leiss (1972: 3ff)) — of the faith in both the desirability and inevitability of progress, which is both analogous, and related, to the faith in science, has militated against any very concerted critical analysis (Tuveson (1949: 1–2); Roszak (1973: 5)).

What remains of interest here is the way in which the emphasis in the dominant meaning of progress has shifted as a consequence of changing political circumstances over the past three centuries. As already noted, the secularisation of progress moved into all areas of European intellectual life in the course of the 18th-century Enlightenment and was epitomised by the notion of infinite improvement — 'perfectibility' — in the human spirit, as encapsulated in the writings of Condorcet (1976) in France and Godwin (1976) in England. The French Revolution precipitated a reaction against the egalitarian implications of these latter texts (Malthus (1970)) and with it came a severe utilitarian reinterpretation of progress: scientific progress would be the handmaiden of economic progress through the medium of technological progress.

The promotion of biological, geological and social, including anthropological, evolutionism in the second half of the 19th century, as aspects of the progressivist doctrine discussed in the foregoing chapter, can be interpreted as a further stage in the 'enlightenment' struggle between secular bourgeois intellectuals and the Church, at the same time extending materialist ideological control over the lower classes at home and in expanding colonial empires overseas (Burrow (1966); Beer (1983)). The ease with which these new interpretations of progress could be adapted for use by revolutionary movements — particularly in relation to Marxism which has (and not without contradiction) attempted to utilise both pre- and postmillennial elements — became increasingly evident towards the end of the 19th century and led eventually, and, as has already been pointed out, especially after the Russian Revolution, to the wholesale rejection of the bulk of 19th-century social evolutionist literature.

Nevertheless, the anti-evolutionist and pessimistic historical interpretations which followed the First World War and Russian Revolution never stood a chance of ousting the core of progressive doctrine. The modern world political system has rejected too great a reliance on ideological means to maintaining inegalitarian social relations and is dependent primarily upon an empirically demonstrable version of progress to hold the social and political system in place (Beckerman (1974: 32, 246); Singh (1989: 152)[15]. That is to say that the majority of the world's population must continue to feel that their lot is improving in material terms if they are going to continue to support the existing political conjuncture. Obviously for the poor peasant in Africa or Asia this can be achieved with relatively little outlay and, in any case, the European revolutionary traditions have no strong purchase in these cultures so that resignation, rather than revolt, is the usual response to lack of resources. For the working classes of the industrialised countries, however, relatively small improvements demand quite substantial resources. But the fear, on the part of the European ruling élite, of working class revolt in a situation of declining resources, in the light of millenarian revolutionary traditions, is far from groundless. Whilst the logic of the ecologists in their questioning of the very possibility, in the face of finite resources, of continuation of this state of affairs for much longer may be perfectly plausible, it is clearly necessary for the movement to confront both the underlying ideological inertia and the political forces which militate against the rejection of progressivism if anything is to be achieved prior to the dénouement which they see ahead.

The New Right appears to be semi-conscious of the problem in that it is concerned to obscure class consciousness and by this means secure a tacit acceptance of their lot by the lower classes, in a situation of economic stagnation and a general recessiveness in terms of the belief in progress. The image is one of an idealised 19th century, when the lower classes were supposed to have known their place, and thus where no demands for progressive material improvements would be made. This is, however, an extremely naïve representation of an age which, in practice, harboured and even nurtured social attitudes that resulted in the momentous emergence of social democracy at the turn of this century. It is laughable to imagine that the Conservative project, seen in any realistic historical perspective, could possess any hope of success in countering the trajectory towards ecological catastrophe that we face. It is unfortunate, however, that it commands enough attention to deflect the concerted development of political and ideological tools powerful enough to provide genuine means to avoid 'ecocatastrophe'. It will take far more than the Conservative project to diffuse the tensions of our inegalitarian society and beyond that to destroy incipient faith in progressivism.

Individualism

The use of the term 'ecology' by the Green movement goes well beyond simply a concern for the preservation of natural processes and a critique of science. As noted earlier in this chapter, it is anxious to assert the constitutive and symbiotic nature of the biosphere and our need to adapt our thinking processes as a foundation for our actions to this. Commoner's (1972a: 29ff) 'First Law of Ecology' stated simply that 'everything is connected to everything else'. The broad propaganda literature of the movement has generally referred to this in terms of embracing 'holism' (Bookchin (1982: 23); Capra (1982: 21); Porritt (1984: 200)). It is difficult to know how aware the movement is of the dangers of adopting this concept where in many a mind it is associated with ideas of authoritarian politics (Lukes (1973: 48)). However, it seems clearer that the movement has been consciously circumspect in attempting any very direct critique of the opposition to the holistic project, namely individualism and beyond that the notion of freedom (Lukes (1973:

124); Capra (1982: 224); Porritt (1984: 116–117)).

Nevertheless, if holism, as the root philosophical concept of the political ecology, is to become more than a 'mystical sigh', adjunct to 'environmentalist kitsch' (Bookchin (1982: 21)), then it will be necessary to undertake an adequate enquiry into the wellsprings of individualism and the mesmeric qualities of the related concepts of liberty and freedom. The subject is, unfortunately, of too great a dimension to treat here to any very satisfactory degree, but its importance dictates that a marker, at least, be placed. The following paragraphs are thus intended to sketch out certain issues that might prove important in a more thorough critique of individualism from an ecological perspective and should be seen as no more than terms of reference for a much more substantial critique at some future date[16].

The concept of individualism is of immense importance to our culture. The term itself has multifarious meanings and ambiguities which relate back to a number of reinforcing origins, and analysis of the various meanings indicates a cluster of related terms and concepts close to the centre of gravity of our cultural cosmology: freedom, liberty, justice, equality, autonomy, privacy, dignity (Lukes (1973)). As with the concepts of science and progress analysed in the foregoing sections of this chapter, the initial approach taken to understanding the power and complexity of the concept of individualism today is one of historic analysis.

At first glance the concept seems to have condensed out of the dissolution of feudalism in Europe and then over time to have acquired new facets and to have broadened and deepened in terms of its meaning and centrality to European thought and action. Walter Ullmann (1967) in his analysis of the individual and society in the middle ages traced the emergence of modern attitudes towards the individual, expressed as a transition from 'subject' to 'citizen'. The rigidly hierarchical nature of medieval society was such that the notion of individual choice in determining social circumstance could not arise. The legalisation of feudal relations around the end of the 12th century, emerging in England from the debate around Magna Carta, indicated the dawning of the possibility of the idea that social relations might not be immutable and that they may be open to challenge.

Whilst the medieval guilds and in general urban life in the Middle Ages included rigidities quite alien to modern urban life, it was nevertheless the growing towns of the late Middle Ages which provided the seedbed for individualistic attitudes. In particular these were associated with the rise of trade, where merchants could improve their own personal standing in the course of their work: there was 'freedom in town air' (Goldmann (1973: 23)). The Bible presented the concept of the nation as a body to which all belonged and served, but a new concept of society, with which individuals were confronted, emerged around the end of the 15th century (Stephen (1983: 123)). Then in Renaissance Italy, 'man' and the dignity of the individual became openly proclaimed (Lukes (1973: 47); Robertson (1933: Ch 4)). But at the simple practical level, legal equality, autonomy and freedom of movement were necessary prerequisites for the development of trade and so were promoted wherever trading interests were in a position to prevail (Goldmann

(1973: 18ff)).

However, as with science, the Renaissance provides us with the prehistory of modern individualism and it is, rather, to the Reformation that we must look for its substantive foundations. H. M. Robertson, in his critique of Weber's thesis on the Protestant ethic, was of the view that the Church was simply not strong enough, in the context of the Reformation struggle, to retain control over the conduct of merchants. He further noted that the emerging notions of 'natural law' were pagan rather than Protestant (Robertson (1933: 131-132)). These arguments, however, are not contradictory to those of Weber, but in addition to them. The Reformation simply broke the hold of the Church over the emerging entrepreneurial class, with Calvinism — despite the wishes of Calvin and the Calvinist Church — providing powerful ideological underpinning for the revolt (Tawney (1947: Ch 4)). The essential contribution of the Reformation to the growth of modern individualism (and its importance dictates that it be discussed at greater length later in this section) was the way in which it forcefully argued against the Church (read society) as arbiter and judge of morality and conduct, placing responsibility upon the individual conscience: each individual must make his own peace with God and prove his worth through his own efforts. This provided moral and religious impetus towards the creation of an essential inner isolation and loneliness of the hypostatised individual that is the hallmark of modern capitalist society (Weber (1976: 104–105, 181–182); Reisman (1950)).

In the course of the secularisation processes of the 17th century (already discussed in relation to the development of science and the notion of progress), this radical religious individualism became woven into social and political theory and into developing secular philosophy. The great innovation of Thomas Hobbes was to construct a conservative social theory upon an a priori assumption of society comprised of nothing more than atomistic individuals. In the first instance, this hypothesis was aimed at justifying higher authority as arbiter to prevent 'war of all against all'. However, with the subsequent development of liberal theory, an alternative vision came to the fore which saw social agreement as being sufficient to achieving a workable society (Locke (1965: Bk.2 Ch.8)); this gained wide acceptance in Rousseau's (1968) republicanism, under the title of the 'social contract'. C. B. Macpherson (1962) pointed to the essential interrelationship between the abstracted individualism of these theories and the concept of property: private property as of the merchant and at root the individual's ownership of the self, with his own privacy, potential for development and marketability. This individualistic view of society was essential to the development of ideas in both the French and Scottish Enlightenment (Goldmann (1973)) and although there was a broad reaction against this individualism in continental Europe during the 19th century starting with Hegel (Lukes (1973)) and broadening out into the development of a range of conservative and radical sociologies (Goldmann (1973: 5)), in the Anglo-Saxon world it remained dominant, initially under the heading of utilitarianism and in the 20th century within an uneasy truce prevailing between economistic 'rational choice' models and sociological explanations (James (1984)).

Earlier in this chapter it was pointed out how science had been created out of the confluence of neo-Platonism and the two apparently contrasting philosophies of rationalism and empiricism. At first it seems a paradox that the thinkers of the Enlightenment could accept, with apparent disregard of contradiction and without attempt at resolution, these contrasting philosophies. However, as Lucien Goldmann (1973: 19) put it:

The answer seems to be that these two philosophies share the same fundamental concept: the treatment of the individual consciousness as the *absolute origin* of knowledge and action.

It was Kant who created the formal synthesis, at the end of the Enlightenment — yielding in practice three forms of the same individualism. It takes comparatively little effort to translate each of these into a psychology and the great importance of psychology as a discipline during the 20th century, divided into apparently opposed approaches — behaviourism, Gestalt and cognitive, corresponding respectively to empiricism, rationalism and Kantianism — testifies on the one hand to the continued widespread adherence to these doctrines and, on the other, to the exaggerated concern of modern culture with the notion of the individual psyche.

Just as the Hegelian and subsequent critical, synthetic and dialectical philosophical attempts have failed to dislodge positivistic science from its pre-eminent position as intellectual arbiter, so these subsequent philosophies have failed to dislodge the primacy of individualistic alternatives. In the course of the 19th century there occurred a resurgence in Protestant-inspired individualistic philosophy, first in the writings of Kierkegaard and then in those of Nietzsche. Both reasserted the Calvinistic doctrine of self-responsibility and this became elaborated into an active rejection of the 18th-century 'objectivist' philosophies and an embrace of a radical subjectivism attaching to the individual human will. Whilst Husserl's phenomenology was somewhat distant from this subjectivism, it did share an antipathy for positive science and it was a synthesis of these neo-Protestant philosophies with phenomenology which resulted in the most extreme of individualist philosophies, existentialism (Warnock (1970)), already discussed briefly in Chapter 3.

Initially formulated by Martin Heidecker in the 1920s, it reached its climax in the work of Jean-Paul Satre in the 1940s and 1950s. The essential intention was to alert individuals to their potential freedom to live life on their own terms, not, however, in the form of advice, but as an urgent moral imperative. The result of following this imperative, according to Satre, was inevitably to encounter anguish, absurdity and ultimately nausea; any attempt to realise human love or any certain moral precepts was doomed to failure. Despite the profound pessimism of this philosophy, it gained a far wider hearing than other philosophical attempts during the middle years of this century, testifying to the peculiar susceptibilities of the age to individualist doctrine.

Further light is shed on the development of individualism in European society by looking briefly at the differences in its configuration and usage in different societies. The term 'individualism' first occurred in France, used by conservatives as a term of abuse directed at Enlightenment influences (Lukes

(1973: Ch. 1)). It meant a kind of selfishness that turns away from contributing to public life and resulting in apathy. This concept of individualism diffused and is basically the interpretation adopted by the ecological critique, in so far as one has been initiated. The term was, however, transmuted into a descriptor of liberal ideals and in the United States has become 'a symbolic catchword of immense ideological significance' (Miller (1967: 75); Lukes (1973: 26)); in Britain, too, it has come to represent liberal values against those of socialism and communism (Lukes (1973: Ch.5)). However, many socialists and communists have not rejected individualism — Jean Jaurès (Lukes (1973: 12)) echoed Oscar Wilde (1956) in asserting that 'socialism is the logical completion of individualism' — and although this could be construed as leading inevitably to contradiction, it is this socialist, rather than the Anglo-Saxon liberal, version of individualism which has been adopted widely in continental societies. This speaks of the self-realisation of human potentialities and desires and promotes a society which will facilitate this. Unlike the liberal vision, this is unlikely to be competitive and by no means necessarily unsocial in form. It must not, of course, be assumed that adoption of this concept of individualism necessarily obviates liberal and further epistemological and practical aspects of individualism found in Anglo-Saxon countries: just that a more equivocal and complex conception subsists against the background of the dominant liberal social and political reality.

Having described the triumphal march of individualism as the transformation of European social, political and cultural life over the past few hundred years — and that of the rest of the world in its train — it is now necessary to take a closer analytical look at certain forces that underlay this process. First it must be stressed that the ideologues of post medieval individualism were not inventing ideas but reviving them. That Descartes' key proposition 'I think, therefore I am' was almost a verbatim restatement of propositions put forward by Saint Augustine over a thousand years earlier (Russell (1961: 353)) may be mere happy coincidence, but that Calvin and the Reformation ecclesiastics, in placing so much emphasis on individual responsibility, were consciously rejecting scholastic teaching and reaching back to the ancient Church, and specifically Augustine, there be no doubt. It will be recalled how earlier in this chapter it was described how Augustine had attempted to save the church from succumbing to the destruction of Rome. This was done by sundering the temporal world from the spiritual and throwing the faithful in upon themselves, to carry forward the legacy of the Church — essentially its moral teachings, but with these preserving the texts and the ritual — through whatever temporal problems that might arise. It is a great paradox that the Augustinian strategy, involving the rejection of reform, revolution or any other temporal salvation (Russell (1961: 360)), should have provided such a powerful ideological basis for a regeneration of temporal power of dimensions far exceeding those of which Rome would ever have been capable. Nevertheless, it was Augustine's allocation of essential moral responsibility to the individual which remains recognisable in the 'Protestant ethic' (Russell (1961: 335)).

Parts of a social explanation of this process have already been presented earlier in this chapter. That Augustine's precepts might, within another context, possess temporal ramifications was quite invisible to Augustine and quite irrelevant in the context of growing political dislocation. Feudalism was an essentially community-based defensive structure directly confronting this context: the feudal village evolved directly out of rampant social disorganisation (Curtler (1920: 4)). The ebbing away of disorder left behind an initially self-reproducing structure which gradually metamorphosed with the growth of economic effectiveness and the irrelevance of the structure. Without wishing to add anything to the substantial debate over the emergence of capitalism out of feudalism (Dobb (1946); Hilton (1976)), it merely requires to be noted here that the incipient pressure of unequal class relations could only be expected to wring changes where the political structure and the ideological system provided inadequate constraint. If Augustine had, for the sake of argument, advocated Confucianism (this being an ideology which arose in similar circumstances in Chinese history, as sketched in a little more detail in the final chapter), then perhaps, as Weber argued forcefully, the development of capitalism would have been inhibited, or perhaps the contending classes would have found alternative ideological underpinnings. It must, however, be stressed that the society and culture which evolved out of the Middle Ages did not invent or choose its ideology freely and the one it inherited was crucial in sowing the seeds of the manifold notions of individualism that inform our lives today.

In completing this line of argument, it is useful to note that whilst Augustine produced a great work of synthesis, we cannot place the origins of our notions of individualism directly at his door. As with our notions of science, so also the origins of our particular notions of individualism originate in ancient Greece and in Judaism. From Greece we inherit the notion of individual competition as virtuous (Andrewes (1971: 216)) and an ascetic attitude towards the enjoyment of consumption (Andrewes (1971: 232ff); Russell (1961: Bk 1 Chs.17–18)), together with certain aspects of an epistemological individualism. Augustine consciously incorporated the last two into his synthesis. From Judaism we inherit our reductive humanism ('anthropocentrism') (Turner (1983: 25)), although aspects of this can also be found in Greek sources, especially Stoicism. The transmogrification of the tribal gods of Mesopotamia — relatively minor entities in the Mesopotamian pantheon (Roux (1980: 92)) — into the jealous God of Israel (Russell (1961: Bk 2 Ch.1)) is one of the momentous events of world religious history, creating, as it did, the sophisticated notion of monotheism and a certain kind of rationalisation of religion as abstract moral and cosmological system. But whilst this single God might suggest individualism, it is rather the Judaic doctrine of the human soul as focus of ultimate value, meaning and salvation that provides the true key to the modern concept of individualism. The Greeks also possessed notions of the soul, as do many religious systems. Their notion of the soul, however, had many manifestations, extending in complex fashion well beyond the individual and, in Plato's version, embracing nature as a complete entity. Aristotle (1976: 35) did not single out the individual human being as the sole possessor of a soul. The stoics, on the other hand, held the individual soul to be paramount (Andrewes (1971: 285)), which is, perhaps, a central reason why stoicism has been looked upon so sympathetically by Christians through the ages. Whilst ecologists (Lovelock (1979); Merchant (1980)) attempt to substitute Greek concepts of the soul for the Judaic, this is initiated against a background of an extremely broad and deep diffusion of the latter notion throughout the modern consciousness, most obviously in Cartesian dualistic rationalism and Anglo-Saxon moral and epistemological individualism.

Moving now beyond the historical derivation of individualism to sketch out certain more theoretical questions, it is first necessary to point out that individualism clearly relates most directly to the larger field of ethics. It concerns what individuals *ought* to do and is criticised because it fails to lead to the behaviour expected within it or even encourages unethical behaviour, but it is an evaluative concept not merely of individuals but concerning society as well. In this light it is useful to discuss the development of individualism in the general context of mechanisms of social structuring.

In recent years anthropologists and some historians — particularly concerned with ancient Greece — have put forward the notion that societies tend towards 'shame culture' or 'guilt culture'[17]. Shame culture involves a situation where actions are predominantly taken for the eyes of others and guilt culture where actions are judged predominantly by the actor. We can say that these represent mechanisms whereby the 'essence of being human' is translated into forms of social existence. Although these are in no way mutually exclusive, with any given 'civilised' culture containing an amalgam of the two expressed in different class and subcultural configurations, nevertheless, the implication is that the evolution of civil society has included a tendency for guilt culture to supersede shame culture. Although we cannot assert a categorical incompatibility between individualistic modes of expression and shame culture, nevertheless, the development of individualism is clearly closely connected with the development of guilt culture. The evolution out of shame culture into guilt culture is the very soul of the notion of freedom but in reality the communal prison becomes one of solitary confinement.

Whilst shame and guilt can be seen to give meaning to structure in society and culture, these do not in practice *create* structure. The creative process, and its results seem to us to lie somehow outside the realm of meaning and to be judged by it only in retrospect. It is possible to speak of a 'ground' of rationality within which shame and guilt become the arbiters in time of what is good and what is bad. These structures — the mechanisms of what is 'other than human' — are what in anthropology and semiology is referred to as myth and ritual. But it covers all that we think of as both aesthetic and rational, be it 'art' or technical procedure, the hunting routine, the operation of a nuclear power station or the performance of a symphonic work.

In his monumental work on social evolution *The Ecology of Freedom*, Murray Bookchin (1982: 114–115) developed the notion of 'organic societies' to describe pre- and early civil societies in contrast with those which emerged in the process of civilisation, writing:

In organic societies, social life more or less approximates this state of affairs. Nature generally imposes such restrictive conditions on human behaviour that the social limits encountered by the individual are almost congruent with those created by the natural world....Accordingly, organic societies do not make the moral judgments we continually generate against transgressions of our social rules. In the preliterate world, cultures are normally concerned with the *objective* effects of crime and whether they are suitably rectified, *not* with its subjective status on a scale of right and wrong....The native may feel *shame* if the transgression is discovered or may lose face as a result of public disapproval, but he or she does not feel *guilt*, notably, an internalised sense of self-blame and anxiety that evokes repentance and a desire for atonement....Guilt and repentance, as distinguished from shame and the practical need to redress the effects of a social transgression, become character traits with the emergence of morality.

Ancient Greece evolved out of tribal societies that were intensely communitarian, but which underwent an extraordinary process of social experimentation (Littman (1974)). A key attribute underlying this process was intense intercommunity and interpersonal competition which had the effect of developing both intellectual independence and *de facto* individualism. Greek scholars generally see Homeric Greece as overwhelmingly a shame culture, with an evolution toward guilt culture informing the Hellenic era (Andrewes (1971: 216)). Christianity is generally seen as overwhelmingly a guilt culture. However, medieval Europe was, rather, predominantly a shame culture: the practice of the confession in the Middle Ages, structured upon Summa (Tentler (1974)), provides a fascinating insight both into the complexities of social control through the period of medieval dissolution as well as the tutoring of that society in the details of guilt structures with which it was launched into the modern world. These provided, as it were, the scaffolding which Luther impetuously cast off (Tentler (1974: 123–124)). At each turn of the social evolutionary screw, it seems, a process of self-enculturation from shame culture to guilt culture ended in an enormous widening of the horizons of the cultures which underwent the process.

Nevertheless, whilst a given society may appear to be predominantly one or other of these types, classes and subcultures within a society might differ significantly from the general. MacIntyre (1967: 37ff) analysed the motivational structures of English class archetypes and concluded that whilst the middle class entrepreneur might be predominantly beholden to guilt structures, the public-school educated upper class was of a more 'tribal' nature, beholden to shame structures. The working classes, too, possess a significant dimension of shame structures. It is significant, however, that the *dynamic* element of modern, individualistic, Enlightenment European society is recognised as being overwhelmingly an expression of middle class guilt culture. The popularity of Robinson Crusoe, since its appearance in the early 18th century, presents the individualist Utopia (Morton (1969: 116)): the reflection of a culture that has the confidence in its guilt-based enculturation process that it can cast its members into any environment and their control over life will remain at root invariant. The shape of the social hierarchy, with its explosive guilt-dominated heart and shame-dominated outer reaches is reproduced also in the messianic European expansionist cultural project. Frederick Turner (1983) dissected the violent process of European domination of the 'New World' which the structure of European moral attitudes made possible, scrutinising the way in which shame culture emerged amongst frontier communities, fearful of 'going native'. And the dark side of these mechanisms was also reflected in the novels of Joseph Conrad, E. M. Forster and others, who explored and reinforced the shame culture that emerged in British colonial communities in Africa and Asia.

Thus, these different inner structuring mechanisms have their corollary in the outer world. Shame culture requires the existence of authority (though not necessarily hierarchical) and an invariant system of norms and standards of human conduct, which in tribal society is transmitted predominantly via mythology. Guilt culture, on the other hand, whilst permissive of social distinction, does not require it and is indeed incipiently disinterested in social problematic (Troeltsch (1931: 55–59)) and suspicious of conscious social enterprise; it bears the word 'freedom' on its banner: freedom from social control. And it is luxuriantly creative of 'rational' structures in the surrounding world of nature and society. In place of authority or uniform moral code, it requires a well-developed law. Shame culture is inherently more restrictive with respect to the forms of social structure within which it can operate effectively, requiring some form of 'community'. Guilt culture provides altogether more expansive terms of reference for social development. Whilst this may lead to the kind of social implosion of the ascetic community or hermit, in the specific instance of Western Europe, with its notion of 'worldly asceticism', the social organisational problematic falls away, presenting an essentially permissive context, dependent upon the inertia of pre-existing attitudes and structures[18] and the contingencies of evolving interests to provide it with orientation and meaning. This is both analogous and related to the structure of science dealt with earlier in this chapter.

Throughout the period of civil society, 'rational' structures — nature absorbed into the structure of human life and organised through exogenous social institutions and structures — remains the ground against which the dynamic shame and then guilt cultures construct social life. In our own era, however, the sheer productiveness of guilt culture in the context of hierarchical society — capitalism and the weird 'dissipative structures' (Prigogine (1980)) of industrialising and urbanising humanity — has generated a framework of rational structures which have become an alternative fate to that represented by nature in the past. We have handed over control of most of our decisions to socially produced mechanisms, physical and organisational. Yet these remain 'irrational', in the sense that they are aspects of a hierarchical society where interests are inherently assumed to be, and hence de facto, antagonistic and where the agreement to abide by common rules remains grudging — the law is just a minor aspect: the operation of office practices, or technical procedures inside the productive process, or the mechanised home and the amazing proportion of human consciousness surrendered to driving cars, are the everyday manifestations of this. Whilst rational culture is no longer for most of us a relation with an unknown nature, but rather with a human-created world, this remains a peculiarly lifeless relation, a dance with the dead. The key to understanding this lies, of course, in the possessive quality of our relationship with the outer and indeed the inner world: an existentialist separation at source of the essential 'I', and of the potential for love and community, from action and production in the world, including the presentation (the marketing) of the self. Whilst the frustration which this generates is extraordinarily productive, it is productive of a world inhabited by the most meagre of empathy, informed merely by instrumental meaning. Both shame and guilt are attitudes informed by fear, mistrust and an intransigent denial of love that is generated by the desolate isolation of the 'I'. They are the hallmarks of civil society as such, that Hobbes seemed to assert as an eternal truth of the human condition[19] but which Rousseau (1964a) recognised for what it is: the essence of civilisation-created individualism. Alasdair MacIntyre (1981: 244–5), in concluding his extensive analysis of moral theory, 'After Virtue', was convinced that the potential for our moral inheritance to continue to hold our political world together is exhausted. We are faced with something analogous to the decline of Rome into the 'Dark Ages' and it is necessary to construct local forms of community to sustain moral and intellectual life through a new Dark Age and defend ourselves against the barbarism of our existing governing structures. This reproduces the vision of Edward Goldsmith (1971) which inspired the production of the 'Blueprint for Survival'. Goldsmith was convinced of, and MacIntyre implied, the need to return to a shame-dominant culture to regenerate a workable moral system.

The 'return' to a local communitarianism need not, however, be of a defensive kind or, indeed, in any way a reaction: the vision of an anarchist Utopia[20] is, indeed, implicit in the Hegelian vision of the development of human capabilities, and more clearly in the Marxist vision of communism, as the ultimate solution to the riddle of civilisation. Political ecology pictures humanity as standing on a fatal threshold of civilisation from which we could collapse backwards into MacIntyre's vision of a new Dark Age — or, indeed, total annihilation — or we can forge a new kind of human existence where shame and guilt culture — community and individual as organising principles — are transcended in a new mode of organising the satisfaction human needs in nature. Satisfaction of the needs of the individual human organism are, of course, important, but individualism based upon an abstract notion of the soul (Lukes (1973: 72n)) must be rooted out and replaced by a caring and sharing process that satisfies human needs organically, working with and through nature. 'Rational culture' becomes the resolution to the cultural problematic as such, but in a form infused with human meaning and empathy so that the structures which it creates are those which are both ecologically benign and accessible to community control, and above all orientated toward satisfying human needs through community self-activity. Infused with the essence of humanity making up the community, the fusion of the individual 'I's, liberated from the prison of civilisation, such a culture would supersede the rational with the empathetic, the aesthetic and the hedonistic, where the outer structures of life *are* that which is essentially human. This would be no system of defence against barbarism, but a supersession of shame-restricted community and benighted guilt-ridden individualism alike: the achievement of Utopia.

Conclusions

The concepts of science, progress and individualism have been immensely productive in extending the realms of the human, in generating social structure and in transforming the relationship between society and nature and, through this, contributing to the restructuring of society itself. The inner assumptions of these concepts, or rather the beliefs and attitudes which they embody, have been that the process of transformation has been both necessary and good, and adherence to these beliefs necessarily involves a continuing faith that ultimately they serve our interests well.

From an ecological perspective, this optimism is seen as unjustified. Whilst it is of little value to cast recriminations at the past, it is certainly possible to conjecture that progress could have given way to a stable form of relationship with nature at any level of scientific knowledge: there is no ultimate understanding of nature although there has clearly developed an ever more effective form of knowledge in terms of society's ability to intervene in and transform nature. The individualism that has informed this progression, and which can be understood as a central motor of the process that stretches back across the entire history of civil society — perhaps being the key term of civilisation as such — can be interpreted at the same time as a great tragedy: corroding away the essential oneness of humanity-and-nature, consciousness-and-nature, to leave the individual human being isolated, lonely and insecure.

But it is not the past which is in question for political ecology. Our problem is simply that these beliefs and attitudes cannot continue to prevail if the biosphere and humanity are to survive in any very happy form, if at all. There is a pervasive belief that the Enlightenment set the terms of reference for the supersession of religion, more specifically Christianity. And whilst some analyses have been concerned with how tenaciously religion has survived at the margins of society, it is assumed to be self-evident that ours is a predominantly secular culture. What this chapter reveals is that the particular process of secularisation that unfolded has only the more effectively concealed the Judaeo-Christian foundations of our system of beliefs and attitudes. The notion that nature is a lifeless thing over against the value of man; the drive towards millenarian ends; and the supreme value of the individual human being: all these are Judaeo-Christian teachings that *remain* central to our putatively secular and rational society.

So, according to political ecology, it becomes necessary to transcend secularisation and construct a system of beliefs, an ideology, which will better serve the needs of future generations by having regard to the needs of nature as the basis for all human existence, and then seeing to the requirements of human consciousness as a whole in order to ensure that the needs of the individual organism can be and are satisfied. But how should this task be approached? In practice, political ecology arose as an intuition rather than any very coherent theory. It is a social movement before it has defined its problematic in any very clear fashion (Enzensberger (1974)). This provides good grounds for optimism in the sense that the movement to change what we do — which is all that matters in the end — rather than what we think is already under way. Elsewhere (Atkinson (1991)) I have analysed and presented the political background to, and programme of, the Green movement and this is therefore not dealt with further here. It remains only to pull the threads of the various arguments developed in this book together and this is the function of the next and final chapter.

Notes

1. The concept of stewardship of nature, developed by Black in the fourth chapter of his essay (1970: 44–57) became popular amongst environmentalists in the mid-1970s and although his putative historical derivation of the concept as a strain of Western attitudes was criticised by Passmore (1980: 30), it must be recognised that Black made no secret of the fact that he was more concerned with building a robust concept than in passive derivation, analysis or exegesis (Black (1970: 118–119)).

2. Paganism and rural superstition appear to environmentalists today as interesting — even beguiling — curios of distant history and distant cultures. However, as recently as the early years in this century, the anthropologist Sir James Frazer, in compiling his massive compendium on magic and religion under the title of *The Golden Bough*, was of the view that the broad mass of the European population was, even then, steeped in such beliefs — a situation which clearly left him apprehensive. See, for instance the quotation in Chapter 3, footnote 3.

3. Winner (1977: 24) wrote: "The consensus of historians of science and technology is that the wedding of science and techniques came only in the late nineteeth century, with most of the progeny of this match arriving in the twentieth". Thomas (1983: 788) wrote: "The difference between the eighteenth and sixteenth centuries lies not in achievement but in aspiration"; (p 790): "The change was less a matter of positive technical progress than of an expectation of greater progress in the future". It is explained below that close functional relations existed between science and changing social relations from the beginning; this relationship is not, however, sufficient to explain the appearance of science, the expectations within which far exceeded its immediate practical worth. It was the German sociologists Weber, Sombart, Tönnies, Borkenau, Troeltsch et al. who investigated this problem in depth and as Borkenau (1934:3) put it: 'Die Naturwissenschaft des 17. Jahrhunderts stand nicht im Dienste der industriellen Produktion obwohl sie das seit Bacons Zeiten gewünscht hätte.'

4. Upon the publication of *Against Method*, Feyerabend was inundated with criticism to which he answered with a book of refutations (Feyerabend (1979)) entitled *Science in a Free Society*. Nevertheless, the 'philosophy of science debate' is still predominantly conducted in terms of 'Popper versus Kuhn'; Feyerabend's (1978: Ch.17) analysis of the Homeric Era as a world view encompassing all forms of 'knowledge', totally distorted by prevalent analytical assumptions imposed upon it from the modern standpoint, possesses great force and subtlety but, it must be realised, comes together with a 'freedom of approach' which clearly remains unacceptable to established debate regarding scientific method.

5. It is often pointed out that on the whole the various Protestant sects were never intended as separate churches but each as a move to reform the one Christian Church. Once separatism had occurred, however, the precedent was there for an infinite regress of repeat performances. The direction of change was generally towards an imagined primitive simplicity and hence towards at once a

conservative reductionism and a self-dissolution which could either mean fanaticism (evangelism on the one hand, the philosophies of the likes of Stirner, Kirkegaard and Nietzsche on the other) or secularisation; the dialectic between these not only characterises Northern European religious life in subsequent years but spilled over into a 'negative dialectic' which could be discerned to continue as the characteristic form of secular political thought in Northern Europe.

6. There was, as Thomas (1973:93) pointed out, an inherent problem for Christians in the separation of creation and creator as manifest in the shift from organicist to mechanist notions of nature and that was the notion that God, once He had set the mechanism in motion, was no longer of any account — indeed a *deus absconditus*; this was clearly an insight to be avoided. In fact a very similar problem had been present in medieval debate surrounding the Great Chain of Being (Lovejoy (1936: 67–79) wherein the perfection of the creation on the part of the creator meant that there was no freedom to alter anything and hence no further function for the creator — or worse, no basis upon which the righteous could demonstrate moral choice.

7. White (1960: 124) wrote: "Suddenly towards the middle of the fourteenth century, the mechanical clock seized the imagination of our ancestors". The image thus preceded its use as analogy for nature as a whole. Otto Mayr (1986) has contributed a valuable analysis of the relationship between social developments and the various uses of mechanical analogy in early modern European history, and particularly in relation to different national cultures.

8. Merton's thesis, first published in 1938, was an attempt at a wide-ranging sociological analysis of the relationship between social and ideological change in 17th-century England on the one hand and the development of science and technology on the other. In the course of his investigation he stumbled on the equation of an enthusiasm for science with active Puritan religious affiliation and followed out this line of investigation as a conscious complement to Max Weber's (1976) thesis on the connection between Protestantism and capitalism. Just as Weber's thesis had generated a massive controversy, so, too, did Merton's analysis of Protestantism and science — though other aspects of his analysis, notably his attempt to show how eager 17th-century English scientists were to achieve practical results, received less attention. Hill accepted Merton's (1970: 112–136) stress on the connection between Protestantism and science and when challenged (Kearney (1964)), answered by extending his conviction in the deep links between these to a Europe-wide phenomenon (Hill (1964)).

These Anglo-Saxon commentaries on the connection between Protestantism and science are referring to utilitarian empiricism rather than a broader interpretation of science. It is important to stress, however, that English empiricism — particularly as expressed by Bacon — is quite useless without some theoretical structure through which to operate. Neo-Platonism and Cartesian rationalism cannot be seen to be in any obvious way intellectually consistent with Protestantism and Copernicanism seems to have become attractive to Protestants mainly because of Catholic persecution of Galileo (Ben-David (1971: 71)). Hill's (1964: 89) note to the effect that the good Catholic Descartes found a more congenial home in Protestant countries only confuses the issue. Protestantism certainly found *use* for these Catholic branches of science — they were, indeed, vital ingredients of Newton's synthesis; but it was unlikely to *generate* these indispensable ingredients.

It is interesting to note that the Protestant Church — Luther and Calvin were both explicit on this — was as opposed to science as was the Catholic Church (Merton (1970: 101–102)) and far from Jansenism promoting science in France, as suggested by Hill (1964: 89), it seems Pascal rejected science in the process of his conversion to Jansenism (Merton (1970: 120)). What made the difference in practice was the avowed individualism of Protestantism that directed the faithful to make their own peace with God. If one sees all the churches as having striven to maintain an intellectual monopoly (that, after all, is one of the main purposes of the church) then the individualistic aspirations of Protestantism can be seen to have opened the door to the demise (or secularisation) of a unitary intellectual life. Whilst, as Merton (1970: 99–101) was at such pains to stress, the contradictions of Protestant doctrine unfolded in ways quite invisible to its promoters, an extension of this view, put by Weber (1976: 72, 182), is that secularisation merely conceals the religious underpinning of modern culture. This latter view is central to this analysis.

9.   That science remained largely separate from technology and, in general, practical problems was argued above. The problem had a clear class dimension. Whilst the bourgeoisie adopted science as a 'practical' ideology in contrast to the ideology of the existing ruling classes, their way of life, and hence involvement in detailed practical problems of the day, was already sufficiently distant for their notion of practicality to be in practice of little practical value. In other words, as Dobb (1946) makes clear, five hundred years of urban development had separated the bourgeois from their class origins as craft artisans and created a substantial social distance between crafts and bourgeois occupations of trade and finance. Zilsel (1942) argued that the 17th-century Scientific Revolution in England had to do with a class coalition between Bourgeois and artisan as part of the more general temporary co-option of the lower middle classes to achieve the aims of the English Revolution. Certainly science seems to have lost its interest in practical problems in England in the latter part of the 17th century (Merton (1970: 204)) and especially the early 18th century, with the centre of scientific enquiry passing over to France (Ben-David (1971: 77)). Meanwhile, however, bourgeois society, *qua* society, proved itself in 18th-century England to be a fertile basis for *technological* advance (Landes (1969: 125)).

10. 'Practicality' for the peasant farmer is clearly something different from that which occupies the mind of the artisan or, again, the merchant. Indeed, the Church liturgy and general intellectual edifice has many practical dimensions (providing sense to otherwise incomprehensible life problems; also providing an economic base for the clergy; etc.) even though this is not advertised as such. All too easily, utilitarianism is imagined to possess its own internal justification whereas in practice what is and is not God's work (ie morally good practice as opposed to morally bad practice) is part of the Protestant idealogical system which is in turn justification for bourgeois values. (Adam Smith (1976: 429–449) exposed this in his telling discussion of 'productive' and 'unproductive' labour).

11. Bruno Latour (1986) wrote (paraphrased in Aronowitz (1988: 293)): "...what counts as scientific knowledge achieves this status by linking itself to power — the power of leading figures in the scientific community and the state, and that of corporations that sponsor and transform research into technology."
     In recent years this insight has been receiving increasingly urgent attention (see *inter alia* Barnes (1974: 102ff; 1977), Singh (1989: Ch.7) and Aronowitz (1988)). As an early expression of this insight from within the ecology movement, Barry Commoner (quoted in Singh (1989: 155) wrote: "Thus, when any environmental issue is pursued to its origins, it reveals an inescapable truth — that the root cause of the crisis is not be to found in how men interact with nature, but how they interact with each other." However, we are still some way from this insight becoming the *central* proposition of the ecological critique which it clearly must

become.

12. Engels succumbed to the fatal positivist trick, which dominated thinking in the period in which he wrote, of converting ontology into epistemology, analysing nature from the point of view of categories imposed by science rather than empathising with nature itself; this then became accepted dogma in the context of Soviet theory of science. Although he made use of the work of Haeckel, he failed to note his suggested programme for 'ecology': at least with respect to the biosphere, this might have proved to be a more fruitful approach to take in seeking a dialectics of nature.

13. Powers (1982: 102–103) noted that Bolzmann's later theory eventually won acceptance within the framework of Einsteinian relativity. This used a statistical approach to bring thermodynamics into the fold of classical mechanics. However:

> "...the statistical interpretation sabotages the very characteristic — namely its irreversibility — which made 'entropy' a candidate for appointment as the 'arrow of time'....This indicates that the search for a physical basis for the directionality of time is confused. Such a search may be motivated by the feeling that 'time' is to elusive to be 'physically real', and that the idea can only be properly secured if it is identified with some other characteristic of things.

> On the other side, a statistical approach acknowledged a 'weak' hypothesis in relation to any strict deterministic science".

14. It is interesting to speculate on the relationship between the suppression of Newton's work on time and the suppression of time throughout the development of classic physics, as discussed in the previous section of this chapter. The spiritual and mystical qualities attaching to consideration of the cosmological role of time clearly influence its radical rejection by the Apollonian — indeed macho — milieu of classic physics.

15. Singh's analysis, completed in 1976 but only published outside India during the 1980s, is an important contribution to the development of political ecology. Its basic thesis is that ecocatastrophe is inevitable unless society is reconstructed on the basis of complete social equality and complete participation in all aspects of our social self-creation — of work. Apropos the use of economic growth as a means to maintain inegalitarian social relations, he quoted Henry Wallich as writing: "Growth is a substitute for equality of income. So long as there is growth there is hope, and that makes large income differentials tolerable". Man, Singh then comments, must liberate himself from a society that knows only how to play Acquisition, a game which must perforce end in disaster.

16. Bookchin is clearly greatly concerned with ethical questions. In his discussion of the evolution of Western ethics and society (Bookchin (1982)), he took 'freedom' as one of the *aims* of an ecological society: it appears as a condition of pre-civil society (p 143) and then, following its subversion and perversion throughout civilisation, is destined to emerge again in ecological society. However, little is said about it in the final chapters of *The Freedom of Ecology* and there remains an undertow of problematic contradiction in the use of the term. Hence also his discussion of the individual (pp 153–166) fails to present a clear analysis. On the one hand the liberal project embodied in: "the 'individualistic' philosophies of Hobbes and Locke emanates from bourgeois notions of selfhood .... mean-spirited, egoistic, and neurotic.... riddled through by cunning and insecurity ... The new gospel of secular individuality conceived the self in the form of *homo economicus*, a wriggling and struggling monad, literally possessed by egotism and an amoral commitment to survival". On the other hand there developed a 'utopistic vision of individuality' initiated by the Greeks and affirmed by 'the so-called individualistic anarchist' Max Stirner as assertion of personality in 'an

increasingly impersonal world'. It might be conjectured that it will prove a herculean task for Americans to root out the concept of individualism and understand the holistic project in its consistent denial of the 'atomistic' and lonely human soul. (See Stephen (1983) for suggestions regarding this problem.)

17. Murray Bookchin (1982: 115n) notes that the anthropologist Paul Radin (1953) and the historian E. R. Dodd (1951) each independently developed the notions of 'shame culture' and 'guilt culture'. The notions diffused from there into the respective literatures.

18. In anthropological terms, one of the most striking features of European bourgeois culture is the insistence with which it repeatedly casts back to the past for rejuvenation of its cultural symbols and structures, so that for all the *material* transformation of society, the outlines of medieval (and to a degree ancient) culture remain clearly visible (the repeated re-emergence of classical architectural style — recently as 'postmodernism' — is an obvious example). The abject lack of cultural self-confidence remains salient.

19. Macpherson (1962: 17–29) argued strongly that Hobbes did not really have it in mind that his version of 'human nature' should be construed psychologically but rather that it presupposed civilization: "Thus in the *Rudiments* the state of war is a hypothetical condition, got by a purely logical abstraction. Yet in calling this hypothetical condition 'the state of nature' Hobbes makes it easy to misread it either as a condition historically prior to civil society or as a hypothetical condition deduced from men's 'natural' characteristics considered entirely apart from their socially acquired characteristics."

20. Lukes (1973: 72n) writes: "For Kropotkin, in a society organised on anarchist principles and 'mutual aid', man would be 'enabled to obtain the full development of all his faculties, intellectual, artistic and moral, without being hampered by overwork for the monopolists, or by the servility and inertia of mind of the great number. He would then be able to reach full *individualisation*, which is not possible either under the present situation of *individualism*, or under any system of State Socialism in the so-called Volkstaat...'" Kropotkin's (1974) *Fields, Factories and Workshops* remains a text of great relevance to political ecology, even today, concerning the organisation of a decentralised anarchist society.

6 Principles of political ecology

The impetus behind the writing of this book has been the desire to deepen and broaden out theory and, at not too great a remove, practice with respect to overcoming the suicidal trajectory which our culture and society are following. In Chapter 2 academic attempts to understand the nature of the ecology movement and its concerns were reviewed and shown to fall very far short of any coherent analysis even with regard to the generally restricted preoccupations of academia, let alone needs of the ecology movement for more coherent theory. The approach taken in this book therefore has been in part to build upon the work of political ecologists coming from a Marxist background and in part to carry out a number of explorations into methodology and epistemology that try to bring the intuitions of the ecologists to bear upon the conventional content and traditions of academic and broader intellectual discourse. The purpose of this final chapter is to attempt to bring an overall order to bear upon the fragments of the foregoing analysis. Because in recent years a substantial debate has materialised around the concepts of 'ecophilosophy' and 'deep ecology' that sees philosphy in relative isolation as the best way to approach the avoidance of ecocatastrophe, it may be useful to enter the main discussion of this chapter by a brief exposition of why ecophilosophy, as it stands, is inappropriate or at least inadequate to the task in hand and hence why the principles of political ecology laid out in the subsequent pages have been chosen as the appropriate vehicle of theory in this field.

Much of ecophilosophy attempts, using reason, rhetoric and recitation, to establish direct links between our consciousness and nature aimed at achieving a mental or ideological reconfiguration that will simply displace pre-existing ideologies. I certainly do not wish to say that these efforts are pointless: much of this now very extensive literature (Davis (1989); Engel and Engel (1990)) is indeed extremely useful by way of background, unearthing the nature and origins of the malfunctioning of our society; indeed, a selection from this literature served to inform parts of the foregoing analysis. However, on the whole it presents us with some very short circuits across what is a very complex and extended problem.

The way in which our society is going about destroying nature is not so much a matter of intention, nor even of a lack of consideration of important questions and issues concerning how we need to care for nature if we are ourselves to survive. It is certainly correct to assert that we need to be less anthropocentric in outlook and action and that we need to be aware of the consequences of what we are doing to nature, how we should establish new ways of understanding the biosphere and how we should change the ways in which we relate to it for our own good. But most people, most of the time are concerned with, and deeply embedded in, ideas and activities that are a very long way removed from 'our destruction of nature' in any general sense. Even when 'ordinary citizens' come across the ideas of the ecophilosophers — virtually never through reading but perhaps from time to time via television — it is in no way obvious how they might weave these insights into their own actions, into their daily lives. The idea that leaders in positions of power in politics and business will be willing to make — or are even capable of making — an effective translation between ecophilosophy and the fine grain of everyday activity is equally unrealistic.

This is not to say that there is no concern to make necessary changes or that changes that are being made are not genuine attempts to address the fundamental issues (though there is certainly a degree of dysfunctional self-righteousness and cynical opportunism at work here (Engel and Engel (1990: 5)). It is indeed remarkable how rapidly, in the late 1980s, activity consciously informed by an awareness of ecological crisis has proliferated, ranging from 'green consumerism', through the commissioning by business and local government of 'environmental audits' to new legislative initiatives to control environmental hazards. But these remain steadfastly 'environmentalist' initiatives in the sense outlined in Chapter 2: addressing the immediate environmental impacts in a fragmented manner but lacking any framework — ideological or practical — through which the totality of the problem might be addressed. As such, they fail to meet the criteria of ecophilosophy and implicitly — and in key respects explicitly — contradict the aims of political ecology.

The ecophilosophers — and indeed their 'practical' support in the actions of Greenpeace, Earth First! and other radical environmental campaign organisations — are concerned with problems that lie a very long way from the everyday lives of most people. And, with few notable exceptions, they are providing virtually no clues as to how to negotiate the distance between everyday life and some other way of doing things that is benign towards nature. Of course this results largely from the fact that they are themselves ignorant, the result of the processes of fragmentation of knowledge and skill which is one of the salient characteristics of our society. Beyond this — and somewhat more problematic — is the continued influence of the proscription upon ideas explicitly aimed at fomenting radical social change. It is more acceptable in intellectual circles to exhort people to take an ethical stance towards nature than it is to call for wholesale change in social and political structures.

But that is precisely what is required if the destruction of nature is to be forestalled. So it is not a question of political ecology, as laid out in these pages, being, as might be construed given the lack of discussion of nature as such, unconcerned with our attitudes towards nature, but rather that if we are in practice to have adequate regard for nature then we will need to change quite fundamentally our social and economic praxis. Thus principles of *political* ecology are concerned in the first instance to effect changes in the social and political machinery that structures our everyday lives, bearing in mind that the ultimate reconfiguration of the way in which these work will have to square with the sustainable self-reproduction of nature. It is necessary to accept culture and society as the central terms of our approach to forestalling ecological destruction; the everyday concerns and actions of 'ordinary citizens' and 'community leaders' will only make informed tracks in the direction of the insights of the ecophilosophers via an adequate understanding of social and cultural structure and process and through a conscious restructuring of this as a whole to produce a set of machinery that is inherently benign in its intercourse with nature.

It was an important part of the argument in Chapter 3 to demonstrate the close interaction of ideology and praxis at the level of everyday activity. It is possible to imagine our way into other worlds and to act upon this imagination. But the constraints on action, and, indeed, the imagination itself, emanating from the real structure of the world — physical, social and psychological — are substantial and complex. Much of the analysis in this book has been concerned to reveal the nature of these constraints but, above all, to demonstrate fallacies in our assumptions about certain constraints and to open up the possibility to reformulate the way we understand our capabilities such as to open up opportunities to move forward in new directions.

The political ecologist, like the environmentalist, starts from an assumption that it is necessary to make choices about how we live our lives in relation to the use of nature. The political ecologist is aware that these are not individual choices but social ones and so is concerned to ask the question: 'Will the choices currently being made by our society satisfy our material and spiritual needs and avoid ecological destruction?' Ten years ago the answer to this was clearly "No", in that not even environmentalism, let alone political ecology, had made any detectable impact on the social and political, encompassing economic, process. Today we can see a significant adoption of environmentalist measures ostensibly designed to address the issue of ecological destruction. But it takes little by way of hard analysis within the framework of an environmentalist perspective to realise that these measures amount in their results to no significant impact at all upon the general destructive trajectory. 'Sustainable growth' as the currently acceptable concept within which changes are politically tolerated, still calls for economic growth. It is quite clear to ecologists that substantially more thought and understanding, and upon that effective action, is required before we have reached a point where we can answer the foregoing question in the affirmative.

For political ecology there are good reasons to suppose that there is a prior question which we must find means to answer in the affirmative before we can meaningfully answer the foregoing question. That is: 'Do we possess a social decision-making structure that is capable of making effective choices to satisfy our material and spiritual needs and avoid ecological destruction?' The purpose of this book is to assist in arriving at a position where this question might be answerable in the affirmative: to lay the foundations for an adequate understanding of the way in which our predicament is determined by the totality of our social and ideological structures at all levels and how we might escape from these to build a sustainable, ecological society and culture.

The format to be used in this final drawing together of the threads of the analysis was outlined in Chapter 3: five dimensions or viewpoints are adopted from which to consider the most appropriate way to understand and thence to solve the ecological problematic. These are not treated simply as individual analytical frames, nor is the sequence adopted coincidental. Each new set of arguments is laid out in the light of the previously accumulated discussion with the intention that the whole sums to a single coherent argument.

The evolution of consciousness

We arrived very suddenly at the edge of the abyss, beyond which lies a very brutal ecological denouement. The passage that took us here was in vital aspects arbitrary and contingent; as Stephen Jay Gould (1990: 14) has put it :

(w)ind back the tape of life...; let it play again from an identical starting point, and the chance becomes vanishingly small that anything like human intelligence would grace the replay.

But where we are today, the way in which social evolution has become a rapidly moving affair propelled by a massive force of inertia, and the ideological and practical, physical accoutrements which validate it and shield us from the full horror of our predicament, are all essentially understandable in terms of the particular route taken. At several points in this book, this problem has been examined from various angles and it remains here to summarise and highlight aspects that are essential parts of the complete picture being sketched in this chapter.

Evolution of the biosphere has never stood still. However, by the standards of our individual experience or that of written human history, evolution of the biosphere has been for the most part an inconceivably leisurely process. That *Homo sapiens* had occupied an ecological niche for some one hundred thousand years before the advent of 'civil society' less than ten thousand years ago would seem to indicate that there was, as for any other species, a distinct relationship between this organism, with its novel form of consciousness and capability to adopt different forms of social organisation, and the rest of nature; not merely hundreds, but hundreds of thousands of generations came and went amongst small bands of people living in equilibrium with their particular piece of nature, evolving means of production, communication and self-expression — microcultures — that explained their particular part of the world and simultaneously regulated their relationships with nature and one another.

In this light, civil society is clearly a runaway phenomenon: an ever-present potential in the existence of human consciousness but aberrant in its manifestation. Until very recently, consciousness of the fact of social evolution, arrived at out of the frame of mind of European Enlightenment, was of a form that insisted that this process possessed some formal structure and could be understood as having a distinct beginning, middle and end. The 19th-century social evolutionists, Spencer, Morgan, Marx and many others (Burrow (1966); Sanderson (1990)) looked insistently for such structures and until very recently it was the conventional wisdom of all social evolutionary theorising that such a structure was there to be found even if there was, perhaps, more than one strand. There is most recently, however (Ingold (1986); Sanderson (1990)) a new consensus emerging which characterises social evolution in the following way: any particular cultural manifestation may be rendered reasonably comprehensible by reference to a discrete set of events that brought it into existence, including both internal creativity and influences from other cultures; as a general process, however, it has been and remains essentially 'chaotic', contingent, arbitrary, without necessary beginning, middle or, most importantly, end. And released from any theoretical evolutionist strictures, what becomes absorbing, fascinating, engaging, beautiful about the process is its sheer luxuriant creativity and inventiveness, the incredible fecundity of cultural manifestations, a vast display of serendipity.

Cultural evolution in the period of civil society has proceeded in step fashion, sometimes rapidly, sometimes gradually, sometimes maintaining a form of equilibrium over quite extended periods. Changes evolve within cultures and/or by the adoption or imposition and reworking of external influences. Typically civil cultures possess, and are conscious of themselves as possessing, coherent political and ideological — religious and ethico-philosophical — structures informing the way in which the lives of individuals are organised. The way in which the sacred and the secular intersect and the structuring effects which these have on particular individuals — and also the way in which individuals organise into interest groups and classes reacting back upon these structures — can take on an almost infinite variety of forms. Above all, what is sacred and what secular is not necessarily immediately obvious either to participants or outside observers. Previous chapters have looked in particular at the unfolding of cultural evolution in Europe between the 16th and 18th centuries and here it is necessary to refer back to this. However, to illustrate how similar and yet how different such processes can be, and might have been in Europe, it is interesting to sketch, by way of an object lesson, certain aspects of the cultural evolutionary path of China between three and two thousand years ago.

Following a period of some 1,000 years as a unified state, from the 7th century BC local powers in China began to grow in strength, usurping central authority and engaging in ferocious feuding and wars (Smith (1974)). This encouraged rapid social and cultural change. Rigid rural social structures broke down and social mobility increased; a new class of 'scholar knights' (shih) emerged to fill the growing demand for knowledge and entrepreneurial skills. Agricultural land came to be bought and sold as a commodity and there was a rapid proliferation of the arts and crafts and in trade; cities of several hundred thousand population grew up and opulent and sophisticated urban lifestyles emerged. Technological development was rapid, responding to the needs of burgeoning consumption and of war, resulting in inventions that found their way to, or were reinvented in, Europe only 2,000 years later. Secular philosophy emerged, concerned to address and find the means to overcome the instabilities of the age, looking on the one hand to ascetic renunciation of the world (Lao Tsu) and on the other back to the morality that had ostensibly secured the stabilities of empires of the past (Confucius) as models.

This age has been compared to the French Enlightenment (de Riencourt (1965)) but if instead it is compared with the Renaissance and this process of rapid cultural development in Chinese history is seen as having encouraged intellectual development that looked, *inter alia*, to the past for guidance, in the manner in which this proceeded in Renaissance Europe, then we obtain some insight concerning the subsequent differences between Chinese history and that of post Renaissance Europe. There was no Judaeo-Christian apocalyptic in ancient China, no Greek science and no Roman engineering. In short, the eventual institutionalisation of an essentially secular ideology originating in Confucius and developed by his followers (Mencius and others) in China, following its reunification some 400 years after Confucius' death, was of a form that did not encourage in practice or theory a linear pattern of development either by leaving sufficient freedom for a dynamic middle class to develop a Chinese equivalent of capitalism (this was forestalled in practice by establishing a meritocratic state bureaucracy, to belong to which became the chief status goal of the ambitious) or by way of eschatological exhortations buried within the philosophy that might encourage dissatisfied social elements to reformulate the social settlement[1]. If Confucius had found other traditions to transmit and amplify to later generations, humanity could have been faced with our present ecological problematic at the time of Christ, resulting from a 'Chinese Enlightenment'. On the other hand, if the Renaissance intellectuals had inherited other ideas from the past — Confucian perhaps, or we might speculate on quite other possibilities — and the structure of society had been other than what it was, then we might not be faced with our ecological crisis even today.

But the fact is that, however contingent the passage may have been, we are now faced with our violent confrontation with nature and it is in relation to this situation that we must rapidly find a way out. It is useful at this point to summarise the conclusions from foregoing chapters with regard to the form of 'Enlightenment' that was the culmination of intellectual developments starting in the Renaissance and which has more or less defined the cultural process that has brought us to the edge. The essential belief embodied in the concept of enlightenment is that there is one universal form of knowledge, termed 'science', that encapsulates the total Truth about the universe and, as part of this, all of human life; this Truth is available for human discovery through the pursuit of 'reason'. The Enlightenment historic project was to discover Truth, whatever this might mean, by way of tearing apart and rebuilding our ways of thinking and our way of life, and that society should flinch at nothing to conform to the rigours of this Truth.

Such a belief is inherently fanatical in that it cannot acknowledge the validity of other ideological standpoints or forms of cultural self-expression, nor can it gain any effective insight into its own origins and impetus. This demonstrated itself in practice in the way in which enlightened European culture smashed its way ideologically and materially through all other cultures and through its own cultural roots; this became possible because of the effectiveness with which this form of the pursuit of truth unlocked the technical means of destruction. Seen as a contingent product of a particular culture, the evidence was reviewed earlier in this book to indicate that the European Enlightenment gained its essential structure from a certain reconstruction of beliefs inherited from Christianity, ancient Greece and the Mesopotamian legacy transmitted via Judaism. It could not acknowledge that it was not the first or only secular ideology to emerge as the dominant form of cultural self-awareness: all other cultural ideologies were seen as necessarily superstitious, false forms of knowledge. Nor could it acknowledge that all forms of knowledge are, in the final analysis, sustained by nothing more than embedded conviction. The fact that other secular ideologies did not lend impetus to an open-ended pursuit of knowledge of natural causality might have lain in a certain wisdom of the potential uncontrollability of the results in a conflictory social setting. The disaster which we now face was always a possibility in that it only took one culture to fail to develop such a form of wisdom, to disgorge itself entirely into an absolute instrumentalism, and this would then possess the capability to force all others to follow its lead.

It is important to be aware of the visions of the possible outcomes of the enlightenment process that emerged in the course of that process. Just as Greek science was pure invention of a past era which was available to subsequent ages to be built into effective ideology, so we have inherited from the Enlightenment a reservoir of ideas about social and political organisation that are embedded in the social consciousness and available for the construction of a new effective ideology. We can divide these quite easily into those which focused on process, based simply on a conviction that enlightenment would eventually lead to some unspecified but worthwhile cultural state — progressivism and revolutionism — and those which were concerned to define the end state and bring it into existence in the here and now — Utopianism.

The process ideologies of Turgot, Condorcet and a proliferation and, certainly in Marxism, deepening of this genre across the 19th century, have provided sustenance and in key respects guidance to the adoption of components of the machinery of progressive cultural development. The Utopian projects and programmes, on the other hand, accumulated ideas and isolated experience but necessarily remained recessive in a situation that insisted on the Truth remaining in the indefinite future beyond the ongoing process. Whilst the Utopian model might be the natural choice of social organisation — as an ideology of arrival — for significant numbers of immigrants to the United States or thoroughly European Jews 'returning' to the Promised Land and establishing Kibbutzim, there would be no way that this could become a generally acceptable model of social organisation within the overall framework of enlightenment ideology. But the Utopian model is available to our society in so far as we are prepared to abandon the millenarian convictions of the Enlightenment. The rich legacy of Utopianism was subject to a brief review in Chapter 4 and as this chapter unfolds, it will become clear how important it is that we recover and develop this legacy as the basis for an escape route — indeed perhaps the only realistic one — from our ecological crisis.

Great emphasis has been placed from time to time in the foregoing text on the problematic nature of the struggle within the Enlightenment in its 20th century manifestation between bourgeois progressivism and Marxist revolutionism. The arguments, laid out in this book, were developing across the 1980s against a background of a strong sense of a subsiding of the heat of the struggle. Then quite suddenly the tension broke in the political sphere, leaving the ideological discourse of Marxism adrift and with it a rising 'postmodern' sense of aimlessness transfusing the whole enlightenment project. It is difficult to overemphasise the way in which the struggle between Marxism and bourgeois progressivism acted as the motor to the whole latter-day enlightenment project, each of these embodying a fanatical moral crusade that insisted that *its* interpretation of the enlightenment project was the correct one; it is this which informed the great pessimism of the Frankfurt School in their doubts about enlightenment. The practicalities of maintaining the form of the political struggle had a peculiar distorting effect on the relationship between theory and praxis. Of particular salience was the way in which the Marxist scenario, involving working class revolution to be followed by a classless, consciously self-managing society, was both acknowledged, as aspiration, and yet suppressed in the practice of 'actually existing socialist' states. It is to a significant degree the rhetorical way in which Marx and Engels (as quoted in Chapter 4) proclaimed this aspect of their scenario, with no practical guidance as to how post revolutionary society might be put into effect — in contrast to the many quite serviceable suggestions emanating from the Utopian tradition — which made the enactment of this suppression of Utopia such a straightforward practical proposition.

Marxism, in being tied to a particular future scenario, laid itself open to refutation in the process of history. As totalising ideology, or 'metatheory', in a situation where culture is rapidly on the move, we should count ourselves lucky for this in that some other form of millenarian ideology, better enured against practical criticism, would have a greater propensity to blunder blindly on, well beyond its practical usefulness; one merely has to look at the extraordinary dysfunctionality of the 'great world religions' attempting to operate in the modern world. Typically we think in terms of possessing a choice of totalising ideologies as given entities — Christianity or Confucianism, Islam or Marxism or whatever — but in practice ideological evolution is a good deal messier than this. There are aspects of the form of analysis and the content of Marxism which are essential to the self-understanding of modern society, having exposed itself so radically to the necessity, with respect to its own day-to-day survival, for conscious self-regulation through the vast extension of instrumental rationality in the operation of the everyday world. It was argued at several points in the foregoing text that the ideological structuring process of the 20th-century enlightenment society has been in essence a 'dialogue with Marx'. Wholesale rejection of Marxism would be a disaster as there really is no coherent alternative capable of giving us an overview of the world created by the enlightenment process. The triumphalism of the bourgeois media in response to the collapse of 'actually existing socialism' is utterly lacking in any sense of its own inner orientation and the consequences that will be unfolding over the coming years in the face of the removal of this structure of opposition to Marxism; the recent manufacturing of a war in the Middle East can be clearly understood in this light and this is but the beginning of what could become a systematic process of cultural degeneration ending in the very self-annihilation feared by the political ecologists.

Metatheory in the form of a consistent Marxism may be in eclipse, as postmodernist rhetoricians insist, and certainly the continued adherence to the complete essential Marxist structure, to which a significant proportion of modern social theorists remain prone, must be deemed a serious problem by political ecologists. The construction of metatheory that will absorb relevant aspects of Marxism and at the same time address the requirements of a strategy that will avoid ecological destruction is required and much of the argument of this book has been intended to lay foundations for just such an exercise. Perhaps the required procedure can be characterised in the following manner: European culture has, over this long period, traversed the sea of civilisation from the land of innocence. The point of arrival at a distant shore is the time of greatest danger: having arrived, it becomes necessary to let down the sails, to engage in a more complex and delicate process of negotiating a landing. The metatheory relevant to our age is a kind of docking procedure which will facilitate our disembarking from the process of history and, via a final stage in the enlightenment, realising the role of human consciousness as the consciousness of nature as a whole.

It must be made perfectly clear that this is not some pre-ordained or ultimately necessary process of arrival. Setting sail onto an unknown ocean can result in shipwreck under way (the demise of culture in course of development) and the location of land is essentially arbitrary relative to the civilizing project. We can say, for instance, that Balinese culture is a perfectly satisfactory resolution of the human condition under a particular set of ecological circumstances. It unites into a continuous cultural fabric cosmological explanation, an immensely rich aesthetics self-expression and an extremely sophisticated development and regulatory system for irrigated rice cultivation; the way of life generally is easy-going and transparent enough for almost anyone to take on any social role as, in practice, they do. Why desire anything more? Why this frantic search for some ultimate Truth (which much of this analysis is dedicated to showing just doesn't exist anyway)? Why this frantic accumulation of material goods and the endless complication of life? The foregoing analysis has attempted to reveal the reasons, but of course in the end it doesn't matter why — though if we realise how pointless it all is then hopefully it becomes easier to abandon it — so much as how we might go about discarding our ridiculous Nietzschean cultural pretensions and living our lives in a more straightforwardly human, that is thoroughgoing gregarious and hedonistic, manner. What chance is there that we will achieve this and not, instead, destroy the whole basis for any reasonable life?

Society and knowledge

The root of the conflict between Marx and his bourgeois opponents lay, of course, in their divergent views as to the role of social structure in the enlightenment process. Bourgeois views were encapsulated in Malthus' attack on Condorcet: on the one side was a vague notion that enlightenment would gradually improve the whole of mankind, with the implication that social inequalities would fade away; on the other lay an assumption that the poor will always be with us, as a natural manifestation, even if circumstances in general were to improve. Marx's view was simply that we cannot expect to achieve a fully enlightened society as long as it is divided into mutually antagonistic interests incipiently or overtly hostile to one anothers' views with regard to what is to be done.

When Marx wrote his famous aphorism concerning the consciousness of men being a function of their social existence and not the other way round, he was doing no more than acknowledging the empiricist views of Locke, as transmitted by Helvetius ('our ideas are the necessary consequence of the societies in which we live'). But he was also questioning Locke's (1965: 375) sanguine view that society is the result of an agreement by the people in a situation where (Locke (1965: 460)) 'the reason men (sic) enter into society, is the preservation of their property' but the vast majority possess no property at all. Rather, people find themselves already situated in a particular form of society, like it or not, and the particular position occupied then colours, indeed forges, the whole way in which they interpret the world. Inevitably variations in function and status engender variations not only in aspiration but, by extension, in understanding. If we are going to truly achieve enlightenment — a state, that is, where we take rational decisions regarding the way in which we organise our mutual relations and those with nature — then it is a prerequisite that we break down the de facto antagonistic relations inherent in an inegalitarian society. For all his espousal of the dialectic, in the final analysis Marx fell in with the disposition of the times that insisted on invoking natural or historical necessity as justification: the Enlightenment would be realised through proletarian revolution.

Whilst Marx may have been wrong concerning his views on the necessity of proletarian revolution as the ultimate stage of enlightenment, there is certainly a compelling logic to his contention concerning de facto antagonistic social relations as precluding the achievement of enlightenment. But it is quite understandable that the bourgeois would be very inventive in finding means to preserve their privileges, in a situation where there was demonstrably a lot to loose, and it should be quite evident that the development of society and politics in the 20th century provides us above all with an illustration of the workings of the dialectic around just this issue. It is quite possible to deconstruct the whole corpus of bourgeois — and much academic and Soviet 'Marxist' — social scientific theorising around the theme of the obfuscation and maintenance of status and privilege and mostly this was perpetrated quite unconsciously as the 'natural' expression of the intellectuals as ideological guardians of bourgeois interests. Such a deconstruction can certainly be carried out in a more sensitive fashion than was the case with orthodox Marxists — notably Lukács (1980) — but on the other hand it is illegitimate to take it to Lukácsian extremes: there were always other facets to the motivation and content of bourgeois 'social science' and, as illustrated in some of the material presented in the foregoing chapters, much of bourgeois theory is far from irredeemably benighted and can be considered useful by way of contributing towards an ultimate reservoir of knowledge in an ultimately enlightened, egalitarian world, should we succeed in achieving one.

It can be argued that in its focus upon modes of theorising about society designed to avoid Marxism or by other means sustaining arguments that implicitly or explicitly lent support to the continuation of privilege — primarily through the medium of positivism — the social sciences were subject to a crucial loss of critical edge with regard to aspects of enlightenment not directly related to this issue. Its unwillingness and in the end inability to confront the rise of fascism is a clear case in point. But it was also incapable of confronting critically the growing complexity, and with this opacity and uncontrollability, or 'overload', of the social system resulting from the proliferation and extension of practical mechanisms for maintaining the political settlement. Whilst Max Weber saw clearly and wrote pessimistically about the extension of bureaucracy and its effects, he was not prepared to accept that the 'withering away of the state' might be a practical proposition, because he was not prepared to accept the abandonment of claims to privilege.

A further problem, when seen from the point of view of any movement designed to push the enlightenment project forward, was the way that the very notion of social change became suspect to a bourgeoisie afraid that this might, as Marx had prophesied, necessarily mean the loss of privilege. Hence we find not only, as mentioned on several occasions in previous chapters, the wholesale abandonment of 19th century evolutionary anthropology but also a studied avoidance of the analysis or even the acknowledgement of social change in a situation of *de facto* change of a violence and rapidity never before encountered in history (Banks (1972: 9); Wertheim (1974)).

It is perhaps of interest that the basic framework of sociology was such that it made it difficult to focus on this question of change. Comte, the inventor of 'sociology', and more broadly the positivist 'philosophy', laid out a postmillennial programme for bourgeois science that assumed that society was now within the framework of the millennium and merely had to apply the correct tools to be able to discover the truth about a reality which would itself succumb to this truth as an absolute determinist programme. When in practice society took turns — not only in the emergence of the labour movement but also the First World War and Russian Revolution and eventually the rise of fascism — that could clearly no longer be considered, at least from their point of view, as meliorative improvement, then bourgeois intellectuals simply labelled it as 'irrational' and washed their hands of any further responsibility. Marxism, as a premillennial framework for the interpretation of social process, whilst in principle more amenable to acknowledging the phenomenon of social change, was in practice only interested in discovering signs of a very specific kind of change, namely that involving the rise of the 'labour movement'. It is only very recently that social change has been acknowledged as an acceptable field of study and various 'new social movements' (in fact mainly old movements that were, in earlier manifestations, unacknowledged as a substantive ingredient of the social process) have become the focus of some attention.

In the latter years of social democracy — from the 1960s on — the importance of the content of social theory as support for the social and political settlement went into decline: we might indeed surmise that the ease with which Marxism made inroads into the universities was precisely because it didn't matter any more what social scientists said[2]. Their residual role was simply to operate the gates at one point of the system of privilege: to restrict the proportion of the population that could claim elevated status or, perhaps more importantly, to impress upon the lower orders, simply by the existence of the university system, a sense of inevitability to their lower status. The ideological means to justifying the settlement was shifting decisively out of academia and, as recent 'postmodernist' discourse has come to express it (Lash (1988)), adopting a figural (audio-visual and tactile) in place of a discursive field of operation. Consumerism had come of age as the chief justification for, and legitimation of, the political settlement.

In contemplating the overall effect of the development of social democracy as an extension of the 19th-century bourgeois version of enlightenment, certain issues arise which could be construed as of great importance to the project of the achievement of the final stage of enlightenment. The vast proliferation of bourgeois status roles in the course of the social democratic era has led to major confusions with respect to the object of privilege. Whilst our society has accommodated itself to this in the sense of continuing to attribute rank to every new functional role, this has nevertheless contributed to a process of deflation of the importance of privilege as such in the social imagination. The massive proliferation of material means to express status and privilege which lies at the heart of the social democratic political strategy — of substituting seduction for repression as the chief means of social and political system maintenance (Bauman (1988)) — has ended up undermining a central pillar of the very *raison d'être* of privilege, namely the relief of physical hardship. Whilst the self-conscious abandonment of the quest for privilege, as manifest in the hippy and communes movements, has, since the late 1960s, played an active practical and ideological role on the margins of society, it might be conjectured that the loss of a sense of the importance of privilege is an important informant of the recent, much broader, 'shift in sensibility' informing the 'postmodern condition' about which a lot more will be said as this chapter unfolds.

There are two, interrelated principles of relevance to political ecology that emerge from this discussion of certain general goals of enlightenment. These aim to achieve a consciously self-regulating society in the face of the ecological abyss, to climb off the roller-coaster of run-away social evolution and actively take responsibility for social organisation into our own hands. One of these principles concerns the requirement to simplify and render more transparent the operations of society and our relationship with nature. The other is concerned to diffuse the tensions within society that result from individualist inegalitarian social relations and the social division of labour by their eradication. The point is to overcome the intrinsic mistrust and misunderstanding which these generate and which hinder the construction of more coherent mechanisms of social decision-making.

From the point of view of political ecology, it appears quite extraordinary how Marx and Engels' messianic enlightenment universalism blinded them to the simple fact that workers whose lives are dominated by extremely fragmented relations with the world would be quite incapable of participating meaningfully in the early stages of their own emancipation without some preliminary experience of handling more diverse aspects of life, being as they were so utterly deprived of the most basic sense of what might comprise a rounded human life. Marx and Engels' (1970: 54) rhetorical discussion in the course of their early years of social theorising, concerning life after the revolution, where the individual would be able 'to hunt in the morning, fish in the afternoon, rear cattle in the evening, criticise after dinner, just as they have in mind, without ever becoming hunter, fisherman, herdsman or critic', was never allowed to inform their view of the *process* of emancipation. Lenin's embrace, *after* the Russian Revolution, of Taylorist modes of industrial management (Braverman (1974: 12)) that could only lead to a *reduction* in the capability of workers to participate meaningfully in social decision-making or personal self-realisation, comprises part of the grotesquerie of socialist 'progress' in the 20th century.

Even Locke and in particular his revolutionary American and French followers (though we should acknowledge the origins of this insight in the English Revolution and the Harringtonian Constitution) were aware to some degree of the systemic nature of politics and society when they affirmed the need for 'checks and balances' in the political realm as means to diffuse power: whilst this in no way intended the destruction of privilege, at least it opened, and left ajar, a door upon the *means* to political and thence cultural emancipation for the whole of society. But this was not a door which Marx and Engels chose to pay attention to and we can be quite certain that this negligence has been the main cause of the failure of Marxism in the political sphere[3].

The Utopians, on the other hand, were more or less aware of the relationship between the way society is structured and the degree to which it might be able to satisfy the rounded human needs of its members and at the same time be amenable to conscious self-management. The Owenites were insistent not only on the universal education of the workforce as a means both to their own self-fulfilment and because an educated workforce is also a more efficient and effective one, but also in the reduction in the size and complexity of the community as a means to simplify the decision-making process and involve the workforce. It is of some interest that whenever concerted movements against Stalinism arose amongst the Eastern European states during the years of Central Planning, almost invariably attempts were made to form councils of self-management at least for the running of industry and with implications for government more generally (Lomax (1972); Fisera (1975);

Ardalan (1980)). A recessive co-operative movement with roots in Utopian socialism has indeed survived, through the social democratic years, across the whole of the European cultural world (Thornley (1982)), particularly marked in Italy and Spain (Leval (1975); Thomas and Logan (1982)), where strong anarchist traditions have taken root, that focus as much on culture and lifestyle as on the organisation of work and government. This recessive tradition of socialism has become more self-aware and assertive in recent years (Bodington (1978); Roberts (1979); Piore and Sabel (1984); Kern and Schumann (1984); Collective Design/Projects (1985); Gorz (1989)).

Political ecology — and in general the Green movement — is much more directly aware of the need for decentralised social and political structures and does not come burdened with the legacy of Marxist suspicion towards anarchist self-activity. Growing directly out of the emancipatory movements of the 1960s and continuing to be directly connected to the various other 'new social movements' emerging at that time — radical feminists, peace and communes — the various 'Green manifestos' (Green Party (Various); Irvine and Ponton (1988); Kemp and Wall (1990)) invariably speak of the need for decentralisation that links in directly to the resolution of the problem of alienation as discussed in Chapter 3 of this book. Political ecology denies that there is any grand trajectory to the enlightenment process — indeed, it rejects the whole notion of progress and enlightenment universalism more generally — and insists that we must build a workable society here and now, within contingent and local constraints and opportunities. It becomes quite evident that this must involve a simplification over the legacy of social democracy and the terms around which this is organised are 'self-reliant regionalism' and the reconstruction of 'community'.

It is not for a theoretical analysis such as this to delve into the practical details of the Green plans and strategies regarding self-reliant regionalism. Suffice it to say that the term is in process, as yet tentative, of gaining technical coherence, through debate and practice on the part of the Green movement, in parallel with the theoretical development of notions of 'bioregionalism' (Sale (1985)) as total reformulation of political, economic, social and cultural process, radically displacing the time-dominated, millenarian, vision of the Enlightenment with a place-dominated vision of a sustainable future. Equally the debates on new forms of community are as yet tentative, gaining sustenance from the communes movement but also investigating the remnants of inherited communities, ethnic communities and communities of interest. It is to be expected that the growth and movement into more assertive practice of these concerns with community will generate both considerable cultural enrichment, but potentially also considerable social tension and conflict.

The solution to this incipient problem of conflict lies in the implementation of the second of the principles outlined above: the undoing of inegalitarian and incommensurable social relations. What has to be emphasised at the outset of the discussion of this principle is that we are clearly confronted with the most delicate aspect of the project of political ecology. An outright assertion in the political sphere of egalitarian ambitions will inevitably incur the resistance, grounded in the fear of losing privilege, to which socialism has been subjected. This would result in the revival of the kinds of distortion of the project which deflected the ambitions of the enlightenment during the earlier part of this century. It would almost certainly destroy the project and, from the environmentalist perspective of political ecology, seal the fate of any happy outcome for civilisation as such. This subject thus needs to be approached with considerable care.

As discussed at some length in the foregoing chapter, political ecology believes in overcoming the multiple dimensions of individualism that dominate enlightenment thought and asserting a holistic mode of thought and action. In the social sphere this means displacing competitive attitudes and modes of action with empathetic, co-operative ones. This must be the philosophical starting point of this particular project. It was pointed out how alien such an outlook is from an enlightenment perspective and, in particular, from the point of view of British 'common sense' philosophy and in general the immediate inclination of our every day thoughts. The arguments sketched out in Chapter 5 need to be developed, debated and disseminated in and by the Green movement in order to effect change at the level of ideological foundations. However, overcoming individualism will not in itself resolve the central problem. Indeed, conservatism has always been suspicious of individualism because it engenders an awareness of social differences and so is incipiently critical of social hierarchy — for all the fact that in practice it has failed to confront it decisively. Conservatism attempts always to hide the fact of hierarchy in order to deflect criticism. In reasserting holistic modes of thinking, political ecology must be highly sensitive to this problem and ensure that the strategy as a whole effectively abolishes social hierarchy at the same time as eradicating individualism.

Ratiocination and debate at the level of high theory will be insufficient in themselves to address the issue effectively and to render the new outlook believable or natural. It is necessary to devise a political strategy aimed at diffusing the divisions which individualism puts between us in practice even more concretely than it does in the ideological sphere. It needs to be emphasised that the co-operative movement and elements also of the Green movement have accumulated considerable experience at a practical level in confronting this problem.

Co-operativism aims simultaneously to practice equal reward regardless of function and at the same time to dissolve the rigid lines between functions (Thornley (1982); Cornforth et al. (1988)). Communes dissolve the boundaries of property and formal relationships and organise on a more pragmatic, empathetic and sharing basis (Rigby (1974); Abrams and McCulloch (1976: 38)). Many organisations of the Green movement itself have experimented with methods of organisation and interaction which similarly dissolve formal social boundaries and promote egalitarianism (Atkinson (1991)). Overwhelmingly the practice has proved more difficult than might at first appear: agreement upon and application of these new kinds of rules of conduct is not easily arrived at out of psychologies enculturated into possessive individualism (Abrams and McCulloch (1976: Ch.7)) and the process of establishing a small stable foundation of co-operatives and communes based upon practical experience in Britain has been slow (Cornforth et al. (1988); Ansell et al. (1989)). But it has been achieved and the potential for the spread of co-operativistic and communistic practices presents us with a realistic route out of the, from the point of view of environmentalism, utterly dysfunctional society which is the legacy of social democracy and which continues to be propelled forward by an inertia that crowds the practicality of the sustainable alternatives out of the social consciousness.

Ten years ago, when the 'new social movements' were small networks of individuals and micro-organisations struggling to formulate their beliefs, translate them into practical programmes and disseminate their message to the rest of the society, there seemed a vanishingly small chance that they could ever make any real impact; they operated in a certain sense like religious groups, driven on by irrational faith in the eventual triumph of their vision of a more rational society. Over a brief period, measurable in months prior to the writing of these lines, the consciousness that informed the Green movement in its early stages in the early 1970s suddenly spread right across society. Notwithstanding a ripple of symbolic gestures (Green consumerism, etc.), very little changed in the material sphere. But, if the theorists of postmodernism are to be believed, beneath the surface there has been a radical loosening of foundations that suddenly presents us with a sense of anticipation of potential as yet unmeasurable. It is certainly possible to interpret the signs as being unmistakably those preceding a spiral into social paranoia of the kind that produced fascism (Harvey (1989: 277)). On the one hand this might be used as an argument for an urgent call for the 'new social movements' to seize the moment and act. On the other hand, it is precisely an uncontrolled spiral into a 'fanatical localism', a forced decentralisation of the kind associated with Cambodia in the early 1980s, that appears as a frightening vision to the postmodernism analysts. This is by no means a trivial problem and will be returned to later in this chapter. But at this point it is simply noted that this is a problem which must be solved in the sphere of political practice rather than here under the heading of theory.

Ecology and consciousness

The texts of ecophilosophy, deep ecology and the gamut of environmentalist writings that have warned us of the probable consequences of our attitudes towards, and actions with respect to, nature, and some of which have enquired into the ideological roots of these, have singularly failed to understand them as manifestations of a thoroughly dialectical affair. The foregoing chapter briefly surveyed the way in which writers in the French and Scottish Enlightenment had sketched out a research programme aimed at investigating the effect of climate and geography on local cultures. Already ample commentary had been made by traders and travellers to other parts of the world to the effect that civilisation of the sort that was in process of unfolding in Europe would be unlikely to develop in the tropics where nature's year-round fecundity made any elaborate planning or sustained hard work redundant.

In the first instance this phenomenon generated a sense of horror: the slothfulness, as they saw it, of the natives of tropical regions was shocking to their cultural sensibilities. However, this soon turned to an attitude of aggressive arrogance that expressed itself both in an implacable racism throughout the literature of the 19th century that dealt with such matters and, of course, in colonial exploitation that was bent not only on economic gain but on eradicating all non-European culture either by conversion to European ideology or by extermination and displacement. The intended Enlightenment research programme materialised only in very partial and distorted form, primarily in the writings of environmental determinists around the end of the 19th century, having been transmogrified into a belligerent theory aimed at nothing more than the justification of European violence towards all other races and cultures; Marx and Engels showed themselves to be hardly more sympathetic than their bourgeois foes to the claims of non-European cultures.

Following the cataclysmic events of the early years of the century and with the rise of counterforces to 19th-century European bourgeois triumphalism, the expression of racism became more circumspect even whilst the fact of exploitation and cultural destruction accelerated unabated against the background of *de facto* adherence to the belief in the messianic enlightenment 'modernising' ideology. Of course the native inhabitants of Asia, Africa and America did not have the material means to defend themselves from the physical onslaught and by extension no platform from which to argue their case. But the Europeans were, from the standpoint of these natives, certainly peculiar in their ceaseless scurrying about generating new projects and generally new things to keep them occupied well beyond what might be deemed necessary for a comfortable life in such conditions. Were they really to be believed in the assertion of the Enlightenment that the whole purpose of science was to make life easier? Certainly they didn't allow themselves any relaxation when the opportunity arose with their settlement in a more climatically congenial environment. On the contrary, they insisted on installing air conditioning and carrying on with life as if they were living in the frigid north.

When Max Weber came to focus his attention on the ideological ingredients of the foundations of modern capitalism, he did so explicitly to counter Marx's 'materialist' explanation. Furthermore, he undertook extensive studies of other ideologies — Judaism, Hinduism, Buddhism and Confucianism — with a view to identifying how these had failed to encourage the development of capitalism elsewhere. Being opposed to materialist explanation as such, Weber would certainly not have been interested in any view that might lend credence to the notion that the 'puritan work ethic' could have arisen in major part out of a pre-existing set of attitudes environed by the physical setting out of which European culture had evolved. Nor did the controversy that arose around Weber's work focus on any such truly materialist approach to the issue. The battle to 'explain' capitalism was entirely one between idealists, believing that ideological invention was sufficient causal explanation, and those who saw the struggle between classes as the causal factor.

Chapter 3 was at pains to argue that 'causality' is generally a complex and structured affair. There really is no conflict between, on the one hand, a belief that the details of European attitudes informing capitalistic practice (and many other aspects of our lifestyle as well) were provided with their essential structure by ecclesiastical texts written in the course of the Reformation; and, on the other, one which acknowledges that the rising middle classes played a crucial role in acting out capitalism in pursuit of what they saw as their self-interest. In a very similar manner to the struggle at the macro-political level between bourgeois and Marxist ideologies, so in respect of the details of European cultural analysis, this squabble over the roots of capitalism failed to take into account the deeper influences of environment on creating the context within which European culture as a whole has developed.

In the end 'understanding' only arises out of some need which may be instrumental, or to satisfy some deeper, perhaps aesthetic, requirement. The fact that there is very little usable literature on the environmental influences upon cultural attitudes[4] is a function of the way in which this notion was abused in the 19th century; that there ensued a strong reaction to this literature; and finally, following the cataclysmic events of the second decade of this century, that the new systems of ideological justification and struggle that emerged found that it had no need for such an investigation, that it would only be an embarrassment.

What is being hypothesised here is that the puritan ideology, upon which Weber placed the responsibility for the existence of capitalism, formed simply the machinery through which the deeper motivating forces of bourgeois ambition, and beyond that a very long cultural prehistory moulded by life in a cold and hostile environment, expressed themselves. Unlike Marx, who rather fancied the macho brute force of capitalism, Weber (1976: 181) was appalled by the effects which 'worldly asceticism', underpinning capitalism, continues to have, writing:

Since asceticism undertook to remodel the world and to work out its ideals in the world, material goods have gained an increasing and finally inexorable power over the lives of men as at no previous period in history. Today the spirit of religious asceticism — whether finally, who knows? — has escaped from the cage. But victorious capitalism, since it rests on mechanical foundations, needs its support no longer. The rosy blush of its laughing heir, the Enlightenment, seems also to be irretrievably fading, and the idea of duty in one's calling prowls about in our lives like the ghost of dead religious belief.

But he failed to ask why puritanism had uniquely favoured an accumulative ascetic strategy where all other forms of religious asceticism had renounced material goods. Perhaps there is a very good real-world reason for this. Where in a tropical or even mediterranean climate a reasonable existence is possible with minimal accoutrements and hence minimal work, in Northern Europe life is miserable and harrowing without substantial buildings and a strategy for accumulating and storing materials over long winters. The contingencies of life under these circumstances require a more highly articulated approach to culture, more oriented to instrumental rationality and engagement with nature, driven on by the fear of want that would quickly follow upon too uninhibited an attitude to consumption.

It is exactly this logic that Weber discovered in his survey of puritan literature, which, as he convincingly argued, informed those crucial middle years of the formation of modern capitalism. The fact that capitalist attitudes continue to 'prowl about in our lives' may, however, be a consequence of their possessing a much older cultural vintage. Certainly of great interest is the light which Weber's analysis throws upon modern consumerism. What an extraordinary contrast is to be found between the role which the same consumer goods play in southern countries in contrast to the north: in the one they become objects predominantly of luxurious display and augmented self-expression as ends in themselves; over the other there hangs a heavy air of responsibility, that consumption is an expression of a duty to accumulate as an end in itself, the objects being but a burden that nevertheless confirms the integrity of the citizen who owns them. The preoccupation with work as the means to accumulate, coupled with the air of sinfulness in uninhibited enjoyment of accumulated things, these are the hallmarks of puritanism and these are still significant features of our present-day culture.

Of course it is precisely this endless urge to accumulate that is in process of precipitating an ecological catastrophe. The defensive strategies of precapitalist Northern European attitudes of planning and careful accumulation turned, under capitalism, into aggressive strategies bent mindlessly upon accumulation at the expense of other cultures, the culture of Northern Europe itself and, above all, nature: in Weber's words, it had 'escaped from the cage'. It is simple enough to assert that to go all the way and destroy nature is to destroy the basis for our existence, to destroy ourselves. We, too, are nature. But there is no coherence between a simple statement of this kind and the complexity and inertia of the machine through which our ancient, environmentally created, cultural motivations operate, and above all that might penetrate to these motivations themselves.

So how do we slay this ghost before it slays us through its possessing of our everyday lives? The first thing that must be said is that there is clearly no one-shot mechanism: it is necessary to work simultaneously at many levels and points in attempts to destroy the impetus of our infernal cultural logic and at the same time to build new structures that will enable our descendants to live easy-going lives in a sustainable relationship with the rest of the Creation. Thus it is necessary to confront the tendency to over-rationalise, over-structure and over-elaborate our mental and physical lives, in ever-renewed reformulations of the puritan ethic, to push alienation out into life way beyond what is necessary to solve our existential needs in a situation of *de facto* technologically created abundance. Relax: we have arrived!

The process of commodification and unlovedness of things that we buy and surround ourselves with, the way we commodify ourselves as objects offered up to the labour market, are not epiphenomena of some mega black box labelled 'capitalism' which cannot be confronted in any form except by its universal overthrow. They are an aspect of our culture which can be taken to pieces and rebuilt piecemeal. On the one hand we are quite capable of turning away from engagement with aspects that are of no material relevance to us — although we may be currently mesmerised by them, such as in viewing television, taking holidays abroad, etc. etc. And on the other hand, above all, we can work at breaking through the walls which we create between us and our immediate satisfaction in one-another, simply as sentient cohabitants of the Creation, and between ourselves and the physical world of nature and human manufacture with which it is perfectly possible to identify, without our having created them as extensions of our own private personalities[5].

However, in themselves, these over-elaborated structures are not the cause but only the consequence of deeper forces and will tend to be rebuilt if the restructuring process is limited to the level of ideology alone, as is attempted by the ecophilosophers. As long as we know that 'others are doing better than us', in circumstances where the main game in town is the achievement of status and privilege — however ephemeral, immaterial, the symbols of privilege might have become (as a piece of functional machinery, a Rolls Royce is a joke in very poor taste; working in a modern office building may have high status but is a highly stressful environment, etc. etc.) — then there is little hope of de-escalating the 'capitalist processes of creative destruction' because it is impossible to command attention even to ask pertinent questions: people are so preoccupied with maintaining and furthering their status. So at the same time as attacking the main ideologies of our times, we must also build alternative social arrangements and aspirations that take the sense of injustice and competition — and, of course, beyond that, the real injustices — out of the way life is currently organised.

But how do we take those inertial forces out of our culture that reproduce our ancient, environed fear of want? There is a well-known passage in one of Marx's (1975: 426) writings which can easily be construed as expressing the teleological, even mystical, side to his thought but which, upon reflection, may help us in this situation. It runs as follows:

No social order is ever destroyed before all the productive forces for which it is sufficient have been developed [this is clearly untrue], and new superior relations of production never replace older ones before the material conditions for their existence have matured within the framework of the old society. Mankind thus inevitably sets itself only such tasks as it is able to solve, since closer examination will always show that the problem itself arises only when the material conditions for its solution are already present or at least in the course of formation.

If we look back to the Enlightenment and in particular the third quarter of the 18th Century, we can see — in what Weber referred to as a 'rosy blush' — a sense developing amongst the emerging middle classes, that life need not be taken so seriously, that a hedonistic, even bacchanalian, existence might be possible. This expressed itself not merely in such literature as *Fanny Hill* and *Tom Jones* and the whole social-critical dimension of the Enlightenment, but also in the Hellfire Club and the *Sturm und Drang* of the early stages of romanticism.

Of course this sensibility was utterly unrealistic, too self-concerned to appreciate the implications of the enormous distance between the lifestyle of this emergent class and that of the broad masses. Inevitably, as E. P. Thompson's (1968: 60) seminal history makes clear, the French Revolution was a very rude awakening that rapidly restored the deep fears that had informed the puritan literature of an earlier generation. The fact was that such a hedonistic lifestyle and its accompanying view of life was quite unsustainable across the population as a whole under prevailing conditions of production, so how else could the material gains of the bourgeoisie be sustained in the face of demands by the rest of the population for a more equitable distribution of growing wealth, but by deception and self-deception and by hypostatising stratagems into 'knowledge' ('political economy') and underpinning all this by brute force.

The 'Behaviourist Dark Ages', as Koestler referred to the period from the early years of this century to the 1960s, were clearly simply the result of a revitalisation, in the face of the Russian Revolution, of the great fear that followed the French Revolution. Regardless of the fact that material possibilities might now have been present to organise society and the production system so that everyone could lead a comfortable life (and one merely has to think of the curtailing of developing productive forces which characterised the 1930s), the knee-jerk response to the Russian Revolution was to disallow coherent reasoning about social organisation, perpetrated not by any small minority bent on maintaining its personal privileges so much as systemic to the cultural structure: the whole European social system willed travail upon itself.

From the point of view of a hedonistic, Utopian sensibility, what is extraordinary about the history of European culture in the 20th century is its refusal to acknowledge and use the products of science and technology to, in Bacon's words, 'relieve man's estate'. The fetishism of armament invention and manufacture and constant warring over what in the end was scarcely more than scholastic ideologising; the insistence on reproducing ridiculously dysfunctional lifestyles that create enormously elaborate structures that then require utterly alienating work to run and maintain; the equally highly structured format of life outside the framework of productive relations; and finally, the dogmatic denial of economic and social justice for so many in a situation where its achievement is no more than a matter of concession: this is the experience of European society, forced upon the whole world, during this century.

So, what might the relevance to this be of Marx's notion concerning the appearance and solution to problems of social and economic organisation? We might conjecture within this hypothesis that the productive forces available to European culture earlier in the century, though providing North Americans with material conditions that might have informed a more easygoing attitude to life, did not in fact extend to the contemplative dimensions of European culture such as to forge essential contact between the fact of material abundance being now permanently available and the deep wellsprings of our culture as informed by the fear of want. Perhaps this has to do with the position which the United States occupies in European culture: 'free' enough to organise society on the basis of efficient and effective capitalism that requires the smashing of dense social structural bonds, but by the same token lacking a deeper sense of the structure of European culture that would facilitate it to indulge in any very fundamental cultural self-examination; on that score it was only when material abundance experienced in North America in the 1920s extended to the heartland of Europe in the 1960s and 1970s that this process of cultural self-examination could start in earnest. On the other hand, perhaps it is simply a question of 'experiential mass': that an insufficient proportion of the politically participating population was exposed to this experience of material abundance until quite recently. Or perhaps there is a time dimension: that a generation must grow up without knowing anything but this material abundance before the belief can begin to take root that this is a natural state of affairs, hence weakening the grip of our ancient fear of want.

Of course one common interpretation of the events of the late 1960s encompassing the campus revolutions, the beatnik and then much broader hippy movements and latterly the rise of the 'new social movements', is that these are attributable in significant measure to the experience of affluence not only in the United States but throughout the heartland of Europe, involving large sections of the population and having been the total life experience of a whole generation. By no means all of these manifestations are libertarian, but libertarianism has nevertheless been a powerful dimension. The failure of 1968 and of the hippy movement can be attributed in large measure to the way in which these manifestations confronted structure merely with image; they did not present, or even attempt to build in anything but the most ephemeral manner, an alternative reality. When the show was over life had to go on and the only life that presented itself was the unreformed, freewheeling reality of yesterday. 1968 was millenarian, not Utopian.

In this light, the New Right is an interesting phenomenon in that it has provided a surface of reaction, of a return to words and images of the past, whilst under the surface massive changes have been under way. Social democracy and the whole edifice of 'organised capitalism' (Lash and Urry (1987)) was too restricting to contain either the continued acceleration of the processes of capitalist development of the means of production or the continued development at a subterranean level of the cultural consciousness of the growth of a libertarian sensibility which manifest itself initially in 1968. The New Right appeared in the guise of the hideous distorting bourgeois ideological reactions to the French and Russian Revolutions, but in practice there was no actual substance against which these might be a reaction: 1968 — or even the Chinese Cultural Revolution — which were clearly events of the past by the time the New Right appeared, were hardly plausible threats to the world social and political settlement. Perhaps we should understand this simply as a wave phenomenon: a fear of structurelessness as a reaction to the advancing spirit of 1968, a vain attempt to resist the growing insistence that in the end, life really isn't such a serious matter as our cultural inheritance has hitherto encouraged us to believe.

On the one hand, the consumerist pseudo-Utopia has produced the most bizarre cornucopia of things such that long before we might fear that there is some need that cannot be satisfied, we find that the means are already on hand, and increasingly sufficiently differentiated, to cater for our every personal whim and foible. Of course the reason that the results are so unloved is that the fear is still alive, expressed as an inchoate denial of the very idea that our genuine needs might ever be satisfied and hence an emotional rejection of every new accoutrement at the moment of possession, the moment the money is paid over the counter: the supermarkets and department stores become the cathedrals where this emotional process is acted out as ritual (Leiss (1978); Devall (1990: 87)). 'Created needs' are no conspiracy of a devious capitalism, they are the condensate of our cultural inheritance, the reality that increasingly insists on the irrationality of our deep-seated fear of want in a world of superabundance (Seabrook (1988)).

On the other hand, there has been emerging in an increasingly insistent way, an already referred to 'postmodern' sense of the emptiness at the heart of the whole process, a feeling that the Enlightenment vision has exhausted itself. Bluntening the edge of beliefs in the 'great ideas' that informed politics earlier in the century and the cultural didactic mission of the middle classes, there is a sense of growing relaxation into simple enjoyment of the kaleidoscope of modern life. Whilst this is in the first instance far from any measurable rejection of the insistent materialist dimension of the age, it is nevertheless losing its utilitarian edge, that requires ownership to validate the experience, replacing this with an appropriation of life as the consumption of a flow of images — a society of the spectacle — in its most obvious form as the crowding out of all other experience by television.

The most dramatic manifestation to date of this loss of inner motivation is the abandonment of 'actually existing socialism' on the part of the Soviet Union and thence the rest of Eastern Europe. But whilst this may be understood as a sudden cracking of the ice following a gradual inner dissolution of ancient fears, what is conspicuously evident is that this does not in any way automatically bring into existence appropriate new structures. Intellectual debate over the postmodern condition continues within the inherited framework of positivist science (indeed this is true also of modern Marxists) in that it focuses almost entirely on attempting to describe what exists and then prophesy what this might mean for the future. Although such analyses may create a frame of mind and general intellectual context which has the effect of reorienting social and political action, they remain firmly this-side of any commitment to structured intervention in the processes with which they concern themselves.

In academic debate, the notion of postmodernism has by no means swept all criticism before it. On the contrary, many, perhaps most, of the commentators on this condition see it as being in some way problematic. At one extreme (Callinicos (1990)) the whole contention that such a condition exists is argued against or, more widely, it is seen as a temporary malaise (Berman (1984)) or a dangerous lurch to the political right (Habermas (1987)). There can certainly be no doubt that there is a radical contradiction between, on the one hand, the progressive loss of any coherent sense of political organisation around consciously formulated social goals, and on the other the ever expanding power of multinational corporate capitalism and the subordination of state power to its ends as highlighted by the collapse of 'actually existing socialism'. And the deflation of the importance of privilege in the social imagination noted earlier has in no way overcome the actuality of social differentials in power and wealth. On the contrary, following the era of social democratic welfarism which saw itself as dedicated to reducing social differentials, these have now dramatically widened and comprise a festering problem drowned out only by the increasing din of consumerist attempted self-indulgence.

But it is also true, as has been noted by many critics (Lash (1988: 331); Harvey (1989: 353-4); Eagleton (1990: 375)), that the postmodern condition creates a new cultural and political context that could be deployed to radical ends. Harvey (1989: 48) notes that 'Curiously, most movements of this sort (ie women, gays, blacks, ecologists, regional autonomists, etc.) though they have definitely helped change 'the structure of feeling', pay scant attention to postmodernist arguments...' (in fact feminist contributions to the postmodernist debate have been accumulating rapidly (Boyne and Rattansi (1990); Nicholson (1990))). Indeed, he notes, some feminists are directly hostile. This hostility stems from the way in which postmodern discourse implicitly disregards the emancipatory project — asserting that sooner or later arbitrary authority will cease to exist — that was such an important strand of the Enlightenment project. There can be no doubt upon a close reading of these texts (Lovibond (1990)) that postmodernism does destroy purchase for the traditional forms of emancipatory strategy and tactics and that the disregard for emancipation and its preoccupation with a form of hedonism which is trenchantly individualistic effectively condone inegalitarian social relations and practice. It is therefore to be expected that those new social movements that focus upon combating social discrimination against particular interests will be, at a minimum, suspicious of the postmodern rhetoric.

The Green movement and its theorists have indeed paid rather little attention to social and cultural phenomena generally and have been quite insensitive to any changes in sensibility within the cultural process except that which concerns a growing awareness that their message about environmental destruction is becoming more widely accepted. It is also true to say that postmodernist debate has had nothing to say about environmental problems: the 'new social movements' are seen as including 'ecologists', but what it is that concerns the ecologists about why and in what way society needs to be rebuilt, makes no appearance in the postmodernist literature whatsoever. The two modes of thought, the two rapidly expanding bodies of literature, appear to be on opposite sides of a chasm.

Political ecology must be concerned to bridge this chasm. It must in general develop a much broader understanding of social and cultural process, its wellsprings and motivations, and the place and potential function of political ecology within this. Being sensitive to the mood and inner directedness of culture grows out of such knowledge. And it also increases greatly its ability to take opportunities as they open up. So much environmentalist and 'deep ecological' rhetoric itself takes on a millenarian edge precisely because it speaks *at*, rather than *to*, social and cultural conditions, imagining that rational explanation of the problem posed by the ecological abyss ahead will bludgeon a deaf and blind populace into 'seeing the truth of their situation' and convince them that they should fall into line behind the movement — which, in reality, is itself much less capable of showing the way out than it generally imagines, requiring a much broader input of ideas from right across society to enrichen those it currently generates from within its own very limited resources.

But political ecology *does* have *some* sense of a way out of our predicament which is in no way the case with the postmodernists who have yet to acknowledge that there is an ecological problematic at all. Whilst there is considerable suspicion amongst postmodernism analysts of any kind of argument that talks of conditions emanating from nature — be they of the environmental determinist kind argued above or of the kind which argues backwards from a future ecological catastrophe[6] — it is incumbent on political ecologists to enter the debate and to argue their proposition and their projects for social and spacial reorganisation as representing the path along which the radical potential of the postmodern sensibility may become a radical actuality of a reorganised world. In the form in which each of these outlooks currently presents its own case, there remains an essential millenarianism. Argued within a common framework it is possible to see a measured path being trodden into what was earlier referred to as the final stages of enlightenment: the construction of a self-managing, bioregionally-based society in sustainable balance with the rest of nature.

The essential argument here is that the driving force of our ancient fear of want is waning as a consequence of the insistence of capitalism to demonstrate at every turn that our needs, however we might fantasise these, can be satisfied. This has been interpreted and analysed in terms of a 'postmodern' sensibility. Although there is a growing acceptance that we may adopt a more hedonistic attitude to life, no structure immediately presents itself to translate this attitude into a genuinely easier-going life for all; on the contrary, it expresses itself as the ultimate achievement of possessive individualism (Rorty (1986)). And so the infernal juggernaut, like the broom of the sorcerer's apprentice, rolls on. The ecologists have seen the inevitable outcome of this process, should it continue much longer unchecked: relief of want will be short lived unless we take the necessary steps to rebuild our relationship with nature such as to reverse the increasingly destructive effects of the machinery of needs satisfaction. There is a definite route out, into a society that internalises responsibility for nature by decentralising production and the related decision-making process and rebuilding society to facilitate and encourage participation in this decision-making, at the same time simplifying lifestyles so that these are easygoing and enjoyable for everyone, requiring relatively little by way of material support. Moreover there are no barriers to implementing such a strategy that are not of our own making, the consequence of our own inhibitions, cultural inertia and a fatal conformity to the existing structures of life. Postmodernist analysts and ecologists are in great need of one another to marry their different interpretations of the state of the world and what to do about it and how to go about it.

As has been stated at several points in this book, the intention here is not to philosophise but, rather, to take a more practical look at how we might go about building a world that will obviate the ecological catastrophe expected to result from continuation of our current cultural trajectory. In so far as certain methodological, epistemological and ontological questions required answering in order to achieve a satisfactory level of explanation for aspects of the argument, these were explored but the result does not in any way add up to a balanced 'ecophilosophy'. However, under the present sub-chapter heading, it is useful, if nothing else, to address the concerns of those who feel the urgent need for such a philosophy at least to provide what Kant might have referred to as a 'prolegomena to an ecological metaphysic'; so here are a few pertinent remarks. Let it be said that if humanity does succeed in banishing the ecological problematic, then such a philosophy will become a necessary aspect of the emerging culture, although we may expect it to be more — as Hegel would have it — insight that emerges at dusk to summarise and contemplate the results of the process, rather than a fully-fledged method with which to achieve an ecological culture.

First we must put positivist science in its place. Whilst this has masqueraded as philosophy since the 18th-century Enlightenment, the fact is that it is no more than methodology which is used, tendentiously, to stifle broader philosophical speculation and synthesis. The attack made upon this by the friends of the Green movement has in some of its manifestations a dangerous tendency towards obscurantism: the assumption that science and its practical progeny alike, must be rejected *in toto*. This has resulted in attempts to revive notions of magic (Berman (1990)) which is no more than to displace one, very effective, methodology with another, the rational for which is entirely unclear, rather than simply putting methodology as such in a more balanced position with respect to the totality of knowledge, understanding, selfconsciousness, wisdom and their uses.

In the foregoing chapter it was pointed out that a philosophy compatible with the aims of political ecology will inevitably be 'organicist', holistic, but that there are many alternative interpretations of what this might amount to. In the first instance, and uncontentiously, this means that it is predominantly interested in differentiation of the interconnected and interactive totality of things, of life and human consciousness as a systemic, organic totality, as opposed to viewing nature and knowledge as being in need of breaking into manageable aspects and disciplines for the purposes of analysis and instrumental utility. It was also suggested that a review of attempts at organicist philosophies of the past — even back to Jacob Boehme, Meister Eckhart and, of course, Greek speculation on nature as well as the philosophies and myths of other cultures — is a worthwhile activity and furthermore that current refocusing of scientific investigation around the concept of 'chaos' is a good deal more useful with respect to the analysis of nature than anything emanating from the traditions of positive science.

As suggested in the adoption by the Green movement from the beginning of the term 'ecology' to describe its intellectual and existential centre of gravity, there is general consensus that a philosophy of a viable future will rest upon the realisation of the promise encapsulated in the 'ecological paradigm'. Whilst the 'science' of ecology and, as its temporal dimension, the 'science' of natural evolution have suffered repression and distortion under the hegemony of positivism, it is now necessary to bring these — or rather the potential within these — into the philosophical forefront. Indeed, considerable re-evaluation of the latter is already in train in a direction of which political ecology cannot disapprove (Gould (1990)) and ecologists have acknowledged the concerns of political ecology both through the ongoing development of their work and in active participation in the Green movement. The extension of this paradigm as it were backwards and forwards to form a framework for the understanding of the inorganic on the one hand and the cultural and thence social (Ingold (1986)) on the other provides us with our starting point.

A philosophy adequate to a viable, ecological future will eschew the esoteric: much philosophising of the past remained scholastic either because it comprised inadequate formulation of its contentions or because it was purposely obscurantist. Whilst there is certainly room for the expression of mystical and aesthetic experience, a sense of respect, of awe, empathy and love, concerning one another and nature that is not rationalised in words — indeed, these are essential — this will lie beyond the purview of philosophy itself. However, what is here being defined as the expression of ideological rationality in our lives must be able to encompass nature and culture, subsuming society, in a single, coherent and balanced framework.

The major problem with what might otherwise be conceived of as the beginnings of a present day organicist philosophy discussed in the foregoing chapter (viz Waddington, Jantsch, Prigogine, etc.) is their inadequacy in accounting for the human (consciousness and society) side of the dialectic. Perhaps it is useful to return at this point to the conceptions of Hegel and Marx with respect to the terms of reference of an adequate secular philosophy. Put in its simplest form, Hegel's 'philosophical system', as sketched in the foregoing chapter, can be interpreted in terms of presenting the active human consciousness on the one hand and nature on the other as dialectical moments unified through cultural and political process. Hegel's development of an understanding of processes of human consciousness can still be studied to great profit. There is, however, little of the content of his philosophy of nature which is still of use in the light of our present day knowledge of nature; furthermore we clearly cannot accept his notion of Lutheran religion and the 19th-century Prussian political settlement as being a final and adequate expression of the potentialities of the dialectic of consciousness-and-nature.

Marx, in common with the immediate followers of Hegel generally, saw Hegel as having successfully resolved the philosophical problematic for all time; the point was now to realise this philosophical resolution in its proper (as opposed to Hegel's false, idealistic) form in the material world. He thus presented himself, and has always been seen by his followers, as having adequately transformed Hegel's framework into a practical tool that subsumed the totality of the Hegelian dialectical framework. However, what in fact happened was that Hegel's notion of consciousness and emerging self-consciousness of humanity was translated into the idea of social process, Marx insisting that consciousness necessarily developed within the practical confines of particular social arrangements. Hegel's second dialectical moment — nature — Marx translated into the way in which society exploits nature through 'modes of production'[7]. In other words nature in-itself was lost in a kind of return to Kant's opposition of phenomena to noumena, the unknowable or, perhaps, the unknown of nature yet-to-be assimilated into consciousness. The excuse which Marx gave for ignoring nature in this way has been appended to the frontispiece of this book because it is so very important to understand the need to re-establish the balance of the dialectical programme which Hegel laid out. In this view, Marx's philosophy is not a 'dialectical materialism' at all but rather a 'dialectical humanism' or perhaps most correctly a 'dialectical socialism'.

The philosophy of a viable ecological future is a true dialectical *materialism* (Murray Bookchin has coined the term 'dialectical naturalism') in that it concerns itself with squaring the truly material, natural process — ecology — with human consciousness, resolved in an appropriate cultural, social and political framework that is capable of operationalising human needs in nature on an everyday basis and into the long term. It is not necessary to be Kantian on the 'nature' side of the dialectic, throwing our arms in the air and declaring it unknowable (rather, we should consider that we now know far too much about nature!) nor is it necessary to back off defining what nature is, in-itself, in the way that science successfully persuaded us to do (substituting method for knowledge), because we are no longer concerned primarily to convert nature into means to satisfy our needs but, on the contrary, to empathise with the processes and rhythms of nature in-itself, of which satisfaction of our needs on a sustainable basis is an indissoluble part.

We might surmise (contentiously: viz. the Marxist debate concerning 'human nature') that Hegel's view of the processes of consciousness were taken as read by Marx. In so far as this requires reworking, the section on 'alienation' in Chapter 3 of this book sketched out some of the issues relevant to a philosophy of ecological consciousness.

Much of this book has focused, however, on the question of cultural, social and political resolution — hence *political* ecology — of the human condition, faced with its current predicament and brought to this point specifically through the instrument of European ideological and social evolution. Of particular salience here, and hence addressed specifically in the foregoing chapter under the heading of 'individualism', is the problematic of ethics and morality, as it effects an ecological society that has annulled conflictory social arrangements and realised an outlook that understands the essentially social nature of human existence, commensurate with an understanding of the essential unity and priority of human consciousness as a holistic entity, where the satisfaction of the needs of others becomes the principle within which the needs of the particular individual are satisfied. Within this framework ethics is resolved into aesthetics. The importance of this principle requires that it is discussed in more detail, which is the function of the following section of this chapter.

The political resolution to the ecological philosophy is, of course, the theory and practice of the Green Utopia. The two principles sketched out in the foregoing section are pertinent here: namely the requirement to organise human activity in nature on a 'decentralised' basis that maintains transparency and manageability across particular ecological and socio-cultural units; and the need to erase fixed social boundaries with respect either to production processes or lifestyles. The details of an ecological culture and politics clearly goes beyond the bounds of an ecological philosophy. But what these principles clearly indicate is that there rapidly develop limits to any *universal* ecological philosophy in that each bioregion, each conjuncture of particular ecosystem and its related human culture will require an ideological system appropriate to itself and itself only.

The role of aesthetics

In Chapter 3 it was emphasised, in discussing the question of ideology, that our immediate inheritance, with respect to the analysis of social phenomena, has avoided consideration of the creative and aesthetic dimension of social process. Here it is intended to spell out the role of aesthetics both in contemporary society and in an eventual ecological society and in order to accomplish this adequately it is necessary to provide somewhat more background than in other sections of this chapter. By way of introducing the subject, however, a few preliminary remarks are in order.

First it is necessary to clarify a little the relationship between morality, ethics and aesthetics as they are to be understood in the following text. It will be recalled from the foregoing chapter that it is envisaged that the achievement of an ecological society will involve, *inter alia*, a decanting of our inherited moral mechanisms of social structuring — guilt and shame — into aesthetic ones. Both morality and ethics must be understood as consequences of an individualistic outlook on life in the context of the actuality of social existence. The assumption that the individual possesses some kind of absolute sovereignty, embodied in the notion of a soul, makes it necessary to spell out the limits which actions emanating from this may have in the real social world, to prevent the destructive clash of individuals, or, by extension, interest groups. Social process in this context is a dead, external framework which constrains and frustrates our inner desires, but with which we must perforce compromise in order to obtain the material benefits that accrue from the agreement to co-operate. This view is clearly spelled out throughout Enlightenment moral and social philosophy.

Morality comprises the negative, coercive aspect of this relation between individual and society, which establishes its roots in obligation. Shame and guilt, as social structuring impulses, inform the construction of moral systems. But, as Williams (1985) points out, there is a more optimistic side to the human condition, even within the framework of civil society, which acknowledges that being human is not merely a lonely individual existence, asserting that our social existence itself possesses a life which is an essential part of us, as expressed in particular through love, the impulse to kindness and in general the deliberate relinquishing of the self in others. Where morality is introspective, ethics is open; ethical systems explore the question of values generally and rather than being concerned only to guard against fear, provide the basis for the realisation of love. Morality involves a legislative discourse where ethics is closer to aesthetic judgement.

Aesthetics thus lies beyond ethics on this scale, beyond the individual and even society as, ultimately, abstract structure embodying the fulfilment of our desires but is also the creative process of achieving this fulfilment, the essential process of living life itself. All of human thought and activity, in the form of culture, sometimes only incidentally but at other times more actively and consciously, creates and clothes itself in the aesthetic: as a kind of inner nature of human existence, there is, ever present, a disposition to appreciate things — even nature as found, but in particular the products of human creativity — for their own sake and to beget them, however utilitarian their immediate reason, as actions and objects in and for themselves objectifying love and our understanding of the rhythms of nature and of the universe. This aesthetic self-expression of human cultures as vernacular objects, rituals, lifestyles and mythologies, tends towards a holistic, coherent unity which becomes the wellspring of all meaning to its members and, seen from outside, the framework holding the society together and ensuring its sustainability in place and time. In the realisation of a society which knows that human existence *is* social existence, which knows that there is no 'human nature' that is not socially given and hence that self-realisation *is* cultural activity and only incidentally activity of individuals, morality becomes redundant and ethics becomes an attribute of aesthetics.

The snag is, however, that aesthetics is available even within the framework of a society fraught with individualistic self-understanding. This means that it can be utilised as a means of deception, as a vital tool for the creation and maintenance of 'false consciousness'. Here the role of 'art', as the conscious separation of aesthetic awareness and creativity for organic cultural process, is of great importance and the discussion which follows is at pains to shed light on this. The process of establishing an egalitarian society requires the clearing away of the aesthetic — in art but also in other domains — which holds a morally-based society in thrall and the construction of aesthetics which express and support social arrangements that have exorcised the individualistic faith. But this is running ahead of the argument.

In the explosive social, political and cultural development of Europe over the past few hundred years, which has been the focus of much of this book, aesthetics has played an important role. This is not merely reflected in the attention paid to the conscious production of art — and the enormous value which this patently commands in late capitalist society as expressed in prices paid for 'masterpieces' and the mass pilgrimages to view such masterpieces — but also in the high priority given to the question of aesthetics in European philosophical discourse more broadly (Eagleton (1990: 1)). It is vital to the achievement of an understanding of where we stand today to review the changing role which aesthetics has played in the unfolding of recent cultural history.

It will be recalled that in the course of the Dark Ages, Christianity consciously turned away from worldly engagement, which was indeed a necessity in so far as the economic — or shall we say the organisational — capacity to engage in elaborate creation, artistic or otherwise, was simply not available. But advancing into the age of scholasticism, this was no longer the case and both the secular social forces and above all the Church encouraged elaborate development of the aesthetic towards the furtherance of their power and their beliefs. The extraordinary development of the gothic cathedral — of engineering and architecture — in the Île de France, guided by biblical exegesis and the litany and absorbing to itself all other arts and sciences (Hugo (1965: 179ff)), laid the foundations for the prominence of the development of conscious aesthetics — of 'high art' and aesthetic philosophy — in modern Europe.

General philosophical positions that unfolded in the course of Enlightenment which have been looked at in earlier chapters expressed themselves also in the development of aesthetic theory. Rationalism equated to a classical aesthetic (Cassirer (1951: 278ff)) that sought invariant rules underlying beauty. It believed in the existence of absolute precepts that summed to absolute truth regardless of human sentiment or appreciation: truth is beauty and beauty is truth. By contrast the sceptical British empiricists denied any truth that was not the product of human passions. Aesthetics to Hume lay in the interpretation of impressions through the human imagination. In so far as a generally valid aesthetic is conceded within this framework, this is attributable to the similarity of the human subjects. For the rationalist, the aesthetic lay at the ultimate point of the discovery of Reason, of the rational structure of nature and a properly organised world; for the empiricist, on the other hand, the aesthetic was the immediate apprehension of the world beyond the human flesh that had to be cleared aside in the process of achieving a better organised — a morally superior — world.

The resolution of this dualism that came to philosophy as a whole only in the German idealism and dialectical materialism of the 19th century, was achieved in aesthetic theory already in the early years of the 18th century in parallel with and directly out of the same roots as the Newtonian synthesis. Tutored in Neoplatonism and a student of John Locke, the Third Earl of Shaftsbury perceived the importance for aesthetics both of the '...'interior numbers' which we discover in every instance of the beautiful reveal(ing) both the mystery of nature and of the physical world' (Cassirer (1951: 314)) and also the psychological process of apprehension and creation of that which is beautiful. And his concern went beyond mere Kantian understanding of the wellsprings of the aesthetic on to the production of art as process. The modern notion of the hypostatised individual artistic genius (the archetype being William Shakespeare), penetrating to a perception of beauty and communicating this through a 'process of pure creation', originates in Shaftsbury's analysis.

Although Shaftsbury laid the foundations for subsequent German aesthetic theory, universally acknowledged as the pre-eminent line of European aesthetic theory, he was nevertheless himself predominantly concerned with moral theory, as was true of Hume and in general of the main line of British philosophical discourse throughout the Enlightenment and beyond. The assertion of the unity of ethics and aesthetics (Eagleton (1990: 41)), locating authority in the creative powers of the individual genius and by this means usurping key ideological powers of the Church, solidified the status of the bourgeois as guardians of social values in a radically unequal society. As Shaftsbury wrote by way of advice to an author:

The genius of (dramatic) poetry consists in the lively representation of the disorders and misery of the great; to the end that the people and those of a lower condition may be taught the better to content themselves with privacy, enjoy their safer state, and prize the equality and justice of their guardian laws. (Quoted in Hill (1969:275).)

The medieval Church had demonstrated how aesthetics could be used as adjunct to textual and liturgical mythology to hold the social settlement in thrall and now the bourgeois could apply it to consolidate their ascent. By asserting the unity of aesthetics and ethics it could be argued that to live aesthetically is to achieve the apogee of virtue. A more clear-eyed assessment simply notes that converting morality into bourgeois lifestyle and etiquette effectively facilitated the deconstruction of the contradiction between beauty in the abstract and in ritual on the one hand and the moral unjustifiability of the prevailing social arrangements on the other.

It is useful at this point to return to the question of the differing intellectual traditions of various European nations, extending the argument in general and specifically with regard to the development of aesthetic theory and practice. Imagine Europe since the Enlightenment as some living organism in which each cultural entity represents a particular organ or characteristic. So we might see Russia as the soul of Europe, Germany as the mind, Italy as the spirit and France as the countenance. Britain would represent the voice and the hand[8], the practical transmission of European culture as a whole to the world beyond, carrying out the hegemonic European project that progressively subjugated then destroyed all other cultures and then moved on to subjugate — and now to destroy — nature as well.

At face value, the empiricist epistemology, so insistent on the power of the human passions, in which all knowledge is deemed to be but an emanation of the sensuous immediacies of empirical life — where life is incipiently ensnared by the clammy embrace of the senses (Eagleton (1990: 32)) — might be expected to emerge from a hedonistic culture uninterested in the world beyond human sensual enjoyment. In practice, however, it will be recalled from earlier discussion that the emergence of modern empiricism was closely associated with the formulation of the puritan form of 'worldly asceticism' involving severe prohibition against all forms of sensuous enjoyment, as a kind of dark warning against any capitulation to the passions and the senses. The restless pursuit of the practical thus results from the flight from sensuous enjoyment, from the nightmare of the passions pressing in upon moral artifice, insisting upon their satisfaction.

Fruitful in feeding notions into the initiation of so many streams of European aesthetic culture — Shaftsbury into German aesthetic theory and Hume disturbing Kant's dogmatic slumbers; Scott feeding into the great French and Russian flowering of the novel; Turner and Constable into Impressionism and the Arts and Crafts movement into the development of modern architecture — the British contribution has otherwise been weak and derivative, tending to lack either developed rationalistic structure or any very fulsome expression of the sensual. This has indeed been true both of aesthetic theory and artistic practice. The acknowledged 'British' artistic genius, and many a theoretician as well, was so often a continental import.

It is broadly acknowledged that the empiricist idiom of British thought has always undermined the development of any very coherent theory — indeed, much British writing sees this as its great strength — and this approach to mental activity, dispersed to every corner of British intellectual life, effectively frustrated any very highly structured creative process of the imagination, for all the empiricist faith placed in the imagination as origin of our actions. Unless it was of a directly practical nature the reasoning process was quickly dissipated, and, beyond its baleful impact on aesthetic creativity, this was wonderfully effective in undermining any propensity to rethink the political and social arrangements[9]. Conversely in channelling creativity into the immediately practical and the instrumental, these thought processes were immensely effective in generating what became known as the industrial revolution coupled into the aggressive exploitation of other cultures and societies. The continental interior could be well left to generate the stuff of a relevant, contemporary European aesthetic culture.

In any case, for all the theoretical importance accorded aesthetics and morals, the reality was that the bourgeois — in particular the English bourgeois — having cast aside the power of royal prerogative and the Church by dint of possessing control over material life, had themselves become the ideological creation of material philosophy that would inevitably handle the contemplative, insightful or beautiful as epiphenomena, fatally devoid of critical edge however angry the critics might be.

Marx's description of this situation, which saw the immediacy of human economic activity as 'base' and all else as 'superstructure', captured the essence not of any deeper human condition, but predominantly of contemporary English bourgeois culture and beyond this, that longer standing northern European fear of want discussed earlier. His ability to achieve this insight lay in the contrasting situation of the German bourgeois from which he came, caught up in markedly different social arrangements and, as expressed by the German theorists themselves enamoured by developments in Britain, over-theorising in the absence of what was deemed to be adequate practical developments. This cultural 'economic imperative', encapsulated and hypostatised in the term 'capitalism' became the characteristic form of European culture as a whole in its restless urge to produce material results first and only secondarily beauty, pleasure and sensuous enjoyment (Williams (1965: 54)).

Nevertheless, the 'cultural division of labour' within Europe and the interaction between societies with significantly contrasting cultural wellsprings, in the context of an enormously productive development of the economic base, yielded an extremely rich aesthetic superstructure. The organic development of romantic music and the bourgeois novel in the 19th century, quite independent of vernacular or classical traditions, are amongst the most complex and impressive phenomena of world aesthetic history and whilst 19th-century architecture was more closely tied to classical precedent, it was nevertheless forced into inventiveness by economically driven technological change presaging new aesthetic interpretations of everyday objects which, in the 20th century, emerged as a full-blown 'machine aesthetic', taking its cue from the forms of functional objects themselves as immediately emergent from the capitalistic production process.

Of course the economic and social processes that this entailed, tearing whole populations away from their roots and depositing them in urban and industrial conglomerations in alien places and foreign lands, conjoined to revolutions in agricultural practice, corroded away vernacular cultural intuitions and practices that had evolved within particular places out of mythical roots, without providing any basis for an appropriate new culture. 'Working class culture' entailed, in the first instance, the radical cultural impoverishment so eloquently described by such as Charles Dickens and

Gustave Doré. Thus whilst the reconstruction of European aesthetic culture could be immediately understood as a coherent reflection and complement to the development of bourgeois society, for the masses of the population this remained a closed realm, esoteric and inaccessible. Their aesthetic experience was one predominantly of destruction as an adjunct to the brutal destruction of their lifestyle (Thompson (1968)).

The calling into question of the impulse to modernity that has emerged in recent years has brought the term itself into the arena of contention. The facts of the case are that the original cultural battle over modernity — the self-acknowledged quarrel between the ancients and the moderns — took place in the early years of the French Enlightenment (Habersmas (1987b: 8)). Modernity represented a notion of time-conditioned beauty in contrast to classical ideas of absolute and eternally relevant rules. The term became common currency in the 19th century to refer to the avant-garde in art embodying, in contrast to the eternal dimension, the contemporary and fashionable, the moral and the passionate, in short, the dynamic aspect of cultural creation.

In terms of aesthetics, it is commonly understood that the modern era starts at the turn of this century. Yet from the definition of the term this makes no sense: if 'modern' is the contemporary and the fleeting, then how can it become a label for an era that continues decade after decade? This contradiction is not one that is easily resolved or dismissed. We are talking of a century in which institutionalised revolution is expected of our own culture and where this is manifestly realised in the economic realm.

The role which 'high art' took for itself, as the accelerating process of modernist 'time-space compression' (Harvey (1989)) burst upon the early years of this century, continued to be that inherited from the Enlightenment: to give aesthetic expression to the spirit of the times and to provide some kind of ethical lead to the social process. Whilst the 19th century bourgeois arts succeeded in fulfilling this role in a coherent fashion, at least for the dominant class, by the turn of the century the accelerating tensions of social and economic change — soon to explode into the First World War and Russian Revolution — became reflected in the aesthetic realm in terms of an incipient incoherence, a breaking apart of the rational from the ethical and both from the sensual. Artistic movements became by turns scandalous and then incomprehensible, running into vacuous over-structured abstraction and atonality or into violent apocalyptic expressionism.

A tendency emerged for opinion to polarise into a fervent embrace of modernism, regardless of where it might lead, or contemptuous dismissal (Berman (1984a: 24)). A handful of Olympian bourgeois moderns succeeded in mastering the contradictions, often, such as in the work of Bartók and le Corbusier[10], by using vernacular forms to instill life into modernist abstraction, creating a set of standards against which 'high art' has been played out across this century. But the revulsion against the politics and culture that had precipitated the First World War generated an anarchist reaction that expressed itself in Dada, evolving into Surrealism, in a forthright rejection of the bourgeois artistic project that could trace its ancestry back to Jean-Jacques Rousseau. For much of the middle years of the century, modernism was rejected by right and left wing orthodoxy alike to be substituted by forms of 'realism' aimed directly at creating an ethical didactic and ostensibly using language and imagery directly accessible to the mass of the population.

One of the highlights of 20th-century aesthetic theoretical debate was that amongst Marxists from the 1920s to the 1960s, concerned to create a relevant aesthetics (Jameson (1971); Taylor (1980)). Major disagreement centred around how the arts might best be employed to promote the ends of the social revolutionary project: expressionism, involving a modernist aesthetic informed by pre-existing popular modes of expression (Kandinsky and Marc (1965), argued in the Marxist context by Bloch), or realism in the form of a classical aesthetic didactic (Lukács, faithful to Marx and Lenin), or some form of socialist realism married either to classical or avant-garde forms (in the latter case by Brecht). In the final analysis, for all the concern of the Marxist theoreticians to see the creation of a mass aesthetic as adjunct to a politics of social transformation, this did not make any major efforts to divest itself of the Enlightenment notion of a 'high art' with superior capacities and pretensions to any aesthetic self-expression of the mass of the people themselves (Taylor (1978)). Marx and thence Marxism remained peculiarly blind to the richness of vernacular aesthetics and the potential of social forces to create and re-create relevant aesthetics out of whatever material lies immediately to hand.

The post Second World War political settlement, ostensibly rent by implacably opposed political ambitions but in practice characterised by a universal adoption of the Enlightenment cultural modernisation project, accepted and disseminated the modernist aesthetic via corporate and bureaucratic management mechanisms. Initially no more than attempts to confirm the modernist impulse of the turn of the century and to continue the process of displacing vernacular modes of expression, post-war modernism thence took on a life of its own of an increasingly anarchic nature in the sphere of 'high art' and of the proliferation of pop culture, in part spontaneous and in part generated and disseminated by the burgeoning capitalist-driven consumer society.

On the one hand, the time and resources were now available to the mass of the population to invent or at least participate in social praxis beyond the utilitarian. However, whilst this might create the space for cultural development, the driving force lay elsewhere. If commodities were going to find markets then they would have to be desirable to succeed, this necessarily involving aesthetics as a major component. With no interest in imposing a didactic upon a disinclined society, but rather openly flattering of sensual predilections to the ends of an exploitative project, the consumer goods industries, the media and above all the advertising industry ate out the heart of modern art, employing and extending its most sophisticated inventions. The shell of 'high art' remained as little more than ritual, tied directly into the confirmation of the class nature of society (Williams (1983: 135)), its content having flowed out and conjoined with multifarious influences to yield an incredibly rich flowering of the aesthetic reaching, in the course of the 1970s and 1980s, into the far corners of society: into domestic lifestyles and workplace procedures, into politics and even of the functioning of bureaucracy. This exuberant growth of the aesthetic, robbing in equal

measure enlightened bourgeois and Marxist attempts to employ the aesthetic
as ethical didactic of their erstwhile authority, was certainly not of a kind that
any but a small minority of the priests of 'high art' could approve: neither was
it respectful of privilege and the superior sensibility of the intellectuals and in
general the established classes, nor was it, conversely, concerned in any
conscious way to promote social change of any kind. And yet it is on this
plane of the aesthetic that the postmodernist sensibility has effected the main
thrust of its criticism of the Enlightenment project, of enlightenment dogma.

Already in the 1950s an anarchist critique of nascent consumer society
sprang up out of the embers of Dadaism and Surrealism, under the title of
Situationism[11]. The importance of this as ideological informant of the
explosive events of Paris in 1968 should not be underestimated and although
the movement dispersed shortly after those events, it can be seen both as
prescient of the emergence of postmodernism and, it might be conjectured,
salient with respect to the role of aesthetics in a future ecological society. The
central concern of Situationism (Debord (1983)) was that modern society is
metamorphosing from a situation where the population was exploited as
workers to one where they are being exploited as consumers, creating a
'society of the spectacle' where the chief mode of social control and
subordination is shifting from repression to seduction.

By the destruction of any sense of community and of the connectedness of
things, the whole cultural cosmos, including the human subject, is being torn
out of its context and manufactured into commodities, all relations are
becoming relations of prostitution. The result is the total loss of participation
in the processes of the creation of life or identification with the increasingly
proliferating products. Desire to possess these is encouraged by whatever
means are effective — and that involves above all the harnessing of the
aesthetic — but satisfaction of these desires is radically denied. The solution to
this problem (Vaneigem (1983a; 1983b)) does not lie in any form of self-denial
but, on the contrary, in breaking through the veil that modern life draws
between ourselves and others, and beyond that nature, and the direct
satisfaction of our desires. It lies in a spontaneous hedonism driven by our
impulse to love. This must involve a thoroughgoing fusion of reason and
passion, living our everyday lives out of a sense of playfulness that invents the
means to communication and participation in the necessarily social decision-
making process, and that radically denies any function for devices, such as
prestige, status and fixed roles, that separate us one from one another. Art,
aesthetics, in this context, transfuses and gives structure to everything in life
(Vaneigem (1983a: 155)):

...the search for new forms of communication, far from being the preserve of painters
and poets, is now part of the collective effort. In this way the old specialisation of art
has finally come to an end. There are no more artists because everyone is an artist. The
work of art of the future will be the construction of a passionate life.

Although first mooted in various disciplinary areas and brought together into
a single analytical framework by Jean-Francois Lyotard (1984) in the late
1970s, it was only in the mid 1980s that the concept 'postmodernism'
suddenly took on its current air of great importance in the academic world[12]

since which there has been a vast proliferation of writing that at once finds difficulty in identifying what is salient about this 'condition' and on the other hand is constantly expectant that it will disappear as suddenly as it appeared. Summarising across a selection of these writings (Jameson (1984); Featherstone (1988); Harvey (1989); Boyne and Rattansi (1990)), there might be said to be a general consensus on the following points with respect to postmodern aesthetics and its influence on contemporary cultural and potentialities for the future more generally.

Postmodernism is not a coherent alternative to modernism and the enlightenment project but rather an acknowledgement and celebration of incoherence that has the effect of undermining the enlightenment project. It is thus a 'change in the structure of feeling' but not a wholesale paradigm shift. A telling aspect is to be seen in its attitude towards history. Although the modernist strictures against historical reference have been cast aside and the arts openly flaunt historical imagery, this brings with it no sense of historic continuity but rather conceals an exhaustion of the modernist teleology behind an ephemeral pastiche. And with this exhaustion, major doubts arise over the credibility of metanarrative, metatheory: there is no longer any widespread belief that a given question only has one true answer. The insistent modernist rejection of relativism is falling away. This has the effect of undermining any moral project and in practice, with the rise of the aesthetic — of figural culture over the discursive — aesthetics becomes the chief mode of social judgement; the continuity of values and beliefs is broken and these become subordinate to style and fashion.

The postmodern sensibility is above all an individualistic one. However, in Richard Rorty's (1986) version, the quest for the discovery of 'human nature' is finally dismissed: another pillar of the modernist universalism falls away. But far from the anguish which this discovery brought upon Satre four decades ago, for the postmodernist this is a signal for an uninhibited project of hedonistic self-expansion guided only by curiosity and the aesthetic. This begs the question, however, that if there is no human nature, then upon what logic or what criteria can the self-expansion project proceed? Perhaps this extreme contradiction in the Rortyan view should be seen as expressing the way in which puritan individualist asceticism insists on maintaining the infinite regress of walls both intersubjective and between subject and object in spite of the realisation of the lack of any content to the subject; and in this we might perceive a structure of perception and understanding ripe for dissolution.

Above all, the incipient radical questioning of the work ethic and of the priority of the 'economic base' over the cultural superstructure is clearly expressed not only by Rorty, but right across the spectrum of postmodern discourse. And yet the loud and insistent process of commodification and simultaneous frustration of desires continues, ignoring the critics of postmodernism. It is widely recognised that postmodernism approaches the realisation of the aims of Dada and Surrealism in the realm of the aesthetic and that as a political project it points in the direction an anarchist, rather than a Marxist, way forward. But it does not go on to recognise the more coherent anarchist project of Situationism, with its insistence on going beyond the destruction of esoteric art and the radical extension of the aesthetic and calls for the destruction of the walls that separate us from the satisfaction of our desires in one another and in the material world which we inhabit.

So what position does political ecology occupy in this context? For its part, and in spite of its origins lying, in part, in the libertarian hippy and 'alternative' movements, the ecology movement has remained overwhelmingly discursive in its relation to cultural dynamics — a problem which, as discussed in Chapter 3, Barthes ascribed to radical (left-wing) politics in earlier decades — and in this way 'unfashionable' relative to postmodernism as 'intellectual preoccupation of the moment'. Furthermore, the movement remains equivocal concerning hedonism in the context of an individualistic consumerist world towards which it is implacably hostile; to this is added in the British case the artfulness with which inhibition of the playful creative impulse is built into the very heart of our culture. On the other hand, the visions of the future constructed by the ecologists, even where they may coincide momentarily with those of postmodernists (such as MacIntyre's vision referred to towards the end of the foregoing chapter), are far too structurally circumscribed and socially committed to make any substantial connection. As already noted, moves towards collaboration, with ecologists acknowledging the importance of hedonism and the aesthetic, and the advocates of postmodernism accepting the need to create a particular future, could be extremely fruitful. But it is necessary to choose strategies and tactics with care.

There would be little purpose in the ecology movement attempting to move into, or combat directly, the frenetic and ephemeral image creation business of advertising, the media and intellectual fad. Whilst there exists a problem of the rapidity with which these institutions have picked up nascent environmental concern and exploited this in the form of 'Green consumerism' and voyeuristic documentary illustrating the destruction of nature, the surface cannot be captured or laid still without first sowing the seeds of an alternative vision within the machinery which generates it, as it were colonising and reworking the machine from within. There is a more serious and hopeful move towards the formation of an alternative ecological consciousness and culture operating through cartoon (Cobb, Batallier and others) and comedy show (Ben Elton), and percolating into pop music and literature; indeed, the art and media worlds abound with concern for ecological destruction (Porritt and Winner (1988: Ch.5)). But although this may well be preparing the ground for political ecology, it is also true that as yet it ventures little beyond the boundaries of environmentalism: raising awareness of the ecological problematic, not yet disseminating notions of ecological lifestyles or any broader alternative symbolic cosmos.

And it is this project which now requires development: an ecological semiotic that, in the fashion of postmodernist figural culture, merges signifier and signified into instant messages about desirable alternative lifestyles and the social arrangements for their realisation. In a fragmentary way the movement has, as it were, drafted out its programme in manifestos and the alternative press. But this requires translation into terms that are compatible with the style of perception which our society has of late come to accept as the valid mode for receiving knowledge and attitudes. Seen from within conventional analytical frameworks informed directly or indirectly by Marxist thinking, there is an a priori assumption that if such an alternative project is seen to be 'against the interests of capital' then it will sooner or later be subverted or suppressed. Whilst modernist and social democratic experience would point to this representing an accurate prognosis, in the context of a growing awareness of the fundamental cultural changes necessitated if the ecological problematic is to be resolved in favour of human survival, the notion of a monolithic phenomenon termed 'capital' becomes questionable and certainly of very questionable conceptual value.

Of course it is in pursuit of breaking open the notion of a monolithic, self-conscious and self-reproducing organism entitled 'capitalism' that the analysis in the foregoing chapter of this book is, in large measure, directed. Capitalism as a phenomenon is the construct of a particular set of attributes that have emerged in the process of evolution of European culture. It might be said to operate through the way in which it is in possession of the social consciousness and beyond that the real structure of society. But this cultural conjuncture is certainly open to being transformed from within through ideological reconstruction and it is this which political ecology sets as its main task.

There is much evidence that elements of the advertising industry[13] and beyond that manufacturing interests are aware well beyond the exploitation of Green consumerism of the implications to them of the ecological problematic, that the end of the road is in sight for its core values centred on the imperative to grow; it should not be forgotten that 'The Limits to Growth' polemic emanated from the heart of capitalism itself. Just how capitalism can be transmogrified into the reconstructed processes of an ecological society is here of concern; this is to a significant degree a project of ideological, and with this semiotic, reconstruction — of the construction of an alternative symbolic universe — that is the responsibility of political ecology and the ecology movement: industry will have no problems interpreting this in terms of alternative production and distribution methods and the problem for the Greens will be to overcome the inertia of the industrial system tending to implement its own internal priorities — in other words the need to change the internal ethic and corporate organisational assumptions of 'business' by way of the implementation of alternative work lifestyles (Handy (1985); Osmond (1986); Robertson (1985; 1990); Dauncy (1988)).

The heart of the problem is not, as the Marxist legacy would lead us to believe, in the organisation of production at all but rather, as is implied by postmodern discourse, in the organisation of lifestyles and, by way of infrastructure, the creation of new concepts of community and the spread of lived practice that realises these concepts (Williams (1983: 195-199)). Where postmodernism advocates the abandonment of the work ethic and the adoption of hedonism, the ecology movement must demonstrate what this means in terms of a truly easy going everyday social praxis.

The aesthetic project of political ecology must clearly go beyond any facile Rortyan individualistic project of self-expansion. It must also move beyond any superficial notion of the admiration of the beautiful or of the individual life lived beautifully. It must adopt the classical notion, embodied in vernacular culture, wherein the need for morality is annulled and the ethical is subsumed into the aesthetic through the creation of social relations and a relationship with nature as a whole which is fundamentally holistic, empathetic and has removed all foundation for conflictory relations that are any more than contingent and essentially playful[14]. This will be embodied in the creation of new, localist vernacular cultures. Certainly any continuation of the use of the aesthetic as means to conceal or regulate social inequality is unacceptable because it cannot work beyond the very short term in which context it will, according to the environmentalist intuitions of political ecology, act as handmaiden not merely to a new totalitarianism, but to the destruction of the biosphere.

The notion of communist society that lay at the end of the Marxist project, as described in the '*Economic and Philosophical Manuscripts*', and that comprised the goal of many a Utopian and anarchist movement, was insistent that ultimately the social and the individual are indissoluble and require no ethics within a framework that operates on an inherently mutualistic basis. It is the supersession of ethical modes of social structuration and functioning by the aesthetic, if they do become heirs to the postmodern sensibility, which will mark the new social movements out as inheritors of the Utopian tradition which a certain strand of the Enlightenment itself was always aware would be the ultimate inheritor of their project. It is in this way, as analysed in the foregoing chapter, that the individualistic dimension not only of postmodernism or capitalism but of the Judaeo-Christian tradition and the whole civilising process itself is annulled in the return of 'human nature', now conscious of its role and potential, to the totality of sentient nature that comprises the biosphere in all its richness.

The ecological future

In a world dominated by competing vested interests, the future is inevitably contentious. In the context of social democratic progressivism, the promise is that all will be better off in the future than in the present and it becomes quite legitimate to fantasise about possible changes in physical arrangements. But serious consideration of changes in social and political arrangements that might alter the ranking of interests becomes problematic. Social analysis — including historiography as well as sociology, anthropology and economics — is not merely concerned with enquiry into structures and content of past and present but also with who will inherit the future and how this will be organised in pursuit of a given configuration of interests. Conservative and liberal ideologues might differ in the degree of shifts in the distribution of benefits in the future between the various interests but not to the point of changing the general order. The struggle over socialism was precisely about changes in the rank order of society.

So it is improbable that any general call for a more conscious and open Utopian speculation and design of the future will find easy acceptance.

Certainly there are those interests who might see such an activity as useful to their ends and, as is argued further below, there may be urgent reasons at the present time, with respect to the general interest, for the development of a more structured consideration of future social arrangements, but such a debate is not going to be achieved easily, indeed, if at all. This is not to say that all aspects of the thinking about the future are proscribed. In the halcyon years of social democracy, corporate and national institutions saw it as a necessary part of their planning functions to understand the context in which their programmes and projects would be inserted into the ongoing social process: the construction of highways and power stations and the implementation of social programmes were accompanied by the development of elaborate technocratic forecasting techniques (Jantsch (1967)) with the restricted function of improving the co-ordination of the processes of economic expansion; there was never any question of introducing consideration of more basic issues of general purpose or of any fundamental changes in social arrangements[15].

Although the foregoing argument comes naturally to us from the perspective of late 20th-century liberal society, it is nevertheless prima facie rather contradictory that a society that believes so strongly in promoting change at the same time suppresses any broad, conscious consideration of the future. This can only be understood in the context of enlightenment ideology as a whole. The notion that society is made up of individual and group interests pursuing their own ends is specifically a product of the Enlightenment. Whether we subscribe to the more brutal line of reasoning put forward by Hobbes, Mandeville, Adam Smith, Malthus and Darwin which acknowledges and applauds conflict and competition or whether we take a more conciliatory view expounded by Locke and Rousseau that sees society as an agreement amongst interests to join together into society, there remains a common belief that society is an artifice made up of sentient individual and group, in the final analysis incommensurate, interests.

But the Enlightenment *also* insisted that the world is progressing towards an ever better state of being. In which case, it is quite possible to contend that the individualist state of affairs prevailing in the early years of enlightenment would eventually give way to a higher rationality. And this is precisely what the more radical enlightenment thinkers — from Condorcet to Godwin and from Marx to Kropotkin — have argued. The general contention here is simply that individualism is a state of mind and of society that will eventually, through the enlightenment process, give way to a mutualistic way of understanding the human predicament and of organising our relationship with nature. Conservatives, subsuming liberals, have imagined that both progress and individual interests can be pursued indefinitely. Of course the emergence of the ecological problematic calls this sharply into question.

In order to combat radical criticism of their stance, conservative interests have assembled layer upon layer of argument that insists that individualism is a necessary aspect of the human condition, a fundamental attribute of human nature. Because it is so widely accepted in our culture as 'common sense', it is an important task for political ecology to refute this contention vigorously and in Chapter 3 some arguments were assembled in this respect under the heading of 'alienation'. To this can be added the historical evidence amassed in recent years indicating the way in which for nine tenths of the time during which *Homo sapiens* has occupied a place in nature, human activity was organised on the basis of mutualism, the last remnants of which survived even into this century. As Rousseau surmised in the early years of the Enlightenment, individualism is a product of the civilising process. The question for us is, therefore, how can we recover mutualistic modes of understanding and action as our cultural centre of gravity?

On the whole the enlightenment radicals, contending that mutualism would emerge as the ultimate stage of enlightenment, argued in terms merely of general notions of progress and through exhortation. Although the Utopian socialists were inventive of numbers of specific mechanisms designed to achieve a mutualistic society, Marx and Engels were alone in designing a whole process of social development that would end in the universal achievement of a mutualistic mode of social organisation. It is worth recalling that this vision understood the importance of the availability of material abundance to the possibility of achieving communist society.

As was argued earlier in this chapter, the class configuration of European society guaranteed that unless abundance was universally available, the bourgeoisie would do everything in its power to destroy emancipatory aspirations amongst the 'lower orders'. Marx understood the importance of the development of technology to the achievement of the conditions of universal abundance as a necessary pre-condition to the abolition of classes and he saw that capitalism was in process of achieving that abundance. The immiseration of the working classes, which was in such evidence in his own day in consequence of the rapid boom and bust cycles of *laissez-faire* capitalism, appeared more and more irrational in the face of the increasing evidence that universal abundance was potentially available if the mode of organisation were to be appropriately refashioned. It was prima facie evident that it was in the interests of the working class to cast off the violent disruptive forces of this productive system without their needing to understand the broader context of problem or solution. Lorenz von Stein's report to the Prussian Government warned already in the 1830s of the way in which the Paris workers would precipitate a communist revolution as a consequence of their predicament (McLellan (1969: 147)) and this tract was enough in itself to inspire German social theorists without their needing to resort to Hegelian logic (Marx (1975: 256)); indeed, the use of Hegelian modes of expression hypostatised facts that might have been applied more pragmatically with greater flexibility and avoiding subsequent adherence to faith in the potential role of the working class well beyond its true functional value.

In retrospect, we can see that Marx and Engels underestimated the power of 'reification' and in general the cultural and ideological inheritance of the working class to inhibit their formulating and acting on the means to overcome their predicament — means, that is, to activate *their* manifest self-interest in the political arena. It was only in the early years of the 20th century, as it became clear that progress towards an ultimately enlightened society was being successfully resisted by bourgeois culture that Marxist theorists — notably Lukács and Gramsci — looked deeper into the wellsprings of existing class ideology and the way in which this held back the working class from adequately forceful pursuit of their class self-interest. But Marxists themselves, enamoured by the notion of proletarian revolution led by breakaway elements of the enlightened bourgeoisie, and then in the face of adherence to the notion that the Soviet Union was in process of traversing and demonstrating the road to communism, were blind to the need to involve the working class in a more structured way in achieving their own emancipation through practical involvement in changing their relationship with social and productive process and via this means changing society itself. And finally, very few Marxists had any sense of the kind of easy going hedonism that the ultimate communist society might involve;[16] on the contrary, it is not difficult to argue that Marxism has been if anything more insistent on maintaining the status of work as social validator than has capitalism (Gorz (1989: Ch.2). There was thus no sense of the need to restructure production and consumption such as to diffuse the underlying northern European sense of the fear of want via a direct involvement of the work-force in achieving abundance on its own behalf.

In the end the strategy of direct opposition to bourgeois resistance to further progressing the enlightenment project, both advocated by Marx and operationalised by Lenin and thence perpetuated by the Soviet state, simply has not worked. Whether, had the anarchist forces in the Russian Revolution prevailed (Makhno, Kronstadt, the return of Kropotkin, etc.) and successfully avoided the onslaught of the implacable opposition by, in particular, the Anglo-Saxon societies, Russia would have demonstrated a more flexible and successful route to communism is questionable and in any case this remains idle speculation. Compromises on both sides gave us — with modest variations from one end of the industrialised world to the other — what we can now see as a particular form of political settlement that has generally here been referred to as social democracy. It might be of some interest, but probably of little real use, to analyse out the degree to which social democracy was a set of bourgeois stratagems aimed at the preservation of privilege as distinct from a general process consciously aimed at improving the material conditions of life of the 'lower orders'. From the point of view of the argument here under consideration, the most important outcome of this — from the outset essentially unstable (Lange (1984)) — settlement has been the obscuring of lines of struggle and development which characterised the initiation of the process. Material abundance has been unquestionably achieved but all sense of the ongoing process of enlightenment appears, at least in the immediate present, to have been lost.

Perhaps advocacy of an oppositional strategy and more generally a coercive theory, that insists that the future *must* unfold in a particular fashion, was the only realistic way for the enlightenment project to be progressed in the 19th century. We have seen across this century how such a strategy, in generating opposition, necessarily engendered arbitrary, unanticipated and, from the point of the common good, dysfunctional social stratagems. Indeed, it is of great interest to any attempt to move the enlightenment project forward to study the many stratagems through which radical movements in the recent past have been rendered impotent (Atkinson (1991)).

But if political ecology is to make headway, as demonstrating the route to the end of the enlightenment project, then it must operate as if it were already there, eschewing all coercive strategies and arguing and acting out the ultimate settlement here-and-now. If opposition persists, then, according to environmentalist belief, we can expect to be precipitated over the ecological abyss simply by the sheer impetus of the direction and structure of our culture; structured opposition on the part of political ecology can serve no useful purpose. And ecologists must be prepared to accept that there is no ultimate reason why it should matter whether humanity, and through it nature's self-consciousness in its current aberrant form, is eliminated from the biosphere. The project of political ecology to rescue humanity is only concerned to rescue an enlightened humanity, not one which persists in meting out oppression upon its own and other species and in general the destruction of the creativity of human culture and nature alike. But this does not mean that we should not think in a structured manner about how to achieve the Green Utopia; anarchy — no coercion — does not mean no structure, no aesthetic. The final paragraphs of this book are concerned to look in a general way at how we might expect the project of achieving Green Utopia to unfold.

So, what forms of speculation about, and design of, the future does political ecology hold to be legitimate? Firstly we must concede that there is more than one possibility simply by way of trajectory out of the present. Secondly, we need to develop ideas about what kind of future we would like and that can be deemed viable. We are not looking to establish one, coercive Truth about the future but, rather, a dialectic between probable futures resulting from inertia of a culture on the move that is in essential dimensions not informed by consciousness on the one hand and on the other images and mechanisms of an eventual self-regulating equilibrium Green Utopia. We may not achieve the Green Utopia and if we do, it is unlikely to be much like the initial images of Utopia which we offer up to the dialectical process. Above all, the concept of 'compromise' is entirely inappropriate. This is not an exercise in horse trading between interests but the development of a mutualistic social and cultural process that internalises the management of nature in accordance with the possible — read, sustainable — and the need to maintain the coherence of the decision-making process and the processes of social and natural metabolism (the productive and reproductive processes).

In Chapter 4, the process of Utopian design was looked at in a certain degree of detail because this is currently so alien to our society. Readers might want to recall or even re-read this at this point. The question of investigating possible futures that could emerge in the absence of efforts on the part of the Green movement need not occupy this text in any great detail. Suffice it to note several possibilities that can be envisaged from here and which would merit investigation in the context of political ecology. What might be the consequences of the continuation of New Right politics, current economic dynamics and the persistence of the postmodern cultural environment? Might we expect a degeneration into global war as the political solution to the failures and uncertainties accompanying the end of social democracy as we saw at the end of the era of liberalism early in this century? Could we expect some precipitate cultural spiral into paranoic politics of a latter-day fascism and if so with what consequences? What might the consequences be of a re-establishment of social democratic managerialism, including 'organised capitalist' industrial co-ordination and technocratic environmental management (Costello et al. (1989))? What variations and elisions of these might it be worthwhile to consider? At what points and in general how rapidly and with what reaction might we expect consciousness of environmental degradation and the various levels of Green perception with respect to solutions to penetrate the social awareness against each of these background scenarios?

Appropriate tools for such an investigation are going to need to be forged by the Green movement and its extending circle of allies. But many a conventional tool of social analysis can be plundered to fruitful effect. Obviously such an approach will need to be pursued with care because all tools, all technologies come burdened with their original purpose and, indeed, the ghost of the context which created them. Consider the technocratic forecasting and sundry modelling techniques mentioned earlier in this discussion. It was noted that they represent an evolution out of the enlightenment concern for 'human perfectibility' and in general the improvement of the human spirit along a route that leaves the spirit behind to increasingly embrace the material; this has now reached a point where human welfare is almost exclusively defined as conterminous with increased supply in the quantity of material possessions and the facilities necessary to 'enjoy' these. Used in the service of developing an understanding of the future context and the construction of Utopias, this 'material bias' needs to be counteracted and augmented with techniques and approaches that assist in understanding social and cultural dynamics and solutions and beyond that recovers more general notions of human desire and the spiritual dimension of life. This does not mean discarding these techniques. Indeed, the Green movement has already made fruitful use of them such as in the development of 'alternative energy futures'. But there is much work to be done before we have adapted them to become appropriate handmaidens to the understanding of possible futures, seen through the eyes of political ecology, or for the design of a mutualistic Utopia built upon the needs of the human spirit and where technology is informed primarily by notions of the aesthetic.

To what degree has political ecology already initiated the development of relevant tools on its own part? The literature of 'deep ecology', ecophilosophy and ecofeminism has had very little of a structured kind to say about historical trajectories or the material and organisational, encompassing the social, side of a Green Utopia. What can be said of this literature is that, notwithstanding some very eclectic and unfocused writing in this vain, the best of it (Berman (1984b); Fox (1986); Hargrove (1989); Naess (1989); Devall (1990)) provides some basis for reconstruction of forecasting tools such as to understand better the human and spiritual 'underside' of the historical trajectory which must be drawn to the fore in the dialectical process of guiding history into the realms of Green Utopia. The work of Bahro and Murray Bookchin is also of great relevance here: although neither has specifically attempted to develop future trajectories along existing lines of evolution (both have been more concerned to portray the construction of a Green Utopia against a background of the critique of past and present reality), they have nevertheless paid considerably more attention to existing social and cultural structures and the problems which these pose for political ecology than have the ecophilosophers and writers on environmental ethics.

An attempt to initiate the dialectic under discussion here that is worthy of note can be found in the work of James Robertson (1985). Starting from the presentation of possible future scenarios, Robertson attempts to show both the unattractiveness and unviability of 'conventional' ('HE': hyper-expansionist) futures relative to the Green alternative ('SHE: sane, humane and ecological). The overall purpose of the exercise is essentially exhortatory and hence undialectical, using conventional views of the future as a foil against which to amplify the attractiveness of the alternative without any further effort to understand the dynamics of real-time phenomena in the historical process. Furthermore this work is very limited in the scope of futures which are considered, and also in the range of concerns with regard to the nature of the Green Utopia aspired to (essentially focusing only on the eradication of the work ethic). Nevertheless, there are the makings of an overall structure that could be of considerable use to the development of a political ecological analytic.

But the dialectical process laid out above is no more than a method for improving the self-awareness and practicality of political ecology in respect of achieving the Green Utopia. In practice, the dialectic will unfold as a process of the self-development of human consciousness and our relationship with the rest of the creation in terms of bringing into existence a new form of social and cultural settlement. Marx and Engels saw the dialectic leading to the creation of communist society as being a function of the change in political consciousness brought about by the internal contradictions of capitalism. The dialectic upon which political ecology focuses is concerned with the materialisation of increasingly intractable environmental problems arising out of the existing relationship between our consciousness — European culture — and nature, between our inherited attitudes and practice on the one hand and the progressive destruction of nature on the other.

Marxists insist that political ecology is unrealistic because it is voluntarist and exhortatory. There is no doubt that most of the literature is indeed exhortatory, simply assuming that the whole world accepts that ecological destruction is upon us and that the job is merely one of pointing to the problem and then, in a few cases, of sketching out a general direction or a few components of a solution. In practice, in spite of the available literature that has increasingly demonstrated the reality of growing environmental problems (but in a context where some analysts also categorically deny the existence of the environmental problematic (Simon and Kahn (1984))), this knowledge has not been immediately translated into an effective line of action. In so far as any coherent answer has been recognised as necessary, then technocratic environmental management has generally been deemed adequate. Whilst the Green movement may have been intuitively correct in its call for fundamentally radical solutions, it could not demonstrate in any substantive way that these were indeed necessary. Above all, the complexity of the interaction of problems and existing reality on the one hand and the profundity of the solutions suggested were — and indeed remain — far beyond the capabilities or resources of the Green movement to confront in a truly coherent manner; indeed, political ecology has so far been no more than a few sketchy lines on an enormous canvas.

Political ecology will come into its own only if and when environmental problems increase in intractability. As noted in the introduction to this book, there is every possibility that the biosphere will be damaged in the coming years by human activity to the point where human life will be unsustainable or worse, to a point just on the edge of survival where life becomes a very wearisome and dangerous existence for the future remnant of humanity. But the growth in environmental problems, should we be fortunate enough for these to materialise in manageable stages, will create the context for re-evaluating ever more fundamentally the configuration of our consciousness. This can be expected to impel the restructuring not only of the political settlement, but the whole configuration of our culture inclusive of social arrangements and attitudes and with this the relationship between human consciousness and the rest of the Creation.

We can thus assert not merely that the dialectic of political ecology is as 'realistic' — grounded in material reality — as is that of Marx in his map of the unfolding of history, but that it goes beyond Marx to the final resolution of the problematic of the dialectic of consciousness in nature. For Marx, the working class became an unconscious instrument, inside of a still-individualistic society, for the creation of a mutualistic society, without nature in-itself ever entering the dialectic; the relationship of humanity with nature lay outside Marxist theory, appended with the footnote that adorns the frontispiece of this book. Political ecology is about the end of individualistic society — civilisation as such — being a direct consequence of the dialectic between consciousness and nature: according to political ecology, consciousness (through the instrument of European culture) has reached the point where it can only either annul individualistic society or destroy the basis in nature of its own existence. So when Marxists insist on looking for a 'social subject' — for an instrument *within* society that possesses the necessary self-interest to shoulder the burden of leading humanity out of social instrumentality as such — then they are falling short of understanding the totality of the dialectical process, they are insisting on a mechanical solution.

We cannot know through what stages the dialectic will mature. The current form of the dialect became active in the first instance with the emergence of the environmental movement in the early 1970s. Its subsequent development has been far from predictable or controllable and it would be a pure assertion of faith to say with any confidence that it will end up with humanity living in harmony with nature into the distant future. The intuitions of the Green movement in their increasingly sophisticated sketches of a sustainable future will need to be experimented with in real time and place. These experiments will surely include much that proves to be socially unviable or ecologically unsustainable. The point is, however, that, in accordance with anarchist theory, 'anything goes': the realisation of the non-universal nature of solutions, the need to develop contingent arrangements in relation to local conditions, moving incrementally out of existing cultures (or rather the remnants of existing cultures), is of great importance. In the end, conscious control over the resulting equilibrium symbiosis of culture and nature will inevitably be centred on the local because that is manageable in terms of the physical wellsprings of human consciousness, namely a manageable number of humans participating in the social and natural metabolic process. Ecological culture, if it comes to pass, will comprise a confederation of locally self-reliant regions based upon mutualist and necessarily egalitarian, relations in which the guiding spirit is an aesthetic self-consciousness that knits together local ecology with social metabolism.

The dialectic of political ecology, of which a small band of environmentalists became the voice in the early 1970s, is making itself felt right across society. Environmental campaigns and then Green political parties gradually infused the social consciousness with an inchoate awareness of the problematic but there seemed to be little in the real world to confirm or reinforce this awareness. Gradually the signs increased: Seveso, Bhopal, Chernobyl; then at the end of the 1980s, the sudden acknowledgement of the global atmospheric effects of our growing use of energy. The first generalised reactions were perceptible quite broadly across society: first signs of an awareness that perhaps our way of life is unviable. But as yet very little acknowledgement of fundamental problems in the form of consciousness with which our society apprehends life, no significant criticism of individualistic modes of thought and action. The field is open for political ecology to develop its programme to the next stage, to prefigure and give structure to the next stage of the dialectic. Hopefully this book can provide some useful ideas to feed into these developments.

Notes

1. Marx made no secret of his abomination of the 'stagnation' of Chinese culture (Anderson (1970: 493) which sheds a certain light on his millenarian sensibilities and by extension on a rather fundamental disagreement between the Marxist sense of cultural time and that of political ecology.
2. The resulting 'crisis of the intellectuals', which is only now being acknowledged for what it is, is a much more striking phenomenon in France than in Britain where, as discussed in Chapter 3, the role of intellectuals — and in particular social scientists — has always been far more modest as an ingredient of social system maintenance.
3. In an oft-quoted passage in Volume III of *Capital*, Marx (1959: Ch.XXVII) wrote of the following: "The co-operative factory of the labourers themselves represent within the old form the first sprouts of the new..." This was, however, in a section that also noted how joint stock companies were increasingly absorbing industry into giant new forms of organisation and he summarised his conclusions as follows: "The capitalist stock companies, as much as the co-operative factories, should be considered as transitional forms from the capitalist mode of production to the associated one, with the only distinction that the antagonism is resolved negatively in the one and positively in the other." It is characteristic of the general interpretation of Marx in the late 20th century that quotations from this passage

(eg Giddens (1981: 35); Mandel (1978)) note that the abolition of capitalism will proceed via the expropriation of the joint stock companies without reference to any role for co-operativism. Whilst it is true to say that co-operativism declined over the early years of this century, thus being less visible to modern analysis, what is important is that modern Marxists have no sense of the importance of co-operativism, as hinted at in Marx's analysis, as a potentional ramp into a co-operative society.

4. The work of Fernand Braudel and his followers was mentioned in the foregoing chapter as having opened up a potentially fruitful line of investigation with respect to geographical influences on history. This has not extended to consideration of the broader question of the connection between cultural inclinations and structures and the physical environment.

5. Whilst acknowledging that the worker in a factory may identify hardly at all with the products for which he (sic) is responsible, in a small way, for creating, the fact is that there is no simple relationship between this situation and the love which he — or his partner — might invest in that product when it enters the home as an accoutrement of the consumer society. It is really the lumpiness and uncontrolledness of the production and consumption processes relative to the sensibilities of the individual lives caught up in it which constitutes the central problem of alienation in our age.

6. David Harvey, a Marxist geographer who has become a major contributor to the postmodernism debate, has in the past argued forcefully against environmental determinism and continues to be suspicious of arguments and projects where space is understood in any kind of deterministic way.

7. Of course Hegel's notion of Nature was in no way a materialist one. On the contrary, Hegel was concerned with the *Idea* of Nature as 'other' than Consciousness, that is realised in the process of self-development, in Spirit. His *'Naturphilosophie'* was thus concerned primarily with the scientific appropriation of nature as it manifest itself in his time, rather than any attempt to follow the route taken by La Mettrie and d'holbach or to develop some framework of his own for the understanding of the natural process as a whole, in-itself. So Marx's translation of Hegel's *'Naturphilosophie'* was consistent with his general procedure of revealing the social process underlying Hegel's idealist philosophy as a whole.

8. Or, if the reference is to the *dissemination* of European culture we might see Britain as representing the male sexual organs both with their macho and their dismissive connotations. Certainly there are few European cultures with less of a feminine side to them than Britain and we might go on to see this same masculinity in the cultural creative process: in at the beginning, at the forefront of mechanical inventiveness, but without significant contribution to the flowering, the truly creative side of culture. Of course Greens would see this as a particularly intractable problem, given the insistence on masculine dominance as the root of the ecological problematic and the need to rebuild our culture to better reflect the feminine.

9. Symptomatic and characteristic of this was the way in which Oliver Cromwell escaped from the confrontation with the written constitution — the 'Agreement of the People' — presented to him and argued by the Levellers, temporarily in control of the army. Britain remains virtually alone amongst industrialised countries — almost alone in the world — in not possessing a written constitution as a manifestation of a *negotiated* settlement between social interests.

10. It is this borrowing of the vernacular which is one of the key characteristics which lifts le Corbusier's contribution to modern architecture so far above the pure

functionalists. But it is manifest nonsense to take vernacular forms out of their immediate cultural context of function, materials, climate and lifestyle and attempt to universalise them. Thus, for instance, for all its inspirational qualities, the surrealistic incongruity of melding architectual forms of the Grisson and Ghardaia (Sahara) in le Corbusier's reconstruction of the pilgrimage chapel at Ronchamp in eastern France.

11. Debord (1983:Para 191): "Dadaism and surrealism are the two currents which mark the end of modern art. They are contemporaneous, though only in a relatively conscious manner, of the last great assault of the revolutionary proletarian movement; and the defeat of this movement, which left them imprisoned in the same artistic field whose discrepitude they had announced, is the basic reason for their immobilisation. Dadaism and surrealism are at once historically related and opposed to each other. This opposition, which each of them considered to be its most important and radical contribution, reveals the inadequacy of their critique, which each developed one-sidedly. Dadaism wanted *to suppress art without realising it*; surrealism wanted *to realise art without suppressing it*. The critical position later elaborated by the *Situationists* has shown that the suppression and the realisation of art are inseparable aspects of a single *supersession of art*"

12. The fact that the debate concerning postmodernism is almost exclusively restricted to academia is plausibly attributed by Bauman (1988) to the 'status crisis' of the intellectuals resulting from the way that the consumer society has usurped their role as providers of "an authoritative solution to the questions of cognitive truth, moral judgement and aesthetic taste", handing this over to capitalist enterprise — the design of consumer goods, media productions, etc. — and the market.

13. Clearly, the advertising industry has been key to the whole phenomenon of 'green consumerism'. However, the main journal of the industry Marketing, has featured articles that make it clear that 'Green' is going to mean far more fundamental changes: (Mitchell and Levy (1989: 28ff)) "Green is not a fad but a revolution.... When Green ideas really take off, people simply won't be 'consumers' any more. They will be conservers.... If Green really takes off, the '90s will be an era of 'less is more'." Their own survey of marketing professionals indicated 'an important and influential minority' of companies that are aware of far-reaching changes ahead to which they will have to respond. The enthusiasm for commissioning 'green audits' of their operation is a certain sign of this.

14. The Situationist concept of playfulness at the centre of human activity ('*Homo ludens*') contrasts with the meaning which our society puts upon this: just as 'art' removes aesthetics out of the realm of common creativity and experience to comprise a weapon in the armoury of class domination, so 'play' is distorted into structured individualistic competitive exercises that become one of the chief symbolic expressions of our individualistic culture.

15. In the 1970s, the author was involved in the use of forecasting techniques for transport planning. These were not only honed specifically to the purpose of justifying highway construction but were even inured against use in favour of public transport as opposed to private cars. It should be added, however, that it was involvement with these techniques that first alerted the author to the environmental problematic and so they can be said to have led, by a circuitous route, to the writing of this book!

16. Marx's renegade son-in-law Ferdinand Lassalle wrote on the subject of abandoning the centrality of work to our society. But in general it has been the

anarchist wing of the radical enlightenment that has insistently criticised the work ethic (Richards (1983)).

Bibliography

Abercrombie, N., Hill, S. and Turner, B. S. (1980) *The Dominant Ideology Thesis*. George Allen and Unwin, London.

Abrams, P. and McCulloch, A. (1976) *Communes, Sociology and Society*. Cambridge University Press, Cambridge.

Adorno, T., and Horkheimer, M. (1979) *Dialectics of Enlightenment*. Verso, London.

Albury, D., and Schwartz, J. (1982) *Partial Progress: the Politics of Science and Technology*. Pluto, London.

Aldermann, Geoffrey. (1984) *Pressure Groups and Government in Great Britain*. Longman, London.

Allaby, Michael. (1971) *The Eco-Activists*. Charles Knight, London.

Allison, Lincoln. (1975) *Environmental Planning*. George Allen and Unwin, London.

Almond, A. and Verba, S. (Eds.) (1980) *The Civil Culture Revisited*. Little, Brown, Boston.

Anderson, Perry. (1964) 'Origins of the Present Crisis'. *New Left Review*, **23**, January–February, 28–53.

Anderson, Perry. (1969) 'Components of the National Culture'. In Cockburn and Blackburn (1969: 184–214).

Anderson, Perry. (1970) *Lineages of the Absolutist State*. Verso, London.

Anderson, Walt. (Ed.) (1970) *Politics and Environment*. Goodyear, Pacific Palisades, California.

Andrewes, Antony. (1971) *Greek Society*. Penguin, Harmondsworth.

Ansell, Vera, Coats, Chris, Dawling, Pam, How, Jonathan, Morris, William and Wood, Andy. (Eds.) (1989) *Diggers and Dreamers: The 1990/91 Guide to Communal Living*. Communes Network, Sheffield.

Apter, David. (Ed.) (1964) *Ideology and Discontent*. Free Press, New York.

Ardalan, C. (1980) 'Workers' Self-Management and Planning: The Yugoslav Case'. *World Development*, **8**, 623–638.

Aristotle. (1976) *The Ethics of Aristotle: The Nicomachean Ethics*. Translated by J. A. K. Thomson, revised edition, Penguin, Harmondsworth.

Aronovitz, Slanley. (1988) *Science as Power: Discourse and Ideology in Modern Society*. Macmillan, London.

Atkinson, Adrian. (1991) *Green Utopia: The Future of Radical Politics*. Zed

Press, London. (Forthcoming)

Atkinson, R. A. F. (1978) *Knowledge and Explanation in History: an Introduction to the Philosophy of History*. Macmillan, London.

Atkinson, William. (1840) *Principles of Political Economy*. London.

Avineri, Shlomo. (1969) *The Social and Political Thought of Karl Marx*. Cambridge University Press, Cambridge.

Bacon, Francis. (1960) *The New Organon and Related Writings*. Anderson, Fulton. H. (Ed.) Bobbs-Merrill, Indianapolis.

Bahro, Rudolf. (1978) *The Alternative in Eastern Europe*. Verso, London.

Bahro, Rudolf. (1982) *Socialism and Survival*. Heretic, London.

Bahro, Rudolf. (1984) *From Red to Green: Interviews with New Left Review*. Verso, London.

Bahro, Rudolf. (1986) *Building the Green Movement*. Gay Men's Press, London.

Baillie, John. (1950) *The Belief in Progress*. Scribner, New York.

Banks, J. A. (1972) *The Sociology of Social Movements*. Macmillan, London.

Barbour, Ian. (Ed.) (1972) *Earth Might Be Fair: Reflections on Ethics, Religion and Ecology*. Prentice-Hall, Englewood Cliffs, New Jersey.

Barbour, Ian. (Ed.) (1973) *Western Man and Environmental Ethics*. Addison-Wesley, Reading, Massachusetts.

Barclay, Harold. (1982) *People Without Government: An Anthropology of Anarchism*. Kahn and Averill, London.

Baren, P. A., and Sweezy, P. M. (1968) *Monopoly Capital*. Penguin, Harmondsworth.

Barfield, Owen. (1957) *Saving the Appearances*. Faber, London.

Barkow, Jerome. H. (1980) 'Sociobiology: Is This the New Theory of Human Nature?' In Montagu (1980: 171–197).

Barnes, Barry. (1974) *Scientific Knowledge and Social Theory*. Routledge and Kegan Paul, London.

Barnes, Barry. (1977) *Interests and the Growth of Knowledge*. Routledge and Kegan Paul, London.

Barnes, B., and Bloor, D. (1982) 'Relativism, Rationalism and the Sociology of Knowledge'. In Hollis and Lukes (1982: 21–47).

Barratt-Brown, M., Emerson, T. and Stoneman, C. (Eds.) (1976) *Resources and the Environment: A Socialist Perspective*. Spokesman Books, Nottingham.

Barrow, J.W. (1966) *Evolution and Society: A Study in Victorian Social Theory*. Cambridge University Press, Cambridge.

Barthes, Roland. (1973) *Mythologies*. Paladin, London.

Barthes, Roland. (1988) *The Semiotic Challenge*. Hill and Wang, New York.

Bateson, Gregory. (1964) 'The Logical Categories of Learning and Communication'. In Bateson (1973: 250–279).

Bateson, Gregory. (1973) *Steps to an Ecology of Mind*. Paladin, London.

Bauman, Zygmunt. (1988) 'Is there a Postmodern Sociology?'. In Featherstone (1988: 217–237).

Bauman, Zygmunt. (1991) *Modernity and Ambivalence*. Polity, Cambridge.

Baumol, W. J. and Oates, W. E. (1979) *Economics, Environmental Policy, and the Quality of Life*. Prentice-Hall, Englewood Cliffs, New Jersey.

Becker, Uwe. (1989) 'Class Theory: Still the Axis of Critical Social Science Theory?'. In Wright (1989: Ch.4).

Beckerman, Wilfred. (1974) *In Defence of Economic Growth*. Jonathan Cape, London.

Beer, Gillian. (1983) *Darwin's Plots: Evolutionary Narrative in Darwin, George Eliot and Nineteenth-Century Fiction*. Ark, London.

Bell, Daniel. (1973) *The Coming of Post-Industrial Society: A Venture in Social Forecasting*. Basic Books, New York.

Bellini, James. (1986) *High Tech Holocaust*. David and Charles, London.

Ben-David, Joseph. (1971) *The Scientist's Role in Society*. Prentice-Hall, Englewood Cliffs, New Jersey.

Bennett, John W. (1976) *The Ecological Transition: Cultural Anthropology and Human Adaptation*. Pergamon, Oxford.

Benson, Douglas. and Hughes, John. A. (1983) *The Perspective of Ethnomethodology*. Longman, London.

Benthall, Jonathan. (Ed.) (1972) *Ecology, the Shaping Debate*. Longman, London.

Berger, P. and Luckmann, T. (1967) *The Social Construction of Reality*. Penguin, Harmoundsworth.

Berger, Peter. (1969) *The Social Reality of Religion*. Penguin, Harmondsworth.

Berlin, Isaiah. (1976) *Vico and Herder: Two Studies in the History of Ideas*. Chatto and Windus, London.

Berman, Marshall. (1984a) *All that is Solid Melts into Air*. Verso, London.

Berman, Morris. (1984b) *The Re-enchantment of the World*. Bantam, New York.

Berman, Morris. (1990) 'The Cybernetic Dream of the 21st Century'. In Clark (1990: 12–32).

Bernal, J. D. (1969) *Science in History*. Fourth edition. Penguin, Harmondsworth.

Berneri, Marie Louise. (1982) *Journey through Utopia*. Freedom Press, London.

Bews, J. W. (1935) *Human Ecology*. Oxford University Press, Oxford.

Black, John. (1970) *The Dominion of Man: The Search for Ecological Responsibility*. Edinburgh University Press, Edinburgh.

Blackburn, Robin. (Ed.) (1972) *Ideology in Social Science: Reading in Critical Social Theory*. Fontana, London.

Bleicher, Josef. (1982) *The Hermeneutic Imagination: Outline of a Positive Critique of Scientism and Sociology*. Routledge and Kegan Paul, London.

Bloch, Marc. (1954) *The Historian's Craft*. Manchester University Press, Manchester.

Bloch, Ernst. (1986) *The Principle of Hope*. Blackwell, Oxford.

Bodington, Stephen. (1978) *Science and Social Action*. Allison and Busby, London.

Bookchin, Murray. (1965a) 'Ecology and Revolutionary Thought'. In Bookchin (1974a: 57–82).

Bookchin, Murray. (1965b) 'Towards a Liberatory Technology'. In Bookchin (1974a: 83–139).

Bookchin, Murray. (1969) 'Listen Marxist!' In Bookchin (1974a: 171–222).
Bookchin, Murray. (1970) 'A Discussion on "Listen Marxist!"'. In Bookchin (1974a: 223–246).
Bookchin, Murray. (1973) 'The Myth of City Planning'. In Bookchin (1980: 133–170).
Bookchin, Murray. (1974a) *Post-Scarcity Anarchism*. Wildwood House, London.
Bookchin, Murray. (1974b) *The Limits of the City*. Harper and Row, New York.
Bookchin, Murray. (1977) *The Spanish Anarchists: The Heroic Years 1936–1968*. Harper Colophon, New York.
Bookchin, Murray. (1978) 'Towards a Vision of the Urban Future'. In Bookchin (1980: 171–191).
Bookchin, Murray. (1980) *Towards an Ecological Society*. Black Rose Books, Montreal.
Bookchin, Murray. (1982) *The Ecology of Freedom: The Emergence and Dissolution of Hierarchy*. Cheshire Books, Palo Alto, California.
Bookchin, Murray. (1983) 'An Appeal for Social and Ecological Sanity'. In Bookchin (1986a: 99–161).
Bookchin, Murray. (1986a) *The Modern Crisis*. New Society Publishers, Philadelphia.
Bookchin, Murray. (1986b) *Urbanisation without Cities*. Sierra Club, San Francisco.
Bookchin, Murray. (1987) *The Rise of Urbanization and the Decline of Citizenship*. Sierra Club Books, San Francisco.
Bookchin, Murray. (1989) *Remaking Society*. Black Rose Books, Montreal.
Bookchin, Murray. (1990) *The Philosophy of Social Ecology: Essays on Dialectical Naturalism*. Black Rose Books, Montreal.
Borgstrom, George. (1965) *Hungry Planet*. Collier, New York.
Borgstrom, George. (1969) *Too Many*. Macmillan, New York.
Borkenau, Franz. (1934) *Der Übergang vom Feudalen zum Bürgelichen Weldbild: Studien zur Geschichte der Manufakturperiode*. Frankfurt am Main.
Bouchier, David. (1978) *Idealism and Revolution: New Ideologies of Liberation in Britain and the United States*. Edward Arnold, London.
Bourdieu, Pierre. (1988) *Homo Academicus*. Polity, Cambridge.
Bourdieu, Pierre. (1990) *Language and Symbolic Power*. Polity, Cambridge.
Boyle, G., Elliott, D. and Roy, R. (Eds.) (1977) *The Politics of Technology*. Longman, London.
Boyne, Roy and Rattansi, Ali. (1990) *Postmodernism and Society*. Macmillan, London.
Bramwell, Anna. (1989) *Ecology in the 20th Century: A History*. Yale University Press, New Haven.
Braudel, Fernand. (1972) *The Mediterranean and the Mediterranean World in the Age of Philip II*. Harper and Row, New York.
Braverman, Harry. (1974) *Labour and Monopoly Capital: The Degradation of Work in the Twentieth Century*. Monthly Review Press, New York.
Bray, John Francis. (1839) *Labour's Wrongs and Labour's Remedy*. Leeds.

Brookes, S. K., Jordan, A. G., Kimber, R. H. and Richardson, J. J. (1976) 'The Growth of the Environment as a Political Issue in Britain'. *British Journal of Political Science*, **6**(2), April, 245–255.

Brookes, S. K., and Richardson, J. J. (1975) 'The Environmental Lobby in Britain'. *Parliamentary Affairs*, **28**(3), 312–328.

Brown, Harold I. (1988) *Rationality*. Routledge, London.

Brown, Harrison Scott. (1954) *The Challenge of Man's Future*, Viking, New York.

Brown, H., Bonner, J. and Weir, J. (1957) *The Next Hundred Years*. Weidenfeld and Nicolson, London.

Brown, Lester. R. (Ed.) (1984–1990) *State of the World: A Worldwatch Report on Progress Towards a Sustainable Society*. Norton, New York.

Bryant, Christopher. (1985) *Positivism in Social Theory and Research*. Macmillan, London.

Burch, William. R. (Ed.) (1972) *Social Behavior, Natural Resources and the Environment*. Harper and Row, New York.

Burgess, Rod. (1978) 'The Concept of Nature in Geography and Marxism'. *Antipode*, **10**(2), July, 1-11.

Burrow, J. W. (1966) *Evolution and Society: a Study in Victorian Social Theory*. Cambridge University Press, Cambridge.

Bury, J. B. (1932) *The Idea of Progress*. Dover, New York.

Buttel, Frederick H. (1975) 'The Environmental Movement: Consensus, Conflict, and Change'. *The Journal of Environmental Education*, **7**(1), 53–63.

Buttle, F. H. and Flinn, W. L. (1978) 'Social Class and Mass Environmental Beliefs: A Reconsideration'. *Environment and Behavior*, **10**, 433–450.

Byrne, David. (1985) 'Just Haad on a Minute There: A Rejection of André Gorz's "Farewell to the Working Class"'. *Capital and Class*, **24**, Winter, 75–98.

Caldwell, L., Hayes, L. and Macwhirter, I. (1976) *Citizens and the Environment: Case Studies in Popular Action*. Indiana University Press, Bloomington.

Callenbach, Ernest. (1978) *Ecotopia: A Novel about Ecology, People and Politics in 1999*. Pluto, London.

Callinicos, Alex. (1990) 'Reactionary Postmodernism?' in Boyne and Rattansi (1990: Ch.4).

Campbell, Bernard. (1983) *Human Ecology: The Story of Our Place in Nature from Prehistory to the Present*. Heinemann, London.

Campbell, Bernard. (1974) *Human Evolution: An Introduction to Man's Adaptations*. Second edition. Aldine, Chicago.

Caplan, Arthur L. (Ed.) (1978) *The Sociobiology Debate: Readings on the Ethical and Scientific Issues Concerning Sociobiology*. Harper and Row, New York.

Capp, B. S. (1972) *The Fifth Monarchy Men: A Study in Seventeenth-Century English Millenarianism*. Faber and Faber, London.

Capra, Fritjof. (1982) *The Turning Point: Science, Society and the Rising Culture*. Flemingo, London.

Carr, E. H. (1964) *What Is History?* Penguin, Harmondsworth.

Carson, Rachel. (1962) *Silent Spring*. Houghton-Mifflin, Boston.
Cassirer, Ernst. (1951) *The Philosophy of the Enlightenment*. Princeton University Press, Princeton.
Catton, William R. Jr. (1982) *Overshoot. The Ecological Basis of Revolutionary Change*. University of Illinois Press, Urbana.
Centre for Contemporary Cultural Studies. (1978) *On Ideology*. Hutchinson, London.
Chadwick, Owen. (1972) *The Reformation*. Penguin, Harmondsworth.
Childe, Gordon. (1951) *Social Evolution*. Watts, London.
Childe, Gordon. (1964) *What Happened in History*. Penguin, Harmondsworth.
Childe, Gordon. (1965) *Man Makes Himself*. Watts, London.
Chomsky, Noam. (1968) *Language and Mind*. Harcourt Brace and World, New York.
Clark, John. (Ed.) (1990) *Renewing the Earth: The Promise of Social Ecology*. Green Print, London.
Clark, J. and Cole, S., with Curnon, R. and Hopkins, M. (1975) *Global Simulation Models: A Comparative Study*. John Wiley, London.
Clarke, J., Critcher, C. and Johnson, R. (1979) *Working Class Culture: Studies in History and Theory*. Hutchinson, London.
Clutton-Brock, T.H. and Harvey, P.H. (1978) *Readings in Sociobiology*. Freeman, San Francisco.
Coates, Ken. (Ed.) (1972) *Socialism and the Environment*. Spokesman, Nottingham.
Cockburn, A. and Blackburn, R. (Eds.) (1969) *Student Power: Problems, Diagnosis, Action*. Penguin, Harmondsworth.
Cohen, Mark Nathan. (1977) *The Food Crisis in Prehistory: Overpopulation and the Origins of Agriculture*. Yale University Press, New Haven.
Cohn, Norman. (1970) *The Pursuit of the Millennium*. Paladin, London.
Cole, H. S. D., Freeman, C., Jahoda, M. and Pavitt, K. L. R. (Eds.) (1973) *Thinking about the Future: A Critique of the Limits to Growth*. Chatto and Windus, London.
Collective Design/Projects. (1985) *Very Nice Work if You Can Get It: The Socially Useful Production Debate*. Spokesman, Nottingham.
Collingridge, David. (1980) *The Social Role of Technology*. Open University, Milton Keynes.
Collingwood, R. G. (1945) *The Idea of Nature*. Clarendon Press, Oxford.
Collingwood, R. G. (1946) *The Idea of History*. Clarendon Press, Oxford.
Committee on Resources and Man. (1969) *Resources and Man*. Freeman, San Francisco.
Commoner, Barry. (1966) *Science and Survival*. Victor Gollancz, London.
Commoner, Barry. (1972a) *The Closing Circle*. Bantam, New York.
Commoner, Barry. (1972b) 'The Social Use and Misuse of Technology'. In Benthall (1972: 335–362).
Commoner, Barry. (1972c) 'The Environmental Cost of Economic Growth'. In Schurr (1972: 30–65).
Condorcet, Marquis de (Caritat, Marie-Jean-Antoine-Nicolas). (1976) *Selected Writings*. Baker, Keith Michael (Ed.). Bobbs-Merrill,

Indianapolis.

Coppleston, Frederick S. J. (1965) *A History of Philosophy, Volume VII, Modern Philosophy, Part I, Fichte to Hegel*. Image Books, Garden City, New York.

Cornforth, Chris, Thomas, Alan, Lewis, Jenny and Spear, Roger. (1988) *Developing Successful Worker Co-operatives*. Sage, London.

Costello, Nicholas, Michie, Jonathan and Milne, Seumas. (1989) *Beyond the Casino Economy: Planning for the 1990s*. Verso, London.

Cotgrove, Stephen. (1976) 'Environmentalism and Utopia'. *Sociological Review*, 24(1), February, 23–42.

Cotgrove, Stephen. (1982) *Catastrophe or Cornucopia? The Environment, Politics and the Future*. John Wiley, Chichester.

Cotgrove, S. and Duff, A. (1980) 'Environmentalism, Middle Class Radicalism and Politics'. *Sociological Review*, 28, 333–351.

Cotgrove, S. and Duff, A. (1981) 'Environmentalism, Values and Social Change'. *British Journal of Sociology*, 32(1), 92–110.

Council on Environmental Quality. (1982) *The Global 2000 Report to the President: Entering the Twenty-First Century*. Allan Lane, Harmondsworth.

Crenson, Matthew A. (1971) *The Un-Politics of Air Pollution*. Johns Hopkins Press, Baltimore.

Crook, John H. (1980) *The Evolution of Human Consciousness*. Clarendon Press, Oxford.

Curtler, W. H. R. (1920) *The Enclosure and Redistribution of Our Land*. Clarendon Press, Oxford.

D'Amico, Robert. (1989) *Historicism and Knowledge*. Routledge, New York.

Daly, Herman E. (Ed.) (1973) *Towards a Steady-State Economy*. Freeman, San Francisco.

Daly, Herman E. (1977) *Steady-State Economics*. Freeman, San Francisco.

Daly, Herman E. and Cobb, John B. Jr. (1990) *For the Common Good: Redirecting the Economy Towards Community, the Environment, and a Sustainable Future*. Green Print, London.

Dauncy, Guy. (1988) *After the Crash: The Emergence of the Rainbow Economy*. Green Print, London.

Davis, Donald Edward. (1989) *Ecophilosophy: A Field Guide to the Literature*. R & E Miles, San Pedro.

Davis. J. C. (1980) *Utopia and the Ideal Society: A Study of English Utopian Writings 1516-1700*. Cambridge University Press, Cambridge.

Dawkins, Richard. (1976) *The Selfish Gene*. Oxford University Press, Oxford.

Day, J. P. (1964) 'John Stuart Mill'. In O'Connor, *A Critical History of Western Philosophy* (1964: 341–62).

de Bell, Garret. (1970) *The Environmental Handbook*. Ballantine, New York.

de Riencourt, Amaury. (1965) *The Soul of China: An Interpretation of Chinese History*. Harper and Row, New York.

Debord, Guy. (1983) *Society of the Spectacle*. Black and Red, Detroit.

Devall, Bill. (1990) *Simple in Means Rich in Ends: Practicing Deep Ecology*. Green Print, London.

Dews, Peter. (1980) 'The "New Philosophers" and the End of Leftism'. *Radical Philosophy*, **24**, Spring 2–11.

Dickson, David. (1974) *Alternative Technology and the Politics of Technical Change*. Fontana, London.

Dobb, Maurice. (1946) *Studies in the Development of Capitalism*. George Routledge, London.

Dobbins, Peggy Powell. (1978) *From Kin to Class: Speculation on the Origins of the Development of the Family, Class Society and Female Subordination*. Signmaker Press, Berkeley.

Dobson, Andrew. (1990) *Green Political Thought: An Introduction*. Unwin Hyman, London.

Dodds, E. R. (1951) *The Greeks and the Irrational*. University of California Press, Berkeley.

Douglas, Mary. (1973) *Natural Symbols: Explorations in Cosmology*. Penguin, Harmondsworth.

Downs, Anthony. (1972) 'Up and Down with Ecology — the Issue-Attention Cycle'. *Public Interest*, **28**(1), 38–50.

Draper, John William. (1927) *History of the Conflict between Religion and Science*. Watts, London.

Dray, William. (1963) 'The Historical Explanation of Actions reconsidered'. In Hook (1963: 105–135).

Drucker, H. M. (1974) *The Political Uses of Ideology*. Macmillan, London.

Dube, Shyama Charan. (1988) *Modernization and Development — The Search for Alternative Paradigms*. Zed, London.

Dumont, Rene. (1974) *Utopia or Else ....* Deutsch, London.

Dunlap, Riley E. (Ed.) (1980) 'Ecology and the Social Sciences: an emerging Paradigm'. *American Behavioral Scientist*, **24**(1), September-October (whole issue).

Dunlap, R. E. and van Liere, K. D. (1978) *Environmental Concern: A Bibliography of Empirical Studies and a Brief Appraisal of the Literature*. Public Administration Series: Bibliography P-44, Vance Bibliographies.

Eagleton, Terry. (1990) *The Ideology of the Aesthetic*. Blackwell, Oxford.

Easlea, Brian. (1980) *Liberation and the Aims of Science*. Scottish Academic Press, Edinburgh.

Edel, Matthew. (1973) *Economies and the Environment*. Prentice-Hall, Englewood Cliffs, New Jersey.

Ehrlich, Paul R. (1972) *The Population Bomb*. Pan/Ballantine, London.

Ehrlich, P. R. and Ehrlich, A. H. (1972) *Population Resources Environment*. Second edition. W. H. Freeman, San Francisco.

Ehrlich, P. R., Ehrlich, A. H. and Holdren, J. P. (1972) *Human Ecology*. W. H. Freeman, San Francisco.

Ekins, Paul. (Ed.) (1986) *The Living Economy: A New Economics in the Making*. Routledge and Kegan Paul, London.

Eliade, Mircea. (1959) *Cosmos and History*. Harper and Row, New York.

Elliott, D. A. and Elliott, R. H. (1976) *The Control of Technology*. Wykeham, London.

Ellul, Jacques. (1964) *The Technological Society*. Vintage, New York.

Elster, Jon. (1985) *Making Sense of Marx*. Cambridge University Press,

Cambridge.

Engel, J. Ronald and Engel, Joan Gibb. (Eds.) (1990) *Ethics of Environment and Development: Global Challenge, International Response*. Belhaven, London.

Engels, Frederick. (1954) *Dialectics of Nature*. Progress Press, Moscow.

Engels, Frederick. (1972) *The Origin of the Family, Private Property and the State*. Lawrence and Wishart, London.

Engels, Frederick. (1976) *Anti-Dühring*. Foreign Languages Press, Peking.

Enloe, Cynthia H. (1975) *The Politics of Pollution in a Comparative Perspective*. Longman, New York.

Enzensberger, Hans Magnus. (1974) 'A Critique of Political Ecology'. *New Left Review*, **84**, March–April, 3–31.

Eurich, Nell. (1967) *Science in Utopia: A Mighty Design*. Harvard University Press, Cambridge, Massachusetts.

Featherstone, Mike. (Ed.) (1988) 'Postmodernism'. Special Edition of *Theory, Culture and Society*, **5**, Nos. 2–3, June.

Ferguson, Adam. (1767) *An Essay on the History of Civil Society*. Kincaid and Bell, Edinburgh.

Ferguson, John. (1975) *Utopias of the Classical World*. Thames and Hudson, London.

Fernbach, David. (1981) *The Spiral Path: A Gay Contribution to Human Survival*. Gay Men's Press, London.

Ferri, Enrico. (1905) *Socialism and Positive Science*. Independent Labour Party, London.

Ferro, Marc. (1987) *The Use and Abuse of History: Or how the Past is Taught*. Routledge and Kegan Paul, London.

Feyerabend, Paul. (1978) *Against Method: Outline of an Anarchistic Theory of Knowledge*. Verso, London.

Feyerabend, Paul. (1979) *Science in a Free Society*. New Left Books, London.

Finley, Moses I. (1986) *The Use and Abuse of History*. The Hogarth Press, London.

Finley, Moses I. (1967) 'Utopianism Ancient and Modern'. In Finley (1986: Ch.11).

Firth, Raymond. (1957) *Man and Culture: An Evaluation of the Work of Bronislaw Malinowski*. Routledge and Kegan Paul, London.

Fisera, Vladimir. (1975) *Workers' Councils in Czechoslovakia 1968–1969*. Allison and Busby, London.

Fox, Warwick. (1986) 'Approaching Deep Ecology: A Response to Richard Sylvan's Critique of Deep Ecology'. *Environmental Studies Occasional Paper No.20*, University of Tasmania, Hobart.

Frankel, Boris. (1987) *The Post-Industrial Utopians*. Polity, London.

Fraser-Darling, Frank. (1971) *Wilderness and Plenty*. Ballantine, New York.

Frazer, James George. (1957) *The Golden Bough: A Study in Magic and Religion*. Abridged edition. Macmillan, London.

Galtung, Johan. (1981) 'Structure, Culture and Intellectual Style: An Essay Comparing Saxonic, Teutonic, Gallic and Nipponic Approaches'. *Social Science Information*, **20**, No.6, pp. 817–56.

Garbarino, Merwyn S. (1977) *Sociocultural Theory in Anthropology: A Short*

History. Holt Rinehart and Winston, New York.

Gardiner, Patrick L. (1959) *Theories of History*. Free Press, Glencoe.

Gardiner, Patrick L. (1974) *The Philosophy of History*. Oxford University Press, Oxford.

Geertz, Clifford. (1964) 'Ideology as a Cultural System'. In Apter (1964: 47–76).

Geertz, Clifford. (1973) *The Interpretation of Cultures*. Basic Books, New York.

Gellner, Ernest. (1982) 'Relativism and Universals'. In Hollis and Lukes (1982: 181–200).

Gellner, Ernest. (1985) *Relativism and the Social Sciences*. Cambridge University Press, Cambridge.

Geras, Norman. (1983) *Marx and Human Nature: Refutation of a Legend*. Verso, London.

Geyer, R. Felix and Schweitzer, David R. (Eds.) (1976) *Theories of Alienation*. Martinus Nijhoff, Leiden.

Giddens, Anthony. (1977) *Studies in Social and Political Thought*. Hutchinson, London.

Giddens, Anthony. (1981) *The Class Structure of the Advanced Societies*. Second edition. Hutchinson, London.

Giddens, Anthony. (1982) *A Contemporary Critique of Historical Materialism*. University of California Press, Berkeley, California.

Giddens, Anthony. (1984) *The Constitution of Society*. University of California Press, Berkeley, California.

Gillette, R. (1972) '"The Limits to Growth": Hard Sell for a Computer View of Doomsday'. *Science*, **175**, March, 1688–1692.

Glacken, Clarence J. (1967) *Traces on a Rhodian Shore*. University of California Press, Berkeley.

Gleick, James. (1987) *Chaos: Making a New Science*. Cardinal, London.

Godwin, William. (1976) *Enquiry Concerning Political Justice and Its Influence on Modern Morals and Happiness*. Penguin, Harmondsworth.

Goldman, Marshall. (1972) *The Spoils of Progress: Environmental Pollution in the Soviet Union*. MIT Press, Cambridge, Massachusetts.

Goldmann, Lucien. (1973) *The Philosophy of the Enlightenment: The Christian Burgess and the Enlightenment*. Routledge and Kegan Paul, London.

Goldsmith, Edward. (1971) *Can Britain Survive?* Tom Stacey, London.

Goldsmith, E., Allen, R., Allaby, M., Davoll, J. and Lawrence, S. (1972) 'A Blueprint for Survival'. *The Ecologist*, **2**(1), January, 1–43.

Goldthorpe, John H. (Ed.) (1984) *Order and Conflict in Contemporary Capitalism: Studies in the political Economy of Western European Nations*. Clarendon, Oxford.

Goldthorpe, J. H., Lockwood, D., Bechhofer, F. and Platt, J. (1968) *The Affluent Worker: Industrial Attitudes and Behaviour*. Cambridge University Press, Cambridge.

Goodwin, Barbera and Taylor, Keith. (1982) *The Politics of Utopia*. Hutchinson, London.

Gorz, André. (1964) *Strategy for Labour*. South End Press, Boston.

Gorz, André. (1969) *Reforme et Revolution*. Editions du Seuil, Paris.

Gorz, André. (1980) *Ecology as Politics*. South End Press, Boston.

Gorz, André. (1982) *Fairwell to the Proletariat: An Essay on Post-Industrial Socialism*. Pluto, London.

Gorz, André. (1985) *Paths to Paradise: On the Liberation from Work*. Pluto, London.

Gorz, André. (1989) *Critique of Economic Reason*. Verso, London.

Gould, Stephen Jay. (1990) *Wonderful Life: The Burgess Shale and the Nature of History*.Hutchinson Radius, London.

Gramsci, Antonio. (1971) *Selections from the Prison Notebooks*. Lawrence and Wishart, London.

Green Party. (Various) *Manifesto for a Sustainable Society*. Green Party, London.

Gregory, Roy. (1971) *The Price of Amenity: Five Studies in Conservation and Government*. Macmillan, London.

Gurvitch, Georges. (1971) *The Social Frameworks of Knowledge*. Blackwell, Oxford.

Habermas, Jürgen. (1976) *Legitimation Crisis*. Heinemann, London.

Habermas, Jürgen. (1987a) *Knowledge and Human Interests*. Polity, Cambridge.

Habermas, Jürgen. (1987b) *The Philosophical Discourse of Modernity*. Polity, Cambridge.

Halfpenny, Peter. (1982) *Positivism and Sociology*. Allen and Unwin, London.

Hall, Gus. (1972) *Ecology: Can We Survive under Capitalism?* International Publishers, New York.

Hall, Stuart. (1977) 'The Hinterland of Science: Ideology and the "Sociology of Knowledge"'. Centre for Contemporary Cultural Studies (1978: 9–32).

Handy, Charles. (1985) *The Future of Work*. Blackwell, Oxford.

Harding, Sandra. (1986) *The Science Question in Feminism*. Open University, Milton Keynes.

Hargrove, Eugene C. (1989) *Foundations of Environmental Ethics*. Prentice-Hall, Englewood Cliffs, New Jersey.

Harper, Peter and Boyle, Godfrey. (Eds.) (1976) *Radical Technology*. Wildwood House, London.

Harrison, J. F. C. (1979) *The Second Coming: Popular Millenarianism, 1780–1850*. Routledge and Kegan Paul, London.

Harvey, David. (1969) *Explanation in Geography*. Edward Arnold, London.

Harvey, David. (1989) *The Condition of Postmodernity*. Polity, Cambridge.

Hawley, Amos H. (1986) *Human Ecology: A Theoretical Essay*. University of Chicago Press, Chicago.

Hawley, Amos H. (1950) *Human Ecology: A Theory of Community Structure*. The Ronald Press, New York.

Hays, Samuel P. (1959) *Conservation and the Gospel of Efficiency*. Harvard University Press, Cambridge, Massachusetts.

Heberle, Rudolf. (1951a) 'Principles of Political Ecology'. In Specht (1951: 187–196).

Heberle, Rudolf. (1951b) *Social Movement*. Appleton Century and Crofts,

New York.

Hegel, Georg Wilhelm Friedrich. (1975a) *Hegel's Logic*. Clarendon Press, Oxford.

Hegel, Georg Wilhelm Friedrich. (1975b) *Lectures on the Philosophy of World History. Introduction: Reason in History*. Duncan Forbes (Ed.). Cambridge University Press, Cambridge.

Hegel, Georg Wilhelm Friedrich. (1977) *Phenomenology of Spirit*. Clarendon Press, Oxford.

Hempel, C. G. (1963) 'Reasons and Covering Laws in Historical Explanation'. In Hook (1963: 143–163).

Hempel, C. G. (1942) 'The Function of General Laws in History'. *Journal of Philosophy*. (Reprinted in Gardiner (1959)).

Henderson, Hazel. (1978) *Creating Alternative Futures: The End of Economics*. Putnam, New York.

Henderson, Hazel. (1981) *The Politics of the Solar Age: Alternatives to Economics*. Anchor, New York.

Herber, Lewis. (1952) 'The Problem of Chemicals in Food'. *Contemporary Issues*, 3(12), 206–241.

Herber, Lewis. (1962 (1973)) *Our Synthetic Environment*. Alfred Knopf, New York.

Herder, J. G. (1968) *Reflections on the Philosophy of the History of Mankind*. Frank Manuel (Ed.). University of Chicago Press, Chicago.

Hill, J. Christopher. (1964) 'Puritanism, Capitalism and the Scientific Revolution'. *Past and Present*, **29**, 88–97.

Hill, J. Christopher. (1969) *Reformation to Industrial Revolution*. Pelican, Harmondsworth.

Hill, J. Christopher. (1975) *The World Turned Upside Down*. Penguin, Harmondsworth.

Hill, J. Christopher. (1980) *Intellectual Origins of the English Revolution*. Clarendon Press, Oxford.

Hill, J. Christopher. (1984) *The Experience of Defeat: Milton and Some Contemporaries*. Viking, New York.

Hilton, Rodney. (Ed.) (1976) *The Transition from Feudalism to Capitalism*. New Left Books, London.

Hindess, Barry and Hirst, Paul Q. (1975) *Pre-Capitalist Modes of Production*. Routledge and Kegan Paul, London.

Hobbes, Thomas. (1968) *Leviathan*. C. B. Macpherson (Ed.). Penguin, Harmondsworth.

Hodge, Robert and Kress, Gunter R. (1988) *Social Semiotics*. Polity, Cambridge.

Hodgskin, Thomas. (1827) *Popular Political Economy*. London.

Hodgskin, Thomas. (1825) *Labour Defended against the Claims of Capital*. London.

Hollis, Martin. (1982) 'The Social Destruction of Reality'. In Hollis and Lukes (1982: 67–86).

Hollis, M. and Lukes, S. (Eds.) (1982) *Rationality and Relativism*. Basil Blackwell, Oxford.

Hook, Sidney. (Ed.) (1963) *Philosophy and History: A Symposium*. New

York University Press, New York.

Horkheimer, Max. (1974) *Eclipse of Reason*. Oxford University Press, New York.

Horton, Robin. (1982) 'Tradition and Modernity Revisited'. In Hollis and Lukes (1982: 201–260).

Hughes, H. Stuart. (1959) *Consciousness and Society*. Macgibbon and Kee, London.

Hugo, Victor. (1965) *The Hunchback of Notre Dame*. Signet, New York.

Hume, David. (1978) *A Treatise of Human Nature*. L.A. Selby-Bigge (Ed.). Clarendon Press, Oxford.

Inglehart, Ronald. (1977) *The Silent Revolution: Changing Values and Political Styles among Western Publics*. Princeton University Press, Princeton, New Jersey.

Ingold, Tim. (1986) *Evolution and Social Life*. Cambridge University Press, Cambridge.

Irvine, Sandy and Ponton, Alec. (1988) *A Green Manifesto: Policies for a Green Future*. Optima, London.

Israel, Joachim. (1971) *Alienation: From Marx to Modern Sociology*. Allyn and Bacon, Boston.

James, Susan. (1984) *The Content of Social Explanation*. Cambridge University Press, Cambridge.

Jameson, Fredric. (1971) *Marxism and Form: Twentieth-Century Dialectical Theories of Literature*. Princeton University Press, Princeton.

Jameson, Fredric. (1984) 'The Cultural Logic of Capital'. *New Left Review*, **146**, 53–92, July-August.

Jantsch, Erich. (1967) *Technological Forecasting in Perspective*. OECD, Paris.

Jantsch, Erich. (1980) *The Self-Organising Universe: Scientific and Human Implications of the Emerging Paradigm of Evolution*. Pergamon, Oxford.

Jantsch, E. and Waddington, C. H. (1976) *Evolution and Consciousness: Human Systems in Transition*. Addison-Wesley, Reading, Massachusetts.

Johnson, Richard. (1979) 'Culture and the Historians'. In Clarke et al. (1979: Ch 2).

Joll, James. (1976) *Europe since 1870: An International History*. Penguin, Harmondsworth.

Jungk, Robert. (1954) *Tomorrow is Already Here: Scenes from a Man-Made World*. Hart-Davis, London.

Jungk, Robert. (1977) *The New Tyranny*. Warner Books, New York.

Jungk, Robert and Müllert, Norbert. (1980) *Alternatives Leben*. Signal-Verlag, Baden-Baden.

Kandinsky, Wassily and Marc, Franz. (1965) *Der Blaue Reiter*. Piper, Munchen.

Kant, Immanuel. (1953) *Prolegomena to any Future Metaphysic that will be able to present itself as a Science*. Manchester University Press, Manchester.

Kateb, George. (1963) *Utopia and Its Enemies*. Collier-Macmillan, New York.

Kaufmann, Walter. (1970) 'The Inevitability of Alienation'. In Schacht (1970: xiii–lvii).

Kavanagh, Dennis. (1980) 'Political Culture in Great Britain'. In Almond and

Vebra (1980).

Kay, J. A. and Mirrlees, J. A. (1974) 'The Desirability of Natural Resource Depletion'. In Pearce and Rose (1975: 140–176).

Kaye, Harvey J. (1984) *The British Marxist Historians*. Polity, Cambridge.

Kaysen, Carl. (1972) 'The Computer That Printed Out W*O*L*F'. *Foreign Affairs*, 50(4), July, 660–668.

Kearney, H. F. (1964) 'Puritanism, Capitalism and the Scientific Revolution'. *Past and Present*, **28**, 81–101.

Kemp, Penny and Wall, Derek. (1990) *A Green Manifesto for the 1990s*. Penguin, London.

Kern, Horst and Schumann, Michael. (1984) *Das Ende der Arbeitsteilung?* Munich.

Kimber, R. and Richardson, J. J. (Eds.) (1974) *Campaigning for the Environment*. Routledge and Kegan Paul, London.

Kneese, Allen V. (1977) *Economics and the Environment*. Penguin, Harmondsworth.

Koestler, Arthur. (1964) *The Sleepwalkers: A History of Man's Changing Vision of the Universe*. Penguin, Harmondsworth.

Kolakowski, Leszek. (1972) *Positive Philosophy*. Penguin, Harmondsworth.

Komarov, Boris. (1980) *The Destruction of Nature in the Soviet Union*. Pluto Press, London.

Kormondy, Edward J. (1976) *Concepts of Ecology*. Second edition. Prentice-Hall, Englewood Cliffs, New Jersey.

Koyré, Alexandre. (1957) *From the Closed World to the Infinite Universe*. Johns Hopkins Press, Baltimore.

Kress, Gunter R. and Hodge, Robert. (1979) *Language as Ideology*. Routledge and Kegan Paul, London.

Kropotkin, Peter. (1974) *Fields, Factories and Workshops Tomorrow*. Colin Ward (Ed.). George Allen and Unwin, London.

Kropotkin, Peter. (1979) *Mutual Aid: A Factor of Evolution*. Extending Horizons, Boston.

Kropotkin, Peter. (1985) *The Conquest of Bread*. Elephant Editions, London.

Kuhn, Thomas. (1970) *The Structure of Scientific Revolutions*. Second edition. University of Chicago Press, Chicago.

Kumar, Krishan. (1976) 'Revolution and Industrial Society: An Historical Perspective'. *Sociology*, **10**(2), 245–269.

Kumar, Krishan. (1987) *Utopia and Anti-Utopia in Modern Times*. Blackwell, Oxford.

Kumar, Krishan. (1991) *Utopianism*. Open University Press, Milton Keynes.

La Piere, Richard T. (1965) *Social Change*. McGraw-Hill, New York.

Labriola, Antonio. (1908) *Essays on the Materialistic Conception of History*. Charles H. Kerr, Chicago.

Lacomber, Richard. (1979) *The Economics of Natural Resources*. Macmillan, London.

Lacomber, Richard. (1975) *Economic Growth versus the Environment*. Macmillan, London.

Lakatos, I. and Musgrove, A. (Eds.) (1970) *Criticism and the Growth of Knowledge*. Cambridge University Press, Cambridge.

Landes, David S. (1969) *The Unbound Prometheus: Technological Change and Industrial Development in Western Europe from 1750 to the Present*. Cambridge University Press, Cambridge.

Lange, Peter. (1984) 'Unions, Workers and Wage Regulation: The Rational Bases of Consent'. In Goldthorpe (1984: Ch.5).

Larrain, Jorge. (1979) *The Concept of Ideology*. Hutchinson, London.

Lash, Scott. (1988) 'Discourse or Figure? Postmodernism as a Regime of Signification'. In Featherstone (1988: 311–336).

Lash, Scott and Urry, John. (1987) *The End of Organised Capitalism*. Polity, Cambridge.

Latour, Bruno. (1986) *Science in Action*. Harvard University Press, Cambridge, Massachusetts.

Leach, Edmund R. (1957) 'The Epistemological Background to Malinowski's Empiricism'. In Firth (1957: 119–37).

Leacock, Eleanor Burke. (1981) *Myths of Male Dominance: Collected Articles on Women Cross-Culturally*. Monthly Review Press, New York.

LeGuin, Ursula K. (1975) *The Dispossessed*. Grafton Books, London.

Leiss, William. (1972) *The Domination of Nature*. George Brazillier, New York.

Leiss, William. (1978) *The Limits to Satisfaction: On Needs and Commodities*. Marion Boyars, London.

Lenski, Gerhard. (1970) *Human Societies: A Macrolevel Introduction to Sociology*. McGraw Hill, New York.

Leval, Gaston. (1975) *Collectives in the Spanish Revolution*. Freedom Press, London.

Lévi-Strauss, Claude. (1968) *Structural Anthropology*. Penguin, Harmondsworth.

Lévi-Strauss, Claude. (1972) *The Savage Mind*. Weidenfeld and Nicolson, London.

Levitas, Ruth. (1990) *The Concept of Utopia*. Philip Allan, London.

Lewis, C. S. (1947) *The Abolition of Man*. Geoffrey Bles, London.

Lichtheim, George. (1967) *The Concept of Ideology and Other Essays*. Vintage Books, New York.

Lipietz, Alain. (1986) 'Les Conditions de Construction d'un Mouvement Alternatif en France'. *Intervention aux Journées de l'AERIP. "Les Enjeux Institutionnels et Politiques de Mars 1986"*, 31 January - 1 February. Mimeo.

Lipietz, Alain. (1987) *Mirages and Miracles: The Crisis of Global Fordism*. Verso, London.

Littman, Robert J. (1974) *The Greek Experiment: Imperialism and Social Conflict 800–400 BC*. Thames and Hudson, London.

Locke, John. (1965) *Two Treatises of Government*. Mentor, New York.

Lomax, Bill. (1972) *Hungary 1956*. Allison and Busby, London.

Lorenz, Konrad. (1977) *Behind the Mirror: A Search for a Natural History of Human Knowledge*. Methuen, London.

Lovejoy, Arthur O. (1936) *The Great Chain of Being*. Harvard University Press, Cambridge, Massachusetts.

Lovelock, James E. (1979) *Gaia: A New Look at Life on Earth*. Oxford

University Press, Oxford.
Lovibond, Sabina. (1990) 'Feminism and Postmodernism'. In Boyne and Rattansi (1990: Ch.6).
Lowe, P. D. and Goyder, J. (1983) *Environmental Groups in British Politics*. George Allen and Unwin, London.
Lowe, P. D. and Rüdig, W. (1986) *Political Ecology and the Social Sciences, The State of the Art*. International Institute for Environment and Society, Berlin.
Luckmann, Thomas. (Ed.) (1978) *Phenomenology and Sociology*. Penguin, Harmondsworth.
Lukács, Georg. (1971) *History and Class Consciousness: Studies in Marxist Dialectics*. Merlin, London.
Lukács, Georg. (1975) *The Young Hegel*. Merlin, London.
Lukács, Georg. (1980) *The Destruction of Reason*. Merlin, London.
Lukes, Steven. (1970) 'Some Problems about Rationality'. In Wilson (1970: 194–213).
Lukes, Steven. (1973) *Individualism*. Basil Blackwell, Oxford.
Lukes, Steven. (1974) *Power: A Radical View*. Macmillan, London.
Lukes, Steven. (1982) 'Relativism in Its Place'. In Hollis and Lukes (1982: 261–305).
Lyons, John. (1968) *Introduction to Theoretical Linguistics*. Cambridge University Press, Cambridge.
Lyotard, Jean-Francois. (1984) *The Postmodern Condition: A Report on Knowledge*. Manchester University Press, Manchester.
MacIntyre, Alasdair. (1967) *Secularization and Moral Change*. Oxford University Press, Oxford.
MacIntyre, Alasdair. (1968) 'The Strange Death of Social Democratic England'. In Widgery (1976: 235–240).
MacIntyre, Alasdair. (1971) *Against the Self-Images of the Age*. Duckworth, London.
MacIntyre, Alasdair. (1981) *After Virtue: A Study in Moral Theory*. University of Notre Dame Press, Notre Dame, Indiana.
Macpherson, C. B. (1962) *The Political Theory of Possessive Individualism, Hobbes to Locke*. Clarendon Press, Oxford.
Maddox, John. (1972) *The Doomsday Syndrome*. Macmillan, London.
Malinowski, Bronislaw. (1948) *Magic, Science and Religion and Other Essays*. Souvenir, London.
Malthus, Thomas Robert. (1836) *Principles of Political Economy*. 2nd edition. London.
Malthus, Thomas Robert. (1970) *An Essay on the Principle of Population*. Anthony Flew (Ed.). Penguin, Harmondsworth.
Mandel, Ernest. (1978) *Late Capitalism*. Verso, London.
Mandel, Ernest and Novak, George. (1970) *The Marxist Theory of Alienation*. Pathfinder, New York.
Mandelbaum, Maurice. (1971) *History, Man and Reason: A Study in Nineteenth-Century Thought*. Johns Hopkins University Press, Baltimore.
Mandelbrot, Benoit. (1977) *The Fractal Geometry of Nature*. Freeman, San

Francisco.

Mann, Michael. (1973) *Consciousness and Action among the Western Working Class*. Macmillan, London.

Mannheim, Karl. (1936) *Ideology and Utopia*. Routledge and Kegan Paul, London.

Manuel, Frank E. (1962) *The Prophets of Paris*. Harvard University Press, Cambridge, Massachusetts.

Manuel, Frank E. (1965) *Shapes of Philosophical History*. George Allen and Unwin, London.

Manuel, Frank E. (1968) *A Portrait of Isaac Newton*. Belknap Press, Cambridge, Massachusetts.

Manuel, F. E. and Manuel, F. P. (1979) *Utopian Thought in the Western World*. Basil Blackwell, Oxford.

Marcuse, Herbert. (1941) *Reason and Revolution: Hegel and the Rise of Social Theory*. Routledge and Kegan Paul, London.

Marcuse, Herbert. (1964) *One-Dimensional Man*. Beacon, Boston.

Maruyama, Magoroh. (1976) 'Towards Cultural Symbiosis'. In Jantsch and Waddington (1976: Ch.10).

Marwick, Arthur. (1981) *The Nature of History*. Second edition. Macmillan, London.

Marx, Karl. (1959) *Capital, Volume Three*. Lawrence and Wishart, London.

Marx, Karl. (1972) *Critique of the Gotha Programme*. Foreign Languages Press, Peking.

Marx, Karl. (1973a) *Surveys from Exile, Political Writings, Volume 2*. David Fernbach (Ed.). Penguin, Harmondsworth.

Marx, Karl. (1973b) *Grundrisse*. Penguin, Harmondsworth.

Marx, Karl. (1975) *Early Writings*. L. Colletti (Ed.). Penguin, Harmondsworth.

Marx, Karl. (1976) *Capital, Volume One*. Penguin, Harmondsworth.

Marx, Karl. (1978) *Capital, Volume Two*. Penguin, Harmondsworth.

Marx, K. and Engels, F. (1965) *Manifesto of the Communist Party*. Peoples Publishing House, Peking.

Marx, K. and Engels, F. (1970) *The German Ideology*. Lawrence and Wishart, London.

Marx, K. and Engels, F. (1975) *Selected Correspondence*. Progress, Moscow.

Marx, Leo. (1964) *The Machine in the Garden: Technology and the Pastoral Ideal in America*. Oxford University Press, New York.

Maynard Smith, John. (1975) *The Theory of Evolution*. Third edition, Penguin, Harmondsworth.

Mayr, Otto. (1986) *Authority, Liberty and Automatic Machinery in Early Modern Europe*. Johns Hopkins Press, Baltimore.

McEvoy, James. (1972) 'The American Concern with Environment'. In Burch (1972: 210–224).

McGuire, J. E. and Rattansi, P. M. (1966) 'Newton and the Pipes of Pan'. *Notes and Records of the Royal Society of London*, **XXI**, 124–125.

McLellan, David. (1969) *The Young Hegelians and Karl Marx*. Macmillan, London.

McLellan, David. (1986) *Ideology*. Open University Press, Milton Keynes.

Meadows, D. H., Meadows, D. L., Randers, J. and Behrens III, W. W. (1974) *The Limits to Growth*. Pan, London.

Meek, R. L. (Ed.) (1953) *Marx, Engels on Malthus*. Lawrence and Wishart, London.

Mellos, Koula. (1988) *Perspectives on Ecology*. Macmillan, London.

Merchant, Carolyn. (1980) *The Death of Nature: Women, Ecology and the Scientific Revolution*. Wildwood House, London.

Merton, Robert K. (1970) *Science, Technology and Society in Seventeenth-Century England*. Howard Fertig, New York.

Mészáros, Istvan. (1970) *Marx's Theory of Alienation*. Merlin, London.

Midgeley, Mary. (1979) 'Rival Fatalisms: The Hollowness of the Sociobiology Debate'. In Montagu (1980: 15–38).

Milbrath, Lester W. (1984) *Environmentalists: Vanguard for a New Society*. State University of New York Press, Albany.

Mill, John Stuart. (1848) *Principles of Political Economy*. 2 Vols, London.

Miller, David L. (1967) *Individualism: Personal Achievement and the Open Society*. University of Texas Press, Austin.

Mitchell, Alan and Levy, Liz. (1989) 'Green about Green'. *Marketing*, 14th September, 28–35.

Montagu, Ashley. (Ed.) (1980) *Sociobiology Examined*. Oxford University Press, New York.

Montagu, Ashley. (Ed.) (1978) *Learning Non-Agression: The Experience of Non-Literate Societies*. Oxford University Press, Oxford.

Montcrief, Lewis. W. (1970) 'The Cultural Basis of Our Environmental Crisis'. *Science*, **170**, 30 October, 508–512.

Montesquieu, Baron de. (1949) *The Spirit of the Laws*. Hafner Press, New York.

Moore, Barrington. Jr. (1967) *Social Origins of Dictatorship and Democracy*. Penguin, Harmondsworth.

Moore, Henrietta. L. (1988) *Feminism and Anthropology*. Polity, Cambridge.

More, Thomas. (1965) *Utopia*. Penguin, Harmondsworth.

Morris, William. (1891) *News from Nowhere*. Reeves and Turner, London.

Morris, Desmond. (1967) *The Naked Ape*. McGraw Hill, New York.

Morton, A. L. (1969) *The English Utopia*. Lawrence and Wishart, London.

Mueller-Vollmer, Kurt. (Ed.) (1985) *The Hermeneutic Reader: Texts of the German Tradition from the Enlightenment to the Present*. Blackwell, Oxford.

Mumford, Lewis. (1922) *The Story of Utopias: Ideal Commonwealths and Social Myths*. Harrap, London.

Myrdal, Gunnar. (1968) *Asian Drama*. Pantheon, London.

Naess, Arne. (1989) *Ecology, Community and Lifestyle*. Cambridge University Press, Cambridge.

Nagel, Stuart. (Ed.) (1974) *Environmental Politics*. Praeger, New York.

Naughton, John. (1982) 'Revolution in Science: 20 Years On'. *New Scientist*, **95**(1317), 5 August, 372–375.

Needham, Joseph. (1954-1971) *Science and Civilization in China*. Four volumes. Cambridge University Press, Cambridge.

Needham, Joseph. (1969) *The Grand Titration*. Allan and Unwin, London.

Negley, Glenn and Patrick, J. Max. (1971) *The Quest for Utopia*. McGarth, Maryland.

Nicholson, Max. (1972) *The Environmental Revolution*. Penguin, Harmondsworth.

Nicholson, Linda J. (Ed.) (1990) *Feminism/Postmodernism*. Routledge, New York.

Norman, Colin. (1981) *The God That Limps: Science and Technology in the Eighties*. Norton, New York.

O'Connor, D. J. (1964) *A Critical History of Western Philosophy*. Free Press, London.

O'Riordan, Timothy. (1981) *Environmentalism*. Second edition. Pion, London.

Ollman, Bertell. (1971) *Alienation: Marx's Conception of Man in Capitalist Society*. Cambridge University Press, Cambridge.

Ophuls, William. (1977) *Ecology and the Politics of Scarcity*. Freeman, San Francisco, California.

Ordway, Samuel H. Jr. (1953) *Resources and the American Dream*.

Osborn, Fairfield. (1948) *Our Plundered Planet*. Faber and Faber, London.

Osborn, Fairfield. (1953) *The Limits to the Earth*. Little, Brown, Boston.

Osmond, John. (1986) *Work in the Future: Alternatives to Unemployment*. Thorsons, Wellingborough.

Outhwaite, William. (1987) *New Philosophies of Social Science: Realism, Hermeneutics and Critical Theory*. Macmillan, London.

Park, Robert Ezra. (1952) *Human Communities: The City and Human Ecology*. Glencoe, Illinois.

Park, R. E., and Burgess, E. W. (1921) *An Introduction to the Science of Sociology*. Chicago University Press, Chicago.

Parsons, Talcott. (1971) *The System of Modern Societies*. Prentice-Hall, Englewood Cliffs, New Jersey.

Parsons, Howard. L. (1977) *Marx and Engels on Ecology*. Greenwood Press, Westport, Connecticut.

Partridge, Ernest. (Ed.) (1981) *Responsibilities to Future Generations: Environmental Ethics*. Prometheus Books, Buffalo, New York.

Passmore, John. (1980) *Man's Responsibility for Nature*. Second edition. Duckworth, London.

Pearce, D. W., Markandya, A. and Barbier, E. B. (1989) *Blueprint for a Green Economy*. Earthscan, London.

Pearce, D. W. and Rose, J. (Eds.) (1975) *The Economics of Natural Resource Depletion*. Macmillan, London.

Pepper, David. (1984) *The Roots of Modern Environmentalism*. Croom Helm, London.

Pevsner, Nikolaus. (1957) *An Outline of European Architecture*. Penguin, Harmondsworth.

Piercy, Marge. (1979) *Woman on the Edge of Time*. The Women's Press, London.

Piore, Michael J. and Sabel, Charles F. (1984) *The Second Industrial Divide*. Basic Books, New York.

Platt, Robert S. (1948) 'Environmentalism versus Geography'. *American*

Journal of Sociology, **53**(5), March, 351–358.
Plekhanov, G. V. (Undated) *Fundamental Problems of Marxism*. Lawrence and Wishart, London.
Plumb, J. H. (1969) *The Death of the Past*. Macmillan, London.
Polanyi, Karl. (1940) *The Great Transformation: The Political and Economic Origins of our Time*. Beacon, Boston.
Political and Economic Planning. (1955) *World Population and Resources*. PEP, London.
Pollard, Sidney. (1968) *The Idea of Progress: History and Society*. C A Watts, London.
Popper, Karl Raimund. (1961) *The Poverty of Historicism*. Routledge and Kegan Paul, London.
Popper, Karl Raimund. (1965) *The Logic of Scientific Discovery*. Harper and Row, New York.
Popper, Karl Raimund. (1966) *The Open Society and Its Enemies*. Two volumes. Fifth edition. Routledge and Kegan Paul, London.
Porritt, Jonathon. (1984) *Seeing Green: The Politics of Ecology Explained*. Basil Blackwell, Oxford.
Porritt, Jonathon and Winner, David. (1988) *The Coming of the Greens*. Fontana, London.
Poulantzas, Nicos. (1973) *Political Power and Social Class*. New Left Books, London.
Poulantzas, Nicos. (1978) *Classes in Contemporary Capitalism*. Verso, London.
Powers, Jonathan. (1982) *Philosophy and the New Physics*. Methuen, London.
Prigogine, Ilya. (1980) *From Being to Becoming: Time and Complexity in the Physical Sciences*. Freeman, San Francisco.
Prigogine, Ilya and Stengers, Isabelle. (1985) *Order out of Chaos: Man's New Dialogue with Nature*. Flamingo, London.
Pryde, Philip. (1972) *Conservation in the Soviet Union*. Cambridge University Press, Cambridge.
Quinn, James A. (1971 (1950)) *Human Ecology*. Archon Books, New York.
Radin, Paul. (1953) *The World of Primitive Man*. Henry Schuman, New York.
Reisman, David. (1950) *The Lonely Crowd*. Anchor, New York.
Ricardo, David. (1973 (1817)) *The Principles of Political Economy and Taxation*. Dent, London.
Richards, Vernon. (1981) *Protest without Illusions*. Freedom Press, London.
Richards, Vernon (Ed.) (1983) *Why Work? Arguments for the Leisure Society*. Freedom Press, London.
Ridgeway, James. (1971) *The Politics of Ecology*. Dutton, New York.
Rigby, Andrew. (1974) *Alternative Realities: A Study of Communes and Their Members*. Routledge and Kegan Paul, London.
Roberts, Alan. (1979) *The Self-Managing Environment*. Allison and Busby, London.
Robertson, H. M. (1933) *Aspects of the Rise of Economic Individualism*. Cambridge University Press, Cambridge.

Robertson, James. (1985) *Future Work: Jobs, Self-Employment and Leisure after the Industrial Age*. Gower/Maurice Temple Smith, London.

Rodman, John. (1980) 'Paradigm Change in Political Science: An Ecological Perspective'. *American Behavioral Scientist*, **24**(1), 49–78.

Roos, Leslie L. Jr. (Ed.) (1971) *The Politics of Ecosuicide*. Holt Rinehart and Winston, New York.

Rorty, Richard. (1986) 'Freud and Moral Reflection'. In Smith and Kerrigan (1986).

Rose, Steven. (1976) *The Conscious Brain*. Penguin, Harmondsworth.

Rosenbaum, Walter D. (1973) *The Politics of Environmental Concern*. Praeger, New York.

Roszak, Theodore. (1973) *Where the Wasteland Ends: Politics and Transcendence in Post-Industrial Society*. Anchor Books, New York.

Rothman, Harry. (1972) *Murderous Providence: A Study of Pollution in Industrial Societies*. Rupert Hart-Davis, London.

Rousseau, Jean-Jacques. (1964a) *The First and Second Discourses*. Robert D. Masters (Ed.). St Martin's, New York.

Rousseau, Jean-Jacques. (1964b) 'Discourse on the Origin and Foundations of Inequality among Men'. In Rousseau (1964a: 77-248).

Rousseau, Jean-Jacques. (1964c) 'Discourse on the Question: Has the Restoration of the Sciences and the Arts Tended to Purify Morals?' In Rousseau (1964a: 31–64).

Rousseau, Jean-Jacques. (1968) *The Social Contract*. Penguin, Harmondsworth.

Roux, Georges. (1980) *Ancient Iraq*. Penguin, Harmondsworth.

Rüdig, Wolfgang. (1983) 'Capitalism and Nuclear Power: A Reassessment'. *Capital and Class*, **20**, Summer, 117–156.

Rüdig, Wolfgang. (1986a) 'Energy, Public Protest and Green Parties - A Comparative Analysis'. Unpublished Ph.D thesis. Department of Science and Technology Policy, Manchester University.

Rüdig, Wolfgang. (1986b) 'Eco-Socialism: Left Environmentalism in West Germany'. *New Political Science*, **14**, 3–37.

Rüdig, W. and Lowe, P. D. (1984) 'The Unfulfilled Prophecy: Touraine and the Anti-Nuclear Movement'. *Modern and Contemporary France*, **20**, December, 19–23.

Russell, Bertrand. (1961) *History of Western Philosophy and Its Connection with Political and Social Circumstances from the Earliest Times to the Present Day*. Second edition. George Allen and Unwin, London.

Sahlins, Marshall D. and Service, Elman R. (Eds.) (1960) *Evolution and Culture*. University of Michigan Press, Ann Arbour.

Sale, Kirkpatrick. (1985) *Dwellers in the Land: The Bioregional Vision*. Sierra Club Books, San Francisco.

Sandbach, Francis. (1980) *Environment, Ideology and Policy*. Basil Blackwell, Oxford.

Sanderson, Stephen K. (1990) *Social Evolution: A Critical History*. Blackwell, Oxford.

Saw, Ruth L. (1964) 'William of Ockham'. In O'Connor (1964: 124–140).

SCEP (Study of Critical Environmental Problems). (1970) *Man's Impact on the Global Environment.* MIT Press, Cambridge, Massachusetts.

Schacht, Richard. (1970) *Alienation.* Doubleday, New York.

Schmidt, Alfred. (1971) *The Concept of Nature in Marx.* New Left Books, London.

Schnaiberg, Allan. (1980) *The Environment: From Surplus to Scarcity.* Oxford University Press, New York.

Schrödinger, Edwin. (1952) 'Are there Quantum Jumps?' *The British Journal for the Philosophy of Science*, **Vol. III**, 109–110.

Schumacher, E. F. (1973) *Small Is Beautiful: A Study of Economics as if People Mattered.* Abacus, London.

Schurr, Sam L. (Ed.) (1972) *Energy, Economic Growth, and the Environment.* Resources for the Future, Johns Hopkins Press, Baltimore.

Schutz, Alfred. (1940) 'Phenomenology and the Social Sciences'. In Luckmann (1978: 119–141).

Schwab, Michael. (Ed.) (1972) *Teach-In for Survival.* Robinson and Watkins, London.

Seabrook, Jeremy. (1988) *The Leisure Society.* Blackwell, Oxford.

Sears. Paul. B. (1953) 'Human Ecology: A Problem of Synthesis'. *Science*, **120**, 959–963.

Sen,Gita and Grown, Caren. (1988) *Development, Crisis and Alternative Visions: Third World Women's Perspectives.* Earthscan, London

Sewell, W. R. D. and Coppock, J. T. (Eds.) (1977) *Public Participation in Planning.* Wiley, London.

Shephard, P. and McKinley, D. (Eds.) (1969) *The Subversive Science: Essays towards an Ecology of Man.* Houghton Mifflin, Boston.

Shusterman, Richard. (1988) 'Postmodern Aestheticism: A New Moral Philosophy?' In Featherstone (1988: 337–355)

Simon, Julian L. and Kahn, Herman. (Eds.) (1984) *The Resourceful Earth: A response to 'Global 2000'.* Blackwell, Oxford.

Singh, Narindar. (1989) *Economics and the Crisis of Ecology.* Bellew, London.

Sklair, Leslie. (1973) *Organized Knowledge.* Hart-Davis MacGibbon, London.

Slater, Phil. (Ed.) (1980) *Outlines of a Critique of Technology.* Ink Links, Birmingham.

Smelser, Neil J. (1960) *Social Change in the Industrial Revolution: An Application of Theory to the Lancashire Cotton Industry 1770-1840.* Routledge and Kegan Paul, London.

Smelser, Neil J. (1962) *Theory of Collective Behaviour.* Routledge and Kegan Paul, London.

Smil, Vaclav. (1984) *The Bad Earth: Environmental Degradation in China.* Zed Press, London.

Smith, J. H. and Kerrigan, W. (Eds.) (1986) *Pragmatism's Freud: The Moral Disposition of Psychoanalysis.* Johns Hopkins University Press, Baltimore.

Smith, Adam. (1976) *An Inquiry into the Nature and Origin of the Wealth of Nations.* Two volumes. R. H. Campbell, A. S. Skinner and W. B. Todd (Eds.). Clarendon Press, Oxford.

Smith, D. Howard. (1974) *Confucius.* Paladin, London.

Specht, Karl G. (Ed.) (1951) *Sociologische Forschung in Unserer Zeit.*

Westdeutscher Verlag, Köln und Opladen.

Spence, Martin. (1982) 'Nuclear Capital'. *Capital and Class*, 16, 5–40, Spring.

Spence, Martin. (1983) 'Soviet Power: Nuclear Energy in the USSR'. *Capital and Class*, 21, 87–96, Winter.

Spencer, Herbert. (1967) *The Evolution of Society: Selections from 'Principles of Sociology'*. Robert L Carneiro (Ed.). University of Chicago Press, Chicago.

Spencer, Herbert. (1852) 'A Theory of Population'. *Westminster Review, New Series*, I(ii), 1 April, 468–501.

Stace, William. (1924) *The Philosophy of Hegel: A Systematic Exposition*. Macmillan, London.

Stapledon, George. (1964) *Human Ecology*. Faber and Faber, London.

Stephen, Chuck. (1983) 'Varieties of Individualism'. *Berkeley Journal of Sociology*, 28, 115–129.

Stern, Fritz. (Ed.) (1970) *The Varieties of History*. Second edition. Macmillan, London.

Steuart, James. (1770) *An Inquiry into the Principles of Political Economy*. Dublin.

Steward, Julian H. (1955) *Theory of Culture Change: The Methodology of Multi-Linear Evolution*. University of Illinois Press, Urbana.

Tatham, George. (1957) 'Environmentalism and Possibilism'. In Griffeth Taylor (Ed.), *Geography in the Twentieth Century* (128–162). Methuen, London.

Tawney, R. H. (1947) *Religion and the Rise of Capitalism*. Mentor, New York.

Taylor, Roger. L. (1978) *Art, an Enemy of the People*. Harvester, Hassocks, Sussex.

Taylor, Ronald. (Ed.) (1980) *Aesthetics and Politics: Theodor Adorno, Walter Benjamin, Ernst Bloch, Bertold Brecht, Georg Lukács*. Verso, London.

Teilhard de Chardin, Pierre. (1964) *The Future of Man*. Collins, London.

Tentler, Thomas N. (1974) 'The Summa for Confessors as an Instrument of Social Control'. In Trinkaus and Obermann (1974: 103–137).

Therborn, Goeran. (1980) *The Ideology of Power and the Power of Ideology*. Verso, London.

Thomas, H. and Logan, C. (1982) *Mondragon: An Economic Analysis*. George Allen and Unwin, London.

Thomas, Keith. (1973) *Religion and the Decline of Magic: Studies in Popular Beliefs in Sixteenth- and Seventeenth-Century England*. Penguin, Harmondsworth.

Thomas, Keith. (1983) *Man and the Natural World: Changing Attitudes in England 1500-1800*. Allen Lane, London.

Thompson, D'Arcy Wentworth. (1961) *On Growth and Form*. Abridged Edition, Cambridge University Press, Cambridge.

Thompson, Edward P. (1965) 'The Peculiarities of the English'. In Thompson (1978: 245–301).

Thompson, Edward P. (1968) *The Making of the English Working Class*. Penguin, Harmondsworth.

Thompson, Edward P. (1978) *The Poverty of Theory and Other Essays*.

Merlin, London.

Thompson, Edward P. (1980) 'Notes on Exterminism, the Last Stage of Civilization'. *New Left Review*, **121**, 3–31.

Thompson, Edward P. et al. (1983) *Exterminism and Cold War*. Verso, London.

Thompson, Kenneth. (1986) *Beliefs and Ideology*. Ellis Horwood, Chichester, and Tavistock Publications, London.

Thompson, William. (1824) *An Inquiry into the Principles of the Distribution of Wealth most Conducive to Human Happiness*. London.

Thornley, Jenny. (1982) *Workers' Co-Operatives: Jobs and Dreams*. Heinemann, London.

Toffler, Alvin, (1973) *Future Shock*. Pan Books, London.

Toffler, Alvin. (1981) *The Third Wave*. Pan Books. London

Toon, P. (Ed.) (1970) *Puritans, the Millennium and the Future of Israel*. Cambridge University Press, Cambridge.

Touraine, Alain. (1974) *The Post-Industrial Society: Tomorrow's Social History. Classes, Conflicts and Culture in the Programmed Society*. Wildwood House, London.

Touraine, Alain. (1981) *The Voice and the Eye: An Analysis of Social Movements*. Cambridge University Press, Cambridge.

Touraine, A., Hegedus, Z., Dubet, F., and Wieviorka, M. (1983) *Anti-Nuclear Protest: The Opposition to Nuclear Energy in France*. Cambridge University Press, Cambridge.

Toye, John. (1987) *Dilemmas of Development: Reflections on the Counter-Revolution in Development Theory and Policy*. Blackwell, Oxford.

Trinkaus, C. and Oberman, N. A. (Eds.) (1974) *The Pursuit of Holiness in Late Mediaeval and Renaissance Religion*. Brill, Leiden.

Troeltsch, Ernst. (1931) *The Social Teaching of the Christian Churches*. Two volumes. Macmillan, New York.

Trop, C. and Roos, L. L. Jr. (1971) 'Public Opinion and the Environment'. In Roos (1971: 52–63).

Turner, Frederick. (1983) *Beyond Geography: The Western Spirit Against the Wilderness*. Rutgers University Press, New Brunswick, New Jersey.

Tuveson, Ernest Lee. (1949) *Millenium and Utopia: A Study in the Background of the Idea of Progress*. University of California Press, Berkeley.

Ullmann, Walter. (1967) *The Individual and Society in the Middle Ages*. Methuen, London.

van Doren, Charles. (1967) *The Idea of Progress*. Praeger, New York.

van Liere, K. D. and Dunlap, R. E. (1979) 'The Social Bases of Environmental Concern: A Review of Hypotheses, Explanations and Empirical Evidence'. Paper presented at the Annual Meeting of the Southern Sociological Society, Atlanta, Georgia.

Vaneigem, Raoul. (1983b) *The Book of Pleasures*. Pending Press, London.

Vaneigem, Raoul. (1983a) *The Revolution of Everyday Life*. Aldgate Press, London.

Vayda, Andrew P. (1969) *Environment and Cultural Behaviour*. Natural History Press, New York.

Veblen, Thorstein. (1969) *The Place of Science in Modern Civilisation and Other Essays*. Capricorn Books, New York.

Vogt, William. (1949) *Road to Survival*. Victor Gollancz, London.

Waddington, Conrad Hal. (1977) *Tools for Thought*. Paladin, London.

Wallerstein, Immanuel. (1974) *The Capitalist World Economy*. Cambridge University Press, Cambridge.

Ward, Barbara and Dubos, René. (1972) *Only One Earth: The Care and Maintenance of a Small Planet*. Penguin, Harmondsworth.

Warnock, Mary. (1970) *Existentialism*. The Clarendon Press, Oxford.

Washburn, S.L. (1978) 'Human Behavior and the Behavior of Other Animals'. In Montagu (1980: 254–282).

Waxman, C. (1968) *The End of Ideology Debate*. Funk and Wagnall, New York.

Weber, Max. (1976) *The Protestant Ethic and the Spirit of Capitalism*. George Allen and Unwin, London.

Weisberg, Barry. (1971) *Beyond Repair: The Ecology of Capitalism*. Beacon Press, Boston.

Westergaard, J. and Resler, H. (1976) *Class in a Capitalist Society*. Penguin, Harmondsworth.

Wertheim, Willem Frederik. (1974) *Evolution and Revolution: The Rising Waves of Emancipation*. Pelican, Harmondsworth.

White, A. D. (1901) *A History of the Warfare of Science with Theology*. Two volumes. Appleton, New York.

White, C. L. and Renner, G. T. (1936) *Geography: An Introduction to Human Ecology*. Appleton-Century, New York.

White, Leslie. A. (1959) *The Evolution of Culture: The Development of Civilization to the Fall of Rome*. McGraw-Hill, New York.

White, Lynn Jr. (1960) *Mediaeval Technology and Social Change*. Oxford University Press, New York.

White, Lynn Jr. (1967) 'The Historical Roots of Our Ecological Crisis'. *Science*, 155(3767), 10 March, 1203–1207.

White, Lynn Jr. (1973) 'Continuing the Conversation'. In Barbour (1973: 55–64).

Whitehead, Alfred North. (1920) *The Concept of Nature*. Cambridge University Press, Cambridge.

Whitehead, Alfred North. (1926) *Science and the Modern World*. Cambridge University Press, Cambridge.

Wickelgren, Wayne A. (1979) *Cognitive Psychology*. Prentice-Hall, Englewood Cliffs, New Jersey.

Widgery, David. (1976) *The Left in Britain 1956-1968*. Penguin, Harmondsworth.

Wilde, Oscar. (1956) 'The Soul of Man Under Socialism'. In Oscar Wilde, *Poems and Essays*. 361-390, Collins, London.

Williams, B. (1985)) *Ethics and the Limits to Philosophy*. Fontana, London.

Williams, Raymond. (1965) *The Long Revolution*. Pelican, Harmondsworth.

Williams, Raymond. (1983) *Towards 2000*. Chatto and Windus, London.

Wilson, Edward O. (1975) *Sociobiology: The New Synthesis*. Belknap Press, Cambridge, Massachusetts.

Wilson, Edward O. (1979) *On Human Nature*. Bantam, New York.

Wilson, Bryan R. (Ed.) (1970) *Rationality*. Basil Blackwell, Oxford.

Wilson, Bryan R. (1975) *Magic and the Millennium*. Paladin, London.

Winner, Langdon. (1977) *Autonomous Technology: Technics-out-of-Control as a Theme in Political Thought*. MIT Press, Cambridge, Massachusetts.

Winner, Langdon. (1986) *The Whale and the Reactor: A Search for Limits in an Age of High Technology*. University of Chicago Press, Chicago.

Wissler, Clark. (1923) *Man and Culture*. Crowell, New York.

Wittkower, Rudolph. (1962) *Architectural Principles in the Age of Humanism*. Alec Tiranti, London.

Woodcock, Alexander and Davis, Monte. (1980) *Catastrophe Theory*. Penguin, Harmondsworth.

Woolfson, Charles. (1982) *The Labour Theory of Culture: A Re-Examination of Engels's Theory of Human Origins*. Routledge and Kegan Paul, London.

World Resources Institute. (1986-1990) *World Resources*. World Resources Institute, Washington DC.

Worster, Donald. (1979) *Nature's Economy: The Roots of Ecology*. Anchor Press, Garden City, New York.

Wright, Erik Olin. (1978) *Class, Crises and the State*. Verso, London.

Wright, Erik Olin. (Ed.) (1989) *The Debate on Classes*. Verso, London.

Young, John. (1990) *Post Environmentalism*. Belhaven, London.

Zerzan, John and Carnes, Alice. (Eds.) (1988) *Questioning Technology: A Critical Anthology*. Freedom Press, London.

Zilsel, Edgar. (1942) 'The Sociological Roots of Science'. *American Journal of Sociology*, **XLVII**, January, 544–562.

Zipf, George Kingsley. (1949) *Human Behavior and the Principle of Least Effort: An Introduction to Human Ecology*. Addison-Wesley Press, Cambridge, Massachusetts.

Index